THE EUROPEAN UNION SERIES

General Editors: Neill Nugent, William E. Paterson, Vince

The European Union series provides an authoritative librai
from general introductory texts to definitive assessments (
issues, policies and policy processes, and the role of memb<

Books in the series are written by leading scholars in their
date research and debate. Particular attention is paid to acc
for a wide audience of students, practitioners and interested general readers.

The series editors are **Neill Nugent**, Professor of Politics and Jean Monnet Professor of
European Integration, Manchester Metropolitan University, and **William E. Paterson**,
Director of the Institute of German Studies, University of Birmingham.

Their co-editor until his death in July 1999, **Vincent Wright**, was a Fellow of Nuffield
College, Oxford University. He played an immensely valuable role in the founding and
development of *The European Union Series* and is greatly missed.

Feedback on the series and book proposals are always welcome and should be sent to
Steven Kennedy, Palgrave Macmillan, Houndmills, Basingstoke, Hampshire RG21 6XS, UK, or
by e-mail to s.kennedy@palgrave.com

General textbooks

Published

Desmond Dinan **Encyclopedia of the European Union**
[Rights: Europe only]

Desmond Dinan **Europe Recast: A History of European Union**
[Rights: Europe only]

Desmond Dinan **Ever Closer Union: An Introduction to European Integration (2nd edn)**
[Rights: World excluding North and South America, Philippines and Japan]

Simon Hix **The Political System of the European Union (2nd edn)**

Paul Magnette **What is the European Union? Its Nature and Prospects**

John McCormick **Understanding the European Union: A Concise Introduction (3rd edn)**
[Rights: Europe only]

Brent F. Nelsen and Alexander Stubb **The European Union: Readings on the Theory and Practice of European Integration (3rd edn)**
[Rights: Europe only]

Nell Nugent (ed.) **European Union Enlargement**

Neill Nugent **The Government and Politics of the European Union (5th edn)**
[Rights: World excluding USA and dependencies and Canada]

John Peterson and Elizabeth Bomberg **Decision-making in the European Union**

Ben Rosamond **Theories of European Integration**

Forthcoming

Laurie Buonanno and Neill Nugent **Policies and Policy Processes of the European Union**

Mette Eilstrup Sangiovanni (ed.) **Debates on European Integration: A Reader**

Philippa Sherrington **Understanding European Union Governance**

Also planned

The Political Economy of the European Union

Series Standing Order (outside
North America only)
ISBN 0–333–71695–7 hardback
ISBN 0–333–69352–3 paperback
Full details from www.palgrave.com

The Dynamics of European Integration

Why and when EU institutions matter

Derek Beach

© Derek Beach 2005

All rights reserved. No reproduction, copy or transmission of
this publication may be made without written permission.

No paragraph of this publication may be reproduced, copied or
transmitted save with written permission or in accordance with
the provisions of the Copyright, Designs and Patents Act 1988, or
under the terms of any licence permitting limited copying issued
by the Copyright Licensing Agency, 90 Tottenham Court Road,
London W1T 4LP.

Any person who does any unauthorized act in relation to
this publication may be liable to criminal prosecution and civil
claims for damages.

The author has asserted his right to be identified as the
author of this work in accordance with the Copyright, Designs
and Patents Act 1988.

First published 2005 by
PALGRAVE MACMILLAN
Houndmills, Basingstoke, Hampshire RG21 6XS and
175 Fifth Avenue, New York, N.Y. 10010
Companies and representatives throughout the world

PALGRAVE MACMILLAN is the global academic imprint of
the Palgrave Macmillan division of St. Martin's Press, LLC and of
Palgrave Macmillan Ltd. Macmillan® is a registered trademark in
the United States, United Kingdom and other countries. Palgrave is a
registered trademark in the European Union and other countries.

ISBN-13: 1–4039–3633–1 hardback
ISBN-10: 1–4039–3633–2 HB
ISBN-13: 1–4039–3634–9 PB
ISBN-10: 1–4039–3634–X paperback

This book is printed on paper suitable for recycling and made from fully
managed and sustained forest sources.

A catalogue record for this book is available from the British Library.

A catalog record for this book is available from the Library of Congress.

10   9   8   7   6   5   4   3   2   1
14   13   12   11   10   09   08   07   06   05

Printed and bound in China

Contents

List of Tables and Figures

Tables

Figures

List of Abbreviations

BB	Bundesbank
BSE	Mad Cow Disease
CAP	Common Agricultural Policy
CDU/CSU	Christlich Demokratische Union Deutschland/Christlich-Soziale Union in Bayern
CEE	Central and Eastern Europe
CFI	Court of First Instance
CFSP	Common Foreign and Security Policy
COREPER	Committee of Permanent Representatives
CSFP	Common Foreign and Security Policy
DG	Directorate-General
DM	Deutsche Mark
DTEU	Draft Treaty establishing the European Union
EC	European Community
ECB	European Central Bank
ECHR	European Convention on Human Rights
ECJ	European Court of Justice
ECOFIN	Economic and Finance Ministers
EEC	European Economic Community
EFTA	European Free Trade Association
EMS	European Monetary System
EMU	Economic and Monetary Union
EP	European Parliament
EPC	European Political Community
EPP	European People's Party
ERT	European Roundtable of Industrialists
ESDP	European Security and Defence Policy
EU	European Union
Euratom	European Atomic Energy Community
GATT	General Agreement on Tariffs and Trade
GDP	Gross Domestic Product
GNP	Gross National Product
IGC	Intergovernmental Conference
JHA	Justice and Home Affairs
MEP	Member of the European Parliament
NATO	North Atlantic Treaty Organization

NTB	Non-Tariff Barrier
PES	Party of European Socialists
PHARE	Poland and Hungary Action for Restructuring of the Economy
PU	Political Union
QMV	Qualified Majority Voting
R&D	Research and Development
RG	Reflection Group
RPR	*Rassemblement pour la République*
SEA	Single European Act
SPD	Sozialdemokratische Partei Deutschlands
TEU	Treaty on European Union
UK	United Kingdom
UN	United Nations
US	United States
WEU	Western European Union
WTO	World Trade Organization

Acknowledgements

This book is a product of my on going fascination with the question of the autonomy and influence of EU institutions *vis-à-vis* EU governments within the European Union.

I have enjoyed the assistance of numerous people in the years in which this book has been under way. I would first like to thank all of the national and EU civil servants that I have interviewed for their insights on the informal politics of IGC negotiations. This has given me a glimpse inside what is an otherwise closed and secretive world. I would also like to extend warm thanks for the help and cooperation of the Swedish Ministry for Foreign Affairs – Department SSSB (Archives) – that went far beyond the call of duty.

I would also like to thank numerous fellow academics for feedback on the arguments presented in this book, particularly Finn Laursen, Jonas Tallberg, Knud Erik Jørgensen, Thomas Christiansen, Neill Nugent, Alexander Stubb, William I. Zartman, Florence Deloche-Gaudez, Ole Elgström, Felipe Basabe Lloréns, Alfred Pijpers, Adriaan Schout, Susanne Boras, Morten Greve, Thomas Pedersen, Georg Sørensen, Anders Wivel, and an anonymous reviewer for valuable feedback in various stages of this research. I would also like to thank my research assistants, Piet Juul Birch and Anne-Mette Hjortebjerg Lund for their hard and often tedious work in plowing through mountains of proposals and press clippings. The author is naturally responsible for any and all errors in the book. I would also like to thank Steven Kennedy at Palgrave Macmillan for his unflagging enthusiasm and support of the project.

Finally, I would like to thank my wife and two sons for their patience with my research, and enduring my many trips to Brussels, London and Stockholm.

Aarhus, Denmark   Derek Beach

Chapter 1

Introduction

Introduction

While EU governments are formally the 'Masters of the Treaties', EU institutions have played a key role in pushing Europe further along the road towards the 'ever closer union' envisioned in the Treaty of Rome by providing direction and oiling the wheels of compromise. Looking at both the deepening of the Union in treaty reform negotiations and the widening of the Union through enlargement, this book recasts the core debate within EU studies on the role and impact that EU institutions have had in the history-making intergovernmental bargains of European integration in the past three decades.

The basic argument of the book is that there is evidence that EU institutions play a significant role even in the most intergovernmental forums of the EU – intergovernmental conferences amending the EU Treaties for either treaty reform or accession (IGCs). Intergovernmentalist theorists have argued that governments are firmly in the driving seat in these grand bargains, whereas supranationalists have contended that EU institutions like the Commission have acted as the motor of the integration process through the exploitation of their roles in daily Community decision-making. This book recasts this debate by going *beyond* the either-or dichotomy found in most of the existing literature on European integration by putting forward a new model that emphasizes the importance of leadership: EU institutions do matter vis-à-vis governments in the actual intergovernmental history-making decisions, but their influence varies according to the leadership resources they possess, the negotiating context and their choice of strategy in the negotiations.

The leadership model serves as the theoretical baseline for the comparative analytical chapters that trace the deepening and widening of the European Union from the mid-1980s until the present. The chapters look at the negotiation of every major IGC since 1985, including the recent 2003–4 IGC, along with the negotiation of the fifth enlargement that was concluded in Copenhagen in December 2002.

This book investigates the roles and impact of three EU institutions:

the European Commission, the European Parliament (EP) and the Council Secretariat in a comparative case study. While the Council Secretariat is not an official treaty-based 'institution' as the other two are, officials in the Council Secretariat do share common institutional interests that make it possible to empirically identify it as a collective 'institutional' actor alongside the Commission and the EP (for more, see the chapters below and Christiansen 2002, 2003). In contrast, while the actual Council of Ministers (Council) is a treaty-based institution, ministers do *not* have common institutional interests to the same degree, and the Council's 'interests' are merely a *sum* of the preferences of the *individual* members taken together.

The oversight of the Council Secretariat in the existing literature is patently surprising, as my findings show that the Council Secretariat was *more* influential than either the Commission or European Parliament in most treaty reform negotiations in the 1990s. The role of other EU institutions such as the European Court of Justice will not be investigated directly, as they play no role in the actual negotiations (see Beach, 2001; Burley and Mattli, 1993; Pollack, 2003; Weiler, 1993).

The following will first describe the basic argument of the book. Thereafter, the rest of this chapter will first briefly discuss in general terms how treaty reform and enlargement negotiations are conducted. The chapter then discusses the definitions of the terms 'leadership' and 'influence' as they are used in this book. Following this, I discuss the assumption of treating institutions as unitary actors. Finally there are a few words on the empirical materials and sources of the book.

The basic argument

It is widely accepted in the literature that EU institutions such as the Commission are influential in daily Community policy-making (Moravcsik, 1995; Peterson, 1995; Pollack, 1997, 2003). But most scholars do not ascribe large roles for EU institutions in the so-called history-making intergovernmental decisions, arguing that national governments dominate this setting (e.g. Moravcsik, 1999a; Peterson, 1995). The basic argument of this book is that EU institutions do matter in the history-making intergovernmental bargains of the EU, but that their impact varies according to the circumstances and their strategic choices.

Leadership can be necessary in the major intergovernmental negotiations in order to overcome two major bargaining impediments. First, complex multilateral negotiating situations such as EU intergovernmental conferences often have very high bargaining costs, which can prevent the parties from finding and then agreeing upon a mutually acceptable outcome. Secondly, even if these bargaining costs can be overcome, there are often coordination problems that can prevent agreement from being reached. For instance, when there are multiple possible acceptable solutions that can be chosen, leadership is often necessary in order to help the parties reach agreement.

Drawing upon rational choice institutionalism and negotiation theory, a leadership model is developed that hypothesizes that EU institutions can play a key leadership role when:

- they have strong leadership resources such as comparative informational advantages;
- they have privileged institutional positions in the negotiations;
- the negotiating situation is complex;
- the distribution and intensity of governmental preferences opens a window of opportunity;
- the issues being negotiated are low salience and technically complex; and
- they choose low-profile and moderate leadership strategies.

While leadership has an altruistic dimension, with the leader assisting the parties in finding an agreement, by providing leadership the leader also gains opportunities to skew the final outcome closer to its own preferred outcome.

This leadership model serves as the theoretical baseline for the comparative empirical chapters that trace the deepening and widening of the EU in the period from the negotiation of the Single European Act in the mid-1980s until the conclusion of the Constitutional Treaty in June 2004.

The case studies show that leadership by EU institutions is particularly successful in two different situations. First, when EU institutions exploit windows of opportunity and privileged institutional positions by tabling moderate proposals that aim at what can be termed the 'upper edge of realism', they often are able to shift outcomes closer to their own interests. The best example of this was the impact of the Commission in the 1985 IGC which negotiated the Single European Act. In the IGC, the Commission was given de facto control over the IGC agenda by the Luxembourg Presidency, enabling the Commission to table a series of proposals that substantively shaped the agenda and skewed the final outcome closer to the Commission's own preferred outcome. Critical to Commission influence was the institutional role given to it by the Luxembourg

Presidency in the negotiations, and the Commission's use of pragmatic agenda-shaping tactics in exploiting the window of opportunity that had opened due to the strong demand for agreement among governments (see Chapter 3). The Commission put forward moderate proposals that were aimed at the upper end of what the member states would realistically accept, leading to a more integrative final treaty than would otherwise have been agreed upon. In later IGCs, when the Commission did not have the same accepted agenda-setting role, governments reacted very negatively to the Commission attempting to table a series of proposals. Further, when the Commission put forward overly ambitious proposals in the 1985 IGC, they were disregarded.

The second type of situation where EU institutions matter is when they facilitate compromise by assisting and advising Presidencies, together with brokering key deals. By playing this type of leadership role, the EU institution gains numerous opportunities to skew outcomes closer to their own preferred outcome. For example, in the 1996–7 IGC that negotiated the Treaty of Amsterdam, the Council Secretariat was able to successfully exploit the possibilities for influence opened by the negotiating context through the use of low-profile agenda-shaping leadership tactics in assisting Presidencies. The Secretariat also used its power of the pen to gain influence in several salient issues, illustrating for example, the 'influence of those who provide draft texts for debate – they run the show' (Stubb, 1998, p. 219).

The argument is not that EU institutions are 'rogue elephants' wildly out of the control, nor that they are even *always* necessary in order for governments to reach an efficient agreement. My claims are more restricted – namely that, given the high bargaining costs and the uncertainty involved in EU Treaty negotiations, the context and the leadership strategies employed by EU institutions *can* allow them to translate their leadership resources into influence over outcomes.

The plan of the book

Following the present introductory chapter, Chapter 2 of this book introduces the two poles of debate within integration theory on whether the grand intergovernmental bargains of European integration are dominated by national governments or by EU institutions. The intergovernmentalist position is first reviewed. The basic argument of intergovernmentalists is that governments are firmly in charge of the EU's intergovernmental negotiations on treaty reform or enlargement.

At the other end of the spectrum, supranationalists such as neo-functionalists argue that EU institutions are influential due to the roles that they play in daily EU policy-making, but they concede that EU institutions play little role in the actual negotiation of the history-making decisions. My argument is that even in the most intergovernmental forum of the EU, there is evidence that EU institutions can matter but, in contrast to supranationalists, they do not always matter.

The theoretical chapter then introduces a leadership model of European integration that contends that EU institutions do possess leadership resources in the history-making negotiations that *potentially* can be translated into influence *contingent* upon the negotiating context and whether the EU institutions choose appropriate leadership strategies in the negotiations. The theory is built upon insights drawn from mainstream negotiation theory and from rational choice institutionalism. The theory is based upon three basic assumptions. First, intergovernmental negotiations in the EU have relatively high bargaining costs that can prevent the parties from reaching a Pareto-efficient agreement. Secondly, actors are treated as boundedly rational, which in short means that bargaining costs matter. Thirdly, the institutional position that an actor is delegated also matters, and can affect both the efficiency and distribution of agreements.

Chapter 3 analyses the roles and impact of the EU institutions in the agenda-setting phase and negotiation of the Single European Act (SEA) in the mid-1980s. As the Single European Act is widely regarded to have been the high point of Commission influence, the analysis will concentrate upon the role of the European Commission, but will also more cursorily look at the impact of the European Parliament and Council Secretariat. The chapter concludes that the Commission did have a strong leadership role in the 1985 IGC, first ensuring that an IGC was convened, and then creating a SEA that had a broader and more ambitious scope than governments would have otherwise agreed upon. But Commission influence had limits, and when the Commission put forward overly ambitious proposals, they had little effect.

Chapter 4 investigates the two parallel IGCs that resulted in the Treaty on European Union in 1991 – the Economic and Monetary Union (EMU) IGC and the Political Union (PU) IGC. The chapter illustrates the importance of low-profile leadership strategies by contrasting the relative success in the PU IGC of the Council Secretariat's low-profile and behind-the-scenes interventions with the failures of the ambitious attempts by the Commission and the European Parliament to gain influence. The importance of possessing a privileged institutional position is also highlighted in the analysis by the chairing role that the Commission President Delors played in the preparation of the agenda on EMU within the Delors Committee prior to the IGC. Delors played a key brokering role that ensured that the Committee wrote a unanimous report which shaped the final EMU outcome.

Chapter 5 investigates the negotiation of the Treaty of Amsterdam. This case clearly shows the impact that context can have upon opportunities for EU institutions to gain influence, together with the impact of inappropriate leadership strategies. The Council Secretariat was very influential in the 1996–7 IGC due to a privileged institutional position – a position that it was able to expertly exploit through the use of low-profile leadership tactics to gain significant influence upon the outcome. The Commission in contrast was marginalized in the negotiations, and played itself even further out of influence by putting forward extremely unrealistic and unacceptable proposals on most issues. The European Parliament was forced to lobby in the margins of the negotiations, but was able to translate gains from daily EU policy-making into influence on provisions regarding its own institutional powers through the use of relatively moderate leadership tactics.

Chapter 6 looks at the 'worst case' scenario for the three EU institutions – the negotiation of the Treaty of Nice in the 2000 ICG. The central issues in the negotiations were the relatively clear-cut and politically sensitive institutional issues relating to Council vote re-weighting and the number of Commissioners. In these circumstances, while there was a high demand for leadership in order to broker a compromise, all three institutions were sidelined by Presidencies – with somewhat predictable results for the final Treaty of Nice. Despite these handicaps, both the Secretariat and Commission were able to exploit the few opportunities they had to provide leadership through the skilful use of low-profile strategies, whereas the EP reverted to its ineffectual strategy of shouting extreme positions from the sidelines.

Chapter 7 analyses the European Convention and the following IGC 2003–4 that negotiated and adopted the Constitutional Treaty. The chapter shows the importance of the shift of the real substantive treaty reform negotiations from the actual IGC to the preparatory phase – the Convention. This shift significantly affected the ability of EU institutions to gain influence. The Convention's draft Constitutional Treaty was a more ambitious result than governments would have agreed upon themselves due to successful EP leadership within the Convention. As a core of governments led by Germany was then interested in adopting the Convention's draft more or less 'as is' in the following IGC, the IGC itself was relegated to being a tidying-up exercise of the Convention's text, with the exception of a handful of contentious institutional issues.

Chapter 8 investigates the negotiation of the fifth enlargement of the EU that led to the Eastern enlargement of the EU, focusing both upon the setting of the agenda prior to the opening of the negotiations, and then the formal negotiations from 1998 until their conclusion in the Copenhagen Summit in December 2002. In comparison to IGC negotiations on treaty reform, the Commission had a much more privileged position in the enlargement negotiations. What is particularly interesting is that the Commission chose to play a pragmatic and low-profile role in the enlargement, assisting governments and finding solutions for problems instead of exploiting its position to push its own agenda. The Commission played in many respects a role similar to the role of the Council Secretariat at its best in IGCs. The Commission facilitated the decision-making process, and without the leadership of the Commission it is highly probable that the process would have creaked to a stop, as no other actor could have lifted the burdens of the technical negotiations, the preparation of realistic draft common positions, and the coordination of the pre-accession aid programs.

The conclusions of the book discuss the empirical findings of the chapters. The basic conclusion is that EU institutions do matter. Outcomes of intergovernmental negotiations do not simply reflect the lowest common denominator, but when EU institutions succeed in providing leadership they are more ambitious and have a broader scope than otherwise would have been agreed. The cases showed first how the *possibilities* for influence through leadership for each of the EU institutions changed due to the changing contexts in the negotiations. Thereafter the chapter analyses the impact of the choice of leadership strategy. What strategies were most effective, and why? These conclusions are then discussed in relation to the existing academic debate. Finally, the conclusion debates the implications of the findings for the democratic deficit in the EU and point towards the future of leadership in the EU.

The object of study – intergovernmental negotiations in the EU

There are two main categories of intergovernmental negotiations in the EU: treaty revision and enlargement negotiations. The first category are intergovernmental conferences (IGCs) held to revise the Treaties. There are currently three major EU Treaties: the Treaty establishing the European Community; the Treaty establishing the European Atomic Energy Community (Euratom); and the Treaty on European

Union. The fourth Treaty, the European Coal and Steel Community, expired in 2002 (see Church and Phinnemore, 2002, pp. 567–74). There are a series of minor treaties, including Accession Treaties.

No major IGCs were held from 1957 until 1985, although minor IGCs had been convened. In these minor IGCs the substantial negotiations took place within the Council. This was followed by a ceremonial IGC that was convened to adopt the final Treaty. Since 1985 the EU has convened six major IGCs where the negotiations took place within the IGC itself. In effect, IGCs are 'constitutional conventions', where history-making decisions are taken by governmental representatives from EU member states that alter the competences of the EU, its decision-making procedures, and the relative balance of power between both EU institutions and between the EU and its member states (Peterson and Bomberg, 1999).

IGCs are based upon Article 48 EU (ex Article N), which states that:

1. The government of any Member State or the Commission may submit to the Council proposals for the amendment of the Treaties on which the Union is founded.

If the Council, after consulting the Parliament and, where appropriate, the Commission, delivers an opinion in favour of calling a conference of representatives of the governments of the Member States, the conference shall be convened by the President of the Council for the purposes of determining by common accord the amendments to be made to those Treaties. The European Central Bank should also be consulted in the case of institutional changes in the monetary area.

The amendments shall enter into force after being ratified by all the Member States in accordance with their respective constitutional requirements.

IGCs are convened either by agreement in the Council under Article 48 EU, or by a binding legal commitment included in a treaty. A proposal to convene an IGC can come from either a member state or from the Commission. The decision to convene an IGC is taken by a simple majority vote in the Council.

There are no formal provisions for how the agenda for an IGC should be prepared, and in the past agendas have been prepared by specific committees, reflection groups, and ad hoc COREPER discussions. There are also no provisions in the Treaties regarding how IGCs are to be negotiated, but a set of norms has developed – the *acquis conferencielle*. IGCs are formally outside of the institutional framework of the EU – they are in effect both international and inter-governmental negotiations between national representatives. But they do draw upon and involve EU institutions to varying degrees, as will be seen in the following chapters. IGCs are chaired by the member state holding the six-month rotating Presidency. The Presidency prepares and chairs all of the meetings and controls the drafting process of the single negotiating text.

IGCs since 1985 have been conducted at three or four different levels, with the exception of the 2003–4 IGC, where negotiations were officially only at the political levels of foreign ministers and heads of state and government levels. The four levels are:

- heads of state and government,
- foreign ministers,
- ambassadorial-level meetings within the Preparatory Group and
- technical meetings among 'Friends of the Presidency'.

The highest level of the IGC is the heads of state or government meeting within the European Council. It is at this level that key deals are brokered and the final treaty is concluded. The next level is Foreign Ministers, who have the overall political responsibility for the IGC. But they are often sandwiched between two levels: lacking the informational skills to follow the lower-level discussions and lacking the political weight of the heads of state and government to strike key deals (McDonagh, 1998, p. 20). In the EMU IGC in 1990–1, the ministerial level negotiations were among Economic and Finance Ministers (ECOFIN).

The Preparatory Group level comprised representatives of foreign ministers. The group meets frequently during IGCs. Most of the IGC negotiations are dealt with at this level, with discussions focusing on detailed and technical questions in what is often characterized as a problem-solving environment. At the lowest level are the Friends of the Presidency, a forum that is used to prepare technical questions for the personal representatives. In the 1990–1 Political Union IGC, the Friends of the Presidency assisted the personal representatives by clarifying points and asking questions on key issues (Mazzucelli, 1997, pp. 61–2, 136). In the 1996–7 IGC this group was charged with discussing questions of simplifying the treaty and in the 2000 IGC the group discussed proposed changes to the EU's judicial system.

The final outcome of an IGC negotiation is a treaty that revises or replaces the existing treaties. The final treaty must then be ratified by member states following upon their constitutional requirements.

Enlargement negotiations are negotiations conducted between the EU and candidate countries within an intergovernmental conference, as accession requires the revision of the treaties. Article 49 EU as revised by the Treaty of Amsterdam states:

> Any European State which respects the principles set out in Article 6(1) may apply to become a member of the Union. It shall address its application to the Council, which shall act unanimously after consulting the Commission and after receiving the assent of the European Parliament, which shall act by an absolute majority of its component members.

> The conditions of admission and the adjustment to the Treaties on which the Union is founded which such admission entails shall be the subject of an agreement between the Member States and the applicant State. This agreement shall be submitted for ratification by all the contracting States in accordance with their respective constitutional arrangements.

After the Commission presents a non-binding opinion on the preparedness of the candidates to the Council, the Council decides upon the principles and procedures to be used in the negotiations (Nugent, 2004; Avery, 2004). The fifth enlargement negotiations were split into two phases.

The first phase was a screening process, where the Commission conducted a detailed examination of the progress made by candidates in transposing and implementing the *acquis communautaire*, or body of EU legislation. The Commission then used this information to prepare draft EU common positions, or negotiating mandates on the terms of the accession, for the Council. The issues in the fifth enlargement negotiations were split up into 31 different chapters.

The substantive negotiations with a candidate state start after the Council has adopted a common position using unanimity. The common position is then delivered by the Presidency to the candidate, after which formal bilateral sessions are held between EU governments and the candidate government at either the heads of state and governments, ministerial or the ambassador level (Avery, 2004). These sessions are chaired by the government holding the Presidency, assisted by the Commission and Council Secretariat (see Chapter 8 for more).

After all of the chapters are closed, a final accession treaty is adopted by the European Council. The fifth enlargement negotiations were for example concluded at the Copenhagen Summit (see Ludlow,

2004a). The accession treaty contains the terms of accession and adjustments to the existing treaties, for example as regards voting weights in the Council (see Church and Phinnemore, 2002, pp. 592–606).

A note on leadership and influence

Leadership is defined in this book to mean broadly any action by one actor to guide or direct the behaviour of other actors towards a certain goal (Underdal, 1994, p. 178). By successfully providing leadership, this allows the leader to influence the final outcome. Therefore a short digression is necessary to detail how this book defines the concept of influence. While the concept of influence is central to political science, its definition is fiercely contested. I will first discuss the definition of influence used in this book and then briefly raise some of the significant methodological problems of measuring influence in actual negotiations.

What do I mean by influence? Influence is here defined as the successful use of leadership resources to change an outcome from what it otherwise would have been in the absence of the action. How then do we know influence when we see it? In order not to open the Pandora's Box of the debate on forms of power and influence too wide, there are two basic types of influence that will be used in this study.

First are the forms of influence that relate to Dahl's classic definitions of power and influence – two terms that he uses synonymously in his work. For Dahl, the analytical focus is observable events. Power/influence is defined as, 'A has power over B to the extent that he can get B to do something that B otherwise would not do (Dahl, 1957, pp. 202–3). However, what if actor A is able to limit the agenda itself to issues that are 'comparatively innocuous' to actor A (Bachrach and Baratz, 1962, p. 948)? Actor A would therefore be able to gain influence over actor B through the use of non-decision-making, preventing certain issues from even being raised and thereby also changing the outcome.

Other theorists have further expanded upon these forms of power and influence. Lukes has pointed to a third form of power, where actor A is able to shape the very interests that actor B acts upon (Lukes, 1974). Therefore 'A exercises power over B when A affects B in a manner contrary to B's [real, objective] interests' (p. 34). Others such as Digeser have gone even further, building upon the work of Foucault to analyse how actors A and B themselves are constructed as subjects, and looking at the sources and effects of norms and values (Digeser, 1992).

However, there are both ontological and epistemological problems with using these additional dimensions of power/influence. At the ontological level, the underlying assumptions of this study are that actors are rational individual agents. By choosing an agency-oriented ontology, I thereby deny that structure determines actor behaviour as is argued by Lukes and Digeser. At the methodological level, I employ a positivistic epistemology that utilizes statements of intention by actors as indicators of their true preferences. In contrast, Lukes argues that we must investigate the real, objective interests of actors, and that stated interests are often the reflections of 'false consciousness'. But this opens up a epistemological Pandora's box, as it can be argued that theorists are always correct no matter what they meet in the real world, as any anomaly can be explained away by contending that the actor was acting based upon 'false consciousness' and not its true interests. Given this and numerous other methodological problems, this study will confine itself to analysing decision-making and non-decision-making.

Returning from this brief discussion of power and influence, how then can we measure the level of influence EU institutions have – that is, how do we know influence when we see it? As is well known, success often has many self-proclaimed fathers.

The simplest method is to measure the correlation between the preferences and proposals put forward by EU institutions and the negotiating outcomes. High levels of correlation would imply that the EU institution had a high level of influence. Yet this method is victim to the problem of anticipated reactions (Bachrach and Baratz, 1963, p. 635). If actor A anticipates what actor B's interests are and only submits proposals that it believes will be accepted by actor B, can we argue that actor A was influential in the negotiations when it was merely putting forward proposals that it knew that actor B would accept? If a Commission proposal merely anticipates what a winning coalition of member states would have accepted anyway, this would clearly *not* be an example of Commission influence over outcomes.

It is necessary to show that an EU institution undertook an observable action that changed the outcome from what it otherwise would have been in the absence of this action. To do this Moravcsik and Nicolaïdis suggest that we look for proposals that were both 'unique' and 'successful' (Moravcsik and Nicolaïdis, 1999, pp. 69–70). However, real-world negotiations are 'one-offs', making it impossible to know with certainty what would have happened if a given actor did not intervene at a given time in a negotiation.

One method to solve this problem is to use counterfactual analysis, attempting to use counterfactual arguments to explain why a high level of supranational influence occurred or did not occur in a given circumstance (Fearon, 1991). The argument used in this book will be basically 'what would have plausibly happened had the EU institution not provided leadership in the given situation'? Would an agreement have been reached without the provision of leadership by the EU institution, and if so, in what manner would it have differed from the agreement that was actually reached? The most serious methodological problem with this type of argumentation is that we naturally cannot know with any certainty what might otherwise have happened (Fearon, 1991, p.173). Therefore we are forced to rely upon the quality of the counterfactual arguments, which can be improved if we base our counterfactual reasoning upon theories and regularities distinct from the hypotheses being tested (Fearon, 1991, pp. 176–7). In this case, what would rational actors in for example a given treaty reform negotiation have done if the Council Secretariat had not brokered a specific deal, based upon what we know from multilateral negotiation theories and rational choice institutionalism?

Can EU institutions be treated as unitary actors?

As an analytical simplification, EU institutions are treated in this book as unitary actors unless otherwise stated. The point of the book is to investigate whether EU institutions were able to provide leadership, and in this respect when institutions present a clear and coherent position vis-à-vis other actors in the negotiations, then the unitary actor assumption is acceptable (Pollack, 2003, pp. 36–7). March and Olsen even go so far as to state that the 'claim of coherence is necessary in order to treat institutions as decision makers' (March and Olsen, 1984, p. 738).

Naturally all three of the EU institutions had internal disagreements, and some of these disagreements did affect the choice and effectiveness of their leadership strategies. For example, during the Convention in 2002–3, the Commission had at times two external 'faces' in the negotiations (see Chapter 7). One was the relatively moderate and pragmatic face of the two Commission representatives in the negotiations. The second face was that of Commissioner Prodi and his aim of a much more ambitious step forward. The result of this split in the Commission came to a head in December 2002, where on the same day each of the two camps published a position paper, creating a situation where the Commission confusingly was speaking with two tongues. But in general, the claim of coherence is justified, as both the Commission and the EP usually adopted a unified position that they then followed during the negotiations.

A note on the empirical material and sources

Finally a few words are in order about the materials and sources that will be employed in this book. All of the intergovernmental negotiations covered in this book took place behind closed doors, and what happened at the negotiating table was confidential. Therefore there is a substantial element of interpretation involved in analysing these secretive negotiation processes.

Primary sources are the main source of information on all of the negotiations covered. First and most importantly, the author has had access to national archives in Sweden and another member state. Secondly, over 50 interviews were undertaken with civil servants from national administrations, selected officials from the Commission, European Parliament, and Council Secretariat, together with several MEPs. The interviews were based upon a standardized questionnaire that was given to the interviewees prior to the interview, though the actual interviews were conducted with some flexibility, and time was spent on motivating interviewees to elaborate or clarify specific events in which it was expected that they were especially knowledgeable. The main focus of the interviews was upon gaining information that was otherwise unavailable about the conduct of the negotiations. The interviews are coded in the book in order to protect the confidentiality of interviewees. Another source of interview information was the archive of over 300 interviews conducted by a team led by Keith Middlemas in the period 1992 to 1994 for the 1995 book *Orchestrating Europe: The Informal Politics of European Union, 1973–1995*. The transcripts of these interviews are deposited at the Sussex European Institute in Brighton, where I consulted them in April 2002.

A significant methodological problem with using interviews as a source is that there are many sources of bias. First, there is the natural tendency for actors to forget details of events over time, or to adapt their recollections to other accounts of the events. Regarding tendencies in the responses, it was expected that national civil servants would have certain incentives to stress the 'rational', state-based character of IGC negotiations, thereby also discounting the role of EU institutions. Somewhat surprisingly therefore, it was often among national civil servants that I found the most frank accounts of Council Secretariat influence in the negotiations.

Further, it was also expected, perhaps counter-intuitively, that officials in EU institutions would have incentives in *downplaying* their own influence. It had been evident that the very high-profile strategy by Delors in the late 1980s and early 1990s had been counterproductive, giving the Commission incentives to shift to a lower profile public role – but this does not mean that the Commission had given up attempting to gain influence. Given this, it is therefore not surprising that Delors himself in an interview with Moravcsik downplayed his own role in the 1990–91 EMU IGC (Moravcsik, 1999a, p. 291).

Another significant problem with interviews of civil servants is the problem of anonymity, which makes replicability difficult. In this study I have attempted as far as possible to corroborate findings using publicly available sources of information.

Other primary sources utilized in this study include the proposals put forward in the IGCs by member states and EU institutions, the reports, articles and opinions published before and during the negotiations, and transcripts of speeches by national politicians and Commission officials.

Secondary sources were also consulted in this study. Surprisingly, much of the literature on European integration merely relies upon 'soft' secondary sources such as newspapers. This is highly problematic, as journalists often do not (or cannot) empirically verify the validity of the public statements of politicians and civil servants. Therefore when using these types of sources, 'accurate statements of fact coexist alongside the most casual of observations and the most opportunistically partisan of *ex post* justifications. National decision-makers often express one position in public and the opposite in private . . . The result? One can find abundant support for *any* plausible conjecture about the causes of European integration' (Moravcsik, 1998, p. 11).

To take account of this, this study draws upon 'hard' secondary sources, meaning accounts that meet the highest methodological standards. For example, the account in this study of the negotiation of the EMU IGC draws upon the authoritative account of the negotiations by Dyson and Featherstone (1999). This work is based upon a series of 440 interviews conducted by the authors, who also had access to the negotiating minutes of the IGC meetings.

Chapter 2

Why and When EU Institutions Matter

This chapter answers two questions. First, why should EU institutions ever matter in the *intergovernmental* negotiations on major treaty reform and enlargement of the Union? Secondly, if EU institutions matter, when should we expect EU institutions to be able to influence the outcome of these negotiations?

The question of the importance of EU institutions for the European integration process has divided students of European integration since the 1960s into an intergovernmentalist camp – which argues that the historical decisions in EU integration are driven by national governments (Baun, 1996; Grieco, 1995; Hofmann, 1966; Milward and Sørensen, 1993; Moravcsik, 1995, 1998, 1999a; Pedersen, 1998) – and a supranationalist camp that contends that EU institutions such as the Commission have acted as the motor of the integration process through their exploitation of their roles in the daily Community policy-making process, leading to a stronger supranational polity that deals with a wider scope of policy-areas than the member states left to themselves would have agreed upon (Christiansen and Jørgensen, 1998; Christiansen, Falkner and Jørgensen, 2002; Haas, 1958, 1961; Lindberg, 1963; Sandholtz and Stone Sweet, 1998, 1999; Schmitter, 1969, 1970).

My argument is that while both sides of this debate contain elements of the truth, the more interesting analytical question is not *whether* EU institutions matter, but *under what conditions* they matter. This chapter puts forward a three-stage leadership model of European integration that answers the question of when we should expect EU institutions to be able to influence the outcome of the major intergovernmental negotiations of the EU. EU institutions will be shown to matter when:

- they possess strong material resources and/or comparative informational advantages;
- they have a reputation for impartiality and/or for the provision of reliable expert advice;

- they have privileged institutional positions;
- the issues being negotiated are technically complex;
- the negotiating situation is complex;
- the distribution and intensity of governmental preferences opens a window of opportunity; and
- when they choose leadership strategies that are appropriate for the negotiating context.

Do EU institutions matter?

The first question though is whether EU institutions ever matter in the intergovernmental grand bargains of European integration? Is the provision of leadership by EU institutions redundant, or does it grant them opportunities to influence final outcomes? While EU institutions have strong formal roles in daily EU policy-making, they have relatively weak formal positions in the intergovernmental negotiations for treaty reform or enlargement (Peterson, 1995). In intergovernmental conferences (IGC) that negotiate treaty reform, none of the EU institutions are formal parties to the negotiations, meaning that they do not have voting rights. Prior to the 2000 IGC, the European Parliament was not even allowed to sit at the IGC table in meetings. While EU institutions have somewhat stronger roles in enlargement negotiations, with the Commission for example providing draft negotiating positions and the European Parliament having to approve the final treaty, only the EU member states and the accession candidates are formal parties to the negotiations. Therefore, EU institutions are only able to provide informal leadership – also termed informal entrepreneurship in the literature. Does the provision of informal leadership even grant EU institutions opportunities to influence treaty outcomes?

The question of the impact of leadership ties into more general theoretical debates in international relations on whether leadership is necessary for the conclusion of international agreements. In the following, arguments are first introduced for why leadership in international negotiations can be necessary, followed by a brief review of the two contending answers to this question within European integration theory.

Why is leadership necessary in international negotiations?

Leadership can in theory be necessary to overcome two major bargaining impediments that can prevent the parties to a negotiation from achieving common gains. Leadership is defined here broadly to mean any action by one actor to guide or direct the behaviour of other actors towards a certain goal (Underdal, 1994, p. 178). But, in the process, by successfully acting as a leader in shaping the agenda or brokering key deals, this gives the leader many opportunities to also influence outcomes for private gain. As discussed in Chapter 1, the term 'influence' is used pragmatically here to mean the successful use of leadership resources to change an outcome from what it otherwise would have been in the absence of the action.

The first bargaining impediment in complex, multi-party negotiations is that parties can have difficulties in finding a mutually acceptable, Pareto-efficient outcome owing to *high bargaining costs* (Bercovitch,1996a, 1996b; Hampson with Hart, 1995; Raiffa, 1982; Sebenius, 1992; Underdal, 1983; Young, 1991, 1999). Bargaining costs are here defined as all of the costs of negotiating an agreement that actors incur, such as the resources that a government must mobilize to acquire detailed information on its own preferences and those of others, and the financial and opportunity costs that governments expend in the search for a mutually acceptable agreement. Pareto-efficient outcomes are outcomes where no party can be made better off without making another worse off, meaning that all of the gains on the bargaining table are realized.

High bargaining costs in a negotiation can affect both the level of common gains of an agreement (*efficiency*) and the division of gains among actors (*distribution*) (see Figure 2.1). High bargaining costs can mean that the Pareto frontier of efficient agreements is cloaked in a 'veil of uncertainty' (Young, 1991, p. 283), with actors lacking the analytical skills and substantive knowledge to accurately determine their own preferences and/or those of other actors (Underdal, 1994, 2002). In such a situation, gains can be left on the table, as actors simply are not aware of the true location of the Pareto frontier (see Figure 2.1). Actors with privileged information on the state of play, and superior analytical skills or substantive knowledge can in theory step in and help the parties get to the Pareto frontier. For example, international mediators in Bosnia in the early and mid-1990s gained privileged knowledge on the preferences of the warring parties through their many bilateral meetings, enabling the mediators to have a better idea of the outer frontier of the zone of possible agreements than the conflicting parties themselves had (Holbrooke, 1998; Touval, 2001). This knowledge proved crucial in the strong mediating efforts by the US in 1995 which led to the resolution of the conflict in the Dayton Accords (ibid.).

Further, high bargaining costs can prevent the parties from

FIGURE 2.1 *The efficiency and distributive elements of a two-party negotiation*

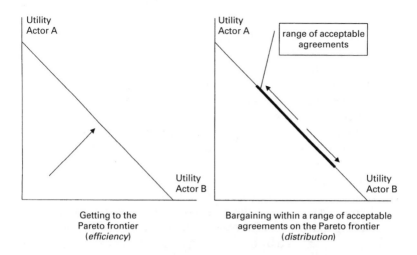

successfully engaging in a negotiation of gains *along* the Pareto frontier (Krasner, 1991; Underdal, 1994, 2992). If negotiations have high costs in terms of the opportunity and financial costs of conducting lengthy multi-party negotiations, and if a formula for a mutually acceptable outcome on the Pareto frontier is not readily discernible due to the highly complex nature of the negotiations, a negotiation can at least in theory break down in a situation where agreement could have been reached with the provision of effective leadership (Underdal, 1994, 2002). One example of this was arguably the Sixth Conference of the Parties to the UN Climate Convention held in The Hague, Netherlands in November 2000. Over 2,200 delegates from 181 states took part in the highly complex and wide-ranging negotiations on the implementation of previous UN agreements on climate change (Dessai, 2001). Yet while the *overall* contours of an acceptable deal were on the table, the parties, and particularly the US and EU, were not able to find a *specific* formula for the distribution of gains despite agreement being within reach (ibid.; *Economist*, 2–8 December 2000a, pp. 21–2). As a result of the immense political and financial costs in extending the negotiations to have another try at finding an acceptable formula, the conference broke down in acrimony.

The second bargaining impediment relates to *coordination problems* that can prevent the parties from agreeing upon an efficient agreement – even if there are low bargaining costs (Garrett and

Weingast, 1993; Krasner, 1991; Stein, 1982). For example, actors can have difficulties finding the Pareto frontier because of the *negotiator's dilemma* (Lax and Sebenius, 1986, pp. 29–45; Young, 1991, p. 284). The negotiator's dilemma relates to the situation where cooperative moves, such as disclosing one's bottom line on an issue, can be exploited by other actors for their own gain (ibid.). Actors can have incentives to *not* reveal their true preferences, or to distort information by, for example, exaggerating the value of their own concessions. In such circumstances, a trusted leader can discuss with each party the nature and intensity of their preferences in an attempt to find the Pareto frontier (Metcalfe, 1998, pp. 424–5; Raiffa, 1982; Scharpf, 1997, p. 145; Stenelo, 1972, p. 54; Tallberg, 2003).

Further, coordination problems can exist in situations where there are *multiple possible efficient solutions* and the parties disagree about the choice of a solution on the Pareto frontier. When competing solutions exist, and where a proposed solution from one party is often perceived to be biased by other actors, leadership can be necessary in order to create a *focal point* around which agreement can converge (Dupont and Faure, 1991, p. 50; Garrett and Weingast, 1993, p. 176; Tallberg, 2002a, p. 7). For example, there were multiple possible 'efficient' solutions to the question of how a single currency could be achieved – ranging from the creation of a parallel 'hard ECU' to a full-fledged economic and monetary union (see Chapter 4).

Integration theory and leadership by EU institutions

Is leadership necessary in complex EU negotiations? Debates in integration theory have echoed the dichotomous debate in international relations on the importance of leadership and informal entrepreneurship. Within the EU context, the controversy has focused upon whether EU institutions are able to play significant roles in history-making decisions. The intergovernmentalist position is basically that national governments, and especially the Franco-German tandem, have been the driving force in the grand bargains of the EU's history. EU institutions do not have a significant role, and any attempt to play a leadership role is seen by intergovernmentalists as either futile or even counterproductive.

Supranationalists counter that leadership by EU institutions, and especially the Commission, has been essential in the integration process, despite the weak *formal* roles played by EU institutions in for example treaty reform. The impact of leadership by EU institutions has led to more pro-integrative outcomes which exceeded what national governments would have agreed upon amongst themselves in the absence of leadership by EU institutions.

Intergovernmentalism

At one end of the spectrum is the intergovernmentalist position, comprised of realist and liberal intergovernmentalist scholars who answer the question of whether EU institutions matter with a resounding 'no' (Baun, 1995; Grieco, 1995; Milward, 1993; Moravcsik, 1998, 1999a; Pedersen, 1998, 2002). Governments are viewed as being firmly in charge of intergovernmental negotiations on treaty reform or enlargement. The history of European integration is seen as a series of celebrated grand bargains between the major EU member states, with outcomes determined by the relative power and preferences of governments.

Underlying these approaches more or less explicitly are the twin assumptions that governments are comprehensively rational, and that negotiations have low bargaining costs. First, national governments in the negotiation of the grand bargains are viewed as comprehensively or fully rational, meaning that they have close to perfect information on their own preferences across the multitude of issues under discussion, and possess the necessary analytical and substantive knowledge to first find the Pareto frontier of efficient agreements, and then agree upon an outcome on the Pareto frontier (see Figure 2.1 above) (see e.g. Moravcsik, 1998, p. 23). Secondly, negotiations are seen as having low bargaining costs, enabling governments to sit down relatively easily at a table and agree upon a Pareto-efficient and mutually acceptable outcome. Questions of the distribution of gains that exist will be resolved in favour of the most powerful actors, with the big bangs of integration being seen as a series of Franco-German compromises (Grieco, 1995; Pedersen, 1998, 2002).

Moravcsik's liberal intergovernmentalist argument is more subtle, but reaches essentially the same conclusion. While he concedes that there can be high bargaining costs in the negotiation of history-making decisions, he argues that the provision of leadership to overcome these bargaining costs is cheap and easy *relative* to the potential gains of European cooperation that result from these grand bargains (Moravcsik, 1999a, p. 273). Governments therefore have strong incentives to mobilize all of the resources necessary to overcome high bargaining costs, creating an over-abundance of leadership. Therefore the provision of leadership by any single actor is redundant, and has no effect upon outcomes. The analyst can therefore proceed *as if* bargaining costs are low, and that leadership provided by a single actor has no effect on negotiation outcomes (ibid.). Given the abundance of leadership provided by governments, the provision of it by EU institutions is therefore 'redundant, futile, and sometimes even counterproductive' (Moravcsik, 1999a, pp. 269–70). Outcomes of the grand bargains reflect patterns of relative actor power, and we should expect that outcomes would tend to reflect the convergence of British, French, and German preferences (Moravcsik, 1999a, p. 273).

Supranationalists

The basic argument of supranationalists is that EU institutions have played a leading role in the integration process, creating and exploiting demands for further integration within the daily Community policy-making process. Neo-functionalism and more recent contextualist theorization will be discussed in the following.

The best known supranationalist theory is neo-functionalism. Neo-functionalism as formulated by Haas, Lindberg and Schmitter, and more recent neo-functionalists such as Burley and Mattli, emphasizes the role of supranational actors as the crucial activators and advocates of further integration (Burley and Mattli, 1993; Haas, 1958, 1961; Lindberg, 1963; Schmitter, 1969, 1970). The analytical focus of most neo-functionalist approaches has been the role of the Commission.

While the Commission has a weak formal role in for example treaty reform negotiations, the Commission has a strong integrative role in daily Community policy-making, cultivating and encouraging further demands for integration based upon functional and political spillover processes. Functional spillover relates to the demands for further integration created by prior decisions, where existing integration in one field then 'spills over' and creates demands for integration in other fields in order to consolidate the gains in the first field (Haas, 1958, 1961; Lindberg, 1963). Political spillover refers to the shifts of actor loyalties and activities as the locus of power shifts from the nation-state to the European level (ibid.).

These demands for further integration, and the cultivation of them by the Commission, create the context in which governments negotiate the grand bargains. Haas for example argues that in the absence of the Commission, intergovernmental negotiations among governments would be trapped in a lowest common denominator dynamic (Haas, 1961, p. 367). An active Commission is able to *upgrade the common interest* by advancing proposals that capitalize upon demands for further integration, leading to higher levels of integration than otherwise would have been the case (ibid., pp. 368, 369). The most celebrated example is the manner in which the Commission exploited the single-market program, arguing that the full gains of the single market could not be achieved without also introducing a common currency (Tranholm-Mikkelsen, 1991).

Newer contextualist approaches, while differing on many episte-mological and ontological points, share the basic structural argument that the outcomes of the grand bargains merely incorporate prior trends in the daily Community policy-making process (context), where EU institutions such as the Commission play key leadership roles. Stone Sweet and Sandholtz's transactional approach argues for example that increases in transnational exchange between member states create a demand from societal actors for more supranational rules to facilitate more efficient exchange (1998, 1999). Supranational actors such as the Commission and the ECJ respond to this in daily policy-making by extending the domain of supranational rules, thereby creating an ever-deepening and self-sustaining dynamic of further integration, led by EU institutions. The grand bargains then merely incorporate these rules into the treaties (1998, p. 12).

Christiansen and Jørgensen's social constructivist approach states that the real big bangs of integration also take place *between* the grand bargains (Christiansen and Jørgensen, 1998, 1999; also Christiansen, Falkner and Jørgensen, 2002; Greve and Jørgensen, 2002). EU institu-tions such as the ECJ and the Commission play a dominant role in interpreting and reinterpreting the treaties in a process of *constitution-alization* within daily Community policy-making, where discourses of common understandings on the interpretation of the treaties are created and developed by EU institutions. They state therefore that 'At most, they [governments] bargained over the way in which existing trends in the integration process . . . were formally incorporated into the treaty' (Christiansen and Jørgensen, 1999, p. 15).

A third variant of the contextual argument is historical institution-alism, which argues for the primacy of long-term factors such as path dependency and organizational factors (Pierson, 1996; Sverdrup, 2000, 2002). Past decisions taken by EU institutions and govern-ments in especially daily policy-making, but also in IGCs, constrain governments in a web of structuring elements that grants EU institu-tions numerous opportunities to gain influence over the process (Sverdrup, 2002).

But when looking at the *actual negotiation* of the grand bargains, most supranationalist scholars concede that EU institutions have little if any role. As put by two leading contextualist scholars in a recent book, 'intergovernmental conferences . . . are practically defined by tough, interest-driven negotiation . . . the grand bargains are, by definition, intergovernmental. The research results are quite predictable when one looks to intergovernmental bargains for evidence of intergovernmental bargaining' (Stone Sweet and Sandholtz, 1998, p. 12). But my argument is that even in the history-making negotiations – the most intergovernmental forum of the EU – EU institutions have leadership resources and institutional positions that can be exploited to gain influence over outcomes. EU institutions can matter even in the most intergovernmental forum of the EU.

A leadership model for when EU institutions matter

While both poles of the leadership debate in European integration studies contain elements of the truth, the sharp analytical divide masks the analytically more interesting question of under what circumstances EU institutions matter vis-à-vis national governments. When are EU institutions able to act as leaders in history-making negotiations, enabling them also to gain influence over outcomes? As importantly, when are they *not* able to act as leaders?

The basic point of my leadership model is that EU institutions possess leadership resources that can be translated into influence over the outcomes of the grand bargains through the provision of leadership, contingent upon the actual negotiating context and their choice of negotiating strategy. While the provision of leadership helps parties achieve collective gain by first finding the Pareto frontier, and then helps the parties agree upon the distribution of gains along the frontier, EU institutions gain opportunities to influence outcomes for private gain in the process.

The leadership model is built upon three basic assumptions. First, intergovernmental negotiations in the EU are seen to have relatively high bargaining costs, which can create bargaining impediments that hinder the achievement of a mutually acceptable, Pareto-efficient outcome. While bilateral negotiations are frequently well-defined bargaining situations in which the parties make concessions until they converge at a mutually acceptable agreement, multilateral and multi-issue intergovernmental negotiations in the EU generally have much higher bargaining costs (Hopmann, 1996, p. 258; Pfetsch, 1999, pp.198–9; Scharpf, 1997; Sebenius, 1983, pp. 308, 1984, 1992). Leadership therefore becomes increasingly important the higher the bargaining costs of a given negotiation (Scharpf, 1997; Young, 1991).

Secondly, actors are realistically seen as boundedly rational (Jones, 2001; Simon, 1997). If actors could be treated as comprehensively rational, then high bargaining costs would not matter. But in the grand bargains of European integration, as in other complex international negotiations, actors can realistically be treated only as boundedly rational. This means that actors are often either unclear about their own preferences or unable to accurately calculate the consequences of different options, and do not *always* possess the necessary substantive and analytical skills to find the Pareto frontier of efficient agreements owing to the many cross-cutting cleavages on large numbers of highly complex and legally technical issues being negotiated (Hampson and Hart, 1995; Zartman and Berman, 1982). Many issues are technically complex, and the consequences of different choices are often difficult to predict and only become apparent years later. As one veteran of treaty reform negotiations puts it, 'Governments and their negotiators do not always know what they want and the situation changes unpredictably with the dynamics of the negotiations where written and oral proposals are floated around the table by all the participants at frequent intervals' (Stubb, 2002, p. 27). In such circumstances, leadership by one or several actors is often necessary to help the parties find a Pareto frontier.

Thirdly, even if we could proceed as if actors in negotiations were comprehensively rational and that the negotiations had low bargaining costs, rational choice institutionalism points out that the possession of a privileged institutional position can grant actors opportunities to provide leadership (Pollack, 1997; Tallberg, 2002a, 2003a). For instance, delegating the role of drafting official negotiating texts to the Council Secretariat grants it a considerable power of the pen that can be used to subtly (and sometimes not so subtly) shift outcomes.

The leadership model is divided into three analytical categories (see Figure 2.2). The first category of variables relates to the leadership resources that EU institutions can possess in intergovernmental negotiations. The second category is the impact of the negotiating context, which determines the size of the bargaining impediments, and whether opportunities exist for the provision of leadership by EU institutions. The third category is whether EU institutions are able to exploit successfully the opportunities available to play a leadership role.

FIGURE 2.2   *How leadership by EU institutions matters – a leadership model of European integration*

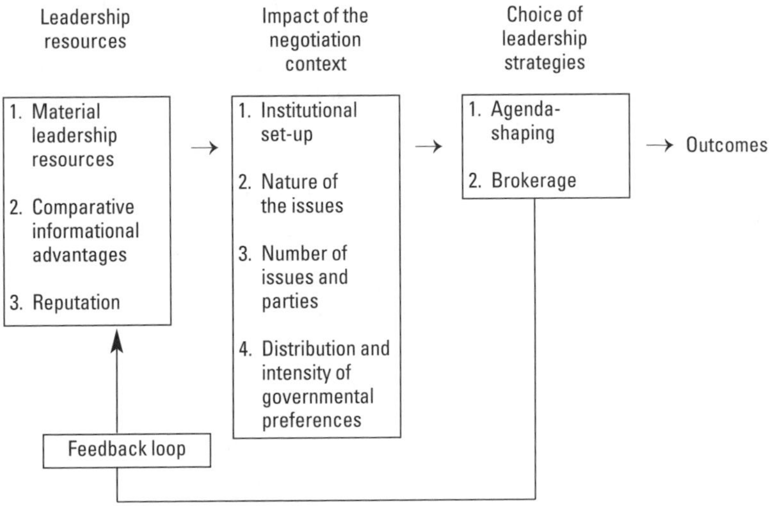

Leadership resources	Impact of the negotiation context	Choice of leadership strategies	
1. Material leadership resources 2. Comparative informational advantages 3. Reputation	1. Institutional set-up 2. Nature of the issues 3. Number of issues and parties 4. Distribution and intensity of governmental preferences	1. Agenda-shaping 2. Brokerage	→ Outcomes

Feedback loop

Leadership resources

There are three overall categories of leadership resources that EU institutions can potentially use to provide leadership in intergovernmental negotiations in the EU, enabling them to also gain influence over outcomes.

Material leadership resources

The impact of material resources echoes work in the realist and intergovernmentalist literature, where the basic argument is that leadership in negotiations is provided by actors with 'muscles'. The facet of material resources that is relevant for EU institutions in intergovernmental negotiations is the ability to link credibly resources that they control in daily Community policy-making with outcomes in intergovernmental negotiations. EU institutions can have the possibility of linking the control of formal powers that they possess in daily Community policy-making with specific issues in the history-making negotiations (Metcalfe, 1998, p. 417; Underdal, 1994, pp. 186–7). This can for example take the form of an EU institution offering a government a budgetary side payment in return for accepting a specific outcome in a treaty-reform negotiation.

Informational leadership resources

Complex, multilateral bargaining situations such as the negotiation of treaty reform or enlargement are, despite extensive preparation at both the national and EU level, often poorly defined negotiating situations, with actors possessing imperfect knowledge of the many complex issues on the agenda, and about their own and the preferences of other actors (Hampson and Hart, 1995; Hopmann, 1996; Midgaard and Underdal, 1977; Pollack, 1997; Stubb, 2002). As actors in these types of negotiations are realistically only boundedly rational, there are natural cognitive limitations upon the negotiating abilities of actors. In such circumstances, the possession of comparative informational advantages can potentially be translated into influence over outcomes.

There are three types of informational resources:

1) levels of substantive technical and legal knowledge of the issues under discussion (content expertise);
2) analytical skills (process expertise), and
3) knowledge of the state of play of the negotiations (Cox and Jacobson, 1973, p. 20; Finnemore and Sikkink, 1998, pp. 899–900; Sandholtz, 1992, pp. 27–8; Wall and Lynn, 1993).

Content expertise has two aspects. Technical expertise of the issues under consideration deals with knowledge of how treaty provisions work at present or the impact of concessions given to new members of the EU. Legal expertise relates to the possession of extensive familiarity with the body of EU law (the *acquis communautaire*), which is vital when drafting treaty texts or estimating the impact of potential revisions.

Process expertise deals with the possession of the necessary analytical skills and experience to be able to digest the hundreds of often very complicated and technical proposals on the many different issues under discussion in a given negotiation. Actors that do not have the necessary process expertise are unable to enter into an efficient joint problem-solving effort aimed at finding a mutually acceptable outcome. Another type of process expertise deals with the possession of the procedural skills necessary to effectively steer a negotiation towards an efficient and mutually acceptable outcome. These skills are usually based upon the institutional memory of a given actor, and learning curves are often present. For example, the Council Secretariat has over time built up an unrivalled institutional memory of how compromises are forged in IGC negotiations.

Finally, turning to the importance of information on actor prefer-ences and the state of play of negotiations, there are two reasons why national delegates in history-making negotiations often do not have detailed information on the nature and intensity of the preferences of other actors on the myriad of issues under discussion. First, individ-ual delegations can have difficulties in keeping tabs on different actor preferences on a wide range of issues. Secondly, delegations are often reluctant to reveal their 'true' preferences due to the negotiator's dilemma (see above). Delegates can for example have strategic reasons for holding their cards in order to see how an issue plays out before revealing their hand (Tallberg, 2003; Underdal, 2002, p. 115).

Moravcsik contends that if governments have incentives to with-hold information from one another, they would also withhold it from EU institutions (1999a, p. 279). Yet EU institutions such as the Council Secretariat are trusted partners, and governments are often more open with the Secretariat than they are with other national dele-gations, or even the Presidency (see below). When this is the case, a trusted actor such as the Council Secretariat can discuss with each party the nature and intensity of their preference in an attempt to help the parties find a mutually acceptable, Pareto-efficient outcome (Metcalfe, 1998, pp. 424–5; Raiffa, 1982; Scharpf, 1997, p. 145; Stenelo, 1972, p. 54; Tallberg, 2003). But by gaining private infor-mation about the zone of possible agreement, the intervening actor can also craft an agreement within this zone that is closest to its own preferred outcome (Lax and Sebenius, 1986).

Reputation

Turning to the third category of leadership resources, a reputation for the provision of leadership in a manner that is broadly acceptable to governments is another resource that actors can possess in intergov-ernmental negotiations (Dupont and Faure, 1991, p. 50; Elgström, 2003; Metcalfe, 1998, p. 420; Wehr and Lederach, 1996). A reputa-tion for acceptable interventions can be based on recognition of the utility of the actor's contributions, the perceived legitimacy of the actor, and/or whether the leader's proposals are close to the centre of gravity of a given negotiation (Bercovitch and Houston, 1996, pp. 25–7; Drake, 2000, pp. 52–5; Haas, 1990, pp. 87–8; Hampson and Hart, 1995, p.18; Hopmann, 1996, p. 225; Menon, 199; Tallberg, 2002a, 2003a; Wehr and Lederach, 1996).

The reputation of a leader can be damaged if the leader is seen to be acting too partially either in the way in which they fulfill a specific institutional role, or as regards promoting a particularly unwelcome outcome (Bercovitch, 1996b, p. 5). When a leader is seen as acting too partially, this can damage their ability to provide leadership in later negotiations. For example, if the EU institution is seen as an expert assistant in the negotiations, then they should not be seen as following political goals (Hooghe, 2001, p. 7).

The impact of previous actions upon reputation of an EU institution is modeled in my theory as a feedback loop from the choice of leadership strategies in previous negotiations, or from other relevant events in daily Community policy-making, and back into the reputation of the EU institution in the next intergovernmental negotiation (see Figure 2.2).

The impact of the negotiating context

The negotiating context matters in that it determines the scope of possibilities that EU institutions have for translating leadership resources into influence over outcomes through the provision of leadership in history-making negotiations. In highly complex situations where there is also a strong pressure for an agreement, the demand for leadership is high, opening many *opportunities* for EU institutions to translate their leadership resources into influence over outcomes.

Institutional position of the EU institution

A widely held conjecture in negotiation theory and rational choice institutionalism holds that how negotiations are structured affects how actor resources are translated into influence over outcomes (Garrett and Tsebelis, 2001; Zartman, 2002). This is particularly evident when we are dealing with highly institutionalized, multilateral negotiations such as history-making negotiations in the EU. The institutional set-up of the negotiation can matter in that actors either can start with or gain a privileged position during a negotiation that can be exploited to influence outcomes (Sebenius, 1984, 1991; Watkins, 1999, pp. 257–8).

Examples of privileged institutional positions in IGCs include being in charge of the drafting of treaty texts, or actually having voting power within a preparatory forum such as the Convention in 2002–3. In the fifth enlargement negotiations, the Commission had a strong institutional position qua its role of monitoring the progress made by candidate countries in implementing the EU's requirements for accession, and its role of providing draft EU positions in the negotiations.

Based upon general conjectures in negotiation theory and in rational choice institutionalism, different institutional positions affect the opportunities and constraints upon actor strategies for providing leadership. We should therefore expect that the ability of actors to successfully provide leadership increases with the level of their formal and informal involvement in the negotiation and drafting process.

The nature of the issues being negotiated

The complexity and/or technicality of issues under negotiation can have an impact upon the ability of actors to provide leadership. If we assume that national delegates in a given negotiation do not have perfect knowledge of the often very complex institutional and legal implications of the issues under discussion owing to high bargaining costs, then we would expect that in complex and/or technical issues, actors such as EU institutions that possess comparative informational advantages would have greater success in providing effective leadership (Meier, 1989, p. 280; Pollack, 1997, pp. 126–7).

The number of issues and parties in the negotiations

Thirdly, the number of issues and parties to the negotiations also matters, in that both can increase the level of complexity of a negotiation provided that they increase the number of cleavages in a given negotiation (Hampson and Hart, 1995, pp. 28–9; Midgaard and Underdal, 1977). When negotiations deal with numerous issues among many different parties it becomes increasingly difficult for the parties to identify possible agreements, while meaningful communication between parties becomes more challenging, if not impossible (Hampson and Hart, 1995, pp. 28–9; Hopmann, 1996; Midgaard and Underdal, 1977; Raiffa, 1982). The increase in the level of complexity of a given negotiating situation increases the demand for some type of leadership to assist the parties in finding a mutually acceptable outcome.

In an EU of 25 member states, even a simple *tour de table* takes several hours, while more substantial negotiations among 25 governments who all possess a veto over the final outcome becomes a physical impossibility. In these types of complex situations, substantive negotiations often move outside of the actual negotiating room, and into more informal settings where the possession of analytical skills and the knowledge of actor preferences are strategic assets that enable leaders to help the parties find a mutually agreeable outcome and, in the process, also grant them opportunities to influence the final outcome. Therefore we should expect that the ability of EU institutions to translate asymmetrically distributed informational leadership resources into influence through the provision of leadership increases with the number of issues and parties to a given negotiation.

The distribution and intensity of governmental preferences

Finally, the distribution and intensity of governmental preferences impacts upon the ability of EU institutions to translate their leadership resources into influence over outcomes in intergovernmental negotiations in the EU. First and most obviously, when governments have strongly held and irreconcilable positions, no zone of possible agreement exists. When faced with such a deadlock, EU institutions have few if any instruments that can be used to push governments towards agreement. For example, in the end game of the 1996–7 IGC it became increasingly clear that governmental positions on the delicate institutional issues were incompatible, and once governments recognized that no compromise was possible they simply agreed to disagree by pushing the resolution of the issue further into the future (see Chapter 5).

When a zone of possible agreement does exist, the impact of EU institutions varies according to two factors. First, when governments have unclear preferences, EU institutions can potentially have greater success in securing their own preferred outcome by for example putting forward proposals that construct a 'focal point' for further negotiations (Garrett and Weingast, 1993, p. 186; Pollack, 2003, pp. 53–4).

Secondly, the strength of governmental preferences also matters for the ability of EU institutions to play a guiding role. When issues are highly politically salient, such as issues with large distributional consequences, we should expect that governments would have incentives to mobilize the necessary resources to reduce bargaining costs. In such issues, governments would therefore keep the negotiations firmly under their control, thereby weakening the bargaining advantages of actors with strong informational leadership resources. In contrast, in less salient issues we would expect that EU institutional actors and other actors possessing strong informational leadership resources would have more discretion in shaping the discussions and outcome (Epstein and Segal, 2000; Meier, 1989, p. 279).

Thirdly, EU institutions can matter when there is a strong demand for agreement and a zone of possible agreements exists, but where governments have difficulties in choosing a specific solution on the Pareto frontier owing substantial coordination problems related to high bargaining costs and strongly held preferences. In this type of situation, a trusted intervener such as an EU institution can step in and potentially broker an agreement, gaining opportunities to choose the outcome that is closer to their own preferred outcome in the process (Carnevale and Arad, 1996; Kressel, 1989; Young, 1991).

The choice of leadership strategy

While the contextual variables describe the *opportunities* that EU institutions have in order to play a leadership role, these opportunities must then be successfully translated into actual influence through the provision of leadership. The literature abounds with different typologies of leadership strategies, but of most relevance for EU intergovernmental negotiations and the provision of leadership by EU institutions are the strategies that involve the use of material and informational leadership resources to shape the agenda and broker outcomes (Metcalfe, 1998, p. 430; Sjöstedt, 1994, p. 242; Tallberg, 2003a; Young, 1991).

Leadership by an EU institution can affect either the efficiency and/or distributive dimension of a given negotiation. Leadership directed towards securing a more efficient agreement involves a variety of agenda-shaping and brokerage tactics to put together a deal that eludes other actors, helping the parties overcome bargaining impediments (see Figure 2.1) (Tallberg, 2003; Young, 1991, pp. 293–8). In the literature this is termed 'entrepreneurial leadership' by Young, and 'instrumental leadership' by Underdal (Underdal, 1994; Young, 1991, pp. 293–8). Appropriate agenda-shaping tactics for instrumental leadership aimed at improving the efficiency of agreements involve managerial agenda-shaping, where the EU institution for example uses its procedural expertise to give advice on managing the agenda to the Presidency (Tallberg, 2003), and brokerage tactics where an EU institutions utilizes its informational advantages to help governments find a mutually acceptable solution (Carnevale and Arad, 1996; Kressel, 1989; Young, 1991). Leadership aimed at improving the efficiency of agreements is often difficult to detect, as it usually involves low-profile tactics and occurs behind the scenes by EU institutions.

Leadership can also be aimed more at shifting outcomes closer to one's own position, that is, along the distributive dimension (see

Figure 2.1). Here leadership involves higher-profile agenda-shaping and brokerage tactics. Looking first at agenda-shaping, this involves advocacy, informational and managerial tactics aimed at putting new issues on the agenda, removing issues, or manipulating the content of existing issues (Kingdon, 2003; Tallberg, 2003). Advocacy tactics deal with putting forward proposals and mobilizing support behind them. Informational tactics are attempts to shape the agenda by providing new information or manipulating existing information in an attempt to, for example, raise the awareness of actors to specific problems (Kingdon, 2003, p. 115). Higher-profile managerial tactics typically deal with manipulating the agenda by, for example, structuring the agenda of the negotiations in such a way that specific issues are prioritized or excluded. Brokerage strategies aimed at the distributive dimension involve EU institutions utilizing their informational advantages to broker an outcome closer to their own preferred outcome (Carnevale and Arad, 1996; Kressel, 1989; Young, 1991).

While high-profile leadership strategies involving, for example, the strong advocacy of extreme positions that are far outside of existing zones of possible agreement are sometimes effective for governments in EU negotiations, and in particular when a government possesses a credible veto threat in intergovernmental negotiations using unanimity, these types of strategies are rarely effective for EU institutions (Bailer, 2004; Schneider and Cederman, 1994; Tsebelis, 1990; Tsebelis and Garrett, 2001). EU institutions seldom possess sufficient material leadership resources, or 'sticks and carrots', to push governments to accept a given solution when it is far from an existing zone of agreement, and they can only in exceptional circumstances utilize informational agenda-shaping to reshape an existing zone of agreement. The only situation where we can expect that these types of tactics will be successful is when the zone of agreements shifts owing to external factors and creates a 'window of opportunity' through which a proposal from an EU institution can pass (Kingdon, 2003, pp. 175–82).

We should therefore expect that the most appropriate leadership strategies for EU institutions involve relatively low-profile tactics aimed at pushing an outcome closer to the institution's own preferred outcome *within* an existing zone of agreement, or when an EU institution advocates a position that is close to that of a key player in the negotiations.

Two crucial factors for all attempts at leadership are whether there exists, first, a demand for leadership to overcome bargaining impediments and, secondly, the coherence, skill and necessary energy with which the EU institution attempts to provide leadership (Bailer, 2004, p. 106; Underdal, 1994).

Conclusion

By incorporating key insights from negotiation theory and rational choice institutionalism into a parsimonious and coherent leadership model, it has been argued in this chapter that EU institutions can have significant influence in the history-making decisions of the European integration process, but that their influence is contingent upon the specific negotiating context and their choice of leadership strategy. EU institutions can play a significant leadership role through the use of leadership strategies when:

- they possess strong material resources and/or comparative informational advantages;
- they have a reputation for impartiality and/or for the provision of reliable expert advice;
- they have privileged institutional positions;
- the issues being negotiated are technically complex;
- the negotiating situation is complex;
- the distribution and intensity of governmental preferences opens a window of opportunity; and
- they choose leadership strategies that are appropriate for the given negotiating context.

This leadership model of European integration serves as the baseline for the empirical analyses in the following chapters of the negotiations of the major history-making decisions of European integration from the mid-1980s until 2004.

Chapter 3

Negotiating the Single European Act

Introduction – the high-water mark of Commission influence

In the early 1980s, there were few signs of cooperation on either side of the Atlantic. The US under President Reagan was locked in an increasingly dangerous arms race with the Soviet Union that threatened to turn the cold war into a much warmer affair. In Europe, the political climate between the ten European Community states had been soured by UK Prime Minister Thatcher pounding her handbag on the Brussels table demanding her money back, while Greece called for a renegotiation of the terms of its membership. Further, the original goal of the EC to create a true common market looked increasingly unrealistic, as governments had introduced a series of non-tariff barriers (NTBs) in response to the second oil crisis in 1979. Political decision-making within the Council of Ministers was stalled, with the Commission proposing detailed harmonization measures to the Council, where the need for unanimity made it almost impossible to reach an agreement (Beach, 2001, p. 61). And yet by the mid-1980s the US was taking the first steps together with the Soviet Union towards détente and later the end of the cold war, while the EC had decided in the 1985 IGC to take a fundamental step to re-launch the Community.

This chapter recounts the European side of the story by looking at the 1985 IGC, and the role that EU institutions, and the Commission in particular, played in it. Why was the Commission such a vital actor in the IGC? After an overview of the course of the negotiations, the chapter looks at what the three EU institutions wanted in the IGC. Following this, I describe why the Commission was in such a prime position to provide guidance and assistance in the IGC, whereas the EP was forced into a subsidiary position. The chapter concludes by showing that the Commission also played its cards astutely in the IGC by both taking an active part in the behind-the-scenes technical drafting process, and by skillfully exploiting its agenda-setting position by tabling moderate and realistic proposals that created a broader and more ambitious SEA than would have otherwise been agreed upon.

The course of the negotiation of the 1985 IGC

The agenda-setting phase – Fontainebleau and the White Paper

Despite the bleakness of the early 1980s for European cooperation, there were several encouraging signs. In 1981 a joint German-Italian initiative was put forward by their respective foreign ministers that proposed the creation of a form of European Union. The Genscher-Colombo initiative called for strengthened economic and foreign policy cooperation, together with the creation of European defence coordination. The European Council was to be granted a stronger role of providing political guidance, while the Council of Ministers would increasingly use QMV (qualified majority voting). But Italy and Germany did not agree on whether the treaties needed to be revised, and therefore the proposal was silent on the issue.

The initiative was received 'with satisfaction' by the London European Council, and subsequently resulted in the non-binding Stuttgart Declaration of June 1983, in which the heads of state and government stated their resolve to 'transform the whole complex of relations between their states into a European Union' by enhancing the role of the European Parliament and the scope of EC activity (Gazzo, 1985a, pp. 29–44). Parallel initiatives were being developed by the European Parliament. In February 1984 the EP adopted the Draft Treaty establishing the European Union (DTEU) (see Gazzo, 1985a, pp. 50–81). Based upon an initiative started by MEP federalist Altiero Spinelli, the draft called for the creation of a more federal constitution for the Community (see below for more).

The year 1984 was a turnaround for the Community. During the French Presidency of the EC in the first half of 1984, several of the outstanding problems that had plagued the Community were solved. After French President Mitterrand's abandonment of his socialist 'dash for growth' in 1983, he became a powerful advocate of European integration as a move to recast his political identity (Moravcsik, 1998, p. 332), even calling for the EP's federalist Draft Treaty to be taken seriously (Gazza, 1985a, pp. 96–7; Wallace, 1990, p. 219). At the Fontainebleau European Council Summit in May 1984, solutions were reached on both the British budgetary contribution and the problems surrounding agricultural spending within the Common Agricultural Policy (CAP) (see Gazzo, 1985a, pp. 96–7).

The Summit also took the first steps towards treaty reform by creating two committees, based upon a joint initiative from German Chancellor Kohl and Mitterrand (Moravcsik, 1998, pp. 352–3). The two committees were the Ad Hoc Committee on a People's Europe (the Adonnino Committee), that would study aspects of the EC directly visible to common citizens, and the Ad Hoc Committee for Institutional Affairs (the so-called Dooge Committee). The Dooge Committee, also called 'Spaak II' as a specific reference to the inspiratory role played by the Spaak committee in the mid-1950s upon the Treaty of Rome negotiations, was to 'make suggestions for the improvement of the operation of European cooperation in both the Community field and that of political, or any other, cooperation' (Gazzo, 1985a, p. 96).

The French representative to the committee put forward a draft report during the committee's second meeting that framed the agenda (Moravcsik, 1998, pp. 360–1). The two primary issues in the report were the extension of qualified majority voting (QMV) and the right of veto power (the Luxembourg Compromise).

Within the Dooge Committee there was a basic cleavage between 'maximalist' and 'minimalist' countries. The 'maximalists' members wanted an increase in the use of QMV in the Community, and were interested in institutional reforms that could lead to an IGC being convened to revise the treaties. The 'minimalists' were only interested in small changes, primarily an informal agreement on increasing the use of QMV in the Council, and were against the convening of an IGC.

An interim report was presented to the Dublin Summit in December 1984, but the report was very vague as no consensus had yet been reached. The final report was to be submitted to the Brussels European Council Summit in March 1985, but owing to the preoccupation of the member states with solving problems in the Iberian accession negotiations, a discussion of the report was postponed to the Milan Summit in June 1985.

The Dooge report detailed ways of improving decision-making through QMV and broadening the Community's scope of action through the completion of the Internal Market and stronger foreign policy cooperation (see Gazzo, 1985a, pp. 123–47). The report advocated a 'homogenous economic area' 'by creating a genuine internal market', setting out these objectives 'without purporting to draft a new Treaty in legal form'. The report did propose that an IGC be convened. Further, the report referred to strengthening the

EMS and liberalizing capital movements. Owing to the strong cleavages in the group, the 'minimalists' included many footnotes in the report, making explicit their opposition to many of the points.

While the Dooge Committee was deliberating, a new Commission was appointed on 17 July 1984, with former French Minister for Economics and Finance and the Budget Jacques Delors being elected Commission President. Prior to taking office on 7 January 1985, President-elect Delors travelled to national capitals in the autumn of 1984, searching for a 'big idea' with could relaunch the integration process (Grant, 1994, p. 66; Moravcsik, 1998, p. 362). Delors raised the questions of monetary union, defence cooperation, institutional reform, and an internal market (Grant, 1994, p. 66; McAllister, 1997, pp. 164–5). Delors was only able to find strong support in France for his own personal priority – monetary union. Germany and Italy for example wanted strengthened foreign policy cooperation (Moravcsik, 1998, pp. 315–16). The only issue that had the support of all ten member state governments was the Internal Market, also called the Single Market (Armstrong and Bulmer, 1998, p. 21; Dinan, 1999, p. 110).

At the March 1985 Brussels European Council Summit, Delors successfully lobbied the heads of state and government to request that the Commission draw up a program and timetable to achieve an Internal Market by 1992 (Dinan, 1999, pp. 111–12; McAllister, 1997, p. 172). This request resulted in the now famous Commission White Paper that was presented in June 1985 prior to the Milan Summit.

The White Paper contained a blueprint and timetable for completing the Single European Market (European Commission 1985). The paper was divided into three chapters: the removal of physical barriers at borders, the elimination of technical barriers to trade in goods and services and the reduction of fiscal barriers. The paper contained almost 300 proposals in which the four freedoms were lumped together in order to prevent the singling out of particularly sensitive issue areas from the others.

The Milan Summit took place on 28–9 June 1985. The Summit endorsed the Commission White Paper as the program for achieving the goal of a functioning Internal Market and decided to convene an IGC to start during the Luxembourg Presidency in the second half of 1985. The contentious decision to convene an IGC despite opposition from the UK, Denmark and Greece will be discussed further below.

The IGC – from Milan to the Kirchberg plateau

The IGC was convened on 22 July 1985 and was planned to be concluded in December 1985 at the Luxembourg European Council Summit. While previous IGCs, such as the one that negotiated the 1965 Merger Treaty that created one set of institutions for all three European Communities, had been negotiated within the framework of the Council and then adopted in a brief ceremonial IGC, it was decided that the actual negotiations in the 1985 IGC would take place within the IGC itself.

The basic mandate of the IGC was for a revision of the treaties which 'should be undertaken with a view to improving Council's decision-making procedures, strengthening the Commission's executive power, increasing the powers of the European Parliament and extending common policies to new fields of activity' (EC Bulletin, 7/8–1985, point 1.1.10).

Two working groups were set up by the foreign ministers to negotiate the reforms. A European Economic Community (EEC) group was set up composed mostly of permanent representatives, called the Dondelinger Group after the Luxembourg chair of the group. This group would discuss the key elements of reform relating to the scope of Community powers and decision-making procedures. A parallel forum was created to discuss reforms to the European Political Community (EPC) that dealt with foreign policy cooperation outside of the supranational Community. The EPC group was composed of political directors who were senior national officials who dealt with foreign policy within EPC. The foreign ministers themselves met six times during the IGC.

The most salient issues in the IGC were: the definition of the Internal Market; the scope of QMV; whether all of the Internal Market measures should come under a 'blanket' QMV clause; the role of the European Parliament (EP); whether economic cohesion policies should be extended; and whether the treaty should include a reference to monetary union (Middlemas, 1995, p. 147; McAllister, 1997, p. 179). The basic cleavage in the IGC was the same as in the Dooge Committee – between the 'minimalists' and 'maximalists' (Budden, 2002, p. 77; Corbett, 1987, p. 244).

The Luxembourg Presidency attempted to chair the IGC using a subdued and neutral approach (Middlemas, 1995, p. 146). As will be discussed more extensively below, most of the negotiations centred upon proposals tabled by the Commission. Further, the Commission played a central role in the actual drafting process of the treaty within a drafting group composed of officials from the Commission, the

Luxembourg Presidency and the Council Secretariat (Interview NAT-20).

Most of the issues were closed by the time of the Luxembourg Summit that was held on 2–4 December 1985. The outstanding issues in the final stage regarded the Internal Market, the powers of the European Parliament and questions of cohesion and monetary union (McAllister, 1997, p. 181). However, despite the heads of state and government spending twenty-one hours negotiating on the matters, they proved unable to solve these issues. A final deal was only reached in a foreign minister meeting on 16–17 December, and even then several loose ends were first wrapped up in a ministerial session held in Luxembourg on 27 January 1986, where the final draft of the Single European Act (SEA) was then approved (Dinan, 1999, p. 119).

The final treaty attempted to complete the Internal Market, primarily by the inclusion of a broader definition of the Internal Market coupled with a blanket QMV clause in Article 100a of the EC Treaty (now, after amendment, Article 95 EC). The article could be used for harmonizing national legislation in order to create a functioning Internal Market (see Table 3.1). The SEA significantly strengthened the powers of the EP through the introduction of the cooperation procedure in Article 189c of the EC Treaty (now, after amendment, Article 252 EC). The scope of the Community (EC) was also expanded through the introduction of new policy competences, including environmental and R&D policies. The transfer of funds through economic and social cohesion funds was also introduced. Finally, the EPC was linked with the Community as a separate inter-governmental pillar.

The SEA was widely seen in 1986 as a 'modest decision', or a 'smiling mouse' (Grant, 1994, p. 74). Delors himself complained at the time that the member states had failed to rise to the challenge, and that they had given birth to a 'monstrosity' (ibid.). Yet as the next few years proved, the SEA was a 'mouse that roared' (ibid.), and the following will show that the Commission had significant influence upon the final outcome. Even Andrew Moravcsik, the foremost proponent of the argument that EU institutions do not matter in IGCs, has admitted that 'supranational actors had a slightly larger influence on outcomes [in the 1985 IGC] than in other grand bargains . . . no government had outlined a package of reforms like the White Paper. Supranational entrepreneurship speeded reform' (Moravcsik, 1998, p. 347).

TABLE 3.1 *The outcome of the 1985 IGC – The Single European Act*

Issue area	Outcome
New policy areas	• introduced new Community competences in environment, economic and social cohesion, and R&D • foreign policy cooperation (EPC) attached to treaties, though as a separate intergovernmental pillar
Reform of existing policy areas	• amended provisions on social policy, monetary provisions, and the Internal Market
Institutional reforms	• increased the use of QMV, especially in the Internal Market through Article 100a of the EC Treaty (now, after amendment, Article 95 EC) • introduced the cooperation procedure • extended the use of the consultation procedure • opened for the creation of a lower European court.

Source: The Single European Act, *Official Journal of the European Communities*, No. L 169/1, 29.6.87.

What did EU institutions want in the 1985 IGC?

The Commission – re-launching the Community through the Internal Market

As was seen above, the completion of the Internal Market was but one of Delors' four main priorities. But while Delors might have preferred monetary union, given the opposition from member states that he would face on this path, he decided to focus the Commission upon achieving the Internal Market (Armstrong and Bulmer, 1998, p. 20; McAllister, 1997, p. 165; Grant, 1994). He sought to 'call the bluff of governments which had constantly proclaimed that they were in favour of liberalism and the enlarged market' (Delors in *Debates in the European Parliament*, Number 2, 328/42, 9 July 1985).

The Commission did not advocate writing a new treaty to replace the existing treaties, as the EP did, but only wanted amendments that could be used to 're-launch' the EC (McAllister, 1997, p. 165). The primary amendment advocated by the Commission was the increase in the use of majority voting in the Council, which would naturally have the beneficial side effect of strengthening the Commission's agenda-setting power. The Commission also wanted to extend Community competence to policies such as environmental, cohesion and monetary policies (Budden, 2002, p. 84; Delors in Gazzo, 1986, pp. 23–7) and to complement the Internal Market with 'social justice' by creating a certain level of harmonization of social rules and standards (McAllister, 1997, p. 165).

Looking at institutional issues, the Commission basically wanted to strengthen its own powers and those of the EP's. The Commission wanted stronger implementing powers vis-à-vis the Council and was advocating a moderate strengthening of the EP, primarily through the introduction of a cooperation procedure (Corbett, 1987, pp. 255–6). Crucial to the Commission's cooperation procedure proposal was that the Commission would have to approve any EP amendments for the changes to have effect, meaning that the EP would in reality only be strengthened vis-à-vis the Council, and not vis-à-vis the Commission.

The European Parliament – towards a federal European Union

The EP was internally split in the early 1980s as to which path Europe should choose to escape from stagnation (Corbett, 1998, pp. 142–60). The basic split was between two groups of MEPs organized in the so-called Kangaroo and Crocodile groups. MEPs in the Kangaroo group focused on the policy direction that Europe should take, arguing for a liberalization of European markets as the way out of the quagmire. More influential for the EP position was the Crocodile group, which had Altiero Spinelli as its chairman and inspiration. The group focused on institutional issues by advocating the creation of a quasi-federal European Union. The Crocodile group succeeded in instigating the drafting of the EP's Draft Treaty on European Union (DTEU), which was approved by the EP plenary in February 1984. The EP intended that the DTEU would then be adopted *as is* by governments. In the following, the DTEU is taken to represent the aggregate institutional position of the EP during the IGC.

The DTEU was a relatively short and simple treaty that would replace the existing treaties with a more federal Union, although the scope of the Union would not be much greater than the existing EC. The DTEU introduced a series of federal principles, such as a form of catalogue of competences and subsidiarity. A form of European citizenship was to be introduced (Art. 3 DTEU), along with the incorporation of certain fundamental rights from the European Convention for the Protection of Human Rights and the European Social Charter (Art. 4 DTEU). Regarding policies, the Internal Market was to be strengthened and different deadlines were to be used (Art. 47 DTEU). Foreign and judicial cooperation were to be incorporated into the treaties (Art. 64–69, 46 DTEU), together with the coordination of economic policies (Art. 50 DTEU). Other policies were to be strengthened, including the environment and education (Art. 59, 60 DTEU).

The EP was to be significantly strengthened through the creation of a co-decision procedure (Art. 38 DTEU), which would be the standard decision-taking procedure. EP budgetary power was to be extended to include all types of Union expenditure, including agriculture (the CAP) (Art. 76 DTEU).

A new legislative instrument, the law, was to replace the existing regulations and directives (Art. 34 DTEU). The use of majority voting was to be significantly extended also (Art. 38 DTEU). The enforcement of Community law was to be strengthened by giving the ECJ the power to sanction member states for their violations, even allowing the ECJ to suspend a government from participating in Council business (Art. 44 DTEU)!

Most controversially, a provision was inserted that would allow the DTEU to come into effect when it was ratified by only a majority of member states representing two-thirds of the Union's population (Art. 82 DTEU).

The Council Secretariat – a stronger Europe with a strong Council

Based upon interviews with former Council Secretariat officials, the Secretariat's overall preferences in the 1985 IGC were basically to solve problems for national governments (Interview EC-3, EC-19, NAT-20). That being said, it was also clear that top officials in the Secretariat did and do have pro-integrative views towards strengthening Europe. And in the careful words of one interviewee, the Secretariat has 'convictions on the *feasibility* of certain solutions' (Interview EC-19). Based on the institutional interests of Secretariat, the Secretariat has often pushed for more Europe, but also a Europe with a strong Council. This would strengthen the institutional position of the Secretariat in comparison to its main 'rival', the Commission. We should also expect that the Secretariat would advocate that new areas of cooperation should be predominantly intergovernmental, with little or no role for the Commission.

The leadership resources of the EU institutions

The material resources of the EU institutions

The Commission had the ability to link budgetary side payments with certain issues in the IGC. The Commission and EP could in theory exploit discretion in the exercise of their formal powers in daily policy-making by linking outcomes they could control in daily policy to IGC outcomes, for example by threatening to withhold an opinion or proposal on an issue in order to force governments to grant them greater powers in the IGC.

The informational advantages of the EU institutions

The role that the Commission plays in daily Community policy-making is well known and does not require extensive elaboration here (see Hix, 1999; Nugent, 2000a, 2000b). It is sufficient to say that given its central role in both the legislative and implementation processes within the Community, this provided the Commission with detailed insights into the substantive aspects of the workings the EC Treaty that were not possessed by any other actor in the IGC (Budden, 2002, pp. 81, 90). In the IGC the Commission had intimate knowledge of most of the dossiers being negotiated in the IGC – especially as regards Internal Market matters. Most of the dossiers were areas where the Commission had decades of policy experience, and therefore the Commission was able to suggest legal changes to existing provisions with a knowledge-based authority that no other actor in the IGC possessed (Budden, 2002, pp. 81, 90). Further, the Commission was able to employ the informational resources of most of its Directorate-generals (DGs) in the IGC, giving the Commission extensive informational advantages vis-à-vis even the largest national delegations. Additionally, Commission Secretary General Emile Noël had been appointed in 1958 and had a breadth of experience in Community affairs that was unsurpassed (Interview NAT-20). Finally, Commission President Delors had a strong sense of what was broadly acceptable to governments based upon his *tour des capitales* prior to his investiture (Drake, 2000, pp. 90–1).

In contrast, the Commission had comparative disadvantages in the foreign policy-related dossiers. While the Commission had been associated with the intergovernmental European Political Cooperation on foreign policy since the 1970s, it had little expertise in the non-trade related areas of foreign relations and only a few officials within the

Commission worked on EPC in the mid-1980s (Nuttall, 1997, pp. 314–6)

The EP had few informational advantages vis-à-vis national delegations. While the exercise of drawing up the DTEU within the Institutional Affairs Committee had given the EP experience in some of the issues, it can also be argued that as the ideas in the text were so far outside of any realistic zone of acceptable agreements, the 'knowledge' gained in the exercise was of little relevance in the IGC.

One comparative informational advantage of the EP was the link between MEPs and national parties and parliaments (Corbett, 1998, p. 86), but the knowledge of what was acceptable nationally did not stop the EP from drafting and then fighting for the DTEU. The size of the staff of the EP Secretariat that dealt with IGC issues was very small in comparison to the officials available to the Commission or national governments (Christiansen, 2002, p. 43).

The Council Secretariat plays an overlooked but nonetheless central role in the EC policy-making process. The Council Secretariat officially provides administrative and technical assistance to the Council of Ministers, and the national Presidency chairing the Council (Sherrington, 2000, pp. 49–53). While the Secretariat played a relatively weak role of '*notaire*' for the Council until the early 1980s, the Secretariat since the appointment of Secretary-General Niels Ersbøll in 1980 had gradually strengthened its role into becoming the 'vital cog' in the EC policy-making process (Westlake, 1999, p. 313; Interview NAT-8).

The Secretariat has played a very important but overlooked role in the day-to-day Community policy-making process within the Council by: 1 providing both legal and policy-related advice to the Council and the Presidency; 2 playing the role of *confidante* and adviser to national delegations and the Presidency; and 3 helping to broker compromises when difficult impasse situations exist (Christiansen, 2003; Hayes-Renshaw and Wallace, 1997; Sherrington, 2000, pp. 49–50; Westlake, 1999, p. 318). Given the central role of the Council Secretariat in Council decision-making, this provided the Council Secretariat with detailed knowledge of the set-up and workings of the treaties, the preferences of member states, and extensive experience with brokering compromises (Budden, 2002, p. 81; Metcalfe, 1998; Westlake, 1999; Interviews EC-3, EC-9, EC-19, NAT-20).

While the Secretariat could not compete with the Commission as regards substantive expertise in the broad range of EC policies, given that the Secretariat only had 177 A grade officials in 1985 in comparison to 2380 Commission A grade officials (1984 figures) (Council

Secretariat, 2002; Stevens and Stevens, 2001, p. 110), and did not have policy-based expertise in the areas under discussion that had until then been outside of the remit of EC policy-making, the Secretariat did have a strong comparative advantage in brokering compromises in comparison to all other actors in the IGC. One former Secretariat official in an interview appropriately called the Secretariat the 'Council *Negotiating* Secretariat' (Interview EC-3). Key Secretariat officials have extensive experience in reading the signals sent by national delegations, and discerning zones of possible agreement and national 'red lines', enabling them to craft compromises that often elude other actors (Interview EC-19).

Furthermore, the knowledge possessed by the Secretariat on how the treaties are structured was unrivalled, especially in comparison with the administrations of smaller member states (Interview EC-3). While member states do have legal experts that understand most of these complex legal problems, national legal experts do *not* sit at the IGC negotiating table when deals are made. As national delegates trust the Secretariat (see below), and as they are also dependent upon the Secretariat for on-the-spot legal advice, this puts the Secretariat in the key position of being able to translate the vague ideas put forward by national delegates into workable draft legal text – giving them numerous opportunities in the process to gain influence over outcomes (ibid.). These advantages are especially evident during small state presidencies, as they do not have the diplomatic resources that larger member states, such as France or the UK, possess in being able to manage the negotiating and drafting process (Interview EC-19).

The reputation of the EU institutions

Given that the matters dealt with in both the Commission's White Paper and most of the dossiers in the 1985 IGC were part of the core bargain made by the member states in the 1957 Treaty of Rome, the issue areas under debate were seen as legitimate areas for Commission intervention. Delors clearly saw the strategic advantages of 'going back to basics and emphasizing one of the original objectives of the Treaty of Rome' (Dinan, 1999, p. 110), especially as governments had been reaffirming their commitment to achieving a functioning Internal Market repeatedly since the Hague Summit in 1969 (see Cameron, 1992, pp. 31–3; Fiedler, 2000, p. 77).

Yet there were no precedents for the proper role to be played by the EU institutions in an IGC, as previous treaty reforms had been negotiated *within* the Council, and then approved by a ceremonial IGC.

Therefore these roles had to be defined prior to the start of the IGC. In the 1985 IGC, most governments chose to treat the IGC like normal Community policy-making, where the Commission plays a key initiating and brokering role (Budden, 2002, p. 90; Dinan, 2000, p. 261; Interview EC-19). And as the Commission was an effective assistant to the IGC during the actual negotiations, the Commission maintained the confidence of governments throughout the negotiations, especially because of the high quality of Secretary General Emile Noël's interventions (De Ruyt, 1987, p. 72; Interview EC-19, NAT-20).

Further, member states trusted Delors personally in 1985 as he had been a colleague of national ministers only six months previously. As French Finance Minister from 1981 to 1983, and thereafter Minister for Economic and Financial Affairs and the Budget from 1983 until his appointment as Commission President in July 1984, he therefore had the confidence of most ministers and heads of state and government, including German Chancellor Kohl (Grant, 1994, p. 58). Finally, the Commission's positions on some issues relating to the Internal Market were strengthened by the close Commission links with transnational business within the European Roundtable of Industrialists (ERT) and civil society (Bornschier, 2000, p. 11; Fielder, 2000, pp. 84–5, 86–8).

Turning to look at the EP, it was clearly an unwanted guest in the 1985 IGC, reflecting both upon its strong advocacy of an extreme position prior to the IGC, and more generally upon the more peripheral role that the EP played in the mid-1980s in Community policy-making. The EP tried to increase the acceptance of it playing a role in the IGC by saying that it was the only 'legitimate representative of all the citizens of Europe', and therefore should have a seat at the IGC table (in Gazzo, 1985b, p. 35), but this fell on deaf ears.

Finally, the Secretariat was seen as a trusted assistant to the IGC, as the IGC was seen to be similar to work within the Council, where they played a similar role of trusted assistant (Interview EC-3, EC-19).

The opportunities for leadership created by the negotiating context

The role of the EU institutions in the 1985 IGC

The Commission was able to secure a privileged institutional position both prior to the IGC and during the IGC itself. Prior to the IGC, the

Commission was able to convince the member states to entrust it to put forward a blueprint for achieving the Internal Market. During the IGC itself, the Commission succeeded in gaining a role similar to its role in daily policy-making.

But Article 236 of the EC Treaty (now Article 48 EU) had little to say about the role of the Commission in an IGC negotiation, except that it could be asked its opinion prior to the IGC and that it could propose an amendment of the treaties to the Council (see Chapter 1). However the Commission acted from the start of the IGC as if it had the same right of initiative in the IGC as it had in daily EC policy-making, and no member state challenged this role (Budden, 2002, p. 90). The incoming Luxembourg Presidency even asked the Commission to put forward a set of proposals in key areas of the IGC, in effect giving the Commission de facto control of the IGC agenda (Interview EC-19; Moravcsik, 1998, p. 365; Ross, 1995, p. 32) – something which the Commission exploited skillfully, as will be seen below.

The Commission was involved in all levels of meetings on the EEC side of the IGC, with Delors attending both the European Council Summits of the heads of state and government and the foreign minister meetings. Delors' role in the European Council was particularly significant, as we will see further below in the section on agenda-shaping. Commission Secretary-General Emile Noël attended the meetings at the preparatory group level. In contrast, the Commission was not as involved in the EPC negotiations dealing with foreign policy matters, which took place in a separate intergovernmental forum in the IGC (Budden, 2002, p. 91).

The Commission also took part in the important task of drafting of treaty articles for the Luxembourg Presidency together with officials from the Presidency and the Council Secretariat (Interviews EC-3, EC-19, NAT-20). Finally, the Commission offered expert legal counsel to the IGC, a role that it shared together with the Council Secretariat's Legal Service (Christiansen, 2002, p. 47; Interview EC-22).

The EP in contrast was relegated to fighting for its views outside of the negotiating room prior to and during the IGC despite repeated attempts to carve a role for itself. Governments denied the EP an active role in the IGC, stating only that they would 'take account in its work of the draft Treaty adopted by the European Parliament', take into account further proposals from EP to IGC, and would submit the final result to the EP for a non-binding opinion (Corbett, 1998, pp. 219, 222–3; Budden, 2002, p. 91). EP delegates were, though, invited to several IGC meetings but no real deliberations took place in these exchanges of opinions (Corbett, 1998, p. 224; Gazzo,1986, p. 8).

The Council Secretariat had a central but not as pivotal a role in the 1985 IGC as it had in later IGCs. It did not act as the secretariat for the Dooge Committee (Budden, 2002, p. 83). During the IGC itself it played a role similar to its role in daily Council business, listening to delegations, preparing drafts and amendments to these drafts, questionnaires, synthesis papers and issue briefs (Interviews EC-3, EC-19, NAT-20). While the Secretariat formally only played a secretarial function for both the IGC and the Luxembourg Presidency, and provided expert legal advice to the IGC, in reality the Secretariat's role was much larger, and it gave both advice on the conduct of the negotiations, played a central role in the drafting of treaty texts together with the Commission, and offered the Presidency assistance in brokering key compromise agreements.

The nature of the issues being negotiated

Most of the issues under negotiation in the 1985 IGC were technically complex, and the future implications of reforms were difficult to predict. For example, when discussing whether to introduce a 'blanket' QMV clause for the Internal Market measures as proposed by the Commission's White Paper, governments were faced with the fundamental problem of how they could accurately predict whether future streams of legislation would benefit them or not in the almost 300 different individual areas called for in the White Paper (see Armstrong and Bulmer, 1998).

The number of issues and parties in the negotiations

The list of items on the agenda for the 1985 IGC was relatively short in comparison to subsequent IGCs. The main issues in both the Dooge Committee report and the Luxembourg Presidency's discussion note for the first IGC meeting in September were: establishing the Internal Market; expanding the EC's field of activity to environmental, cultural, health, education; and strengthening judicial cooperation and external policies (in Gazzo, 1985a, pp. 123–47; 1986, pp. 17–19). Institutional issues included strengthening the EP and executive powers of the Commission, and extending majority voting in the Council (ibid.). As these issues fell into the basic 'maximalist'/'minimalist' cleavage, the negotiating situation was relatively simple (see next section). Therefore, despite there being 12 governments negotiating in the IGC (delegates from the ten existing member states together with representatives of Spain and Portugal), the basic cleavage in the IGC reduced this complexity to two basic positions.

The distribution and intensity of governmental preferences

There was a basic consensus in the mid-1980s that reform was necessary, but governments disagreed about the form it should take. The basic cleavage in the 1985 IGC was between the 'maximalist' states who favoured strengthening EC institutions and increased EC competences, and 'minimalists', who first opposed convening an IGC, and then once they were overruled, wanted to limit the IGCs' scope to only include measures needed to achieve the Internal Market (see Figure 3.1 below) (Budden, 2002, p. 77).

Yet given the irreconcilability of the positions of the two coalitions, especially on questions of institutional reform and the scope of an extension of EC competences, this created a situation where leadership was necessary in order to first find a mutually acceptable compromise, and then assist the parties in achieving agreement.

Further, the issues on the agenda of the IGC were formulated in broad terms, with multiple possible outcomes in each issue area. The ambiguity of the issues on the agenda can for example clearly be seen in the Dooge Committee Report, where very vague wording is included regarding cohesion policies which should be aimed at 'the promotion of solidarity amongst the Member States aimed at reducing structural imbalances which prevent the convergence of living standards, through the strengthening of specific Community instruments and a judicious definition of Community policies' (in Gazzo, 1985a, p. 128). The vagueness of the agenda allowed the Commission to provide leadership by translating these broad priorities into actual treaty texts.

Additionally, there was relatively tight window for the negotiations. After the breakthrough at Fontainebleau in June 1984, there was an opportunity for reforms, but most governments also wanted to finish the negotiations prior to the coming Iberian enlargement in the start of 1986 (Budden, 2002, pp. 87–8). This created a situation where leadership was required to help the parties match their strong demand for agreement with the relatively tight window for agreement – a

FIGURE 3.1   *Major cleavages in the 1985 IGC negotiations*

demand for leadership that the Commission under Delors skillfully exploited.

Yet while many of the dossiers were very technical, there were also many issues that had clear political and/or economic costs for member states: most evidently the free movement of persons, but also the free movement of services. For the UK, the extension of Community competences in general was a politically sensitive issue (NAT-22). Institutional questions were very sensitive, especially regarding the powers of the European Parliament. Here it was difficult to construct easy trade-offs, as granting the EP increased powers was in many respects an either/or issue. Finally, the issue of foreign policy cooperation was seen to be 'high politics', and was therefore seen by member states as a no-go area for either majority voting or increased involvement by EU institutions (Corbett, 1987, pp. 251–3).

However, the overall picture was one of low political salience for most of the dossiers, largely due to the fact that most of the provisions under discussion dealt with deregulation, or 'negative integration', where governments only have to agree to *remove* existing barriers to trade, which is in the interests of all parties, whereas in so-called 'positive integration', governments *also* have to agree upon a common EC policy to *replace* the previous national measures (Hix, 1999; Majone, 1996; Scharpf, 1997).

Leadership by EU institutions in the 1985 IGC

Given the negotiating context of the IGC, the Commission was in a prime position to play a strong leadership role. The Secretariat had some opportunities, whereas the EP was relegated to the sidelines. Were any of the EU institutions able to exploit the opportunities they had in the IGC successfully to provide leadership? And if they did provide leadership, what effects did this have upon the efficiency and distribution of gains in the IGC?

Leadership by the European Commission

The Commission actively attempted to shape the agenda prior to the IGC, seizing the opportunity that had opened after the Fontainebleau Summit in May 1984 in first defining a formula for the Internal Market, and then mobilizing support behind it. Later, the Commission linked the Internal Market with the treaty reforms necessary to achieve it.

The Commission defined the form and scope of the Internal Market in its now famous White Paper, tabled days before the Milan Summit in 1985. Although most of the provisions in the Paper were pulled out of Commission desk drawers, the Paper was more than just the mere compilation of existing ideas argued by Moravcsik (Moravcsik, 1999a, pp. 293–4). What was novel about the White Paper was the way in which the proposals were linked, together with an overall timetable that ended in 1992 (Armstrong and Bulmer, 1998, pp. 309–10; Dinan, 1999, pp. 112–13). Additionally, the scope of the proposals in the White Paper opened many opportunities for spillover dynamics, which could then be cultivated to create future demands for integration in related policy areas.

Officials inside the Commission were aware of the many possibilities for spillover, and they therefore actively sought to *downplay* the implications of the White Paper by, for example, not openly stating in the report that the free movement of capital implies a form of monetary union (Middlemas, 1995, pp. 146, 148–9). Further, the potential implications of the proposals were cloaked in the technical language used (Dinan, 1999, p. 112; Sandholtz and Zysman, 1989, p. 115). Finally, as the Paper was tabled only ten days before the Milan summit, this prevented member states from drawing up counter-proposals (Middlemas, 1995, p. 143).

The Commission then turned its efforts to linking the White Paper with a potential IGC on institutional reform through informational tactics. Delors for example gave a series of speeches prior to the Milan Summit where he argued that the Internal Market as depicted in the White Paper could only be achieved if an IGC introduced majority voting for Internal Market regulations, thereby linking the common desire among the member states for completing the Internal Market with treaty reform (Dinan, 1999, p. 113).

At the Milan Summit, Delors played a key role in the decision to convene an IGC – a controversial decision that was termed a 'coup' by some participants (Interview NAT-20). A month before the Summit, the Italian Presidency submitted a draft mandate for an IGC (Gazzo, 1985a, pp. 161–3). The UK tabled a counter-proposal attempting to avoid an IGC by calling for strengthened foreign policy cooperation and an informal agreement to improve decision-making in the Council (Gazzo, 1985b, pp. 24–6; Grant, 1994, p. 71; Middlemas, 1995, p. 144). A joint Franco-German counter-proposal on a draft Treaty on European Union was put forward the day before the Summit started, but its ten articles dealt almost exclusively with foreign policy cooperation (Gazzo, 1985b, pp. 18–21; McAllister, 1997, p. 174). Delors in a meeting with President Mitterrand told him that he thought that the Franco-German proposal looked like the Fouchet Plan (Grant, 1994, p. 71). This influenced Mitterrand to subsequently pull back his support from the proposal, which then was not discussed in-depth at the Summit (ibid.).

Therefore, on the first day of the Summit a consensus was forming around the UK proposal for an informal agreement that would avoid an IGC (Moravcsik, 1998, p. 363). The interventions of the Commission changed this. In debates in the European Council, Delors argued vigorously that if the member states were serious about implementing the White Paper to complete the Internal Market, they would need to change the treaties in an IGC. To combat the paralysis in the Council, Delors proposed amending three articles so that the Council could decide Internal Market measures by QMV, while also strengthening the powers of the EP (Corbett, 1998, p. 216; Grant, 1994, pp. 71–2).

Delors' arguments helped swing the debate against the UK position (Interview NAT-20). Italian Prime Minister Benito Craxi, who chaired the Summit, asked the foreign ministers to prepare a proposal to amend the treaty at the end of the first day of the Summit. This would be the tried method of agreeing amendments to the treaties *within* the Council, and then convening a ceremonial IGC to ratify them. Yet this procedure required unanimity as the results of an IGC have to be accepted by all – something that clearly did not exist due to British, Danish and Greek resistance to changing the treaties.

In meetings through the night, the Italian Presidency, together with Commission officials, decided instead to force a decision under Article 236 of the EC Treaty (now Article 48 EU) on the convening of an IGC, which only required a simple majority vote (Dinan, 1999, p. 115; Grant, 1994, p. 72; Interview NAT-20; Moravcsik, 1998, p. 363). When the Summit started the next day, Craxi called a vote under Article 236 on convening an IGC – seven governments voted for, while the UK, Denmark, and Greece voted against. The convening of an IGC was by no means predestined, but was 'almost as much as a result of accident than of strategy' (Armstrong and Bulmer, 1998, p. 33), and was a process in which Delors played a key role (Interview NAT-20).

During the IGC itself, the Commission was extensively involved in the negotiations, playing a 'determining role' (De Ruyt, 1987, p. 70). This involvement took two primary forms. First, the Commission was invited by the Luxembourg Presidency to present a set of proposals for reforms in key areas, granting the Commission a privileged agenda-setting role that it skillfully exploited (Ross, 1995, p. 32; Interview EC-19). Secondly, the Commission took part in the behind-the-scenes working group that drafted all of the treaty texts in the IGC, together with officials from the Luxembourg Presidency and Council Secretariat (Interview EC-3, NAT-20).

In the following, I will focus on the more visible leadership role of the Commission that aimed at influencing the distributive dimension of the negotiations, where the Commission's shaping of the agenda through tabling proposals and brokering deals resulted in a Single European Act that arguably had a broader scope and created a stronger Europe than governments left to themselves would have agreed upon. The Commission's leadership shifted outcomes away from a narrow focus on the Internal Market to also include flanking measures such as cohesion policies, social policies, and foreign policy cooperation in the final treaty, and also created a stronger Europe by expanding the use of QMV to more measures than governments originally intended (Interview EC-24).

The Commission exploited the role delegated to it by the Luxembourg Presidency by tabling thirty proposals on a wider range of subjects than the member states had envisioned in for example the Dooge Committee Report. In comparison, only twenty-eight proposals were put forward by member states (Corbett, 1987, p. 244). The most important Commission proposals included proposals on: the definition of the Internal Market; institutional provisions; cohesion, environmental and social policies; monetary cooperation; and the executive powers of the Commission (Corbett, 1987).

Debates in the 1985 IGC centred on the Commission proposals (Corbett, 1987; Ross, 1995, p. 32). In the words of Budden 'it was the Commission's proposal around which member government preferences coalesced. Left to their own devices, member governments might have determined this particular point of balance amidst their scattered policy preferences. In the historical context of the rushed 1985 IGC, however, it was the Commission that played this role' (Budden, 2002, p. 81). But the Commission was doing more than just *anticipating* what governments wanted, and several of their successful proposals were clearly outside of what the member states had indicated that they wanted in the Dooge Committee Report.

The Commission's proposal on the definition of the Internal Market argued for a very broad formula that envisioned an area without frontiers, 'in which persons, goods and capital shall move freely under conditions identical to those obtaining within a member state' (in Gazzo, 1986, p. 48). The Commission proposed that a 'blanket' QMV clause should be introduced with the exception of the free movement of persons, and that implementing measures could be adopted by the Commission except where Council unanimity was required. Finally, the Commission proposed that if EC legislation was not enacted by 1992, automatic mutual recognition would be introduced – in effect giving the 1992 deadline direct legal effect that could be enforced before the ECJ.

This broad definition was opposed by among others the UK, France and Germany (Budden, 2002, p. 82; Corbett, 1987, p. 245; McAllister, 1997, p. 180), and during the negotiations the scope of the Internal Market was slowly whittled to a mere 'common market', together with a long list of exceptions to QMV. Delors lamented publicly in late November that the text had 'more holes than Gruyère', and lobbied both Mitterrand and Kohl to restore the original Commission proposal (Grant, 1994, p. 73). This resulted in a joint Franco-German initiative that returned to the Commission's original proposal (ibid.; De Ruyt, 1987). But in the final weeks of the IGC, member states reinserted some of the restrictions on QMV, although the scope of QMV in the SEA was arguably wider than it would have been in the absence of the ambitious Commission proposal, with QMV applicable for about two-thirds of the measures in the White Paper (Dinan, 1999, p. 118). Finally, a declaration was inserted that stated that the date 1992 would *not* create automatic legal effects, thereby ensuring that the Internal Market was a *political* objective and not a *legal* obligation.

On the institutional issue of the powers of the EP, there were three basic positions in the debate: granting full co-legislative powers to the EP in a co-decision procedure (Germany and Italy); a moderate strengthening of the EP by introducing a new cooperation procedure (Commission and a majority of member states); and keeping the status quo (UK and Denmark) (Corbett, 1987, pp. 243, 255–7). The final text was based upon the Commission's proposal (Corbett, 1987, p. 257), but was actually tabled by the Council Secretariat (Interview NAT-20).

On the question of the structure of the final treaty, the Commission proposed very early in the IGC that a single treaty should be drafted, composed of a section of joint provisions, and then two separate sections on the reforms of the Community and on foreign policy cooperation (EPC). This was met with scepticism from most member states (Dinan, 1999, p. 117). The French put forward a similar proposal, but the French version envisioned the creation of an intergovernmental European Union with its own secretariat (Corbett, 1987, p. 254). Delors used strong advocacy tactics in the IGC endgame in an attempt to convince foreign ministers at a meeting on 19 December to include the EPC within the treaties, and to strengthen the common elements of the treaty (Grant, 1994, p. 74). The ministers subsequently strengthened the federal rhetoric in the preamble, and coupled the EC and EPC together, calling the whole treaty the *Single European Act* (ibid.; Corbett, 1987, p. 254). But while the name of the final treaty was inspired by Delors, the creation of a single act was an idea broadly accepted by the member states (Dinan, 1999, p. 117; Grant, 1994, p. 74).

The Commission proposal on cohesion policies was the point of reference for the IGC debates. Poorer member states such as Greece and Ireland wanted to create an explicit link between their acceptance of the Internal Market and increased financial transfers (Corbett, 1987, p. 245). Proposals were tabled by the Commission, France, Ireland and Greece, but while the final outcome was based upon the Commission's proposal, governments peeled away the most controversial aspects of it, including a reference to social and working conditions and a proposed reform of social funds (Corbett, 1987, pp. 248–9; Gillingham, 2003, p. 234; Ziltener, 2000, p. 63).

The Commission succeeded in shaping the debates on environmental policy and social policy (Corbett, 1987, pp. 249–51). Again, while certain reservations were inserted into the text by governments, the Commission's proposal formed the focal point around which member state preferences converged (ibid.). In social policy, for example, the Commission put forward a proposal that argued for creating minimum standards in regulations governing working conditions, although it was not as ambitious as a similar Danish proposal (ibid.). Ross argues that the Commission was afraid of a strong British reaction to such proposals from the Commission, and therefore it 'hid' its advocacy behind the Danish and French social proposals (Ross, 1995, p. 33). The Commission proposal also included a proposed article for dialogue between management and labour at the EC level, which could lead to contractual agreements (ibid.). Both of these provisions were adopted by the IGC (Corbett, 1987, pp. 250–1) but as regards minimum standards in working conditions, the final outcome was closer to the Danish proposal.

The Commission was less successful when it tried high-profile strategies such as advocating positions that were far outside of existing zones of possible agreements. The best example of this was in the negotiations of strengthened monetary cooperation, where no real zone of possible agreements existed. Britain was opposed to any reference to monetary policy whatsoever, whereas Belgium, France, Ireland and Italy wanted strong monetary provisions in the final treaty. In the face of these disagreements, the Commission in September and October smartly dropped its initial strong advocacy of monetary references in the treaty (Moravcsik, 1998, p. 372), and instead tabled a modest proposal in November that would have codified the existing cooperation, together with references for future progress that could include monetary union (Corbett, 1987, p. 247).

Governments, as we would expect in such a highly contentious issue, maintained tight control over the negotiations by allowing the negotiations to be conducted by finance ministers, who were more focused on economic details than broader political considerations (Corbett, 1987, p. 247; Moravcsik, 1998, p. 365). But Delors did play a role in brokering the final compromise, where Germany accepted the modest reference to monetary union in the SEA in exchange for French acceptance of the free movement of capital (Grant, 1994, p. 73). British fears were allayed by stating that any further changes would require an IGC. The deal inserted three extra indents into the preamble referring to monetary union, along with a new chapter that obliged member states to attempt to ensure the convergence of their economic and monetary policies.

Despite the disappointing outcome for the Commission on monetary cooperation, Delors put a brave face on it by saying that the inclusion of the reference to monetary union had in itself been a victory for the Commission. 'It's like the story of Tom Thumb lost in the forest, who left white stones so he could be found. I put in white stones so we would find monetary union again' (Delors, in Grant, 1994, p. 74).

A final area where Commission attempts to play a leadership role failed were in the debates on the executive powers of the Commission. Both the Commission and the Netherlands tabled proposals to strengthen the Commission's implementing powers. But governments preferred the Dutch approach, and only adopted the Commission's suggestion that the Council could reserve powers for itself in specific cases by unanimity – a Commission suggestion that paradoxically weakens the Commission's powers vis-à-vis the Council in comparison to the pre-SEA equilibrium (Corbett, 1987, pp. 254–5; Grant, 1994, p. 74).

But overall, the Commission had a strong leadership role in the IGC, ensuring first that an IGC was held, and then that the IGC drafted a Single European Act with a broader and more ambitious scope than would otherwise have been achieved. Debates in the IGC centred on the Commission's proposals (Ross, 1995, p. 32), and the Commission played a key drafting role behind the scenes in the IGC. Observers note that the Commission provided between 60 and 70 per cent of the wording of the final SEA (Grant, 1994, p. 75; Moravcsik, 1998, p. 370).

Three factors were crucial for the success of Commission leadership in the SEA. First, by linking the White Paper with the IGC negotiations, the Commission expanded the range of issues to be discussed in the IGC (Cameron, 1992, p. 51), creating both new zones of possible agreement in certain issue areas, and shifting existing zones of agreement closer to Commission preferences in others. Secondly, the Commission's proposals were relatively realistic in most dossiers, attempting to maximize outcomes *within* existing zones of possible agreement. While these small shifts taken individually were perhaps not revolutionary, on an aggregate level they led to a more ambitious SEA than governments would have agreed upon themselves in the absence of Commission leadership. Finally, the Commission played a key role in improving the efficiency of the negotiations within the behind-the-scenes drafting process, and participants point out that most of the 'raw material' of the IGC came from the Commission, with Secretary-General Noël especially active in ensuring that the negotiations were efficient through the provision of instrumental leadership (NAT-20).

Moravcsik contends that the Commission only mattered in relatively technical and unimportant issues (Moravcsik, 1998, p. 370, 1999a), and therefore at most was 'limited to advancing innovative proposals and offering direct encouragement early in the negotiations in order to coordinate governments and social actors not yet aware of possible agreements' (Moravcsik, 1999a, p. 298). Yet when we investigate areas where the Commission was influential, there appears to be little correlation between the political salience of the issue and the influence of the Commission. Most telling are the significant fingerprints of the Commission in the sensitive issues of the definition of the Internal Market and cohesion policies. Further, the final SEA arguably had a much broader and more ambitious scope than would have been agreed by governments. Finally, the very decision to call an IGC was to a large degree a product of Commission leadership, though contingent upon the acceptance of the Italian Presidency to the Commission's strategy.

Leadership by the European Parliament

While the Commission played a key leadership role in the 1985 IGC, ensuring the increased efficiency of the negotiations while also shifting outcomes to create a broader and more ambitious SEA than would otherwise have been agreed upon, the EP had no direct role in the negotiations. Was the EP able to overcome this handicap and succeed in influencing outcomes in the 1985 IGC?

The EP's strategy prior to the IGC was to attempt to pre-empt any reform efforts of governments by drafting its own Draft Treaty on European Union (DTEU). Spinelli, for example, argued that while a proposal for further integration would *gather* momentum in the EP, a similar proposal would only *lose* momentum in an IGC (Corbett, 1998, p. 144). The EP's DTEU was an ambitious treaty framed in legal text that was intended to *replace* the existing Community with a more federal European Union. But by advocating such an extreme and unrealistic outcome, the EP had little impact on the debates prior to and during the IGC.

The EP attempted to build support for the DTEU by: lobbying governments both individually and collectively, using contacts with national political parties, lobbying national parliaments, and contacting interest groups, NGOs and academics (Jacobs, Corbett and Shackleton, 1995, pp. 301–2). But while governments paid lip-service to the DTEU, with for example the Dooge Committee Report stating that the negotiation of a draft European Union treaty should be 'guided by the spirit and the method of the draft treaty voted by the European Parliament' (in Gazzo, 1985a, p. 144), the DTEU was in reality politely but resolutely shelved by governments prior to the IGC, and there is little evidence that it had any significant impact whatsoever in the negotiations.

The EP was then denied any formal role in the IGC itself. The EP did have moral support from parliaments in Belgium and Italy, which both adopted resolutions calling for the DTEU to be ratified as is, and Italy said that it would reject the SEA if the EP did not support it (Jacobs, Corbett and Shackleton, 1995, pp. 302–3). In the IGC end-game, the EP attempted to force member states into improving the provisions on the EP in the SEA by threatening to either reject the 1986 budget, censure the Commission, or withhold its mandated opinion on the IGC (Budden, 2002, p. 93). But these threats were not seen as credible by governments, and despite stating in its resolution on the SEA that the results were 'unsatisfactory and [the EP] is unable to accept in their present form the proposed modifications to the EEC Treaty, particularly as regards the powers of the European Parliament' (in Gazzo, 1986, p. 105), the EP was unable to block the outcome (Armstrong and Bulmer, 1998, p. 31; Budden, 2002, p. 82; Fielder, 2000, p. 85).

And the EP had little impact even on the issue in which it had the greatest interest – the strengthening of its institutional position. The EP was not granted greater powers in the budgetary procedure, and although the EP's role in Community decision-taking was strengthened through the introduction of the cooperation procedure, it was national governments supported by the Commission and Council

Secretariat, and not the EP that drove the process (Corbett, 1987, p. 257; Interview NAT-20; Rittberger, 2003, pp. 217–20).

Concluding, the EP had little impact upon the SEA. Forced to shout from the sidelines, the EP's cause was not helped by advocating an extreme position that was so far outside of any realistic zone of possible agreements that the DTEU was not relevant either as a focal point for debates, as the Commission's proposals were, or as a source of ideas for proposals and treaty texts drafted by other actors.

Leadership by the Council Secretariat

The Council Secretariat played a subdued role in the 1985 IGC in comparison to later IGCs. The primary functions of the Secretariat were assisting the Luxembourg Presidency in drafting texts (together with the Commission), and brokering outcomes (Interviews EC-3, EC-19, NAT-20). Given the limited resources of the Luxembourg Presidency, the Secretariat naturally had a role to play in assisting the Presidency to ensure that the negotiations reached an outcome – in negotiation theory terms the Secretariat ensured that the negotiations were efficient. But in comparison to later IGCs, there were few instances where the Secretariat significantly influenced the final outcome, that is, affected the distributive dimension by shifting the final outcome closer to its own preferred outcome along the Pareto frontier (see Figure 3.1).

The Secretariat did though play a key role during the IGC in listening to national delegations, and helped the Luxembourg Presidency solve outstanding problems that could have blocked agreement (Interview NAT-20). One example of the Secretariat's crucial assistance was in the environmental dossier, where Denmark had a problem relating to the environmental chapter. Denmark feared that an EC-level environmental policy would lead to a degradation of Denmark's high standards of environmental protection, and therefore the Danes fought for the inclusion of a treaty-based guarantee that high national standards could be maintained – the so-called environmental guarantee (Lyck, 1992). The Secretariat found a formula that solved the problem in a way that was acceptable to both Denmark and the other parties by stating that common policies 'shall not prevent any Member State from maintaining or introducing more stringent protective measures compatible with this Treaty' (Article 25 SEA) (Interview NAT-20). This environmental guarantee became a crucial selling point for the SEA in the consultative referendum that the Danish Conservative government decided to hold in order to prevent the Social Democrats from vetoing the SEA in the Danish parliament in 1986.

Conclusion

This chapter has illustrated *when* and *why* the Commission was influential in the IGC and why the other institutions were less influential. While the 1985 IGC was the high-water mark of Commission leadership, it was also constrained leadership, meaning that there were outer limits to the Commission's ability to influence the final agreement set by governmental preferences. The Commission ensured a more efficient negotiation, while also shifting outcomes closer to its own preferred outcome, creating a final SEA that had a broader scope and strengthened Europe more than governments would have agreed

TABLE 3.2 *Conclusions – leadership in the 1985 IGC*

Issue area	Outcome
New policy areas	• Environmental policy – Commission proposal formed focal point, whereas Secretariat found formula for the 'environmental guarantee' to assist Denmark • Cohesion policy – Commission proposal formed focal point for debates, but governments removed most controversial aspects • Foreign policy – Commission leadership led to the creation of a *Single* European Act, including the foreign policy provisions
Reform of existing policy areas	• Social policy – Commission advocacy important alongside Danish and French efforts, with the UK acting as the brake • Monetary policy – Commission tabled modest proposal with little effect, as the issue was controlled by governments • Internal Market – Commission leadership ensured broad definition, although governments did insert some restrictions on the use of QMV
Institutional reforms	• Cooperation procedure – final proposal based upon Commission proposal, but submitted by Council Secretariat • Commission executive powers – Commission unable to strengthen its own powers, and final outcome closest to Dutch proposal

upon if left to themselves – in Haas' terms, the Commission 'upgraded the common interest' (Haas, 1961, pp. 368, 369). Key to the success of Commission leadership was:

- the possession of strong comparative informational advantages;
- the trust of governments;
- the nature of the issues involved;
- the key agenda-setting role delegated to it in the IGC; and
- the use of a two-pronged pragmatic leadership strategy, where Delors worked at the political level using low-profile tactics aimed mostly at the distributive dimension, whereas Emile Noël skillfully operated at the more technical level.

In contrast, neither the EP nor Secretariat had a substantial impact on the final SEA.

If we look at the most salient issues in the final SEA as illustrated in Table 3.2, the Commission did have significant influence upon outcomes when it advocated ambitious but realistic positions. First, the scope of the definition of the Internal Market was broader than it would have been without Commission leadership. The Commission also ensured that the final treaty was a single treaty, including the foreign policy provisions. Commission leadership was also important in environmental and social policies and in the actual decision to convene the IGC. But when the Commission advocated proposals far outside of what was broadly acceptable to governments, it had little influence. The provisions on monetary cooperation are a case in point. Finally, the Commission had little impact upon the content of the foreign policy provisions as governments did not see the issue as an area for legitimate Commission activity.

Chapter 4

Negotiating the Treaty of Maastricht

Introduction – building the European Union

The growing asymmetry in economic and political power between Germany and its neighbours within a European context became an evermore pressing problem in the late 1980s. On the economic side, the European Monetary System (EMS) introduced in the late 1970s was intended to stabilize exchange rates between its members. But by the mid-1980s, the German DM had become the de facto anchor currency, forcing other EMS countries like France to unilaterally adopt the same monetary policies as Germany, irrespective of whether they were appropriate or not for their own economy. In the late 1980s this resulted in considerable tensions between Germany and its partners, and most critically a Franco-German crisis after the German Bundesbank (BB) failed to assist the French franc in 1987, which as a consequence was devaluated (Heisenberg, 1999, pp. 89–95). This led to strong demands from France and Italy for a single currency to replace the asymmetric EMS and German economic hegemony (Dyson and Featherstone, 1999, p. 3). In order to take some of the political pressure off French President Mitterrand in the run-up to the presidential elections in April 1988, German Foreign Minister Genscher publicly backed the Franco-Italian calls for a single currency (Heisenberg, 1999, pp. 102–3). These demands for reform led to the creation of a working committee that was to study how an Economic and Monetary Union (EMU) could be achieved, and later for an IGC on EMU.

On the political side, the fall of the Berlin Wall in November 1989 sent political shockwaves through Europe (Baun, 1995–6; Wood, 1995). Germany's neighbours were concerned about the policies a reunified Germany would follow, especially in Central and Eastern Europe. German politicians were equally concerned and wanted to reassure their partners about German motives (Gillingham, 2003, pp. 276, 279). A key aspect of this reassurance strategy was 'Einbindung' – that is, voluntary restraint by binding oneself in institutions (Grieco,

1995; Pedersen, 2002). These concerns, together with calls for creating a more democratic Community, led to demands that a parallel IGC be held to politically bind Germany into Europe.

This chapter investigates the negotiation of these two parallel IGCs. Why was the Commission so successful in providing leadership in the agenda-setting phase of the EMU IGC, but then failed spectacularly in the actual IGC negotiations? Why was the Council Secretariat so effective a behind-the-scenes player? After looking at the course of the negotiations and what the EU institutions wanted in the IGCs, the chapter discusses the relevant leadership resources that the three institutions possessed. Finally, the chapter analyses the impact of the negotiating context, and whether the three EU institutions were able to successfully provide leadership in the IGCs. Was the Treaty of Maastricht an intergovernmental bargain or did EU institutions matter?

The negotiation of the 1990–1 IGCs

The agenda-setting phase of the EMU IGC – the Delors Committee and the three draft EMU treaties

The demands for reform of the EMS led the Hannover European Council Summit in June 1988 to create a committee to study how to achieve EMU. This committee, which came to be called the Delors Committee after its chairman, Commission President Delors, was composed of heads of national central banks together with several independent monetary experts. The Delors Committee produced a report that was presented to the Madrid Summit in June 1989 (Committee for the study of the EMU, 1989), where it was accepted as the basis for further work. The Summit also decided that an IGC would be convened with the view to creating an EMU. The drafting of the report in the Delors Committee is discussed more extensively below.

Later, in December 1990 the Commission tabled a draft EMU treaty (European Commission 1991a). Together with texts from France and Germany, the three texts formed the substantive agenda of the IGC (Christoffersen, 1992, pp. 33–4; Dyson and Featherstone, 1999, p. 727). An alternative British market-led 'hard ECU' plan was published in June 1990 that suggested that a new currency should be introduced alongside existing currencies, and while it would be linked to the strongest currency, it would *not* automatically lead to a single currency (Dyson and Featherstone, 1999, p. 613; Forster, 1999, pp. 53–4). The idea only gained support from Spain, and was laid to rest in April 1991 (Dyson and Featherstone, 1999, p. 640).

The agenda-setting phase of the PU IGC – ad hoc preparation within the Council

In contrast to the careful preparation of the EMU IGC, the Political Union (PU) IGC was haphazardly prepared. The idea to actually convene a second parallel IGC was first raised in an EP resolution in March 1990, which called for the creation of a 'European Union of a federal type' (European Parliament 1990). The call for a PU IGC was echoed in a Belgium memorandum, and later a Franco-German joint letter to the Irish Presidency of Spring 1990 that called for tackling the democratic deficit, creating more efficient institutions, together with the adoption of a common foreign and security policy (CFSP) (reprinted in Laursen and Vanhoonacker, 1992, p. 276).

The Dublin Summit in April 1990 decided to ask foreign ministers to investigate whether a second IGC was needed (Christoffersen, 1992, p. 23), resulting in a 'reflection document' that was presented to the second Dublin Summit in late June 1990. The Summit decided unanimously to convene a second parallel IGC to discuss four topics: the goal of political union; democratic legitimacy; the institutional effectiveness of the Community; and the unity and coordination of the EC's external policies (Christoffersen, 1992, pp. 23–4).

The PU IGC agenda was then discussed at the ambassadorial level within COREPER. The preparations were unstructured and disorderly, and one participant characterized the debates and subsequent drafting of a working paper on the agenda as being 'all over the place' (Interview NAT-23). Despite the best efforts of the Italian Presidency in the second half of 1990, the PU IGC agenda as agreed in the Rome Summit in December 1990 was imprecise and vague, reflecting both the unclear ideas that governments had about the issues in the PU IGC, and the desire to avoid isolating the British by taking too strong stances on increasing Community competences before the IGC started. Five topics were on the agenda: democratic legitimacy; the effectiveness and efficiency of the Union; an extension and strengthening of Community policies; CFSP; and the creation of some form of European citizenship (reprinted in Laursen and Vanhoonacker, 1992, pp. 318–21).

The course of the EMU IGC negotiations – building upon the Delors report

The two parallel IGCs were convened in Rome on 14 December 1990, although the start of real negotiations would have to wait until the Luxembourg Presidency took the reins in the first half of 1991.

The basic cleavage in the EMU IGC was between the so-called 'economist' and 'monetarist' approaches to monetary integration. 'Economists' such as Germany, the Netherlands and Denmark argued that EMU should not be created before economic cycles in the national economies had converged (Dyson and Featherstone, 1999, pp. 29–30). Without this convergence, an EMU would be unstable. The 'monetarist' position of Belgium, France and Italy contended that a common currency would create economic convergence, as governments would be forced to create the conditions necessary for the survival and functioning of the EMU (ibid.).

Most of the negotiations in the EMU IGC were, though, about details, as the broad outlines of EMU had already been agreed in the Delors Report (Corbett, 1993, p. 41). By mid-April 80 per cent of the final EMU text had been agreed by governments (Mazzucelli, 1997, p. 103). But several issues were still outstanding, including:

- whether a fixed timetable for the transition to the third stage should be adopted;
- what form the stage two institution should have;
- what role the Commission should have;
- how strong the economic policy aspects of EMU should be;
- the form of convergence criteria; and
- whether opt-outs should be given.

The Luxembourg Presidency managed to find solutions to several of these issues, and it was for example agreed that a relatively weak institution would be created in stage two (EMI), and that stage two would be relatively short (Ross, 1995, p. 154).

The Dutch Presidency in the second half of 1991 put forward its first EMU draft treaty in August, although the IGC first discussed it in September 1991. One of the outstanding questions at that point in the negotiations was whether there should be opt-outs, and what form they should take. While the UK had signaled that they might accept an opt-out, without a satisfactory solution for the UK there were real fears that they would veto the outcome of the IGC. The basic debate was therefore whether a temporary opt-out should be given, or whether the treaty should include an explicit, general 'opt-out for all' clause; something that was opposed by both the Commission and most member states (Corbett, 1993, pp. 41–2; Dyson and Featherstone, 1999, p. 438). The first Dutch EMU draft treaty suggested a general opt-out clause that met with strong protests and was then removed (Dinan, 1999, p. 145). The final outcome on this point was only reached in the last weeks of the IGC, where a pragmatic formula for opting-out was formulated together with protocols for the UK and Denmark (see below). Other issues that were agreed upon in the first Dutch draft treaty included the convergence criteria, and the starting date for stage two of EMU (Ross, 1995, pp. 185, 187).

Despite the introduction of a new Dutch draft EMU treaty in October, there was still no agreement on the questions of whether a fixed timetable should be introduced or the manner in which transition would occur to the third stage (for example, the number of required participants and which institution would take the decision to move to the third stage) (Ross, 1995, p. 187). Regarding the fixed timetable, the basic cleavage was between the French and Italians who wanted a fixed date, and the German and Dutch position of no transition to stage three prior to economic convergence. Yet in late November, Kohl publicly weakened Germany's position by stating that he was seeking an irreversible EMU in order to lock future German politicians into the common currency (Dyson and Featherstone, 1999, pp. 442–3). This movement by Kohl created an opening for France and Italy to table a compromise proposal which called for a vote on the third stage in 1996, and if stage three did not start then, it would *automatically* start in 1999 among the qualifying countries (Grant, 1994, p. 200). This proposal was agreed upon at the final meeting of the finance ministers on 2–3 December.

The actual Maastricht European Council Summit on 9–10 December 1991 was therefore a non-event as regards the EMU negotiations, with agreement being announced on the first day of the summit. This rather orderly negotiation process contrasted starkly with the chaotic negotiations in the parallel PU IGC.

The course of the PU IGC negotiations – from the pillar to the tree and back again

The discussions in the PU IGC started on the basis of a working paper drawn up by Personal Representatives together with the Rome Summit conclusions (in Laursen and Vanhoonacker, 1992, pp. 318–21). Despite the relatively unclear agenda, the Luxembourg Presidency had high ambitions for the PU IGC (Christoffersen, 1992, p. 34).

Early discussions centred on justice and home affairs (JHA) matters, and whether and how to create a common foreign and security policy (CFSP). In JHA, four options were presented in January, ranging from creating a Schengen-like cooperation outside of the treaties, to a full communitarization of JHA policies, meaning that they would be placed within the supranational first pillar of the

Community (Corbett, 1993, pp. 48–9). Based upon IGC discussions, the Luxembourg Presidency chose the rather pragmatic third option of elaborating a full set of treaty provisions, but not deciding whether they should be intergovernmental or supranational.

The salience of the debates on foreign policy increased after the start of the Gulf War in January 1991, which again exposed European impotence in foreign affairs – a situation which would become even more apparent after the failed attempts by the Community to stop the outbreak of conflict in Yugoslavia in the summer of 1991. A key Franco-German proposal was put forward in February, which proposed that a CFSP should include all aspects of security, including defence, and that in the long term the Western European Union (WEU) should be incorporated into the suggested European Union (in Laursen and Vanhoonacker, 1992, pp. 333–5; also in Corbett, 1993). The idea of incorporating the WEU into the EU met with strong opposition from the 'Atlanticist' countries (Netherlands, Denmark and the UK), and attempts to reconcile these two positions failed in several meetings in the spring of 1991 (Laursen, Vanhoonacker and Wester, 1992, p.13).

Another salient issue during the first months of the IGC was whether to strengthen the role of the EP in Community decision-making. There were many views on the issue ranging from the German position that favoured creating parliamentary co-decision vis-à-vis the Council to British opposition to any change in the status quo. German and Italy put forward a maximalist joint declaration in April, which argued that no legislative act should be passed without co-decision (in Corbett, 1993).

The first comprehensive draft treaty text was tabled in April by the Luxembourg Presidency (in Corbett, 1993). Based upon a French idea that was then fleshed out by the Council Secretariat, the first Luxembourg draft treaty comprised three pillars. The existing supra-national Community would form pillar one, while CFSP and JHA would be attached as separate *intergovernmental* pillars, meaning that the Commission, EP and ECJ would have little if any role in them. The draft treaty introduced the principles of subsidiarity and citizenship, together with amendments to existing policies and the introduction of new policies such as consumer protection and public health. Drawing from a Commission proposal, the draft also proposed the creation of a new type of EC act – the law – which would be adopted using co-decision. The actual CFSP provisions envisioned only a slight strengthening of existing foreign policy cooperation within the EPC, although QMV was suggested for imple-menting certain decisions. The JHA provisions were relatively close to the final outcome, with only several relatively minor changes; for example a reference to the European Convention on Human Rights was included (Corbett, 1993, p. 49).

Despite its best efforts to locate the median of national positions, the first Luxembourg draft was met with criticism when it was presented. Several member states felt that it was not ambitious enough, while others felt it went too far (Laursen, Vanhoonacker and Wester, 1992, p. 15). The Dutch and Belgium governments were quite critical about the structure of the treaty, especially as regards the incorporation of two intergovernmental pillars into the treaties. The UK and Denmark were opposed to the potential use of QMV in CFSP and the implications of the incorporation of the WEU into the Union. But despite this critique, it was also agreed that the Luxembourg draft could serve as the basis for further negotiations. This strengthened the Luxembourg Presidency's resolve to attempt to conclude the IGC before the upcoming Dutch Presidency. Several delegations supported this ambition, as for example France had fears that the Dutch Presidency would be excessively partial to their own pro-integrative national interests (Christoffersen, 1992, pp. 35–6).

The Commission tabled amendments to the first Luxembourg draft in an attempt to replace the pillar (also called temple) structure with a tree structure that would ensure a single treaty framework (trunk) together with special arrangements for CFSP and JHA (branches). When these amendments were discussed in an informal ministerial meeting held in Dresden on 2–3 June, all of the member states except France, Denmark and the UK appeared to support the change to a tree structure (Laursen, Vanhoonacker and Wester, 1992, p. 16).

In its revised draft treaty that it presented to the IGC on 18 June, the Luxembourg Presidency maintained the pillar structure, but strengthened the common elements of the treaty and inserted a reference to the EC's federal goal (ibid.). The second Luxembourg Draft Treaty was accepted by the heads of state and government in the Luxembourg European Council Summit on 28–9 June as the basis for further negotiations in the IGC.

The Dutch Presidency in the second half of 1991 was plagued by internal disagreement on what overall strategy they should follow – problems that proved to be near catastrophic for the PU IGC. The Dutch Presidency was in August and September run from the Dutch Foreign Ministry in the Hague, with little input from either the Dutch Permanent Representation in Brussels or from the Council Secretariat (Interviews NAT-3, EC-19). During August the Foreign Ministry prepared a new draft treaty that would scrap major elements of the second Luxembourg Draft and replace them with a single pillar treaty which substantially strengthened the role of the EP and where the aims for the intergovernmental CFSP were lowered. The Dutch originally planned that they would first introduce their draft to governments that were seen to be sympathetic, but word got out that the Dutch were working on a radical new draft (Christoffersen, 1992, p. 37). The Dutch then postponed its presentation until the end of September, when they presented their full draft treaty.

On September 30, in what has gone into EU lore as 'Black Monday', the Dutch presented their draft treaty. The draft was resoundingly rejected by ten of the twelve delegations as the basis for further negotiations (Corbett, 1998, p. 310). The main criticism was that the draft clearly broke what had been agreed upon in the Luxembourg Summit's conclusions in June – even antagonizing those who preferred a more federal treaty structure (Ross, 1995, p. 172). In the face of massive opposition, the Dutch were embarrassingly forced to return to the second Luxembourg draft as the basis for further negotiations (Christoffersen, 1992, pp. 97–7; Christiansen, 2002, p. 48). Responsibility for the Dutch Presidency also shifted to the Dutch Prime Minister, assisted by the Dutch Permanent Representation and the Council Secretariat (see below) (Interviews EC-3, EC-19).

In the final months of the IGC, discussions continued on the defence and security dimensions of CFSP. A shift in the British position in September/October led to a joint British–Italian statement on 4 October that opened the possibility that the WEU could be used as the EU's defence arm, and that the WEU would act as the European pillar of NATO (Corbett, 1993, p. 47; Laursen and Vanhoonacker, 1992, pp. 413–4; Ross, 1995, p. 181). Following this breakthrough, ministers met on 7 October, where the overall contours of an agreement were reached on including an article on defence; later to be supplemented with elements from a Franco-German draft article submitted in mid-October (Christoffersen, 1992, p. 250; Laursen and Vanhoonacker, 1992, pp. 415–8; Laursen, Vanhoonacker and Wester, 1992, p. 18).

The Dutch tabled a new draft treaty for the ministerial meeting held in Noordwijk on 12–13 November. The main difference between it and the second Luxembourg draft was that the EP's role was strengthened, there was a suggestion that the Commission should be reduced to one member per member state, together with five additional junior Commissioners, and that visa policy could be transferred in the future to the supranational first pillar through a so-called *passerelle* (bridging clause), whereby governments in the Council could agree unanimously to transfer the policy to the first pillar (in Corbett, 1993).

There were several outstanding questions left in the weeks prior to the Maastricht Summit which risked derailing the PU IGC. One of the most problematic issues was the economic cohesion issue, where Spain warned that it would potentially veto the final treaty unless a 'satisfactory solution' was reached. As will be shown below, agreement on this was only reached in the actual Maastricht Summit.

Another unsettled issue was social policy, where the UK threatened to veto the treaty if it contained any references to this policy, while other member states threatened a veto if social policy was absent from the treaty (Christoffersen, 1992, pp. 126, 128; Forster, 1999, pp. 92–3)! A deal was brokered by the Commission and the Dutch Presidency in the dramatic dying hours of the Maastricht Summit (see below). After thirty-one hours of hard negotiations, the member states approved the Treaty on European Union, also called the Treaty of Maastricht (see Table 4.1, p. 72).

What did the EU institutions want in the 1990–1 IGC?

The Commission – developing a more effective and democratic European Community

Tables 4.2 and 4.3 illustrate the preferences of the European Commission in both of the IGCs, based upon opinions and proposals presented before and in the first months of the IGCs. In general, the two IGCs formed part of what Ross has termed Delors' 'Russian Dolls strategy', where Delors' final goal of a Social Europe would be achieved through five distinct steps (Gillingham, 2003, pp. 260–93; Ross, 1995, pp. 39–50). The first step was the SEA, followed by the first multi-annual budgetary agreement (Delors I) and the creation of strong social policy provisions (Social Charter in 1989). The next layer of Delors' Russian doll was an EMU and political union, which would after a second multi-annual budgetary agreement lead to his vision of Social Europe.

Looking first at EMU, a common currency had been a priority of President Delors since 1985 (see Chapter 3). On the form that EMU should have, Delors and his cabinet supported the 'monetarist' position on most issues, though on institutional matters they were closer to the German approach of an independent monetary authority with price stability as a key goal. But Delors wanted price stability supplemented with the goals of high levels of growth and employment. Delors also believed that the EMU should have a strong economic

TABLE 4.1 *The outcome of the 1990–1 IGCs – The Treaty on European Union*

Issue area	Outcome
First pillar – Provisions amending the Treaty establishing the European Community	
Introduction of new policies	• creates an Economic and Monetary Union (EMU):
	– three-stage process with a fixed timetable, with the introduction of a single currency in the third stage at latest in 1999
	– relatively strict economic convergence criteria during the transition
	– creation of a weak monetary institution at the start of stage 2
	– monetary policy to be determined and conducted in the third stage by the ECB, which is fully independent of both the member states and the EC institutions
	– temporary opt-outs for member states that do not qualify, and with more permanent opt-outs for Denmark and the UK
	• included new policies: developmental, education, public health, consumer protection, trans-European networks, and the competitiveness of industry
Modification of existing policies	• strengthened R&D policy, environmental policies, and economic and social cohesion
	• adopted a Social Protocol, strengthening Community social policies but with an opt-out for the UK
Institutional changes	• QMV in Council considerably extended
	• co-decision introduced
	• scope of cooperation procedure revised, scope of assent extended
	• reform of the Commission, including EP approval of the Commission
	• Committee of the Regions established

→

→	
Issue area	*Outcome*
Institutional changes (continued)	• ECJ given ability to fine member states for failing to fulfill treaty obligations

Second pillar – Common Foreign and Security Policy

Scope	• includes all questions of security, even the eventual framing of common defence policies
Institutional issues	• can adopt common positions 'when necessary'
	• can adopt joint actions by unanimity in the European Council, then implementation by QMV in the Council
	• EU can request WEU to elaborate and implement defence decisions
	• non-exclusive right of initiative for Commission, and EP shall be consulted on main aspects and basic choices

Third pillar – Justice and Home Affairs

Scope	• deals with: asylum and immigration policy, 3rd country nationals, combating fraud, immigration and drug addiction, judicial cooperation in civil and criminal matters, customs cooperation, and police cooperation to combat terrorism and drug trafficking
Institutional issues	• joint positions adopted by unanimity
	• joint actions adopted by unanimity, then can decide that implementing measures to be adopted by QMV
	• can draw up conventions for member states to adopt
	• coordination between relevant administrative departments

Source: The Treaty on European Enion, *Official Journal of the European Communities*, No. C 224/1, 31.8.92.

TABLE 4.2 *The preferences of the European Commission in the EMU IGC*

Issue area	Commission preferences
Convergence criteria	• relatively weak and not rigidly defined convergence criteria • in the 3rd stage a system of incentives should be used instead of sanctions for member state transgressions
Tasks and organization of the ECB	• monetary policy to be determined and conducted by the ECB, which is fully independent of both the member states and the EC institutions • strong emphasis on price stability, coupled with focus on high levels of growth, employment and cohesion between the member states
Fiscal transfers and other economic policies	• interested in prominent economic-policy pillar of EMU, with EC-wide fiscal transfers, structural adjustment, an EC-wide industrial policy, and certain labour market policies
Institutional issues	• strong role for Commission in EMU policy-making, e.g. in multi-annual economic guidelines, and exchange rate policy • strong role for European Council, for example in the decision to start stage 3 of the EMU
Procedures for transition	• fixed timetable • short stage 2 starting on 1 January 1994 • creation of ECB at start of stage 2 • decision on 3rd stage by 1997, with the Commission and Council submitting reports to the European Council, which then decides whether the conditions for the 3rd stage have been met • temporary opt-outs for member states that cannot participate

Sources: European Commission, 1990a and 1990b; Dyson and Featherstone, 1999, p. 718.

pillar, with an EC-wide industrial policy and certain labour market policies. The Commission also, not surprisingly, wanted to have a strong role for itself in EMU.

Delors had as his long-term goal the creation of a federal Union where the Commission would be the political executive, but he only expected that the outcome of the present PU IGC would be a small step towards this goal – an '*Acte Unique Bis*' (Delors in Grant, 1994, p. 135), although he became more ambitious during the IGC. On the issues, the Commission argued for the creation of a single treaty on European Union with common institutions for all policies, with certain exemptions for foreign and justice policies.

The Commission did not want broad extensions of Community competences, but instead focused upon harnessing perceived spillover by calling for increased competences in areas directly related to the Internal Market, such as social policies (see Table 4.3). The Commission also pushed for an increase in the effectiveness of EC policies through the use of QMV, and by strengthening the enforcement of EC law through national courts (Beach, 2001, pp. 97–8; Tallberg, 2003b, pp. 78–80). The Commission was opposed to the broad introduction of co-decision, and instead advocated a minor adjustment to the cooperation procedure. Later in the IGC, the Commission proposed that a new type of act, laws, could be adopted using co-decision in a limited number of areas.

The Commission advocated compiling all of the provisions dealing with external policies into a single chapter. In the common trade policy, the Commission argued for an across-the-board extension of Commission competences to include negotiations in trade in services, capital and intellectual property. In CFSP, the Commission wanted to introduce the use of QMV, and gradually incorporate the West European Union (WEU) into the Union.

The European Parliament – another shot at a federal European Union

Overall, the basic preferences of the EP in the IGCs were along the lines of the DTEU, although some of the details were modified to take account of developments since 1984 (Corbett, 1998, p. 292). But different reports from EP committees were advocating different strategies to reach this goal. In the Colombo Report, the EP called for the creation of a federal 'Constitution for Europe' which would also include foreign policy, whereas the Martin Reports proposed more specific changes to the existing treaties (Corbett, 1998, pp. 293–4; European Parliament, 1990; Vanhoonacker, 1992).

TABLE 4.3   *The preferences of the European Commission in the PU IGC*

Issue area	Commission preferences
Structure of treaty	• create a unitary, single pillar treaty structure (tree) with common institutions • leave the way open for a form of federal union

New policies and reform of existing policies within the first pillar	• selective increases in EC competences, primarily in policy areas that are related to the Internal Market such as:
	  – social policy – the Commission wanted to incorporate the Social Charter into the EC with QMV in the new provisions
	  – trans-European networks
	  – and the free movement of persons, including common policies vis-à-vis third-country nationals
	• increase the effectiveness of environmental and R&D policies
	• create single chapter on energy policies
	• create EC cultural policy with respect for the subsidiarity principle
	• introduction of EC citizenship as a complement to national citizenship
	• extension of common trade policy to services, intellectual property and investment
	• creation of common development policy
	• improve economic and social cohesion policies
	• move CFSP and JHA into the first pillar, with certain restrictions

Expansion of QMV	• QMV extended to all issue areas except constitutional and a restricted number of sensitive issues

$\rightarrow$

Looking primarily at the reforms advocated in the Martin Reports that were adopted by the EP plenary as the official position for the IGC, the thrust of the changes called for the creation of a single pillar Union with a single currency and common foreign policies. The Union was to have broader competences, including in environmental, social and economic cohesion, and cultural policies.

→	
Issue area	*Commission preferences*
Institutional changes	• strengthen the executive powers of the Commission
	• introduce the subsidiarity principal in connection with a revised Article 235 of the EC Treaty (now Article 308 EC)
	• strengthen the role of national courts as the enforcers of EC law
EP powers and decision-making	• did not support co-decision, but merely wanted an extension of the cooperation procedure to allow the Commission's second reading proposal to stand unless rejected by simple majority of Council
CFSP procedures	• QMV in common foreign policies in areas determined unanimously by European Council
	– common policies initiated by Presidency, Commission, or simple majority of member states
	• creation of common security policy, with long-term objective of common defence in compliance with NATO commitments
	• unanimity in common security policy, with possible dispensations;
	• external representation by Council Presidency, Commission, and where appropriate by previous and next Presidencies
	• no jurisdiction for the ECJ
	• EP kept informed of developments
Relationship with WEU	• gradual incorporation of WEU into EU
JHA procedures	• stronger policies with Commission role

Source: European Commission, 1991a.

The EP advocated the introduction of the protection of fundamental rights into the treaties, together with the introduction of European citizenship and the subsidiarity principle. QMV was to be extended to all areas of policy except constitutional and certain foreign policy issues. The executive powers of the Commission were to be extended, while the enforcement of Union law was to be

TABLE 4.4   *The preferences of the European Parliament in the 1990–1 IGCs*

Issue area	European Parliament preferences
Structure of treaty	• replace the existing treaties with a federal 'Constitution of the Union'
New policies and reform of existing policies within the first pillar	• increases in Union competences, such as: – environmental policies, social policy, R&D and cultural policies • strengthen economic and social cohesion policies • create an economic and monetary union with an independent central bank, based upon an automatic and mandatory timetable • introduce fundamental rights • create a subsidiarity principle • introduction of Union citizenship
Expansion of QMV	• QMV extended to all issue areas except constitutional issues and the extension of Union competences
Institutional changes	• strengthen the executive powers of the Commission • strengthen the enforcement of Union law by allowing the Commission to create European Inspectorates that would investigate member state compliance, and by granting the ECJ sanction powers • proposed that the Council should meet in public when adopting legislation →

strengthened by the creation of 'European Inspectorates', who would investigate member state compliance, and by allowing the ECJ to sanction member states.

Finally, the EP argued for a substantial increase in its powers, both through the introduction of a co-decision procedure, and by extending its powers to include all aspects of the budget including agriculture, the appointment of the Commission President, and in IGC negotiations.

$\rightarrow$	
Issue area	*European Parliament preferences*
EP powers and decision-making	• introduce a co-decision procedure • extend EP budgetary powers to all aspects of the budget by removing the distinction between compulsory and non-compulsory expenditure • grant the EP the right to elect the Commission President based upon a proposal from the European Council • give the EP the right of initiative when the Commission fails to respond to a request for a proposal from a majority of MEPs • grant the EP powers in IGC negotiations by extending the assent procedure to IGCs, and by allowing the EP to submit proposals to the IGC before it starts • called for the creation of a federal Union to be negotiated by representatives of governments and the EP
CFSP procedures	• QMV in CFSP, with certain veto and opt-out options • give the Commission the role of external representative of the Union for all aspects of external policy • grant the Commission the right of initiative, while the Council retains the right to define policy • expand the scope of CFSP to security policy

Sources: European Parliament, 1990; Corbett, 1998, pp. 287–94.

The Council Secretariat – another step towards a stronger Council-based Europe

As with the 1985 IGC, the preferences of the Secretariat in the 1990–91 IGCs are relatively difficult to reconstruct, as there were no public pronouncements by key Secretariat officials on the issues under debate – in contrast to later IGCs. Based upon interviews with current and former Secretariat officials, the Secretariat did not have strong interests in most of the issues in the IGC, and attempted to 'serve' the member states by assisting them in finding a mutually acceptable agreement (Interviews EC-19, NAT-20). That being said, there are indications that the Secretariat when, faced with a choice, chose the solution that strengthened its own institutional position by, for example, advocating that new areas of cooperation should be more Council-based. Commission officials in the IGC believed that the Secretariat was even actively seeking to *limit* Commission powers (Ross, 1995, p. 71). The Council Secretariat wanted more Europe, but also a more Council-based Europe (Interviews EC-3, NAT-20).

Changes in the leadership resources of EU institutions since 1985

The material resources of the EU institutions

While the Secretariat had no material resources that it could draw upon in the IGCs, both the EP and Commission did have material resources based upon their formal powers in daily Community policy-making. Of particular relevance for the Commission were its agenda-setting powers in the Community budget, granting the Commission the possibility to offer budgetary side-payments to actors. For the EP, of most relevance was the manner in which it had exercised its existing powers. The EP had creatively attempted to create de facto powers for itself that would make it easier for governments to accept a *de jure* entrenchment of them in the treaties (Corbett, 1992; Hix, 2002). For example, despite not being mandated in the treaties, the EP had since 1980 acted *as if* it had the right of approval of the Commission through a vote of confidence (Corbett, 1992, p. 293). By voting in plenary on the issue, this created a situation where, despite having no formal powers, if the EP voted against the Commission it would have been difficult for governments to uphold the appointment – thereby creating a *de facto* vote of confidence for the EP where no formal power existed (Hix, 2002).

The informational advantages of the EU institutions

The informational advantages of both the Commission and Council Secretariat are primarily the result of their roles in the daily Community policy-making process and prior participation in IGCs. The EP had few informational advantages.

As was pointed out in Chapter 3, the Commission has unsurpassed substantive knowledge of the workings of the treaties. Looking at changes since 1985, the overall staff of the Commission had increased 22 per cent by 1990 (European Communities, 2000, p. 47), but most of this increase was due to the Iberian enlargement. A total of 3,640 A grade staff dealt with Community policy-matters in 1990 (Huang, 2002, p. 5). In comparison, while national governments have many more civil servants, they also deal with a much larger gambit of policy areas than purely Community matters. In relation to the IGC, a participant recounted that the Commission could study particular issues in an 'almost scientific' manner, creating issue briefs of unrivalled quality (Interview EC-3).

In the issues in the IGC, the Commission did not have the depth of expertise that national central banks and finance ministries had in monetary affairs. In the EMU IGC, the basic problem for the Commission was that the ECOFIN (economic and finance) ministers who controlled the negotiations had 'accumulated vast experience and reputation and had their own closeted networks with a complex infrastructure of meetings, lunches, and telephone calls. The legal and technical resources of Delors and the Commission, and their networks, were no match at this level of negotiation' (Dyson and Featherstone, 1999, p. 744).

In the Delors Committee that prepared the EMU IGC agenda, Delors acted in a personal capacity which prevented him from tabling drafts and briefs prepared by the Commission services – and thereby cut him off from that source of information and assistance. But Delors saw this as a small price for ensuring that central bankers were also kept at arm's length from ECOFIN ministers (Dyson and Featherstone, 1999, p. 716). And Delors personally had a long experience in monetary affairs from his career that started in the *Banque de France*, and later as French Finance Minister (1981–3) and Minister for Economic and Financial Affairs and the Budget (1983–4). This experience did give him a comparative advantage vis-à-vis heads of state and government in monetary issues, and both Kohl and Mitterrand used Delors as an alternative source of expertise to their own national administrations during the EMU IGC (Dyson and Featherstone, 1999, pp. 692, 702).

In the PU IGC, the Commission had no informational advantages in foreign and security policy questions (see Chapter 3). But in the economic aspects of foreign policy, such as trade policy, the Commission had strong comparative advantages. And in Internal Market-related issues such as social and environmental policy, the Commission was able to fully mobilize its informational resources.

Turning to the EP, the Committee on Institutional Affairs had commissioned numerous reports on various aspects of further treaty

reform since the 1985 IGC, including reports on institutional procedures, the WEU, fundamental rights, and the democratic deficit
(Corbett, 1998, p. 276). While members of the EP did gain significant
insight into many of the issues on the IGC agenda, the radical nature
of many of the EP proposals made the 'expertise' and 'knowledge' of
the EP less relevant for the IGCs, either directly or indirectly as
sources of ideas and inspiration. The size of the EP's Secretariat had
increased by almost 500 since 1985, but much of this was due to the
Iberian Accession (European Commission, 1986, p. 36; 1991c, p.
388). And the size of the staff assisting the Institutional Affairs
Committee was very small in comparison to either the other two EU
institutions, or national governments (Christiansen, 2002, p. 43;
Corbett, Jacobs and Shackleton, 1995, p. 119).

The Council Secretariat's comparative informational advantages
in the 1990–91 IGCs were primarily based upon its institutional
memory of the 1985 IGC and daily Council policy-making, and
knowledge of how the treaties are structured. While the Secretariat
had only 206 A-grade officials in 1990 (General Secretariat of the
Council, 2002), they were in close contact with national delegations
throughout the process and had a very accurate picture of the state of
play throughout the IGCs (Interview EC-19).

The reputation of the EU institutions

Riding on a wave of success in the late 1980s generated by the
success of the SEA and the 1992 program, Delors was widely seen as
'Mr Europe'. But buoyed by this enthusiasm, Delors and the
Commission increasingly took high-profile political stances in pursuing Delors' long-term goal (see above). 'Delors, like Icarus before
him, appeared to believe he had wings. His self-confidence soared to
new – and dangerous – heights. He believed the Community capable
of a leap towards closer union and no longer thought constitutional
reform could wait' (Grant, 1994, p. 134).

There were, though, storm clouds on the horizon, as governments
showed signs of becoming increasingly sceptical of supranational
cooperation. In many respects, the backlash was a product of the
success of the Community, for as the EC became increasingly active
it also provoked national reactions (Grant, 1994, p. 136). Members of
Delors' cabinet were aware of this, and as one member put it in spring
1991, 'Before we could count on being ahead of other people strate-
gically. We knew what we wanted and they were less clear, partly
because they didn't believe that anything much would follow from
the decisions we asked them to make. Now they know that we mean

business and they look for all the implications of our proposals. There are huge numbers of new things on the table and it will be much tougher going from now on' (Leygues in Ross, 1995, p. 137).

Pulling in the other direction was Delors' close relationship with German Chancellor Kohl that had been built during 1989–90. This relationship was built upon Delors' unflagging support of German reunification (Grant, 1994, pp. 131–4; Gillingham, 2003, p. 279). It is also important to distinguish between the PU and EMU IGC. While the Commission was viewed with scepticism in the PU IGC, Delors had strong credentials in monetary policy. Further, he had attended the Basle meetings of the Committee of EC Central Bankers since 1985, and had cultivated networks of politicians and experts in monetary policy, strengthening his acceptability among key actors (Dyson and Featherstone, 1999, pp. 694, 696–7, 708).

As in the 1985 IGC, the EP was clearly an unwelcome guest in the IGCs, although it did attempt to bolster its legitimacy by building closer links with national parliaments through the so-called 'assizes' (see below). In contrast, the Secretariat was perceived to be a trusted and valued assistant to national delegations (Interview EC-3, NAT-20). The Secretary-General of the Secretariat, Niels Ersbøll, had attempted to maintain the perceived neutrality of the Secretariat by developing a *déontologie,* or a professional administrative ethos, where the Secretariat was to work quietly behind the scenes (Ersbøll in Westlake, 1999, p. 314; Interview EC-19). Instead of sitting behind the microphone, the Secretariat would use the ear of the Presidency (ibid.).

The opportunities for leadership created by the negotiating context

The role of the EU institutions in the two IGCs

The Commission was not invited to play the same agenda-setting role in the 1990–91 IGCs as it had in the 1985 IGC. The Commission did though play a key role in the preparations of the EMU IGC through the chairing role that Delors had in the so-called Delors Committee (see below). But after the two IGCs started, the Commission pulled itself out of the behind-the-scenes drafting group that together with Council Secretariat officials assisted the Luxembourg Presidency in preparing texts for the IGC, opting instead to play a more political leadership role of tabling proposals and attempting to mobilize support for them (see below). During the Netherlands Presidency, the

Commission though was invited to help the Dutch prepare their ill-fated Draft Treaty (see below).

As in the 1985 IGC, the EP was kept outside of the IGC negotiating room. But delegates from the EP were able to hold several meetings, or inter-institutional preparatory conferences, with foreign ministers and finance ministers prior to the IGC, where they exchanged opinions (Corbett, 1998, pp. 295–6). The EP was also able to get its foot inside the IGC door by securing the right for the EP President to address the start of IGC Ministerial meetings, and also that the inter-institutional preparatory conferences would continue during the IGC (ibid., p. 296).

The formal mandate of the Council Secretariat was for it to play a secretarial function for both the IGC itself and the Presidencies chairing the negotiations. The Secretariat was also granted a monopoly on the provision of legal advice to the IGC: a task it had shared with the Commission in 1985 (Christiansen, 2002). In reality, the Secretariat's role was much larger, and it had a crucial role in the drafting process and in assisting Presidencies in finding and achieving agreement. The level to which Presidencies chose to rely upon the Secretariat varied, with some relying extensively upon Secretariat advice and assistance and others choosing to go it alone.

First, the Secretariat advised Presidencies on setting meeting agendas and the overall conduct of the negotiations, and in finding and brokering compromises. This advice and assistance was based upon: the Secretariat's institutional memory from Council business and the 1985 IGC; the knowledge gained by the Secretariat through taking part in IGC meetings at every level; and informal contacts with national delegations. The Secretariat also took part in the bilateral 'confessionals' held between the Presidency and individual delegations prior to European Council Summits. The confessionals are held prior to European Council Summits during IGCs between individual delegations and officials from the Presidency and (usually) the Secretariat. Presidencies use these meetings to tease out possible solutions by attempting to find the 'real bottom line' of national delegations (McDonagh, 1998, p. 23). As the Secretariat took part in most of these meetings during the 1990–1 IGCs, this gave it an overview of the state of play of the negotiations that was greater than any single government, and arguably even greater than the individual Presidencies, who had naturally not taken part in the confessionals held by other Presidencies during the IGC. However the Presidencies had the advantage of information garnered from the traditional tour of capitals by national officials and politicians prior to European Council

Summits which the Secretariat was not party to, and other informal meetings held during the IGC.

Secondly, in the drafting process member states often put forward relatively vague ideas that need to be translated into actual legal text (Interview EC-3). In both of the IGCs, all of the draft Presidency texts with the exception of the first Dutch Draft Treaty in the PU IGC, were written and developed by the Secretariat, granting the Secretariat the 'power of the pen' (ibid.). The development of the texts took part in close collaboration with the Presidencies, where the Secretariat would state for example, 'If you want cooperation in this issue-area, then it can be done in this way, while you should also be careful about this' (ibid.). The Secretariat would then develop an initial text for the Presidency, and then after consultations with the Presidency, it would prepare a final draft.

Thirdly, the Secretariat provided expert legal counsel to the IGC, and the head of the Secretariat's Legal Services took part in all IGC meetings at all levels. Importantly, while the Secretariat itself only works through the Presidency, the head of the Legal Services, Jean-Claude Piris, was an independent actor in the IGC, acting as the legal adviser to the IGC with the function of answering questions from national delegates, and also taking the floor on his own initiative when he deems it necessary. In contrast to the normal Secretariat role, Piris had his own microphone in IGC meetings.

The monopoly on the provision of legal expertise in the IGC granted the Secretariat opportunities to shift the agenda by being able to state that there was no other *legal* course of action than its own viewpoint. As argued by Christiansen, 'in the absence of recourse to judicial review of individual aspects of the negotiation results, the "legal advice" of the Council's legal service on proposals for draft articles is authoritative and can therefore constitute a constraint on the possibilities for treaty reform' (Christiansen, 2002, p. 47). As is well known to EU law specialists, the meaning of specific provisions of EU law such as treaty articles is often ambiguous and open to different interpretations ranging from a literal interpretation that often will downplay the scope and strength of Community competences, to a purpose-oriented (teleological) method of interpretation aimed towards the preambles goal of building an 'ever closer union' (Hartley, 2003). Evidence exists that key lawyers in the Legal Services sometimes use teleological methods of interpretation based upon their pro-integrative and pro-Council views. As will be seen in Chapters 5 and 6, some indications of this can be seen in the non-papers produced by the Council Secretariat on questions such as the legal personality of the Union.

The nature of the issues being negotiated

The issues in both IGCs were technically complex. The monetary issues involved were technically complex, for while the overall question of creating a single currency was relatively clear-cut, only insiders from national central banks and national finance ministries fully understood the technical intricacies of the issues. The PU IGC faced similar problems. Questions like the structure of the treaties involved difficult legal problems that few delegations could tackle. Further, the haphazard preparation of the PU IGC also contributed to the difficulty with which many delegations had in coming to terms with the issues, making them dependent upon the provision of outside expertise in many issues. In many of the sessions prior to and during the IGC, ministers did not even receive texts or agendas prior to meetings (Interview EC-24)!

The number of issues and parties in the negotiations

In comparison to the 1985 IGC, the negotiating situation in the two parallel IGCs was very complex. While the 1985 IGC agenda had been relatively short, the agendas for the two 1990–1 IGCs were very long, with hundreds of salient points under debate. One indicator of the complexity is simply the length of the two treaties. While the SEA took up 29 pages in the *Official Journal*, the final Treaty of Maastricht filled a total of 130 pages (No L 169 of 29.6.87; No C 224 of 31.8.92). And while the negotiating situation in the 1985 IGC was significantly simplified by the overreaching 'maximalist'/'minimalist' cleavage, there were few cross-cutting cleavages in the 1990–1 IGCs. In theory, the sheer complexity of the negotiating situation therefore created a strong demand for leadership to overcome these high bargaining costs.

The distribution and intensity of governmental preferences

Figures 4.1 and 4.2 illustrate the distribution of preferences in the two IGCs. In Figure 4.2 the two main cleavages in the EMU IGC are illustrated. The first cleavage was basically whether a single currency should be created or not, whereas the second cleavage split advocates of the 'monetarist' and 'economist' approaches towards monetary union. While many of the issues were resolved in the Delors Committee's report (Committee for the Study of EMU, 1989), several salient issues were open when the IGC started, including

FIGURE 4.1 *Major cleavages in the EMU IGC*

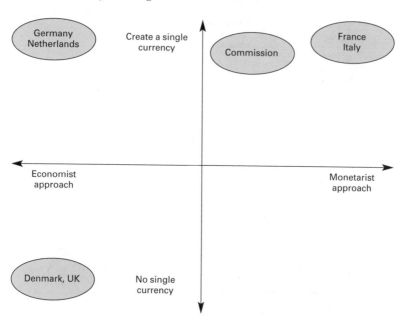

questions of the independence of the ECB, how strong the economic pillar of EMU should be, the procedures for the transition to stage 3, and whether transition should be forced with a timetable or not.

The issues were also politically sensitive in the EMU IGC. The question of creating a single currency struck at the very heart of national sovereignty. In Germany, for example, there were heated verbal exchanges between the Bundesbank (BB) and the government both before and during the IGC (Dyson and Featherstone, 1999, pp. 390–34, 434–7), whereas in the UK the issue contributed to the replacement of Prime Minister Thatcher with John Major in November 1990 (Forster, 1999, pp. 55–6).

In the PU IGC, the pattern of cleavages was more fluid and complex. The first of the two most important cleavages split advocates of more supranational cooperation such as the Commission, Italy, the Netherlands, Germany and Belgium, with those who argued for intergovernmental solutions, such as the UK and France. The second cleavage pitted proponents of a stronger Europe that would increase the scope of cooperation and make existing cooperation more effective, against governments like the UK that basically were satisfied with the status quo, with some exceptions. In reality, the negotiating situation was much more complex, and other cleavages

FIGURE 4.2 *Major cleavages in the PU IGC*

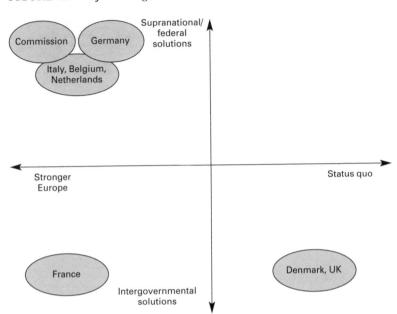

were also important, such as whether stronger economic cohesion policies should be introduced – an issue that pitted the poorer member states against their partners. This complex situation coupled with the strong demand for agreement to solve the German problem created a negotiating situation where there was a strong demand for the provision of leadership.

Many of the issues in the PU IGC were politically sensitive. Issues such as the structure of the treaties involved highly political questions such as whether foreign policy cooperation should be within the supranational Community, or remain intergovernmental. Other sensitive issues included justice and home affairs cooperation and social policy.

Leadership by EU institutions in the 1990–1 IGCs

The two IGCs presented different possibilities for leadership by EU institutions. While none of the EU institutions had strong comparative informational advantages in the EMU IGC, the Commission could potentially gain significant influence over the developing EMU agenda given the role it was granted in the Delors Committee. The chaotic preparations and complexity of the issues in the PU IGC created a strong demand for leadership. Were any of the EU institutions able to successfully provide leadership in either of the IGCs? And if so, what were the effects upon the efficiency and distributive elements of the negotiation?

Leadership by the European Commission

The context of the two IGCs presented different opportunities for the Commission to play a leadership role. As will be seen below, the Commission through institutional politics was able to secure for itself a privileged position within the Delors Committee; a position that Delors exploited skillfully through relatively low-profile leadership tactics within the committee to ensure that EMU would become a reality, and that further negotiations would take place on the basis of the Delors Report. The Commission in the PU IGC chose a much higher profile strategy, eschewing getting its hands dirty in the drafting process but instead opted to openly advocate highly ambitious outcomes. What were the effects of these two different strategies in the IGCs?

Building on the perceptions of Commission successes in the SEA and '1992' program, the Commission attempted to play a much higher profile role in the 1990–1 IGCs in comparison to the 1985 IGC. This was particularly evident in the PU IGC, where Delors attempted to take the next step in his Russian-dolls strategy. The Commission even went so far as to put forward whole draft treaties in both IGCs that were clearly far outside of what a majority of member states wanted (see below).

Investigating first the leadership strategies of the Commission in the EMU IGC, the Commission did prove successful in its attempts to shape the pre-IGC agenda. One example of informational tactics used by the Commission to push for EMU after the approval of the SEA was the decision by Delors to set up a group of experts under the leadership of Tommaso Padoa-Schioppa to analyse the policy implications of the liberalization of capital movements in the EC in the context of the Single Market. The report produced emphasized the spillover from the Single Market, pointing out that the free movement of capital, autonomous national monetary policies, and exchange-rate stability in the EMS formed an 'inconsistent triangle', and that 'hard choices' were necessary on some form of monetary union (see Dyson and Featherstone, 1999, pp. 710–11; Grant, 1994, pp. 116–17; Padoa-Schioppa, 2000, pp. 83–92).

As momentum began building for a decision on monetary union, Delors was concerned that if the agenda-setting phase was handled by finance and economy ministers it would quickly become bogged down in technical details (Dyson and Featherstone, 1999, p. 712). Delors therefore attempted to shift the venue for monetary union discussions to a more favourable institutional forum through managerial tactics, attempting to create a forum where national governments could not act as gate-keepers over the EMU agenda.

There are strongly contrasting accounts of the source of proposals on both the creation and composition of the Delors Committee. Most of the literature, including the authoritative account by Dyson and Featherstone, argues that Delors attempted to capitalize upon his close relationship with German Chancellor Kohl during the German Presidency in the first half of 1988, and that he both persuaded Kohl that the time was ripe for a decision on EMU (Dyson and Featherstone, 1999, p. 712; Grant, 1994, p. 119), and that a group of central bankers should be created to set the parameters for a debate on EMU (Dyson and Featherstone, 1999, pp. 712–13; Grant, 1994, pp. 119–20; McAllister, 1997, pp. 201–2; Ross, 1995, p. 81). Delors allegedly pointed out to the heads of state and government that prior to every significant step forward in integration, a group of experts had been entrusted with preparing the agenda. For example the Spaak Committee prepared the Treaty of Rome IGC agenda (see Haas, 1958, pp. 514–17). Delors argued that if EMU was to be achieved it should be prepared in the same manner (Dyson and Featherstone, 1999, p. 712).

Delors further believed that by co-opting central bankers into the agenda-setting process, and by securing their signatures on the final committee report, the report on EMU would be able to draw upon their legitimacy in strengthening the push for EMU. Delors also lobbied Kohl to *not* appoint Bundesbank (BB) President Karl-Otto Pöhl as chair of the committee, as Delors feared that he would obstruct the progress of the committee, given his known opposition to giving up the German DM in favour of a 'weaker' currency (Dyson and Featherstone, 1999, p. 713). Delors did not lobby Kohl directly to be given the chair, but instead used his cabinet to lobby on his behalf (ibid., p. 713). At the Hanover European Council Summit in June 1988, Delors was given the chair of the committee, and the Summit agreed that the committee should be composed of central bank governors, assisted by three external experts.

Moravcsik contends that the decision to create a committee came from French Finance Minister Balladur, who sent a letter to his colleagues in January 1988 advocating EMU, and that German calls for EMU preceded Delors' attempts to get EMU back on the agenda in the spring of 1988 (Moravcsik, 1998, pp. 433–4). Regarding the composition of the committee, Moravcsik argues that Kohl, backed by Thatcher, insisted that the committee be composed of central bankers (ibid., p. 434). Delors supposedly wanted the committee to be composed of independent experts, but, backed by the French, was only able to secure the participation of three experts on the committee (ibid.). Moravcsik does not investigate the decision-making behind giving Delors the chair, only arguing that it was proposed by Kohl (ibid.).

Given the weight of evidence, while it is probable that Delors was not very influential in the decision to put EMU on the official agenda during the German Presidency, as his calls were preceded by both Balladur and Genscher, there is strong evidence for the claim that Delors was able to influence the decision on the institutional forum, allowing for the creation of an expert committee of (almost) like-minded central bankers. Why Delors would argue for a committee of independent experts is left unclear by Moravcsik – and is all the more puzzling given that Delors had cultivated the group of EC central bank governors since 1985 by attending their monthly meetings in Basle with the express purpose of gaining their confidence (Dyson and Featherstone, 1999, p. 708).

Of further interest is the question of the mandate of the committee. According to Grant, Kohl asked Delors to write the conclusions of the Hanover Summit regarding EMU (Grant, 1994, p. 120). Delors then exploited this to exclude unwanted items from the mandate. Critically, the question in the mandate was not *whether* a single currency could be achieved, but only *how*. This echoed the mandate of the Spaak Committee in 1955, which had been asked *how* a common market could be created, and not *whether* it should be created. This wording in the Spaak Committee mandate then 'trapped' France into accepting the creation of a common market in the subsequent IGC (Haas, 1958, p. 514.).

Within what came to be known as the Delors Committee, Delors actively worked to shape the EMU agenda. Prior to its first meeting, Delors decided to focus on the technical points of how to create an EMU in order to avoid strong disagreements among the members (*Agence Europe*, 12–13 September 1988, No. 4850, p. 5; Dyson and Featherstone, 1999, pp. 715–16; Verdun, 1999, p. 318). Delors also took a series of confidence building steps in order to win the favour of central bankers, especially BB President Pöhl – for example, Delors decided to hold the meetings on the home turf of the central bankers in Basle and not in Brussels (Dyson and Featherstone, 1999, pp. 714–15, 717). Other confidence-building tactics aimed at creating a positive, problem-solving environment included using English instead of French – English was the working language of the central bankers (Dyson and Featherstone, 1999, pp. 714–16).

Delors also held a series of bilateral meetings with BB President Pöhl in order to gain his confidence, and also giving him the concessions that he needed to placate his critics within the BB (Dyson and Featherstone, 1999, p. 715) Further, Wim Duisenberg, head of the Dutch central bank, had both Delors' and Pöhl's confidence. Delors used Duisenberg as a broker between the views of the Commission and like-minded delegations and those of the BB (Dyson and Featherstone, 1999, p. 717). Through clever mediation and brokerage, Delors succeeded in getting Pöhl to sign the final report – which at the start was by no means a foregone conclusion!

Delors did much of the drafting of the report himself, but the degree to which he shaped the final report is strongly contested. While some argue that 'there wasn't a phrase in the final report which he didn't author' (Mingasson in Ross, 1995, p. 82), Moravcsik and others argue that the final report was based upon the BB proposal to the Committee, and that Delors' role was merely being a coordinator and *rapporteur* (Heisenberg, 1999, pp. 105–7; Moravcsik, 1998, p. 291).

The truth is probably in between these two positions, for while Pöhl was able to shape the overall contours of the report, especially regarding most of the institutional aspects of the proposed European Central Bank, Delors successfully exploited his power of the pen to insert certain Commission priorities, including a strengthened economic pillar to EMU, and a 'mischievous' reference to an automatic progression from the 2nd to the final stage of EMU that was clearly opposed by the BB and others (Committee for the Study of EMU, 1989; Interview NAT-23).

But Delors' primary significance in chairing the Committee was achieving a unanimous report, and in particular securing the signature of Pöhl on the final report. The unanimous report significantly strengthened the probability that some form of EMU would be accepted by the member states.

The Commission had less success in shaping the EMU agenda during the French Presidency in the second half of 1989 on questions relating to when to convene the IGC or on how the IGC would be conducted. While both Mitterrand and Delors wanted the IGC to start within six months of the Strasbourg Summit, they were blocked by Kohl, who wanted the start of the IGC to be after German elections that were scheduled for November 1990 (Moravcsik, 1998, p. 437). The Commission also attempted to influence how the IGC negotiations would be conducted. Delors was concerned that negotiations between ECOFIN ministers would at worst lead to no agreement, or at best put EMU into a separate intergovernmental pillar of the treaty (Dyson and Featherstone, 1999, p. 723). Therefore Delors argued that foreign ministers should conduct the negotiations in the hope that they would focus more on the overreaching political arguments (ibid.). Yet despite his best efforts, Delors was unable to prevent the overall responsibility for the EMU negotiations being entrusted to ECOFIN ministers (Dyson and Featherstone, 1999, p. 723; Moravcsik, 1998, p. 437).

During the Italian Presidency in the second half of 1990 that prepared the official mandate for the IGC, the Commission attempted to shape the agenda by issuing a communication on EMU in August 1990 (European Commission, 1990a). The communication echoed the Delors Report by advocating a short stage 2 with a strong institution, and further argued for a substantial economic pillar to EMU. Other ideas included a suggestion that stage 3 could begin when at least eight member states approved a proposal from the Commission on the transition, and that temporary derogations to stage 3 could be granted to countries with severe economic difficulties. These points were then echoed in the Commission's Draft Treaty on EMU in December 1990 (European Commission, 1990b). This draft treaty substantially shaped the debates in the IGC, although there is disagreement on how significant it was to the IGC agenda. Corbett and Ross argue that it formed the basis of the discussions (Corbett, 1993, p. 39; Ross, 1995, pp. 153, 155), whereas Christoffersen (1992, pp. 33–4) and Dyson and Featherstone (1999, p. 727) point out that while it was influential, the French and German draft treaties were also very important (Christoffersen, 1992, pp. 33–4; Dyson and Featherstone, 1999, p. 727). There are also indications that this relatively high-profile Commission attempt to shape the agenda raised concerns among many member states, who saw the Commission draft treaty as pre-empting the work of the IGC, and several member states therefore reacted very negatively to the Commission proposal (Grant, 1994, p. 151). The Commission was also excluded from the drafting of the official mandate for the IGC by the Italian Presidency, which was then agreed at the second Rome Summit in December (Dyson and Featherstone, 1999, p. 516).

During the Luxembourg Presidency in the first half of 1991, the Commission was not directly involved in the behind-the-scenes drafting of Presidency texts for either IGC. The Commission had been invited by the Luxembourg Presidency to take part in the drafting process, but according to insiders, Delors from the start decided to only send low-level officials to the Presidency's group, whereas both the Secretariat and the Presidency sent high-level officials (Interviews EC-3, EC-19, NAT-20). After several months the Commission withdrew its officials from the group altogether, opting instead for more high-profile advocacy tactics in both of the IGCs (Interview EC-3).

Throughout the spring of 1991, Delors continued to push for a stronger economic pillar to EMU (Ross, 1995, p. 86) and, for example, reacted negatively to the German draft treaty in February for its lack of reference to economic policies (Dyson and Featherstone, 1999, p. 728). The Commission put forward a proposal that called for financial assistance in the case of serious economic difficulties in a member, but the proposal met with a strong negative reaction from a majority of member states, and although the final treaty did contain a financial assistance clause, it was far from what the Commission had originally proposed (Dyson and Featherstone, 1999, p. 732).

In the issue of convergence criteria, Moravcsik contends that the Commission vigorously opposed German demands for strict convergence criteria throughout the whole IGC (Moravcsik, 1998, p. 439). But there is evidence suggesting that the Commission changed its views regarding the desirability of strict criteria in early spring 1991, and came to see strict criteria as a means of ensuring an autonomic transition from stage 2 to 3 (Dyson and Featherstone, 1999, pp. 729, 735). The Commission did not, however, share the German's views on *what* the criteria should be, and as will be seen below, during the Dutch Presidency attempted to introduce more growth-oriented criteria.

The Commission also fought to maintain its traditional institutional role in EMU. The French draft treaty on EMU had severely restricted the role of the Commission and the EP in EMU, and the Commission feared that this would result in an EMU as an intergovernmental fourth pillar (Dyson and Featherstone, 1999, pp. 729–30; Reprinted in Corbett, 1993, pp. 247–53). While the final treaty did not fully extend the Commission's role to all aspects of EMU, significant portions of the EMU include a strong role for the Commission. Yet we cannot solely attribute this outcome to the success of Commission agenda-shaping tactics – according to participants the Commission's successful opposition to an intergovernmental EMU was as easy as 'shooting into an open goal' (Dyson and Featherstone, 1999, p. 730). Dyson and Featherstone point out that French representative Pierre de Boissieu was successful in dissuading the French government from advocating an intergovernmental fourth pillar solution for EMU. De Boissieu's strategy was to make a trade-off between French acceptance of placing the EMU within the first pillar in exchange for the acceptance by other delegations of intergovernmental pillars for both CFSP and JHA (ibid.).

One particularly successful Commission proposal was the formula for countries to opt out of the single currency. The British had firmly declared that they would not join the single currency, but had also signalled that they might decide *not* to veto the EMU if they were given a satisfactory opt-out (Forster, 1999, pp. 67–70). In May, Delors had in an informal ministerial meeting put forward a proposal that suggested that no member state would be obliged to join the single currency, but at the same time that no member state could block the start of the third stage of EMU (Ross, 1995, p. 154). This proposal formed a focal point for further discussions on the UK opt-out, and the final protocol introduced by the Dutch Presidency in the last week of the IGC was largely inspired by the Commission's proposal (Corbett, 1993, p. 42).

In general though, key Commission officials realized towards the end of the Luxembourg Presidency that the EMU agenda was set, and that the remaining outstanding questions of EMU would only be solved by the heads of state in the IGC end-game (Ross, 1995, p. 155–6). But the internal assessment was also that the Commission could be satisfied with its efforts, as EMU was seen to be running on 'tracks' laid by the Commission (ibid.).

While the Commission was quite happy with Dutch attempts to rewrite the agenda in the PU IGC (see below), the Commission was upset with how the Dutch Presidency handled the EMU dossier (Dyson and Featherstone, 1999, p. 743). In particular it felt that the Dutch had too strong opinions on some of the issues, and that in several instances they were excessively partial to their own preferences in breach of the traditional Presidency role of 'honest broker' (ibid.). Further, as the Dutch were not dependent upon the Commission's informational resources on EMU (ibid.), and Dutch Presidency's preferences on EMU did not overlap with the Commission's, the Dutch did not draw upon the resources of the Commission to assist them in the EMU IGC. In contrast, in August and September the Dutch drew extensively upon the Commission in the PU IGC, as their views on the PU IGC overlapped with the Commission's (see below). The Dutch draft treaty on EMU was in contrast prepared with help from the Germans (Grant, 1994, p. 183).

When the Dutch EMU draft treaty was debated on 9 September, Delors attempted to fight against the provision in the Dutch draft that proposed forming a two-speed EMU, with the third phase starting when at least six states had satisfied the convergence criteria over two years, and that the members of EMU could veto any state from joining if they felt they had not met the strict convergence criteria (ibid.). Delors then suggested additional convergence criteria, including levels of youth and long-term unemployment (Dyson and Featherstone, 1999, pp. 735–6). While Delors' proposals on additional criteria foundered, a majority of states did back Delors' opposition to the automatic use of the criteria as advocated by the Dutch and Germans (ibid.; Grant, 1994, p. 183). Yet it was French and Belgian opposition to the strict German demands, and not clever advocacy by the Commission, that ensured that a 'criteria plus trend' formula would apply for the transition to stage 3 (ibid.).

The Commission fared better in other aspects of the EMU discussions. Delors had for example long advocated a strong role for the European Council in the decision on the transition to stage 3 of EMU, in the belief that heads of state would see a broader political context than ECOFIN ministers (Dyson and Featherstone, 1999, p. 729). While this formed the final outcome, whether the Commission proposal shaped the agenda or whether the Commission merely proposed what it believed the member states would accept anyway is difficult to discern. Additionally, there are few indications that this was an especially salient point, and a strong role for the European Council was also included in the French draft treaty from January 1991.

In the EMU IGC end-game, the Commission attempted to broker an outcome regarding the introduction of a fixed transition timetable. The basic cleavage was between the French and Italians, backed by the Commission, who wanted a fixed date for the transition to stage 3 of EMU, whereas Germany and several other delegations wanted economic convergence prior to any transition to the final stage. An opportunity for a compromise came in late November when Kohl signalled that Germany was seeking an irreversible EMU in order to commit future German leaders to EMU (Dyson and Featherstone, 1999, p. 737). Yet Delors also believed that a compromise proposal tabled by the Commission would be seen as 'imposing'. Therefore Delors and his cabinet lobbied the French government to table a compromise proposal (ibid.). At the Maastricht Summit a winning compromise proposal was put forward by France and Italy that called for a majority vote at the end of 1996, and if stage 3 did not start then, it would automatically start in 1999 (Grant, 1994, p. 200). However, there is little evidence that this compromise was due to the provision of leadership by the Commission (Dyson and Featherstone, 1999, p. 738).

Concluding, the EMU IGCs agenda was significantly shaped by Delors in his capacity as chair of the Delors Committee. However, after the report was produced the Commission's ability to provide leadership in the IGC declined. The resulting lack of success of Commission leadership during the IGC is especially evident when we see how governments watered down the economic pillar of EMU (Corbett, 1993, p. 43). But by the start of the IGC the Commission had already achieved its main goal – the creation of a single European currency.

The PU IGC in contrast became a nightmare for the Commission because of a combination of poor strategy and rising anti-Commission sentiments among governments during the IGC. During the agenda-setting phase of the PU IGC, Delors first gave a series of speeches in late 1989 and early 1990, where he argued that a parallel IGC to EMU should be convened to reduce the democratic deficit and deepen the EC's executive authority (that is, the powers of the Commission). Yet available evidence indicates that the decision to convene the PU IGC was a Franco-German bargain, and was not the result of the Commission's advocacy (Dinan, 2000, p. 257; Grant, 1994, p. 129–30; Ross, 1995, p. 89; Wester, 1992, p. 206).

After the decision was taken to convene a PU IGC, the Commission pushed for the creation of an expert group to prepare the agenda, but was rebuffed by the member states, who decided that it should be prepared by COREPER, where national concerns dominate (Dyson and Featherstone, 1999, p. 722). Yet the Commission surprisingly did little internally to prepare itself for the PU IGC, and only presented a brief opinion prior to the convening of the IGC (Wester, 1992, pp. 206–7).

As was seen above, the Commission had pulled itself out of the Luxembourg Presidency drafting group, removing an important tool from its leadership toolbox. But giving up this role appears to have been deliberate, with Delors believing that the Commission could achieve more by not getting its hands dirty in the detailed behind-the-scenes drafting and advising process, and instead use strong political advocacy tactics at the highest level, putting forward proposals and building support for them, while mobilizing opposition to competing proposals (Interview EC-19; NAT-20).

The Commission tabled a series of proposals during 1990–1 (European Commission, 1991a). The first proposals were basic statements of positions, while from March the Commission began formulating them in draft legal text (Ross, 1995, p. 90). If we look across the issues, the Commission's proposal for a strong European citizenship provision was first put forward in the Commission's Opinion on 21 October 1990 (European Commission, 1991a, pp. 69–78). Yet the idea of European citizenship had already been discussed within

COREPER prior to this (*Agence Europe*, 19.05.90, No. 5258, pp. 3–4), and had been given substance by the EP's Martin's II Report from July 1990 and the Spanish proposal of 24 September 1990 (in Laursen and Vanhoonacker, 1992, pp. 282–91, 325–32). The final provisions in the Treaty of Maastricht are also closer to the Spanish proposal (Christoffersen, 1992, pp. 111–16), though the final text was relatively weak in comparison to the Spanish text, and only contained the relatively non-contentious provisions on voting rights in local and EP elections as advocated by the EP.

In CFSP, the Commission had already put forward in March 1990 a proposed draft chapter that called for incorporating all external policies into one chapter (European Commission, 1991a, pp. 85–114). But the Commission proposals had little impact upon the negotiations, which were led by the Franco-German tandem with the UK acting as the brake. The member states showed little interest in Commission proposals for a communitarization of foreign policy (that is, moving it into the supranational first pillar), or for strengthening the Commission's role in the common trade policy (Christoffersen, 1992 pp. 221–66; Interview EC-3; Moravcsik, 1998, pp. 450–1; Ross, 1995, pp. 95–6). However, it can also be argued that the Commission was aware that its proposal would not be accepted, but that it put forward a 'blue-sky' proposal in the hope that it could shape the agenda by pushing certain actors closer to accepting a watered-down version of the Commission's proposals, or at worst that it could influence the agenda for future treaty changes (Ross, 1995, p. 96).

The Commission's proposal to create a new EC act (laws) that would be adopted by co-decision, and that would then allow the Commission to fill in the details without the approval of either the Council or EP was unanimously rejected in the IGC, although the idea of creating a new type of EC act was supported by a majority of member states, and was included in the first Luxembourg Draft Treaty (Christoffersen, 1992, pp. 199–200). Further, the Commission proposals for the areas to which the new law would be applied, such as agricultural policy, were also rejected, with for example Germany calling it of 'centralizing inspiration' (Ross, 1995, p.100). The term 'law' was first removed in the second Dutch Draft Treaty in November 1991, and a declaration was attached to the final treaty to the effect that the 1996 IGC would look at the question again (Declaration 16 on the Hierarchy of Community Acts).

Regarding the discussions on co-decision, the Commission was not very successful in shaping the debates. The Commission had been against co-decision in its original IGC opinion, and in its proposal in

March 1991 had argued for a strong role for the Commission and a relatively weak role for the Parliament in the procedure (European Commission, 1991a, pp. 115–23). This proposal had very little impact upon the discussions, and governments saw it as a 'wholly absurd' attempt to increase Commission powers (Forster, 1999, p. 140).

Worse was to come for the Commission. Based upon a draft report produced by the Secretariat, Germany put forward a proposal for co-decision that considerably weakened the role of the Commission (Moravcsik, 1998, p. 456; Christoffersen, 1992, pp. 194–6). While the Commission succeeded in preserving its right to withdraw a proposal in the final co-decision procedure both before and after the Conciliation Committee in the event that the Committee had not adopted the proposal, the Commission was unable to prevent the member states from accepting that the Council could adopt amendments to a Commission proposal by QMV while it was in the Conciliation Committee, whereas in other procedures the Council could only amend a Commission proposal by unanimity unless the amendments were approved by the Commission (Christoffersen, 1992, pp. 195–6; Grant, 1994, p. 197). Additionally, the final article states that the Commission cannot withdraw a proposal while it is being discussed in the Committee (Article 189b, now after amendment Article 251).

The Commission fared slightly better in protecting its prerogatives in other areas. For instance, a strong coalition of governments including Germany and Italy had suggested giving the EP the right of legislative initiative alongside the Commission, but the Commission succeeded in preventing it through strong opposition by Delors in the Noordwijk foreign ministers conclave on 12 November 1991 (Christoffersen, 1992, p. 206; Grant, 1994, p. 197).

Turning to social policy, Delors as his second step in his Russian-doll strategy had since 1988 advocated strengthening the EC's social dimension as a complement to the Internal Market by creating common minimum standards in the workplace, together with EC-level dialogue between employers organizations and trade unions. These efforts led to the adoption of the Social Charter in 1989 by all governments except the UK (Falkner, 2002, p. 197; Grant, 1994, pp. 83–7). In the PU IGC, the Commission tabled a proposal in March 1991 that would introduce QMV in the areas of the Social Charter and that would increase the role of organized interests at the EC level. The Belgians put forward a similar proposal in January 1991, and Falkner argues that the Commission collaborated with the Belgians, using them as a front to put forward what was in essence a Commission proposal (Falkner, 2002, p. 111). The Belgian and Commission proposals did then set the substantive agenda in the IGC (Christoffersen, 1992, pp. 122–6; Falkner, 2002). While this tactic is often used by the Commission, it is very difficult for the analyst to detect, as neither the Commission nor national delegates have incentives to reveal this type of collaboration.

However, in the face of opposition, the scope of QMV in the social policy provisions proposed by the Commission were reduced in the first Luxembourg Draft and further in Dutch drafts in the fall of 1991 (Christoffersen, 1992, pp. 124–6; Ross, 1995, p. 183). To counter this, the Commission encouraged the Social Dialogue ad hoc group, composed of representatives from EC-level trade and employers unions, to write a letter to Dutch Prime Minister Lubbers urging him to reinstate the Commission social policy proposal (Forster, 1999, p. 89; Ross, 1995, p. 183). The Dutch Presidency responded to the letter by agreeing to reincorporate most of the Commission proposal into its non-paper presented to the Noordwijk foreign ministers meeting on 12 November, though there were still substantial reductions in the scope of the provisions in comparison to the Commission's original proposal (Ross, 1995, p. 183).

The final stages of the negotiation of the social policy provisions dealt with finding a way to avoid a looming British veto (Forster, 1999, p. 92). UK Prime Minister Major had clearly indicated that he would *not* accept an 'opt out', but he did begin to consider a compromise if the provisions were kept outside of the EC Treaty (Christoffersen, 1992, pp. 126–7; Forster, 1999, p. 92). The Commission in the Maastricht Summit was able to step in and provide a legal formula that was acceptable to all of the member states, and that substantively was based upon the original Commission proposal with certain reductions in the scope of QMV. The Commission used materials produced in advance by the Commission's Legal Services to create a legally binding Social Protocol that enabled the 11 member states to 'opt in', creating an agreement formally outside of the EC but that could act within EC structures, and that stated that measures adopted using the Protocol would not be applicable to the UK (Ross, 1995, p. 191; Moravcsik, 1998, pp. 453–4). The importance of this Commission intervention should not be downplayed as Moravcsik does (1998, p. 454, 1999a, p. 292), as it is probable that if the Maastricht Treaty had not included strong social policy provisions, both France and Italy would have vetoed the final treaty as a whole, whereas if the provisions had been included within the Community itself, the UK would have vetoed the final treaty (Christoffersen, 1992, pp. 126, 128; Forster, 1999, pp. 92–3).

The Commission's proposal on economic and social cohesion dealt with small modifications of the existing treaty provisions and were for the most adopted. More importantly, as will be discussed below, the Commission played an important brokering role between the poorer member states, especially Spain, and the rest of the member states on whether to adopt more drastic amendments of the existing cohesion provisions.

Commission proposals to introduce QMV into R&D framework decisions and that would increase the role of the Commission in their implementation were opposed by several member states, and were vetoed by the UK in the final stage of the IGC (Christoffersen, 1992, pp. 154–6). The Commission also proposed a new treaty chapter for energy which was not approved by the member states.

The Commission faired better in its proposals in other areas such as environment policy, although its viewpoints were shared by pro-environmental member states such as Denmark and Germany (Christoffersen, 1992, p. 142). On trans-European networks, the Commission was the main agenda-setter. The Commission used informational leadership to build support for its proposal, arguing that the full benefits of the Internal Market would not be realized unless greater progress was made (Christoffersen, 1992, p. 158). The final outcome was close to the Commission's proposal, although southern member states were able to strengthen the cohesion aspects of the provisions in comparison to the original Commission proposal (ibid.).

Most of the other Commission proposals were relatively minor, except the proposals on the enforcement of EC law and the structure of the treaties. Regarding the first, the Commission's quite revolutionary proposals for strengthening compliance with EC law by increasing the powers available to national courts to enforce EC law were not adopted, and governments instead opted for a sovereignty-friendly UK proposal that would amend Article 171 of the EC Treaty (now Article 228 EC), enabling the ECJ to fine member states for non-compliance (Beach, 2001, pp. 97–8; Christoffersen, 1992, p. 219; Tallberg, 2003, pp. 78–80).

Finally, the Commission strongly advocated a single treaty structure (the tree), although its proposals also opened certain restrictions in the sensitive areas of foreign policy and justice and home affairs. Following the presentation of the pillar structure in the first Luxembourg Draft Treaty, the Commission submitted an amendment that would replace the pillars with a tree structure (Christoffersen, 1992, p. 37; European Commission, 1991a, pp. 173–7; Ross, 1995, p. 146). In the explanatory memorandum that was attached, the

Commission stated that 'the IGC should be guided by the basic think-ing which has been behind the construction of Europe for 40 years now, namely that all progress made towards economic, monetary, social or political integration should gradually be brought together in a single Community as a precursor of a European Union' (European Commission, 1991a, p. 176).

The Commission attempted to mobilize opposition to the pillar treaty structure, and Delors travelled to national capitals in an attempt to convince leaders of the merits of a tree structure (Grant, 1994, p.190; Moravcsik, 1998, p. 460). Commission pressure paid off (temporarily), and a strong coalition backed Delors' calls in the 2–3 June Dresden meeting of foreign ministers for a revision of the first Luxembourg draft, including Germany, Spain, Italy and Holland – leaving only France, the UK, Ireland and Denmark openly supporting the pillar structure (Grant, 1994, p. 190; Christoffersen, 1992, pp. 53–4). In the aftermath of the 'battle of Dresden', the Luxembourg Presidency strengthened the common elements of the treaty in their second draft text, and included a federal reference in the preamble (Christoffersen, 1992, p. 54; Grant, 1994, pp. 190–1). This appears to have appeased most governments, but not the Commission or the Netherlands (Grant, 1994, p. 191). The second Luxembourg Draft was subsequently adopted as the basis for further negotiations by the heads of state and government at the Luxembourg European Council on 28–9 June.

At the start of the Dutch Presidency, the Commission encouraged and assisted the Dutch Foreign Ministry in producing a single pillar structure in their Presidency draft treaty, and the Dutch consulted high-level Commission officials close to Delors as they prepared their draft (Christoffersen, 1992, p. 37; Interview EC-3; Ross, 1995, p. 171). That the Dutch drew upon the Commission and not the Secretariat was primarily due to the overlapping preferences of the Commission and Dutch on issues such as the structure of the treaty, where both advocated a single pillar structure.

This intervention in favour of the Dutch draft was fateful for further attempts by the Commission to shape the agenda on the struc-ture of the treaties, as siding with the excessively partial Dutch Presidency significantly reduced the acceptability of future Commission interventions. After 'Black Monday', the Dutch drew less upon the Commission, and the Commission became increasingly isolated in its attempts to advocate a more ambitious outcome during the last months of the IGC (Dinan, 2000, p. 263).

In the final months of the IGC, Commission attempts to advocate a stronger common framework were ignored both by the 'new' Dutch

Presidency and by other governments (Grant, 1994, pp. 197–8), and the final treaty structure chosen was based upon the second Luxembourg Draft, with a vague reference to a more federal Europe in the preamble and strengthened common provisions.

The Commission did have success with several attempts at brokerage. One was the deal crafted by the Commission on the issue of economic and social cohesion. Spain, together with several of the poorer member states, demanded a substantial increase in the financial transfers between member states in order to compensate them for the strong demands that would be made upon them by strengthened EC environmental policies and the EMU convergence criteria – in effect saying 'if you want EMU it will cost you'. Further, Spain wanted a clause inserted into the treaty that would ensure that national contributions to the EC budget reflected the relative wealth of the member state as a whole – that is, a national proportionality clause (Christoffersen, 1992, pp. 135, 137; Grant, 1994, pp.196–7; Gil Ibañez 1992, pp. 108–10). Spain signalled that it might not sign unless the treaty included these measures, whereas net contributors were concerned about the financial implications of these changes, and strongly opposed the introduction of a national proportionality clause into the treaty article on the EC's own resources (Christoffersen, 1992, p. 137).

The Commission in the IGC end-game was able to utilize its material leadership resources to broker a compromise that prevented a negotiating breakdown. Delors in behind-the-scenes meetings with the foreign ministers from Greece, Ireland, Portugal and Spain assured them that they would receive increased structural funds in the next EC budget, which ensured Spanish support for including strengthened EC environmental policies and EMU into the final treaty (Moravcsik, 1998, p. 446). Delors also helped broker a deal in the final negotiations on a proportionality clause, helping the Dutch Presidency find a satisfactory solution that would appease both sides of the conflict (Grant, 1994, p. 200). The result was a legally binding treaty protocol that stated that the member states intended to take 'greater account of the contributive capacity of individual Member States in the system of own resources, and of examining means of correcting, for the less prosperous Member States, regressive elements existing in the present own resources system' (Protocol, 15).

Yet, overall, the Commission had little success in providing leadership in the PU IGC. The basic problem for the Commission was that it was advocating an extreme policy position, fighting for an enhancement of its own powers and for a single pillar treaty framework. The

Commission in many instances behaved more like a 13th member state. The Commission also had a poor working relationship with the Luxembourg Presidency. During the Dutch Presidency, by backing the first Dutch Draft Treaty, the Commission severely damaged its ability to act as a trusted instrumental leader. For example, a compromise proposal by the Commission on a solution to the question of the WEU-EU relationship was simply ignored by the Dutch Presidency (Grant, 1994, p. 199; Ross, 1995, p. 184), and Delors increasingly resorted in the PU IGC end-game to openly admonishing governments for their lack of progress and ambition both within the IGC and to the press – but with very little success (see *Agence Europe*, 28.11.91; *Financial Times* 21 November 1991).

Leadership by the European Parliament

The EP and its members were very active both before and during the IGC in an attempt to guide governments towards the EP's goal of a closer union. But as with the SEA IGC, the combination of the EP's peripheral role and an extreme position led to the situation where the EP was mostly relegated to shouting to deaf ears from outside the negotiating room. A notable exception was in the question of the EP's own powers, where the EP successfully linked its formal powers in daily policy-making with outcomes in the IGC.

Prior to the IGC, the EP attempted to set the agenda with a series of reports. The EP attempted to show that the SEA was an inadequate response to the challenges facing Europe. Reports were drafted on subjects including the democratic deficit (Toussaint report), the costs of non-Europe (Catherwood), a report on the first year of application of the SEA (Graziana), on fundamental rights (De Gucht), and a final report on how European Union could be achieved (Herman report) (Jacobs Corbett and Shackleton, 1995, p. 303).

Corbett argues that the EP shaped the agenda regarding the decision to convene a parallel PU IGC through a resolution in November 1989 that asked the Institutional Affairs Committee to begin to prepare a draft treaty, and that the first EP reports then significantly shaped the agenda (Corbett, 1992, pp. 273–4). But while the EP resolution was then echoed in Belgian and Italian calls for an IGC, the main impetus in convening the PU IGC was the Franco-German letter and the strong German interests in convening a parallel PU IGC.

The EP proceeded to draft three reports, entitled the Martin Reports that contained the EP's positions drafted in treaty language. In an effort to build support behind the EP's proposals, the EP proposed holding a conference of representatives of national parliamentarians and MEPs (Corbett, 1998, pp. 296–300). The 'assizes' were then held in Rome in November 1990, and were composed of two-thirds national parliamentarians and one-third MEPs. The 'assizes' adopted a declaration by 150 to 13 that endorsed all of the EP's main proposals for the IGC (Jacobs, Corbett and Shackleton, 1995, p. 304).

The EP also succeeded in carving out a small role for itself in ministerial discussions both prior to and during the IGC. Prior to the IGC, four inter-institutional meetings were held, and during the IGC monthly meetings were held between the foreign ministers and twelve MEPs in an inter-institutional committee, together with a Commission representative (ibid.). An EP delegation also toured national capitals during the IGC, holding meetings with national governments (Corbett, 1998, p. 312). Finally, the EP President spoke at numerous IGC meetings, including European Council Summits (Corbett, 1998, p. 312).

Did this activity translate into effective EP leadership in the IGCs? The answer based upon the evidence in the EMU IGC is simply 'No' (see Dyson and Featherstone, 1999). Regarding the PU IGC, the picture is somewhat more complicated. While Corbett argues that the EP's 'early formulation of a precise and detailed set of proposals was crucial in providing a focus for all those concerned with preparing or discussing the IGC ... In the compromises that emerged from the IGC, it obtained a far from negligible proportion of its aspirations' (Corbett, 1998, p. 342). Yet the overall conclusion with the exception of EP powers is that the EP in most issues in the PU IGC was ineffective.

If we look at important issues in the PU IGC such as the structure of the treaty or extension of QMV, there are few indications that the EP's advocacy played a role, as the EP's position was far from the centre of gravity of the debates. And neither the Dutch nor Luxembourg Presidency utilized EP proposals as sources in the drafting of texts (Interviews EC-19, NAT-20). Most revealingly, despite the EP passing a resolution in late November that threatened to reject the treaty unless significant changes were introduced (*Agence Europe* No. 5615, 23.11.91:3–4), the final Treaty of Maastricht was far from what the EP had advocated. Whether governments perceived this 'threat' as credible is also questionable, as under then Article 236 of the EC Treaty (now Article 48 EU) the EP has no right of assent over the final treaty!

The notable exception to the lack of success of EP leadership was in the issue of EP powers, where the EP was able to shape the agenda and outcomes on a few select points. In the issue of the right of the EP to approve the Commission with a vote of confidence, the EP had since 1980 acted *as if* it had the right to a vote of confidence despite the lack of a treaty-based power to do so (Corbett, 1992, p. 293; Stacey, 2003, p. 943). When the EP then advocated the granting of a treaty-based *de jure* right to approve the Commission, it was in effect only asking governments to entrench existing practices (Corbett, 1992, p. 293). Yet despite this, the PU IGC only granted the EP a non-binding right of 'consultation'. The EP also pushed strongly for the terms of the Commission and EP to coincide, and although the demands were met with open hostility from many governments, they did make it into the final treaty (Corbett, 1992, p. 293).

In other EP-related issues, there is little evidence that the EP was influential. Most notable was the lack of EP success in its attempts to extend its budgetary authority to all aspects of the budget, including agriculture. On the creation of a co-decision procedure, this was a major fighting point for the EP that was included in the final treaty. But the creation of the co-decision procedure was arguably due to German leadership. The draft that was adopted by the IGC was also based upon a German proposal, and revealingly, the EP was unable to gain equal footing in the procedure. The procedure agreed at Maastricht allows the Council in a third reading to reject any EP amendments to a proposal. The Council position then becomes law unless the EP can muster an *absolute* majority against it. The EP only has the power of veto, and cannot amend a Council position in the third reading (for analysis, see Garrett and Tsebelis, 1996; Scully, 1997; Tsebelis and Garrett, 1997). The EP also asked for a limited right of initiative, but these calls were beaten back by successful Commission opposition (see above).

Concluding, there is little evidence that the EP was influential in the two IGCs. The EP had a peripheral role in the IGCs, and its position was not helped by it advocating extreme outcomes. Even as regards its own prerogatives the EP was, with few exceptions, unable to shape the agenda or the outcome.

Leadership by the Council Secretariat

Looking first at the negotiations of the EMU IGC, there are few indications that the Secretariat was able to provide leadership either prior to or during the IGC. The basic problem was that the Secretariat had no real comparative informational advantages in monetary policy, with the real expertise possessed by national central bankers and finance ministry officials (Tsoukalis, 2000, p. 155).

Secondly, a large part of the technical drafting of EMU provisions took place prior to the IGC within the Delors Committee, to which the

Secretariat was *not* a part. If we investigate the agenda-setting phase after the Delors Committee, the Council Secretariat played no substantial role in the Guigou group, which was set up by the French Presidency in the summer of 1989 to further prepare the EMU IGC agenda by drafting questions in response to the conclusions of the Madrid European Council Summit in June 1989.

Turning from the agenda-setting phase to the start of the actual negotiations, during the Italian Presidency that presided over the convening of the IGC, the Secretariat was kept out of the drafting of the proposed conclusions of the Rome Summit on EMU that would open the IGC. The intention of the Italian Presidency was basically to 'keep control of the wording' (Dyson and Featherstone, 1999, p. 516). During the Luxembourg and Dutch Presidencies, the Secretariat took part in the committee that prepared draft texts on EMU, together with officials from the Presidency (and the Commission for the first months of the IGC) (Interview NAT-20; Moravcsik, 1998, pp. 440–1). This involvement was more technical than guiding, as ECOFIN ministers and national civil servants controlled the process (Interview EC-19), and there are only a few examples of leadership by the Secretariat. One example was in the final stage of the IGC, where the Dutch draft text on the mechanism for the transition to the final stage of EMU called for ratification by national parliaments (Interview NAT-20). Kohl was afraid that the German legislature would in the future block German transition to stage 3, and therefore the Secretariat found a text that solved their problem (ibid.).

The lack of Secretariat leadership in the EMU IGC contrasts with the Secretariat's relative success in influencing the PU IGC outcome, with many of the salient features of the Political Union agreement skewed towards Secretariat preferences following its successful provision of leadership (Christoffersen, 1992, p. 33; Ross, 1995, pp. 84–5, 271 n.19). Member States generally had vague ideas about what they wanted out of the PU IGC (Interview NAT-20). There had been little preparation of the agenda, and many of the most salient issues, such as the structure of the treaty, were legally complex. This complexity and lack of preparation created many opportunities for the Secretariat to provide leadership aimed both at the efficiency and distributive dimensions.

The Secretariat helped in the preparation of the agenda for the member states prior to the IGC, for example by drafting a non-paper in May 1990 on the agenda based upon COREPER discussions on possible agendas for a PU IGC (*Agence Europe*, 19.05.90, No. 5258:3–4; 21/22.05.90, No. 5259:3–4). According to Secretariat officials, they knew that governments 'wanted more foreign policy cooperation, more democratic legitimacy', but these vague concepts had to be translated into concrete ideas and options upon which governments could then negotiate (Interview NAT-20). Unfortunately given the closed and ad hoc nature of these proceedings, it is difficult to discern whether certain points were put on or excluded from the agenda by the Secretariat.

During the Italian Presidency in the second half of 1990, the Italians did not rely extensively on the Secretariat in preparing the IGC agenda, although the Secretariat did assist the Italians by circulating questionnaires to member states to assess their positions, and wrote the draft of a report to conclude the COREPER and ministerial discussions on the PU IGC agenda (Mazzucelli, 1997, p. 62). This draft was then adopted by the foreign ministers without amendment as the basic text for the Rome II Summit, but with the available evidence it is again difficult to discern whether and where the Secretariat succeeded in shifting the agenda in the report. And in the final preparations of the Rome Summit Conclusions, the Italian Foreign Minister took full control of the drafting process and excluded the Secretariat (Dyson and Featherstone, 1999, p. 516; Moravcsik, 1998, p. 448 n. 142).

This situation changed dramatically with the Luxembourg Presidency. As was politely put by Ross, 'The Luxembourgers were not overly endowed with global statesmen', meaning that they lacked the leadership resources necessary to guide the negotiations towards an acceptable outcome (Ross, 1995, p. 90). In contrast to the 1985 IGC, the 1991 Luxembourg Presidency drew extensively upon the services of the Secretariat, which gave them greater power than 'anyone on the Delors team was happy to see' (ibid.). The Secretariat for example prepared all of the questionnaires that were distributed in advance of IGC meetings to ascertain national positions on issues (Moravcsik, 1998, p. 448).

The Secretariat used informational tactics to convince the Luxembourg Presidency of the merits of the Secretariat's legal formula for introducing restrictions upon EC competences within new articles in the EC Treaty, for example in culture, education, or the Social Chapter (Interview EC-3). There had been many proposals from member states to the IGC for new treaty provisions within these areas, but they were only accepted by sceptical member states *after* the Secretariat tabled a satisfactory legal formula for restricting certain EC competences in the new articles. This new formula echoed Secretariat interests in moving away from the use of Article 235 of the EC Treaty (now Article 308 EC) by increasing the scope of EC competences while at the same time restricting the powers of the Commission and other competing institutional actors in the new policy areas.

The Secretariat was also very important in one of the most salient issues in the IGC: the legal structure of the treaty. The original idea of creating a treaty split into three pillars – two intergovernmental pillars together with the existing supranational EC pillar – had come from French representative Pierre de Boissieu (Interview EC-19; Moravcsik, 1998, pp. 449–50). Yet de Boissieu's pillar idea was only a vague metaphor, and it then had to be translated into a concrete legal reality – something that arguably only the Secretariat was able to do with its extensive knowledge of the structure of the treaties coupled with the acceptance among governments of its leadership (Interview NAT-20, EC-19). Crucially, without a workable legal formula for a pillar framework, it is unlikely that a final agreement would have been reached on including either the CFSP or JHA into the treaties.

The production of a workable legal formula was a task that only the secretariat or the largest member states had the technical and legal expertise to do. But whereas a proposal from the Quai d'Orsay or the Foreign and Commonwealth Office would have been seen by other governments as partial to their own intergovernmentalist preferences, given the Secretariat's reputation as a trusted assistant among governments, the legal formula that it proposed was seen to be balanced and digestible. Further, the Secretariat consulted all twelve governments while it was drafting the formula, ensuring that it was broadly acceptable by all before it was introduced to the IGC (Christoffersen, 1992, pp. 34–5). The pillar structure in the first Luxembourg Draft Treaty was presented to the IGC on 12 April 1991, and was accepted as the basis for further negotiations by national delegates (Christoffersen, 1992, p. 35).

The Dutch Presidency that took charge of the IGC in the second half of 1991 did not rely on the Secretariat during August and September. The Dutch Foreign Minister, who had overall responsibility for the Dutch Presidency until after 'Black Monday', saw Secretariat Secretary-General Ersbøll as a 'skeptical Dane' who did not share the Dutch Foreign Minister's federal vision of the EC (Interview EC-25; Ross, 1995, p. 171). The Dutch Foreign Minister also thought that the head of the Secretariat's Legal Service, Jean-Claude Piris, was advocating in his interventions 'Fouchet'-like ideas to create a more intergovernmental EC (Interview NAT-3).

While Ersbøll in his discussions with Dutch Prime Minister Lubbers in August and September was informed that the Dutch were proceeding with their work on the basis of the second Luxembourg

Draft Treaty, the Dutch Foreign Ministry was actually busy working behind his back on an alternative Draft Treaty that would replace the Secretariat's pillar structure with a Commission-inspired unitary treaty framework (Christoffersen, 1992, p. 37; Interview EC-3). The Dutch Foreign Ministry utilized its own officials to draft the first Dutch Draft Treaty, and did not consult the Secretariat or even its own Permanent Representation in Brussels! The Council Secretariat became aware of the intentions of the Dutch Foreign Ministry, and warned them that they should be more cautious and that their reading of the state of play was incorrect (Interview EC-19).

By then departing so strongly from the Luxembourg Draft, which had been agreed upon as the basis for further negotiations at the Luxembourg Council Summit in June 1991, the Dutch Presidency overstepped the invisible line of acting too partially, and thereby antagonized the other delegations – even including those who preferred a more federal treaty structure. In the face of the massive rejection of the Dutch first draft, the Dutch were embarrassingly forced to abandon their proposal and return to the Luxembourg draft as the basis of the negotiations (Christiansen, 2002, p. 48; Christoffersen, 1992, pp. 37–8).

After the Dutch failure, the overall responsibility for chairing the Dutch Presidency was transferred to the Dutch Prime Minister, who was assisted by a small team of experts drawn from the Dutch Permanent Representation in Brussels and the Council Secretariat (Interview EC-3, NAT-20), giving the Secretariat opportunities to provide leadership, and thereby influence the agenda and outcome of the IGC.

In the final months of the IGC, the Secretariat put forward the winning legal formula for decision-making in both the co-decision and cooperation procedures, providing a formula that placated both those delegations that wanted a substantially stronger EP role and those that either favoured the status quo or were concerned about the weakening of the powers of the Commission (Interview EC-3). The Secretariat's Legal Services drafted a report that suggested that the Commission's right to withdraw proposed legislation in a proposed Conciliation Committee within the co-decision procedure should be removed (Moravcsik, 1998, p. 456). This idea was then taken up in the German proposal on co-decision that shaped the final outcome, where tellingly the final co-decision procedure weakened the Commission in comparison to the Council. Whereas the Council in other procedures is only able to amend a Commission proposal by unanimity, the co-decision procedure allows the Council to adopt previous Council or EP amendments to a proposal that were rejected by the Commission using QMV in the Conciliation Committee, contingent upon acceptance of the changes by the EP within the Conciliation Committee.

During the final stage of the IGCs, the Secretariat's role shifted to assisting the Presidency in the brokering of key deals. One example of Secretariat brokerage was the assistance provided by the Secretariat's Legal Services to the Commission in brokering a deal on the Social Protocol in the Maastricht Summit (Grant, 1994, p. 202).

Concluding, while the Secretariat only played a minor part in the EMU IGC, it was an important leader in the PU IGC by helping governments translate vague ideas into legal text and in finding solutions to specific problems.

Conclusion

This chapter has shown the impact of the negotiating context and choice of leadership strategy on the ability of EU institutions to provide leadership. While the Commission was very successful in the agenda-setting phase of the EMU IGC owing to its privileged institutional position and choice of low-profile leadership strategies, in the PU IGC the Commission threw off its cloak and attempted to play the role of the 'Champion of Europe'. But the Commission's ambitions outran its ability to achieve them, with Delors fundamentally misjudging the zones of possible agreement in the PU IGC (Gillingham, 2003, pp. 260–1). The Commission also surprisingly decided to not 'get its hands dirty' in the behind-the-scenes drafting process – a scene where Emile Noël had such great success in the 1985 IGC as a complement to Delors' leadership at the political level. The lack of Commission success is illustrated in Table 4.5.

The EP was again sidelined with the exception of certain extensions of its own powers. Here, the EP was successful in translating material leadership resources into influence over outcome. The EP had created de facto powers by creatively exploiting discretion in the rules governing its formal powers in daily policy-making. Once a de facto power was created, this made it easier for governments to accept a de jure entrenchment of the right in the treaties. But while the EP did succeed in translating a de facto right to be consulted on the appointment of the Commission into a de jure right, the tactic had limits, and governments only granted the EP a *non-binding* right (see above).

The Council Secretariat, on the other hand, was coming into its own right as the 'unseen hand' in the IGC negotiation process. Leadership by the Secretariat did significantly increase the efficiency

TABLE 4.5   *Conclusions – leadership in the 1990–1 IGCs*

Issue area	Outcome
First pillar – Provisions amending the Treaty establishing the European Community	
Introduction of new policies	• EMU – basic contours of agreement agreed in Delors Committee, where the German Bundesbank set the broad framework, and where leadership by Delors ensured that agreement was reached
	– fixed timetable – Franco-German compromise in endgame
	– decision-making – Commission prevented creation of intergovernmental 4th pillar, but acceptance was due to French strategy of a trade-off between a (semi)-supranational EMU in exchange for intergovernmental 2nd/3rd pillars
	– economic convergence criteria – French/German/Belgian compromise of 'criteria plus trend'
	– stage 2 institution and independence of ECB – despite Franco-Italian pressure, issues were firmly controlled by Germany
	– temporary opt-outs – Commission brokered outcome
	• citizenship – EP and Spanish advocacy influenced outcome
	• Commission leadership on other issues such as trans-European networks
	→

of the negotiations by ensuring that governments could first find and then reach a mutually acceptable outcome in Maastricht (Moravcsik, 1999a). When Presidencies such as the Dutch did not rely upon the Secretariat, there was little the Secretariat could do to provide leadership. Yet the lessons of 'Black Monday' are that a Presidency ignores the advice of the Secretariat at its own peril.

Secretariat leadership also affected the distributive dimension of

$\rightarrow$

Issue area	Outcome
Modification of existing policies	• environmental policies – Danish/German/Commission leadership • economic and social cohesion – Commission brokered outcome • Social Protocol – Belgian/Commission collusion shaped agenda – the Commission with Secretariat assistance brokers compromise with UK in endgame
Institutional changes	• pillar structure – French backed idea that was fleshed out by Council Secretariat • introduction of 'laws' – Commission kept issue on agenda, but unable to push governments to accept it • introduction of co-decision – German-led process, backed by EP • EP right of initiative – Commission prevented the introduction of EP right despite German and Italian pressure to do so • reform of the EP to approve Commission – EP leadership ensured the creation of non-binding vote of approval • ECJ fines – UK leadership

Second pillar – Common Foreign and Security Policy

     • Franco-German leadership, although 'Atlanticist' countries acted as brake on full incorporation of WEU into EU and UK/ Denmark acted as brake in extension of QMV

Third pillar – Justice and Home Affairs

     • German leadership with France advocating intergovernmental solutions, and UK as brake

the negotiations, particularly as regards ensuring a more intergovernmental outcome that strengthened the Council, and thereby also the Council Secretariat. This was evident in both the issue of the structure of the treaty and the co-decision procedures. Directional leadership by the Council Secretariat was though contingent upon acceptance by the Presidency and the distribution and intensity of governmental preferences.

Chapter 5

Negotiating the Treaty of Amsterdam

Introduction – Maastricht left-overs

Upset with the lack of progress towards a more federal Community in the PU IGC, Germany supported by several other like-minded member states put forward the idea that another IGC should be held in 1996 to review the functioning of the intergovernmental pillars of the EU (Mazzucelli, 1997, p. 163). This resulted in the inclusion of a sub-paragraph in Article N of the Treaty on European Union (now, after amendment, Article 48 EU), which stated that an IGC should be convened in 1996 to examine possible reforms of CFSP, JHA, the scope of co-decision and an extension of the scope of EC competences.

Two other events in the mid-1990s also significantly influenced the agenda of the upcoming IGC. First was the rapid development of the EU's relations with the Central and Eastern European countries, with the prospect of an Eastern enlargement of the EU becoming an evermore real prospect as the 1990s progressed (see Chapter 8). It was clear that it would be necessary to reform the EU's institutions if the EU was to function effectively and democratically with perhaps 27 or more member states. Could a Commission college with 40 members function? What about a European Parliament with up to 1,000 members? And what of voting weights in the Council? If the then current voting weights were merely extrapolated to the acceding member states, this could lead to a 'tyranny of the smalls'.

Secondly, the Danish 'no' in June 1992, and the narrow French 'yes' shocked the EU establishment, and put demands for a more democratic union closer to its citizens onto the centre of the agenda for the upcoming IGC.

This chapter analyses the role and impact of EU institutions in the 1996–7 IGC that discussed these sensitive questions of institutional balance, democracy and efficiency. While the 1985 IGC was the high-water mark of Commission influence, the Treaty of Amsterdam is the Secretariat's magnum opus. The chapter first looks at what the

EU institutions wanted in the IGC and the relevant leadership resources they possessed in the negotiations. The chapter then describes the negotiating situation, where a combination of a bewilderingly complex negotiation and a privileged institutional position created a situation where the Secretariat had many opportunities to provide leadership – opportunities that it exploited skillfully through the provision of low-profile and behind-the-scenes agenda-shaping and brokerage.

The course of the negotiation of the Treaty of Amsterdam

The agenda-setting phase – discussing the Maastricht left-overs and preparing for EU enlargement

The agenda-setting phase started formally with the European Council meeting in Corfu in June 1994, which set up a Reflection Group to prepare the IGC agenda. The mandate of the Reflection Group was to elaborate ideas and options on possible revisions of the provisions that were to be examined according to the Maastricht Treaty, and other issues relating to democracy and enlargement (European Council 1994).

Shortly after the Corfu Summit, an important paper was put forward by the CDU/CSU Parliamentary Group in Germany (the so-called Lammers/Schäuble paper), that proposed a strengthened 'hard core' within the EU, and more effective foreign and security policies (CDU/CSU, 1994). The idea of a 'hard core' coming from within Kohl's own party provoked strong reactions and fears among Germany's neighbours (Beuter, 2002). But the paper also provoked debate on new institutional arrangements in an enlarged EU, a discussion which eventually paved the way for the new flexibility provisions contained in the Treaty of Amsterdam.

The Reflection Group was convened in Taormina in June 1995, and over six months prepared a report that was presented to the December Madrid Summit. The Group, chaired by the representative of the Spanish Presidency Carlos Westendorp, was composed of representatives of each member state, along with a representative of the Commission, and two observers from the European Parliament. The Council Secretariat acted as the secretary and adviser to the group.

The final report was very vague and merely canvassed the different views among governments (Reflection Group, 1995). There was no attempt to create a unanimous report like the Delors report that prepared the EMU IGCs agenda. The primary problem was simply that many member states, so shortly after the Maastricht ratification problems and with enlargement still a far-off possibility, were simply not very interested in a new IGC (Dehousse, 1999, pp. 3–4). The report was approved by the European Council Summit in Madrid in December 1995. The Madrid Summit Conclusions also set the practical arrangements for the IGC, including the decision that the IGC would finish in June 1997 under the Dutch Presidency, in an effort to postpone the conclusion of the IGC until *after* the expected Labour victory in the upcoming British elections, which were to be held at the latest in May 1997.

The course of the negotiations – the crooked path from Turin to Amsterdam

The IGC started during the Italian Presidency in the first half of 1996. Unfortunately for both the Italian Presidency and the IGC itself, Italy plunged into political chaos two months before the planned start of the IGC. Prime Minister Lamberto Dini resigned on 12 January 1996, and attempts to create a new government without a parliamentary vote failed, leading to a planned general election to be held on 21 April. A caretaker government was set up under Dini until a new government could be formed after the elections. However, this government lacked the political clout to be able to effectively lead the IGC negotiations – creating a political vacuum that, as will be seen below, the Council Secretariat was able to exploit quite effectively.

A series of papers and proposals were put forward by member states in the months prior to the start of IGC (see the chapters in Laursen, 2002). The Commission also put forward its official opinion on the convening of the IGCs in February 1996 (European Commission, 1996).

The IGC was officially launched in Turin on 29 March 1996. Based upon the Reflection Group report, the three main themes were to be an attempt to bring the EU closer to citizens, institutional reform, and creating more effective external policies. Meetings were held on all three topics in the first months of the IGC. Especially important in this phase was the joint Finnish/Swedish proposal on a security and defense dimension that suggested the EU should undertake the so-called 'Petersberg' tasks – for example, peace-keeping and peace-making (CONF 3832/96). However, it was already clear that any real negotiating breakthrough would have to wait until after the UK election scheduled to be held at latest in May 1997 (Dehousse, 1999, p. 13) – if the breakthrough ever came at all.

The negotiating climate deteriorated further due to the BSE crisis. On 21 May 1996, the UK, in protest of the beef boycott imposed by the EU's Veterinary Committee, announced an 'empty chairs' policy in the Council. While the British boycott of Council sessions did not directly affect the IGC meetings, it 'hung like a dark cloud over meetings', preventing real progress in the IGC (Svensson, 2000, p. 87). Even after the crisis was defused in June 1996 at the Florence Summit, the UK continued its combative stance towards the IGC, putting forward a 'Court-bashing' proposal to the IGC in July 1996 (Beach, 2001, pp. 103–4; CONF 3883/96), and Prime Minister Major even threatened to veto the outcome of the IGC in November 1996 unless a satisfactory solution was found to the British problems relating to the Working Time Directive (Beach, 2001, p. 161).

An informal ministerial conclave was held in Rome on 17 June to prepare the Florence European Council. There was progress on many issues, but little on the central issues of institutional and external action reform (Svensson, 2000, p. 91).

The Florence European Council concluded a deal with the UK that settled the BSE crisis. A progress report on the IGC was submitted, but member states were not willing to commit on detail – in effect the conclusions were those of the Reflection Group report, merely noting areas of consensus and disagreement (European Policy Centre, Issue 9, July/August 1996, p. 2). The conclusions did though give the incoming Irish Presidency a mandate to prepare a draft treaty on the three main topics on the IGC agenda (European Council, 1996a).

The Irish Presidency worked hard with the aim of presenting a draft treaty to the Dublin European Council to be held in December. The negotiating strategy by the Irish was a Secretariat-inspired strategy of 'successive approximations', attempting to gradually translate general positions into precise legal treaty text (McDonagh, 1998, pp. 75–7; Svensson, 2000, p. 110). The Irish started by presenting general introductory notes as bases for discussions in IGC meetings. In the light of member state responses they revisited the text and then put forward 'Suggested Approaches' (McDonagh, 1998, pp. 76–7).

One of the more significant events in the fall of 1996 was German Chancellor Kohl raising the possibility of a Maastricht III IGC in the event that the 1996–7 IGC did not reach an agreement on the institutional dossiers (*Agence Europe*, 04.10.96, p. 3). This sparked a strong reaction from the other member states, which accused Germany of not wishing to achieve anything substantial in the present IGC (*Agence Europe*, 04.10.96, p. 3; *Financial Times*, 18.09.96).

An informal European Council Summit was held on 5 October in Dublin in order to inject political impetus into the negotiations by allowing heads of state and government to discuss the issues. Following the meeting, the Irish started preparing the actual Outline Draft Treaty. In the first week of November a cluster of officials from the Irish Presidency, the Secretariat and Commission cloistered themselves in a castle in Ireland in order to hammer out an approach for the Irish Draft Treaty (McDonagh, 1998, pp. 104–5). Bilateral confessionals between the Irish Presidency and national delegations, assisted by the Secretariat, were then held in the last week of November in an attempt to discern potential zones of agreement (McDonagh, 1998, p. 109).

The Irish Draft Treaty was presented formally to a conclave of Foreign Ministers on 6 December (CONF 2500/96) and although it was greeted positively, many areas of contention were simply side-stepped – for example no draft article on flexibility was in the draft. The Draft Treaty was then presented to the Dublin European Council on 13–14 December. But the discussions of the IGC in the Summit would be overshadowed by a heated debate on the EMU Stability Pact between the French and Germans (Svensson, 2000, p. 126).

The Irish Draft was divided into five parts. The first section dealt with an Area of Freedom, Security and Justice. There were still substantial disagreement on the manner and scope of communitarization of parts of the third pillar (JHA) (McDonagh, 1998, pp. 171–2; Svensson, 2000, p. 120), and the question of the integration of Schengen into the EU was side-stepped completely (Svensson, 2000, p. 120). The Schengen Agreement had been adopted in 1985 by the Benelux countries, France and Germany in an effort to gradually abolish frontier controls, supplemented by a Convention in 1990 to implement the agreement. The Schengen Agreement was an intergovernmental agreement outside of the EC. The second section dealt with the Union and the Citizen. Issues in this section were for example employment and the environment. In the former, the Irish proposed a new treaty chapter that was supported by all delegations except France, Germany and the UK. The third section was entitled an Effective and Coherent Foreign Policy. While consensus was emerging on issues such as the external representation by a troika of past, present and future Presidencies and on issues such as the inclusion of the Petersberg tasks in CFSP, the EU–WEU question was very controversial, and would only be solved at the Amsterdam Summit (McDonagh, 1998, pp. 117–20). Little progress was made in the fourth section on the Union's Institutions, and it was also clear that this was also an issue that would only be solved in Amsterdam

(Stubb, 2002, p. 81; Svensson, 2000, p. 121). Finally, the negotiation of the fifth section on Enhanced Cooperation (flexibility) had not really started, and no draft articles were put forward by the Irish.

The incoming Dutch Presidency primarily focused on the issues that had been by-passed in the Irish Draft Treaty, particularly EU–WEU relations, flexibility, institutional questions and third pillar matters such as the incorporation of Schengen into the EU – something that was a pet project of the Dutch Presidency. While substantial progress was made in the issues of reform of the third pillar and flexibility in the spring of 1997, and the Dutch submitted an addendum to the Irish Draft Treaty to a ministerial meeting in Rome on 25 May (CONF 2500/add1/97), the real negotiations got under way after the Labour Party victory in the UK general elections held on 1 May 1997. The new Blair government indicated that the UK would support moves towards more QMV and co-decision, a reform of the EU institutions, and the incorporation of the Social Charter into the treaty (McDonagh, 1998, p. 184).

An informal European Council Summit was held in Noordwijk, Netherlands on 23 May to discuss an informal Dutch draft treaty entitled 'Compilation of texts under discussion' (SN 2555/97). During the meeting, the issue of institutional reform lost steam (Dehousse, 1999, p. 14) as the sharp cleavage between large and small states showed that it would be difficult to reach agreement without a major push coupled with a willingness to compromise. Large states such as France wanted a re-weighting of Council votes *prior* to an extension of QMV. Smaller states such as Belgium warned about linking re-weighting with an extension of QMV, as re-weighting risked creating 'winners' and 'losers' in Amsterdam. Others such as Denmark and Sweden were adamant about not giving up 'their' Commissioner. As the demand for a solution on these issues was low in Amsterdam, the final outcome would be to (again) push the painful decisions into the future (see Chapters 6 and 7).

The final stage of the IGC was partially upset by the surprising results (at least for French President Chirac) of the French general election held on 25 May. Chirac had called for parliamentary elections in April, as he was certain that he would win a strong majority, yet the elections were won by the Socialist leader Lionel Jospin, who became Prime Minister on 1 June – starting a new period of *cohabitation*. The change in French governmental representatives upset the preparations for the Amsterdam Summit, and in particular the traditional Franco-German collaboration that had proved influential in prior IGCs (Deloche-Gaudez, 2002, pp. 149–50).

The Amsterdam European Council Summit was held on 16–18

June. After numerous non-IGC topics were dealt with at the Summit, focus turned to the Dutch draft treaty (CONF 4000/97). As the Summit started, there was still substantial disagreement on the text of the revised third pillar, external policy questions relating to the common trade policy and EU–WEU relations, and the final balance of the flexibility provisions. Agreement was reached during the first day of the Summit on incorporating the Schengen *acquis* into a reformed intergovernmental third pillar (Svensson, 2000, p. 161). Yet attempts to find a compromise on the institutional questions failed, with the dinner on the first night of the summit breaking up without any positive results (ibid., p. 162).

On the second day of the Summit, the Dutch Presidency put forward a working document that attempted to accommodate the first day's discussions (CONF 4000/97/Add.1). During the afternoon a compromise was reached on EU–WEU relations, agreeing to closer relations with the possibility of full inclusion, while also not prejudicing NATO relations (McDonagh, 1998, p. 192). A deal was also brokered on the common trade policy (see below for more).

The final issues of institutional reform and flexibility were first settled late in the night of 17 June. While there was progress on an extension of QMV and co-decision, despite Kohl pulling back his support for a significant extension of QMV, an agreement on the re-weighting of Council votes and the number of Commissioners slipped out of the hands of the heads of state and government (McDonagh, 1998, p. 193).

There are contrasting accounts on the reasons for this bargaining failure. First, Spain was unwilling to compromise, as it did not feel they were receiving sufficient compensation for giving up its second Commissioner, which it had gained during its accession negotiations in return for being placed in a tier lower than the big four on Council voting weights (Lloréns, 2002). Second was the somewhat surprising (at least to outsiders) blockage of a more far-reaching extension of QMV by German Chancellor Kohl, who was under domestic pressure from the German *Länder* to block QMV being extended to policy areas that were under their remit (Beuter, 2002; Nugent, 1999, pp. 79–80). Thirdly, the pressure for solving the questions relating to enlargement was generally perceived to be relatively low in mid-1997, given that enlargement negotiations with the candidate countries had yet to be opened.

Some participants believed that if the issues had been given several more hours, then a deal could have been reached. Others noted that both France and Spain were very aggressive and undiplomatic, and created the impression that they were launching an attack on the smalls. This soured the negotiating climate, and made compromise impossible. A final explanation was that the Dutch Presidency had simply placed the issue too far down on the agenda, and when the Summit finally reached the last points, it was simply too late and the meeting turned into chaos.

A deal was however reached on flexibility in the early hours of the 18th (Stubb, 2002, pp. 99–101). Flexibility was dropped from the second pillar (CFSP) in favour of a constructive abstention clause. The trigger for flexibility in the other pillars was to be QMV, though with the right of a national veto in the case of strong national interests. Finally, the Commission was given the final say in first pillar flexibility.

What did the EU institutions want in the 1996–7 IGC?

The Commission – advocating a single Community

The Commission entered the IGC with publicized preferences, and in this respect resembled a national delegation. The Commission, based upon its perception of its role as the guardian of the treaties and the common European interest, was partial to the strengthening of EU-level competences, and particularly the prerogatives of supranational institutions like the Commission, European Parliament, and European Court of Justice, although the Commission did not argue for a strong increase in the *scope* of EC competences (European Commission, 1996) (see Table 5.2).

The Commission's Opinion prior to the start of the IGC prioritized among the issues put forward in its submissions to the Reflection Group (Gray, 2002). The overall priority of the Commission was to prepare the EU for enlargement through the extension of QMV, while communitarizing as much as possible of the intergovernmental pillars, that is, transferring policies from intergovernmental to supranational decision-taking. One further priority was to create a stronger role for the Commission in the common trade policy.

During the IGC, the Commission attempted to push the outcome towards the highest possible level of European integration, sometimes admonishing national delegates for their lack of ambition. The Commission also saw it as its mission to protect the Community from what it saw as intergovernmental encroachments, such as the '*1 bis*' solution to JHA proposed by France, and protecting its own institutional prerogatives, such as its monopoly on the right of initiative in the first pillar.

TABLE 5.1   *The outcome of the 1996–7 IGC – The Treaty of Amsterdam*

Issue area	Outcome
Re-weighting of Council voting weights	• Protocol on the Institutions stating that would be reviewed in new IGC
Size and reform of the Commission	• Protocol on the Institutions stating that would be reviewed in new IGC
Co-decision	• reform of the co-decision procedure, strengthening the role of the European Parliament • extension of co-decision to most legislative measures in the first pillar, with the notable exceptions being agriculture, tax harmonization, and trade policy
Reforms of other institutions	• no fundamental reform of the ECJ as suggested by both the UK and France
Extension of QMV	• limited increase in QMV in certain policies, including social and employment policies, public health, equal opportunities, research framework programs, and customs cooperation
Flexibility	• introduced strict flexibility provision in the first pillar, but excluded areas of exclusive EC competence, and had strict conditions for its use • no specific flexibility provisions introduced into second pillar (CFSP) – only constructive abstention • flexibility provisions introduced in third pillar (JHA) that are similar to the first pillar flexibility provisions
CFSP	• QMV in joint actions and common positions with unanimity for other decisions

$\rightarrow$

The European Parliament – a more pragmatic go at building a more federal Europe

The EP's positions prior to and during the 1996–7 IGC marked a dramatic departure from the past. While the EP had advocated a federal Union in both the 1985 and 1990–1 IGCs, the EP tabled more

$\rightarrow$

Issue area	Outcome
CFSP (*continued*)	• Commission's role increased in CFSP • incorporation of Petersberg tasks (peace-keeping and peace-making activities) • closer institutional cooperation between EU and WEU, with a view towards a possible incorporation of the WEU into the EU should the European Council so decide • creation of CFSP 'High Representative' by strengthening the Secretary-General of the Council Secretariat
JHA	• communitarized over a 5-year period visas, asylum, immigration and other policies related to the free movement of persons. Some restrictions on the role of the Commission and the ECJ in the new policy areas • all policies except visas decided by consultation with unanimity. After 5 years, Council decisions will be taken with co-decision • introduced measures into remaining third pillar to combat organized crime, terrorism, drug addiction and drug trafficking • Schengen *acquis* incorporated into third pillar • ECJ given limited jurisdiction within remaining third pillar • measures introduced to promote a balance of efforts in receiving refugees

Source: Treaty of Amsterdam, *Official Journal of the European Communities*, No. C 340, 10.11.97.

realistic demands in 1996–7 (Maurer, 2002, p. 420). Based upon the EP's opinion on the IGC adopted by the plenary in March 1996 (European Parliament, 1996z), the EP's main priorities were:

• the increased effectiveness of the Union through the extension of QMV, including in CFSP;

TABLE 5.2 *The preferences of the Commission in relation to the key issues in the 1996–7 IGC*

Issue area	Commission preferences
Reforms of the first pillar	• incorporate the Social Protocol into the Community • introduce employment policies • increased openness • 'clarify' the operation of the common trade policy • attempt to simplify and codify the treaties, creating a two-tiered treaty split into constitutional and legislative parts
Re-weighting of Council voting weights	• introduce form of double majority
Size and reform of the Commission	• reduce number to one per member state
Decision-making	• reduce procedures to three: decisions adopted on EP opinion, assent, and co-decision • extend and simplify co-decision. It should apply to all acts of a legislative nature • extend the use of the assent procedure, especially to decisions on 'constitutional' matters such as IGC's
Reforms of other institutions	• increase the effectiveness of the enforcement of EU law, giving the ECJ a stronger role

$\rightarrow$

- a limited increase in Community competences, mainly focusing on social policy, the creation of an employment chapter, and the partial communitarization of JHA; and
- an increase in the powers of the EP, including the extension of co-decision, EP budgetary powers, an equal footing of the EP in co-decision, and granting the EP a legally binding vote of confidence on the investiture of the Commission.

The EP was also concerned about the introduction of flexible integration and wanted to protect the Community through the use of strict safeguards.

→	
Issue area	*Commission preferences*
Reforms of other institutions (*continued*)	• strengthen the fight against fraud
	• introduce cap on EP of 700 members
Extension of QMV	• make QMV the general rule
Flexibility	• introduce flexibility with strict guidelines
CFSP	• create a single external relations chapter
	• establish a European identity in security and defense matters, including the Petersberg (peace-keeping and peace-making) tasks
	• incorporate WEU into EU
	• QMV should be norm for decision-making
	• other improvements, including a 'joint analysis unit' composed of Commission and national experts
JHA	• communitarize JHA, especially relating to the free movement of persons, including asylum and immigration. Preserve the intergovernmental nature of judicial cooperation in the criminal field and police cooperation
	• introduce into the new provisions QMV voting, while also giving the Commission the power of initiative, and extend the jurisdiction of the ECJ
	• incorporate Schengen into the treaty

The Council Secretariat – towards a more intergovernmental union

As in previous IGCs, while the Council Secretariat formally only had a secretarial function, there were many indications that it had its own pro-integration agenda that did not merely reflect member state preferences. Several key officials in the Secretariat published articles prior to the IGC (most under pseudonyms such as Justus Lipsius, authored by Jean-Claude Piris), making it much easier to illustrate the preferences of the Secretariat in relation to the issues on the IGC agenda (see Ersbøll, 1994; Charlemagne, 1994; Lipsius, 1995). However, in comparison to larger institutions like the Commission, individual personalities are very important in the Secretariat, and different officials within the Secretariat often have strongly diverging views on the issues. Therefore we must be careful in aggregating the views of select officials to the Secretariat as a whole.

With these caveats in mind, the Secretariat had strong institutional interests in increasing the strength and scope of policy areas dealt with at the European level, but only if the role of the Council was strengthened in the process. Institutional issues were especially important to the Secretariat as they had intimate knowledge of what works and what does not work in the EU through their daily work in the Council (Interview EC-7). They were quite pragmatic in their views in contrast to the Commission or EP, believing that an incremental first step was often a better way of achieving a final goal than a single 'big bang' decision that might not be accepted by the member states.

Looking at several of the issues on the agenda of the IGC, while the Secretariat was in favour of flexibility, they were also interested in strong safeguards in order to protect the *acquis communautaire* (Lipsius, 1995). The Secretariat was interested in more QMV, with Piris arguing for the 'quasi-elimination' of unanimity (Lipsius, 1995, pp. 258–9). Ersbøll had advocated prior to his replacement in 1994 for extending the use of QMV in CFSP, but also pragmatically stated that if CFSP is 'communitarized', it would 'result in a complete blocking of the much-needed effort to build the Common Foreign and Security Policy foreseen by the Treaty' (Ersbøll, 1994, p. 416). Piris argued in favour of a much simplified two-tiered treaty, with a short treaty that would merge the EU and the EC into one legal entity, and would only include the most fundamental provisions, whereas all of the other provisions of the treaties would be contained in protocols.

Changes in the leadership resources of EU institutions since 1991

The material resources of EU institutions

Both the Commission and the EP possessed certain material leadership resources that potentially could be translated into bargaining leverage in the negotiations. But while the Commission could play the budgetary card in the 1990–91 IGCs, there was little to indicate that this could be used again. Of primary interest therefore were the attempts by the EP to link its power of assent in the Eastern enlargement negotiations with outcomes of the 1996–7 IGC, together with the powers the EP possessed in daily Community policy-making.

First, the EP attempted to link its assent in the enlargement negotiations with the IGC outcome (Maurer, 2002, p. 420) but as governments simply did not see this threat as credible, it was not a relevant leadership resource that could be drawn upon.

Secondly, the EP had updated its rules of procedure after the TEU to try to create a de facto equal footing for itself in the co-decision procedure (Hix, 2002, p. 273). In the TEU provision, if the two institutions did not find a joint text in the Conciliation Committee, the Council could confirm its position, leading to the adoption of the act despite potential EP opposition. The EP's revised rules of procedure dictated that in a situation where the Council attempted to reaffirm its position, the EP would both: invite the President of the Council to 'justify the decision before the Parliament in plenary'; and call on the EP plenary to reject the Council text (in Hix, 2002, p. 273). On the first occasion where the Council attempted to re-affirm its own position, the EP acted *as if* it had a veto by rejecting in plenary the Council's position, and thereby created a credible de facto EP veto, as it was politically difficult for the Council to then merely trump the EP's vote irrespective of the fact that the EP veto had no legal effect. The creation of this de facto veto then made it easier for governments to accept a *de jure* entrenchment of an equal footing for the EP in the IGC (ibid., pp. 274–5).

The informational advantages of EU institutions

The informational advantages of the EU institutions were primarily the result of their roles in the daily EU policy-making process, and prior participation in IGCs. As discussed in Chapters 3 and 4, member states are often dependent upon the Commission for substantive information on the actual working of provisions of the EU Treaties – information which is naturally vital when revising the EU Treaties in an IGC. If we look at the analytical resources possessed by the Commission, the Commission staff had grown by 20 per cent since 1990, although a large portion of this increase was due to the 1995 enlargement of the EU (European Communities, 2000, p. 47). In comparison to the 1985 and 1990–1 IGCs, Delors had, prior to his departure in 1995, set up an IGC Task Force composed of ten senior officials to deal specifically with the 1996–7 IGC (Gray, 2002). Many of the officials had taken part in IGCs before, including the head of the IGC Task Force, Michel Petite. The Commission representative in the IGC, Commissioner Oreja, was, however, a first-timer and was generally seen as weak in the negotiations (Interviews NAT-5; NAT-9).

The EP was able to draw upon a growing experience in the issues under debate, especially as regards the powers of the EP. Since the early 1980s, the EP's Institutional Affairs Committee had debated and followed IGC-related issues. In the 1996–7 IGC, David Martin, who had been the rapporteur for the PU IGC proposals, was appointed co-rapporteur by the Constitutional Affairs Committee for the preparation of the EP's proposals for the IGC (Corbett, Jacobs and Shackleton, 2003, pp. 299–300).

The appointment of Elisabeth Guigou and Elmar Brok as the two official EP representatives that would follow the IGC was a good choice, in that they represented the two largest parties in the EP, and Guigou's political talent supplemented Brok's knowledge of the details well (Interview EC-2). Finally, an EP Task Force on the IGC was also set up that produced briefings on the state of play and other issue briefs during the IGC (Maurer, 2002, p. 409). The total staff of the EP Secretariat had increased by 490 to 3,493 from 1990 to 1995, but a major portion of this increase was due to the addition of two extra working languages in 1995 (European Commission, 1991, p. 388; 1996, p. 456). The actual staff assisting EP Committees and the EP representatives was very small in comparison to those of both the Commission and Council Secretariat, and national governments (Christiansen, 2002, p. 43; Jacobs, Corbett and Shackleton, 1995, p. 119).

Chapters 3 and 4 discussed in detail the lesser-known role of the Council Secretariat in the EU policy-making process. The size of the Council Secretariat had increased since 1990 by 19 per cent, with 246 A grade officials in the Secretariat in 1995 (General Secretariat of the Council, 2002). Both the Irish and Dutch, as small state Presidencies, were dependent upon the assistance of the Secretariat both in terms of its substantive expertise and its knowledge of how to broker EU compromises, given that they did not possess the diplomatic resources of countries such as France or Germany. Furthermore, when we look at prior participation in IGCs, while national representatives and civil servants rarely have attended more than one or two IGCs, the representation of both the Commission and especially the Council Secretariat have been remarkably constant since the 1985 IGC. This gave both institutions an institutional 'memory' and personal experience with IGC negotiations that no other actor in the IGC had.

In European Council Summits during the IGC, the Council Secretariat and Commission, together with the relevant Presidency in charge, had comparative informational advantages vis-à-vis governments (Interviews NAT-6, EC-6, EC-7; McDonagh, 1998, p. 211; Svensson, 2000, p. 160). Governments were represented only by their head of state or government together with one other minister, both of whom were naturally not familiar with the technical details of the proposals on the table before them. Experts from national delegations were only able to participate indirectly through the so-called 'Antici' room, where the Secretariat briefed delegations through a complicated (and archaic) system on what was happening within the European Council itself (McDonagh, 1998p. 190; Svensson, 2000, p. 160), after which delegations were able to send experts in briefly to assist their politicians. However, given the time delays involved, the system prevented national experts from steering politicians.

In contrast, the Secretariat and Commission officials sitting at the table took part in the entire IGC negotiation process, including the more technical negotiations, and therefore had detailed knowledge of the dossiers. This informational asymmetry was further strengthened by the working methods used by both the Irish and Dutch Presidencies. Both Presidencies refrained from introducing draft legal texts until the last moment prior to final European Council Summits in order to prevent a proposal from being, 'examined too closely by the [national] experts before being entrusted to the Heads of State and Government' (Petite, 1998, pp. 3–4), thereby enabling both the Presidencies and the Secretariat, and sometimes the Commission, to utilize the asymmetry of technical knowledge to their advantage in the Summit negotiations.

The reputation of EU institutions

The basic problem for the Commission in the IGC was that it was perceived by many delegations as being excessively partial to its pro-integrative agenda, based upon the Commission's reputation from the PU IGC (feedback loop) and the manner in which Delors had attempted to push integration in the late 1980s and early 1990s (Dinan, 1997; Gray, 2002; Peterson, 1999). President Santer also had a low level of acceptance, as he was nobody's first choice as Commission President (Peterson, 1999, p. 53). The lack of acceptability of Commission leadership forced the Commission to attempt to play the role of an unwanted guest *without* a vote, but *with* an extreme policy position.

The EP through its words and actions sought to signal that it would attempt to play a more constructive role in the 1996–7 IGC than in previous IGCs. In the Reflection Group proceedings, the two EP representatives, 'enjoyed a high degree of acceptance in the Reflection Group. On no occasion were they considered as foreign bodies' (Commission official in Maurer, 2002, pp. 420–1). And during the IGC, the 'Parliament's striking sensitivity to the concerns of all Member States, including smaller Member States, enhanced its credibility' (McDonagh, 1998, p. 59). Yet this credibility was not enough to win over the several governments who were still principally opposed to EP involvement in the IGC.

Looking at the Council Secretariat, crucial to its ability to intervene effectively in the negotiations was the fact that it was still widely accepted and trusted as a useful agenda-shaper and broker. While many national delegates were aware that the Secretariat had its own agenda, they accepted the Secretariat's role because of: the functional utility of having the Secretariat to broker deals and offer technical, administrative and legal advice during the IGC; and the trust relationship between the Secretariat and governments built up in daily contacts within the Council of Ministers (Interviews NAT-4, NAT-2, NAT-3, NAT-6). Importantly, most member states trusted that the Secretariat would not step over what they viewed to be an invisible 'red line' of excessive partiality in either the handling of the negotiation process or in pushing certain substantive outcomes.

But governments did sometimes perceive that the Secretariat's interventions were excessively partial (Dehousse, 1999, p. 6). As will be seen below, the Dutch Presidency did not trust the Secretariat's impartiality in the debate on the integration of Schengen into the EU. On the legal side, several governments believed that the Secretariat's Legal Services were excessively partial to their own pro-integrative interpretations of EU law. One indication can be found in a meeting of Permanent Representatives in October 1996, where Piris said that the ECJ had declared that the EU must act together in external trade negotiations. The UK afterwards questioned whether this was really what the ECJ had said, implying that they believed that Piris was misconstruing what the ECJ had said in a pro-integrative direction.

The opportunities for leadership created by the negotiating context

The role of EU institutions in the 1996–7 IGC

The Commission had a relatively weak position in the IGC. The Commission did not regain the privileged, behind-the-scenes institutional position of being part of the draft process that it had enjoyed in the 1985 IGC. However, the Commission was again allowed to attend all IGC meetings including the European Council Summits, and to submit proposals to the IGC (Dinan, 2000; Gray, 2002). Additionally, national delegations and Presidencies in the IGC often drew upon the substantive expertise of the Commission, for example by inviting opinions from the Commission on specific proposals, or by asking the Commission for advice during the drafting process.

The EP was granted two seats in the Reflection Group meetings in 1995 (McDonagh, 1998, p. 58). The EP then campaigned for a role in the IGC itself, arguing that as the IGC was being convened to prepare the Union for enlargement, and as the EP must approve of enlargement, the EP should therefore have a significant role in IGC (Lodge, 1998, p. 486). Further, the EP argued that as it was the only directly elected EU institution, it should take part in the IGC to lend the process democratic legitimacy (ibid.). Both France and the UK opposed it taking any part in the IGC. A compromise was reached that allowed the EP to be 'associated closely' with the IGC without being a formal party (McDonagh, 1998, pp. 57–9). The EP was allowed an exchange of views between the EP President and ministers at the beginning of each IGC ministerial session, and once a month the Presidency would hold a working meeting between IGC representatives and EP delegates, and would keep the EP informed of progress in the IGC (ibid.).

The Council Secretariat's role in the 1996–7 IGC was based upon a mandate given to it prior to the opening of the IGC by the European Council. Its basic function was, as in previous IGCs, to support the IGC itself and the Presidencies in charge of the negotiations. The role played by the Secretariat in the 1996–7 IGC was similar to the role it played in the PU IGC, and therefore it will not be reviewed here. One difference though was the privileged position that the Secretariat gained in the Friends of the Presidency Group that was created in January 1997 to discuss the simplification of the treaties (see CONF 4100/1/97).

The nature of the issues

Most issues in the IGC were relatively technical and complex (Stubb, 1998, p. 17). If we look at the agenda, major issues such as flexible cooperation, the competences of the Commission in international trade negotiations, and the communitarization of certain Justice and Home Affairs (JHA) policies were all highly complex institutional issues, making national delegations dependent upon expertise from both the Secretariat and Commission. While governments had undertaken extensive preparations prior to and during the IGC, creating a relatively 'information-rich' environment (Pollack, 1999; Moravcsik and Nicolaïdis, 1999), most governments lacked the resources to fully study the implications of different choices in all but a few prioritized areas, making them dependent upon the informational resources of other actors such as the Secretariat.

The number of issues and parties in the negotiations

In the 1996–7 IGC, fifteen governments were negotiating over two hundred salient issues. The sheer size of the agenda is illustrated by the 141 pages of the Irish Draft Treaty from December 1996 (see CONF 2500/96). If we look at the charts on the state of play published by the European Policy Centre or the European Parliament during the IGC, the complexity of the situation is clear (European Parliament, 1996a, 1996b; European Policy Centre, 1996–7). In this complex negotiating situation, leadership was necessary to help the parties find and agree upon an outcome.

A factor that made governments even more dependent upon leadership was that, in contrast to previous IGCs, most of the negotiation sessions in the 1996–7 IGC were simply *tour de tables*, with each delegate merely stating their position without any real debate or shifts in actor positions (Interview EC-6; Dehousse, 1999). This was most evident at the Foreign Minister level of the IGC, where ministers often had locked mandates that prevented any real negotiation (Dehousse, 1999, pp. 8–9; Gray, 2002). Therefore, leadership was even more necessary *between* IGC meetings by either the Presidency or EU institutions in order to find winning solutions in this complicated wilderness.

The distribution and intensity of governmental preferences

Figure 5.1 illustrates but a few of the many major cleavages in the IGC. The figure is simplified, as there were many other important cleavages that are not depicted such as flexibility, and not all of the governments are depicted. However, as can be clearly seen even in the highly simplified figure, there was no obvious zone of possible agreements, with few cross-cutting cleavages. This complexity made governments very dependent upon bargaining skills of the Presidencies and the Council Secretariat in order to find zones of agreement on more than 200 issues in the IGC.

Governments had strong preferences on many of the issues, especially regarding the institutional issues, where many smaller member states were very concerned about giving up 'their Commissioner'. The issues in the so-called 'institutional triangle' were very sensitive issues involving delicate questions of national power and prestige. The three sides of the triangle were: the re-weighting of votes in the Council; the number of Commissioners; and the extension of QMV. For example, the zero-sum issue of the

FIGURE 5.1 *Major cleavages in the 1996–7 IGC negotiations*

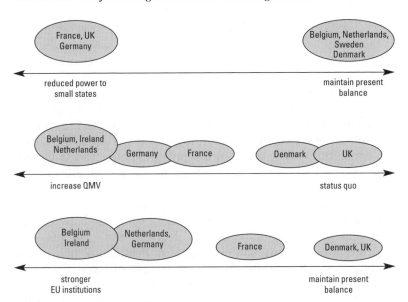

re-weighting votes in the Council of Ministers pitted member states directly against each other, where the gain of one country would result in a relative loss of voting power for another country. Other sensitive issues in the IGC were CFSP issues, especially security and defence.

Further, despite the IGC being called to prepare the EU for Eastern enlargement, a decision on the issues was not seen as pressing, as realistic estimates put the first accession at 2002/2003 at the earliest, enabling the EU to easily convene another IGC to tackle these sensitive issues immediately prior to enlargement (Dehousse, 1999, pp. 3–4, 23–4; Devuyst, 1998, p. 626).

Leadership by EU institutions in the 1996–7 IGC

The negotiating situation in the 1996–7 IGC was immensely complex, creating a strong demand for leadership. Were any of the EU institutions able to successfully provide leadership in the negotiations, helping the parties find and agree upon an outcome, while also gaining opportunities to skew outcomes closer to their own preferred outcome in the process?

Leadership by the European Commission

The Commission had close connections with several of the Presidencies during the IGC, and was involved with the drafting process both directly by being consulted by Presidencies, and indirectly by submitting proposals to the IGC that were incorporated into later Presidency draft texts.

The overall strategy of the Commission in the IGC was to play a lower-profile role in comparison to the 1990–1 IGCs. The strategy was to not put forward whole draft treaties, as governments felt this pre-empted its work. Instead, the Commission would table individual proposals and attempt to build support for them behind the scenes (Gray, 2002, p. 383).

Looking first at the importance of being directly involved through consultations with Presidencies, the close links between the Commission representative to the Reflection Group (Spanish Commissioner Oreja) and the Spanish Presidency helped the Commission influence the developing agenda of the IGC (Dinan, 1997, p. 209; Gray, 2002; Svensson, 2000, pp. 47–8), leading to a final Reflection Group report that in many respects echoed the Commission report on the functioning of the treaties from May 1995 (European Commission, 1995b; Reflection Group, 1995).

During the IGC itself, Presidencies often drew upon both the expertise of the Commission and legitimacy of being the 'guardian of the Community'. For instance the Irish Presidency invited the Commission to take part in the drafting process of the Irish Draft Treaty together with the Council Secretariat in Kilkea Castle in November 1996 (McDonagh, 1998, pp. 104–5). Additionally, the Council Secretariat routinely sent copies of the drafts that it produced to the Commission, allowing them to reply and suggest amendments (Interview EC-6).

There were differences during the IGC in how involved the Presidency allowed the Commission to be. This depended upon whether the agenda of the Commission reflected the agenda of the given Presidency. Most notably, the Dutch Presidency often drew upon the Commission in the drafting process, even running through whole draft treaties prior to their introduction to the conference (Gray, 2002). This was due to the overlapping of Dutch and Commission preferences in many issue areas, especially regarding Schengen and JHA.

Did this involvement allow the Commission to influence outcomes? One example of Commission success were the provisions for communitarizing a hard core of JHA policies that the Commission drew up for the Irish Presidency prior to a ministerial meeting in September 1996 (CONF 3912/96). These provisions then formed the basis for later Irish proposals (CONF 3924/96; CONF 2500/96), and significantly influenced the final treaty text (den Boer, 2002, p. 519). While the Commission's proposal could have been a case of anticipating the consensus of member states based upon the state of play in the IGC, given the technical expertise that the Commission had regarding the existing provisions for the free movement of persons, and its legitimacy of being the 'guardian of the treaties', it can be argued that the proposal from the 'guardian' of the treaties for the transferal of JHA policies to the supranational first pillar was a 'unique' solution that would not have been successful had it come from any other actor.

Turning to leadership through tabling proposals, there are several examples where a Commission proposal provided a focal point around which the negotiations converged. The Commission's proposal for a formula regarding the extension of co-decision (CONF 3882/96) was first proposed by the Irish Presidency as the focus for debates, and then was taken up in the draft texts produced by the Netherlands Presidency (CONF 3839/96). The provisions then strongly influenced the final treaty text, although the Commission was greatly assisted by having Germany as a strong backer of the formula (Beach, 2002; Gray, 2002). Moravcsik and Nicolaïdis contest this point, arguing that when we look at the policy areas that the Commission had selected in its proposal, they are negatively correlated with the articles included in the final treaty (1999, pp. 70–1). However, this misses the point, in that the Commission's formula provided the winning solution, which is not discounted by governments removing certain sensitive issue areas such as CAP and taxation from the list (Gray, 2002, p. 391).

Another Commission proposal that formed the basis for further discussions was regarding the size of the Commission post-enlargement. The Commission suggested postponing the issue until the number of member state exceeded twenty, which was then picked up by Germany in the final months of the negotiations and formed the final outcome.

Yet the overall picture for the Commission is a relative lack of success for its attempts at providing leadership, even in issues that were a major priority (Dehousse, 1999, p. 9). A good example was regarding the question of the extension of Commission competences in the common trade policy. While the Commission did succeed in putting the issue on the agenda, it was unable to push sceptical governments towards accepting a stronger solution than the one brokered by the Council Secretariat (see below). And in issues like CFSP, while it spoke at meetings, its interventions had no impact.

One problem was that the Commission did not speak with a single voice, and presented too many viewpoints during the IGC, as the Commission was represented by different officials at different levels in the IGC (Gray, 2002; Interviews NAT-2, NAT-6). In the European Council Summits, for example, while the President of the Commission, Jacques Santer, was a very experienced politician, he lacked the legitimacy and force of personality that enabled former Commission President Jacques Delors to (often) be such an effective operator within European Council Summits.

Leadership by the European Parliament

The EP played a more constructive role in the 1996–7 IGC than in previous IGCs (Interview EC-3). During the IGC, the EP was kept well informed of progress and the state of play through its participation in IGC meetings and formal and informal meetings with delegations. Participants note that on some issues it was important for governments to secure the approval of the EP's delegates to make further progress (ibid.). Guigou and Brok worked effectively as a team, and in meetings where they took part, one would start the meeting while the other would reserve his/her time until the end so they would get the last word in (Interview EC-2).

During the Spanish Presidency, the Council Secretariat used the EP's opinion on the IGC as a source of ideas, although the EP position did overlap closely with the Commission's (Interview EC-6). During the IGC itself, the EP tabled proposals on several priority issues instead of tabling whole draft treaties as in previous IGCs.

As seen above, one of the priorities of the EP was to strengthen the EU's employment policies. The EP tabled a proposal in July 1996 on employment (CONF 3891/96), and throughout the IGC the EP advocated the inclusion of a separate chapter or title devoted to employment policies. The EP's views echoed those of a large majority of governments – Sweden was especially very active while there were several governments who were opposed, notably Germany due to concerns about new expenditure (Tallberg, 2002b; McDonagh, 1998, pp. 84–5). Although the outcome was less ambitious than either the EP or Sweden had wanted, the continued advocacy by the EP during the IGC was influential in achieving the final result (Interview EC-2, EC-3).

Regarding the powers of the EP, one example of successful EP leadership was in the reform of the co-decision procedure to put the

EP on equal footing with the Council. As was described above, the EP had exploited its formal powers in the existing co-decision procedure, creating a *de facto* equal footing for itself in the procedure. During the IGC, the EP tabled a proposal to amend the co-decision procedure to give the EP *de jure* equal footing (CONF 3881/96). In the autumn of 1996, governments held strongly opposing views regarding whether they should accept the change (McDonagh, 1998, p. 155). The EP won over sceptical governments by arguing that the change had no real cost, as the EP already had *de facto* equal footing (Hix, 2002, p. 275; Interview EC-2; Stacey, 2003, pp. 941–3). The EP also succeeded in using similar tactics regarding the introduction of a binding vote on the appointment of the Commission, utilizing the material leadership resources from daily policy-making to influence outcomes in the IGC (Hix, 2002, p. 277; Stacey, 2003, pp. 944–6). But governments learned from this and introduced more precise wording in new treaty provisions regarding the EP so as to prevent the EP from exploiting the discretion in broadly formulated provisions in the future (Hix, 2002, pp. 275–6).

But overall, while the EP was more successful than in the past, it was still in a subsidiary position. And the EP did not succeed in its priority issues. The best example of the lack of EP success was with respect to its own budgetary powers, where the EP not surprisingly advocated the removal of the distinction between 'compulsory' and 'non-compulsory' expenditure. To simplify the budgetary procedure, the EP suggested that 'The easiest way to do this would be to provide for all categories of expenditure to follow the procedure that currently applies for "non-compulsory expenditure" ' (CONF 3810/97, p. 3). While the EP has strong powers as regards non-compulsory expenditure, the EP had little say in compulsory expenditure, which included large budgetary items like agriculture. Due to British and French opposition, these proposals were not adopted by the IGC, illustrating the limits of EP leadership in traditional IGCs.

Leadership by the Council Secretariat

As shown above, the Secretariat had a privileged institutional position in the negotiation of the 1996–7 IGC, giving it numerous opportunities to influence the agenda. In the work of the Reflection Group that was charged with preparing the negotiation agenda, the Secretariat wrote questionnaires that were used as the basis for discussions (e.g. SN 2488/1/95 Rev 1). The Secretariat inserted several of its priorities into the questionnaires, for example including legal personality and a hierarchy of norms (points 6 and 8). Flexible cooperation was downplayed as the Secretariat was concerned about the potential implications that flexibility could have upon the Community if introduced without sufficient safeguards. The contents of the report raised the suspicions of the Spanish Presidency, which believed that the Secretariat was excessively pushing its own agenda, and in consequence the Spanish Presidency drafted most of the later material for the RG without assistance from the Secretariat (Svensson, 2000, p. 56). After the Spanish took control, there is no evidence to indicate that the Secretariat was able to significantly shape the content of the final report.

The political vacuum left by the political crisis in Italy during its Presidency created an opening for the Secretariat to provide leadership, which it effectively filled. The Secretariat was given a carte blanche by the Italian Presidency, and was put in charge of preparing and presenting negotiation materials to the IGC. The Secretariat exploited this by inserting points that reflected its own agenda (Svensson, 2000, p. 83). The pro-Council slant was especially evident in the papers produced on the powers of the Commission and EP (Interview EC-5). One instance was in a proposal that the Secretariat produced on the powers of the EP prior to the start of the IGC in March 1996 (CONF 3812/96). In the proposal, the Secretariat proposed weakening the Commission by granting the EP the right of legislative initiative alongside the Commission, and extending co-decision (Gray, 2002, pp. 392–3). The Secretariat also wrote most of the conclusions for the June Florence European Council Summit towards the end of the Italian Presidency (ibid.).

The Irish Presidency in the second half of 1996 had a close relationship with the Council Secretariat, and, for example, most of the draft texts came from the Council Secretariat in the Justus Lipsius building, though guided and sometimes amended by the Presidency (McDonagh, 1998, pp. 44, 104–5; Gray, 2002). But all available evidence indicates that the Irish did not lose control of the process, although there is one notable exception, and the Irish were able to provide the leadership of the IGC that the Italian Presidency delegated to the Secretariat (Gray, 2002).

The only example during the Irish Presidency where it can be argued that the Secretariat succeeded in significantly shaping the agenda was in the presentation of a non-paper on flexibility tabled after the Dublin II Summit in December 1996 (SN/639/96 (C 31)). Breaking with tradition, the Secretariat submitted the non-paper on its own initiative, and it was not asked for by either the Presidency or any government, although both the Irish and Dutch Presidencies had agreed to its distribution (Interview EC-9; Stubb, 1998, pp. 217–18).

The Secretariat's sceptical attitude towards flexibility is clearly seen in the non-paper, which argues for strict conditions. Secretariat officials felt at the time that the debates in the IGC were too 'theoretical', and they wanted to both alert governments to the risks involved, and attempt to move the debate forward by proposing treaty texts upon which further negotiations could be conducted (Interviews EC-6, NAT-7). One insider goes so far as to say that the Secretariat was not only an 'advocate' of flexibility, but also became the 'judge' of the form of flexibility embodied in the final treaty (Stubb, 1998, p. 218).

While parts of the non-paper reflected the state of play in the IGC negotiations, the Secretariat also inserted many of its own ideas, and the non-paper formed a focal point for the subsequent debates on flexibility and shaped the outcome. Of the innovative ideas presented by the Council Secretariat, the following made their way into the final treaty of Amsterdam. First, the eight conditions for the use of flexibility were included almost word for word in the subsequent Dutch draft article in February 1997, and in the final Treaty of Amsterdam (Stubb, 1998, pp. 218–19). The state of play at the time was for the introduction of positive and/or negative lists of areas *instead* of conditions.

Secondly, the Secretariat argued that flexibility should *not* be used for CFSP, which also turned out to be the final outcome in the Treaty of Amsterdam. At the time, both France and Germany were arguing that flexibility should be used primarily in CFSP (see Stubb, 1998, pp. 199–200; joint Franco-German letter in Agence Europe, Europe Daily Bulletins, No. 6871, 11/12/96; and European Parliament, 1996b, p. 27)! The financial provisions contained in the Secretariat's non-paper were also adopted, with a few exceptions. The Secretariat also suggested only allowing MEPs from participating member states to vote. This was opposed by most governments, but it kept popping up in Presidency drafts due to insistence by the Secretariat (SN 639/96 (C 31), Art. F, TEU (Dispositions institutionnelles); see Stubb, 1998, pp. 218–19 footnote). It was not adopted in the final treaty.

The Dutch Presidency chose to draw more upon the Commission during its Presidency in both drafting texts and assessing the state of negotiations (Gray, 2002, p. 393). But the Secretariat still played an influential role in drafting texts for the Dutch Presidency, although relations were perhaps not as 'cordial' as they had been between the Secretariat and the Irish Presidency (Svensson, 2000, p. 139).

In complex and technical issues that were not high priorities of the Dutch Presidency (including flexibility and legal personality), the Secretariat had substantial room for manoeuvre when drafting texts, enabling it to skew the texts so they echoed its own institutional preferences. On legal personality, the Secretariat, and in particular Director-General of the Secretariat's Legal Service Jean-Claude Piris, strongly advocated the creation of an independent legal personality for the Union (Interviews NAT-9, NAT-10; Lipsius, 1995). The question of legal personality is a complex legal question in which Piris as a highly skilled international law expert had a comparative informational advantage in relation to national delegates. While many member states supported creating some form of legal personality for the Union, there were several prominent opponents, including France and the United Kingdom (European Parliament, 1996a, p. 27). Given the lack of interest of the Dutch Presidency, it is very likely that the issue would have disappeared from the agenda if it had not been for the constant advocacy of the Secretariat. Irish diplomat Bobby McDonagh even presented Piris with a T-shirt during the IGC with the caption 'The Legal Personality of the Union' (Interview EC-9). Further, Piris attempted to use informational tactics with sceptical governments like the Danish by providing briefs and interventions that repeated that legal personality did not involve any transfer of sovereignty. Although the Secretariat was able to keep the issue on the agenda, the final result was far from what Piris hoped for (see Church and Phinnemore, 2002, p. 118).

In dossiers where the Dutch Presidency had strong interests, it often did not draw upon the Secretariat for assistance – most evidently in the issue of incorporating Schengen into the Community. The Secretariat was opposed to this both owing to its concern about the legal implications of incorporating the entire Schengen *acquis* into the EU's *acquis,* and based upon institutional interests in not having the Schengen secretariat incorporated in the Council Secretariat. The Dutch believed that Secretariat hesitancy was evident in the provisions that it drafted on Schengen, and therefore chose to rely upon their own staff, assisted by officials from the Commission.

The dossier where the Secretariat arguably played the strongest leadership role in the IGC negotiations was in the negotiations on the simplification and consolidation of the treaties. The Secretariat had succeeded in putting the issue on the agenda during the Reflection Group in October 1995, where it tabled a non-paper on the need for simplification and consolidation (SN 513/95). The points raised in the Secretariat's paper were incorporated directly into the IGC mandate. The Legal Services then produced three more reports for Presidencies on the issues, where the key issues were a proposed merger of the treaties, the removing of obsolete articles, and a renumbering of the treaties.

In January 1997 the Dutch Presidency set up a Friends of the Presidency Group to negotiate the issues that had been put on the agenda by the Secretariat (McDonagh, 1998, p. 186). Most delegates were very dependent upon Secretariat expertise. Yet while most of the points on the agenda were very technical, some points had political implications, such as the merger of all of the treaties into one treaty. The Secretariat attempted to guide the negotiations towards a significant simplification, but only succeeded in removing some obsolete articles and renumbering the treaties, and the complete overhaul of the treaty that it advocated to make it easier to use and more accessible was not accepted (see Church and Phinnemore, 2002, pp. 46–8).

In the final stage of the IGC, the Secretariat was able to use brokerage tactics to find compromises on several highly politicized issues. In these issues, there was a strong demand for agreement but also strong divergences of opinion, creating a strong demand for the provision of leadership through brokerage to help the parties find an agreement.

The best example of this was the negotiation of the common trade policy (Article 113 of the EC Treaty (now, after amendment, Article 133 EC), where the debate was about whether Commission competences in external negotiations should be extended to all aspects of trade negotiations, including trade in services, investments and intellectual property. In the final weeks of the IGC, consensus was building on a German proposal that would grant the Commission across-the-board competence, but with a long list of exceptions (CONF 3912/97). On the last day of negotiations, the Commission dropped its support of the German proposal owing to the ever-growing list of exceptions, and it looked like the outcome would be no agreement (Gray, 2002, p. 391; Interview NAT-9). However, the Secretariat's Legal Service stepped in and brokered a compromise, exploiting its legal expertise and knowledge of the bottom line of all delegations to craft a deal that arguably no other actor could have achieved in the Summit, as national legal experts were not in the actual meeting room.

The revision did not grant the Commission exclusive competence *in practice*, but the new section five of the article did open up for the transferal of competences *in principle* through a unanimous Council vote (a so-called *passerelle*). This solution echoed the pragmatic preferences of the Secretariat, which has a long-term strategy that Europe is best built through small incremental steps that are acceptable to governments. This view was vindicated in the 2000 IGC, as the principled acceptance by the member states of Commission exclusive competence in Amsterdam influenced the debates in the 2000 IGC, and resulted in a significant extension of Commission competences within Article 133 EC (Galloway, 2001, pp. 106–11).

Concluding, by being intimately involved in the negotiation and drafting of treaty texts in the IGC at all levels, the Secretariat played a key leadership role, helping parties translate their relatively vague ideas into actual treaty text. Through low-profile agenda-shaping tactics, the Secretariat was able to use the power of the pen to gain influence in several salient issues, illustrating the 'influence of those who provide draft texts for debate – they run the show' (Stubb, 1998, p. 219). However, this guiding role was also dependent upon the acquiescence of the Presidency in charge, and when the Secretariat attempted to openly advocate its own positions, it was generally unsuccessful, as was seen in the question of Schengen. Further, despite strong advocacy, when governments were strongly opposed to an issue, there was little the Secretariat could do, as we saw above regarding the question of the complete overhaul of the treaties within the Friends of the Presidency to create a simplified single treaty.

Conclusion

The 1996–7 IGC was a 'high-water' mark for the Secretariat's influence, whereas the Commission and the EP were largely unsuccessful in their attempts to make the most of their weak institutional positions. The following will discuss briefly why the Secretariat was relatively successful, and why the EP and Commission failed.

The 1996–7 IGC was in many respects a 'most-likely' case for EU institutional leadership. The negotiations had very high bargaining costs and there were few cross-cutting cleavages to simplify the situation. This created a strong demand for leadership to first find possible agreements, and then help the parties agree upon a final outcome. Of the three institutions, the Secretariat was in the best position to provide leadership.

While the EP acquitted itself better than in previous IGCs and did play a constructive role in the negotiations, the EP with few exceptions was unable to influence outcomes (see Table 5.3). The basic problem for the EP was that governments did not see the EP as a legitimate party in an *intergovernmental* conference. Despite emerging from the IGC as the major institutional winner, the increase in EP powers was more due to German leadership. Basically, Germany saw an increase in EP powers as a politically correct way to increase German power in the EU vis-à-vis other governments. Germany argued that it favoured an increase in democracy in the EU through

TABLE 5.3 *Conclusions – leadership in the 1996–7 IGC*

Issue area	Outcome
Institutional 'triangle'	• lack of strong leadership in issues leads to acceptance of Commission compromise to postpone reform • extension of QMV – Germany acts as brake in IGC endgame
Reform of co-decision	• reform of the co-decision procedure – EP's creation of *de facto* equal footing eased the acceptance of a *de jure* entrenchment • extension of co-decision – Commission provided formula, while actual extension due to German leadership
Reforms of existing policies	• employment – coalition led by Denmark and Sweden, and backed by EP, with Germany as brake • common trade policy – German leadership until endgame, where the Secretariat brokered a compromise that averted a no agreement outcome • Secretariat provided leadership in the simplification of the treaties process, with UK and Denmark acting as brakes
Flexibility	• issue championed by France and Germany, but actual form included in the treaty based upon the strong leadership role of Secretariat
CFSP	• Franco-German leadership, with UK and the neutrals acting as brakes • Petersberg tasks – Finnish/Swedish proposal formed focal point for debates and outcome • CFSP 'High Representative' – Secretariat proposal bridged gap between UK and French views
JHA	• Commission provided formula for the scope of the communitarization of JHA • Schengen – Dutch Presidency provided leadership backed by Commission • strong coalition of UK and France, backed tacitly by Germany drove issue of weakening ECJ, with final outcome restrictions on ECJ role in new powers granted to Community

strengthening the EP – but the real German motive was to strengthen the institution where it had more weight than France and the UK.

The Commission also tried to play a more constructive role than in the PU IGC, but was unsuccessful in most issues. The lack of impact of the Commission was compounded by poor negotiating tactics and extreme positions. In Community matters, the Commission was though more successful in the provision of leadership, with examples including the formula for the extension of co-decision, and the formula for the scope of the communitarization of JHA policies. In other issues such as CFSP, the Commission had no impact.

The Council Secretariat played a key leadership role in the IGC, although the main effect of its leadership was to increase the efficiency of the negotiations. But by wielding the pen in the IGC in a relatively innocuous manner on most issues, the Secretariat was able to subtly shift outcomes closer to its own pro-integrative/pro-Council viewpoint. When the Secretariat attempted to promote its own views too openly, Presidencies cut the Secretariat out of the loop, clearly illustrating the limits of Secretariat leadership. This was most evident during the Dutch Presidency on the issue of Schengen.

Chapter 6

Negotiating the Treaty of Nice

Introduction – the institutional triangle revisited

The negotiation of the 2000 IGC was in most respects a least likely case for the ability of EU institutions to gain influence over outcomes. The negotiating context created few opportunities for EU institutions to provide leadership. The issues were simply not conducive to leadership provided by EU institutions. Issues such as re-weighting of Council voting weights were relatively simple, but they were also 'life-or-death' matters that pitted governments directly against each other. The negotiating situation itself was also relatively simple, with only a few well-known cleavages, and governments generally knew the positions of other governments on most issues. This poor context for EU institutional leadership was especially evident during the French Presidency in the second half of 2000, where the French even went out of their way to alienate and patronize the Commission. French President Chirac, for example, politely reminded Commission President Prodi during the Nice Summit that 'it is up to the member states to decide these matters' (Interview NAT-4). In the crucial negotiations in the IGC end-game, the French Presidency attempted to undertake all of the leadership functions itself – with somewhat predicable results for the overall gains made in the final agreement.

This chapter investigates what went wrong for EU institutions in the 2000 IGC, but also why the institutions were nevertheless able to gain some influence on the margins. The chapter first reviews the course of the negotiations of the 2000 IGC, and thereafter looks at the preferences of the three EU institutions. Next, the analysis shows that the EU institutions possessed limited opportunities to play a leadership role in the IGC, but that both the Commission and the Council Secretariat were able to employ leadership strategies that gave them some influence over the final Treaty of Nice. The conclusion discusses what types of leadership strategies were most effective in conditions that were definitely not conducive to attempts by EU institutions to play a leadership role.

The course of the negotiation of the Treaty of Nice

The agenda-setting phase – dealing with the Amsterdam left-overs

The contours of a compromise on the politically sensitive institutional triangle were increasingly clear in the dying hours of the Amsterdam Summit (McDonagh, 1998, p. 193). Yet the fundamental reform of the EU's institutions to prepare for an upcoming Eastern enlargement slipped out of the grasp of the prime ministers and presidents in the last minutes of the Summit (ibid.), even though this reform was arguably the main reason for convening the 1996–7 IGC.

In a typical Euro-fudge, it was decided to postpone the settlement of the institutional triangle by inserting an institutional protocol into the Treaty of Amsterdam mandating that a new IGC would be convened to tackle the questions of re-weighting of votes and the size of the Commission at least one year prior to the date when the membership of the EU exceeds twenty (Protocol 11). Additionally, declarations were attached that both discussed the 'special situation' for Spain (Declaration 49), and stated that the IGC should also 'address' the extension of QMV (Declaration 57). Therefore, just as a large part of the agenda for the 1996–7 IGC consisted of 'Maastricht left-overs', so the main topics for the 2000 IGC were primarily the politically sensitive 'Amsterdam left-overs'.

It was a political necessity for the IGC to end by late 2000 in order to make way for the conclusion of the difficult fifth enlargement negotiations that were scheduled to be concluded by the end of 2002 (see Chapter 8). But it was also decided to *not* set up an official group to prepare the agenda for the 2000 IGC. Instead, more informal discussions were held in COREPER and in the Council of Ministers similar to those that prepared the Political Union IGC in 1990–1. The conclusions of these meetings were then discussed in European Council summit meetings in 1999, and formed the basic agenda for the IGC.

The primary debate prior to the IGC was on the scope of the agenda – a debate that started in May 1999 in the first COREPER meetings on the IGC and would continue throughout the IGC itself. On one side were the proponents of a minimalist agenda, who felt that the IGC should only deal with the 'Amsterdam left-overs' in order to expedite a quick enlargement. On the other side were advocates of a more comprehensive reform aimed at ensuring that the institutional structure of the EU could still function in an EU of up to twenty-seven states (Galloway, 2001; Gray and Stubb, 2001). The Cologne

European Council in June 1999, which gave the upcoming Finnish Presidency the mandate to draft a report for the IGC, temporarily settled this debate by stating that the IGC would only deal with the three issues in the 'institutional triangle' (European Council, 1999a, paragraphs 52–4).

The debate on the scope of the agenda continued during the Finnish Presidency in the second half of 1999, focusing especially on whether to include the questions of flexibility or enhanced cooperation, but the Finns settled on a compromise in their IGC report (see below). The report opened the possibility of the upcoming Portuguese Presidency to 'propose additional issues to be taken on the agenda' (European Council 1999b paragraph 16). It was also decided that the matters of security and defence and the creation of an EU charter on fundamental rights would take place in two separate but parallel forums that would also be concluded at the Nice European Council summit in December 2000.

The course of the IGC negotiations – from Brussels to the (not so) Nice Summit

The IGC was officially convened on 14 February 2000 after both the Commission (European Commission, 2000a) and the European Parliament (European Parliament, 2000a) gave their opinions as mandated by Article 48 EU.

The Portuguese held the Presidency during the first half of 2000, during which they attempted to expand the agenda of the negotiations beyond the institutional triangle (CONF 4716/00). In the first months of the IGC, the issue of flexibility gradually made its way onto the agenda, being first discussed officially in an informal Representatives Group meeting in April 2000 (Stubb, 2002, p. 110). Flexibility was then put on the official agenda in the Feira report on the IGC's progress to the European Council (CONF 4750/00). Despite some progress on certain issues, such as the extension of QMV, the real bargaining in the IGC had yet to start, especially as regards the delicate questions of the size of the Commission and re-weighting of votes, where large and smaller member states were pitted directly against each other (Galloway, 2001; Laursen, 2001, p. 25).

The incoming French Presidency surprisingly decided to scrap the Feira report that had been approved by the European Council, and instead started almost from scratch by posing more conceptual questions rather than the usual IGC strategy of whittling away disagreements based upon a single negotiating text using techniques such as bracketing and the listing of options (Gray and Stubb, 2001).

Unfortunately for the efficiency of the negotiations, the French Presidency was beset by internal difficulties that made it very difficult for it to function effectively as a leader in the negotiations. Among the problems were: *co-habitation* and the internal coordination problems that this raised between a Socialist Prime Minister and a neo-Gaullist *RPR* President (Lequesne, 2001); the clashes of personality between European Affairs Minister Moscovici and Foreign Minister Védrine; and the question of whether the Presidency should be Paris-based or coordinated by the French Permanent Representation in Brussels.

The general impression from other delegations was that the French were excessively partial towards their own interests and did not listen to the concerns of other delegations (Interviews NAT-7, NAT-8, NAT-9). Examples of French partiality in their chairing of meetings and in the drafts produced included: openly advocating the shift of the locus of power in the EU towards the larger member states; promoting the introduction of flexibility into the second pillar contrary to what a large majority of governments wanted; and attempting to block the extension of QMV to common trade issues that were sensitive to France, especially in cultural and audiovisual matters, despite a clear majority in favour (*Agence Europe* No. 7755 11.07.2000; Gray and Stubb, 2001; Interview NAT-9; Schout and Vanhoonacker, 2001).

While the negotiation of dossiers such as flexibility and the extension of QMV were managed relatively well, with consensus developing on most points (*Agence Europe* No. 7792 06.09.2000; No. 7803 21.09.2000 and No. 7812 04.10.2000; Gray and Stubb, 2001; Schout and Vanhoonacker, 2001, p. 14;), the Presidency decided to postpone the resolution of the most sensitive issues until the final Nice Summit; where the French strategy appeared to be to put the heads of state and government under the gun in Nice to accept a compromise package, making them more prone to give in on national positions. The French upped the stakes by stating that they 'preferred failure [to agree in Nice] to an unsatisfactory agreement' (*Agence Europe* No. 7812 04.10.2000).

The informal Biarritz European Council on 13–14 October was the first opportunity for the heads of state and government to tackle head-on the major institutional questions in the IGC. Prior to the summit, France had, in informal and highly secretive consultations with the other four large member states, agreed in meetings between state secretaries that they would all accept an equal rotation of seats in a future Commission comprising fewer members than the number of member states (Interview NAT-4). This coordinated position put pressure on the smaller member states to accept a capped

Commission, as it removed the small state argument that they would not be treated equally in a capped Commission (Schout and Vanhoonacker, 2001, p. 18). At the same time, this proposal was the source of considerable indignation among the smaller member states, as they saw it as undermining the implicit bargain contained in the institutional protocol in the Treaty of Amsterdam, where the smaller member states indicated acceptance of a re-weighting of votes skewed towards the larger member states in return for guarantees that the smaller member states could keep their Commissioners.

No formal agenda was produced prior to the Biarritz summit, and the meeting almost collapsed during the first dinner in a row between the large and smaller member states after the French Presidency openly stated that the smalls should just accept the deal given to them (*Agence Europe* No. 7821 16.10.2000; Galloway, 2001, p. 48; Schout and Vanhoonacker, 2001, p. 18)! However, the summit arguably 'cleared the air' (Gray and Stubb, 2001, p. 12) and perhaps paved the way for agreement in Nice; but it had also became clear that no substantive agreement on the major issues would occur before Nice. After Biarritz, the meetings continued in the IGC, and in late November at the Val Duchesse informal Preparatory Group meeting, a number of lower-profile issues were concluded.

The Nice European Council summit, held from 7 to 11 December, was intended to conclude the IGC. But the 'seven shirter' summit quickly descended into chaos as the previous eighteen months of preparation were thrown out the window (*European Voice*, 14.12.00; Gray and Stubb, 2001, p. 10). While there was broad agreement on most of the dossiers of the IGC, including flexibility, two of the key institutional questions that were the very *raison d'être* of the IGC were unresolved as the heads of state and government arrived in Nice (Gray and Stubb, 2001). These were the questions of the re-weighting of votes and the extension of QMV to certain sensitive areas, particularly areas of the EC's common trade policy.

Furthermore, the negotiations were chaired haphazardly by the French, with participants noting strong internal French disagreements on whether their strategy should be to solely protect French national interests, or whether they should also act as a defender of the European common interest (Interviews NAT-9, NAT-6, NAT-7). Additionally, the French team in the summit was mainly composed of Paris-based civil servants who had not followed the IGC as closely as their Brussels-based colleagues, and were not as skilled at leading European meetings (Interviews NAT-6, NAT-7).

The actual bargaining on the two key issues only started on 9 December, which had originally been planned to be the last day of the summit. The French Presidency had on the evening of the 8th held a series of bilateral confessionals with each delegation, assisted by the Council Secretariat, attempting to find possible compromises on the key issues. On the 10th, the French then tabled a series of new proposals that were quite different from those that had been put forth prior to the Summit (Gray and Stubb, 2001). The bargaining then continued chaotically until 4.40 a.m. on the 11th, where the provisional text of the Treaty of Nice was agreed upon.

Looking at the two most salient issues in the last days of the summit, the discussion on the re-weighting of votes degenerated into a crude clash between the large and smaller member states, and within these groups between France and Germany, and Belgium and the Netherlands regarding the parity of voting weights. On the 10th, the French Presidency tabled a pro-large state proposal on voting weights that: compensated Spain in terms of voting weights for giving up its second Commissioner; kept Franco-German parity in voting weights; and introduced a demographic 'safety net' that mandated, if one government asked for it, a proposal under QMV must be adopted by governments representing 62 per cent of the EU's population. While this proposal was supported by the large member states, the proposed deal strongly upset the smaller member states – and was not helped by the strongly partial chairing of the discussions by the French Presidency (Schout and Vanhoonacker, 2001, p. 20; Interviews NAT-4, NAT-1). Once the second set of re-weighting tables was rejected by Portugal and Belgium, who were supported by Austria, Finland, Greece, and Sweden later on the 10th, the French had no alternative proposal (*Agence Europe* No. 7860 12.12.2000). Portuguese Prime Minister Guterres called the proposals an 'institutional *coup d'Etat*' by a 'directorate of large States' (ibid.).

The negotiations then spun dangerously out of control, and the French Presidency appeared to be more interested in maintaining Franco-German parity than in brokering a fair compromise (Schout and Vanhoonacker, 2001, p. 21; Interviews NAT-4, NAT-1). The French even proposed that the negotiations on the issue should be closed and taken up by the next Presidency in the spring of 2001 (ibid.)! A majority of governments demanded a new proposal based upon the Commission's proposed simple double majority solution – but the French Presidency after long debates and bilateral discussions reintroduced its own proposal, with the crucial difference that many of the medium-sized countries gained an additional vote. This was accepted by all of the governments except the Belgians, which demanded and got compensation for accepting that the Dutch gained more votes that themselves (*Economist*, 2000a; Interviews NAT-9,

NAT-4). The final outcome was a messy horse-trade that resulted in a 'triple majority voting' system, and many mistakes crept into the table that had to be ironed out after the conclusion of the IGC (see Table 6.1) (Interview NAT-9; Schout and Vanhoonacker, 2001, p. 21).

After Tony Blair made it clear that the UK would not accept QMV for taxation and social policy, attention turned to the extension of QMV and Commission competences in common trade matters (Galloway, 2001, pp. 106–9). The basic cleavage here was between the advocates of a significantly strengthened role for the Commission in the negotiation of trade agreements for services and intellectual property coupled with QMV, and those that were opposed to all or parts of this extension, including the French, who feared that QMV would limit France's ability to protect its audio-visual, cultural and health sectors (Galloway, 2001, p. 108; Meunier and Nicolaïdis, 1999). After intense negotiations between the French Presidency, assisted by the Council Secretariat, the Commission and the Finnish delegation, a legally complex formula broadly based upon a Commission proposal was agreed upon, which expanded the scope of Community competences while also excluding the sensitive sectors (see below). That the French accepted this outcome can in part be attributed to the fact that they had the Presidency, which led them to be more accommodating towards an extension of competences and QMV than they perhaps otherwise would have been.

What did the EU institutions want in the 2000 IGC?

The Commission – towards a more effective enlarged Union

While the Commission's overall institutional interests was to strengthen the power and prestige of the Commission, the Commission had learned from the intergovernmental backlash of the mid-1990s that it should try to play a lower profile public role while also trying to gain support from the European Parliament for its advocacy of a more ambitious outcome in the 2000 IGC. Table 6.2 shows Commission preferences across the main issues in the IGC (Europaudvalget, 2000c; European Commission, 1999b, 2000a and 2000b; Petite, 2000).

The Commission's main aim was to ensure that the 2000 IGC prepared the EU for the upcoming enlargement. It therefore advocated an ambitious agenda in order to ensure the effective operation of the institutions in an EU-27, although some of its proposals were aimed more at setting the agenda for the next IGC that was already

TABLE 6.1   *The Treaty of Nice*

Issue area	Outcome
Re-weighting of Council voting weights	• a re-weighting of voting weights was agreed that gave larger member states relatively more voting power, and a declaration was attached that transposed these numbers to an EU of 27 members • the thresholds for majorities and minorities were changed • a population threshold of 62 per cent was introduced
Size and reform of the Commission	• a deferred capping of the size of the Commission once the EU reached 27 members was agreed, though the actual number was not agreed upon. An equal rotation system will then be put in place • certain reforms to the organization of the Commission were undertaken, primarily strengthening the president's powers internally in the Commission
Size of the European Parliament and the extension of co-decision	• a re-allocation of the number of national seats in the European Parliament was undertaken • co-decision was extended to fifteen treaty provisions

$\rightarrow$

looming on the horizon (Petite, 2000, p. 62). The two central priorities of the Commission in the 2000 IGC were the extension of QMV coupled with the extension of Commission competences in Article 133 EC. Another major issue for the Commission was the simplification and consolidation of the treaties.

The European Parliament – a new pragmatism?

While the European Parliament (EP) has traditionally been the most federalist-oriented EU institution in its opinions in IGCs, the EP's positions in the 2000 IGC followed the more pragmatic path adopted in the previous IGC. But the EP in its opinion on the convening of the IGC called for a much wider and more ambitious agenda than had been approved in the Helsinki European Council Summit conclusions

$\rightarrow$

Issue area	Outcome
Reforms of other institutions	• significant changes in the composition and functioning of the ECJ were agreed, including the transferal of a large portion of routine cases to the Court of First Instance and the new judicial panels
Extension of QMV	• QMV was extended to 37 treaty provisions, with 8 more articles at various future dates going over to QMV • in Article 133 EC, the potential recourse to QMV was expanded subject to legally complex conditions. The potential scope of EC exclusive powers was also expanded to include trade in services and certain aspects of intellectual property, allowing the Commission to negotiate trade agreements in these issue areas
Flexibility	• the veto option was removed from 1st and 3rd pillar flexibility • the conditions for the use of flexibility were relaxed • an enabling clause was inserted into the 2nd pillar

Source: Treaty of Nice, *Official Journal of the European Communities*, C 80/1, 10.3.2001

(see Table 6.3) (European Parliament, 2000a). While some of the proposals for institutional change were more pragmatic than the Commission's – for example stating that the size of the EP could exceed 700 during an interim period – other proposals were highly ambitious, such as calls for ten per cent of the seats of the EP to be elected in EU-wide elections from 2009, or for the constitutionalization of the treaties into a single supranational Union.

A priority of the EP was that QMV and co-decision should become the general rule in legislative decision-taking. The EP also wanted to be able to elect the Commission President from a list of candidates proposed by the European Council. Another proposal called for a change in treaty reform methods, including 'greater democratic control over the process of drafting and adopting changes to the treaties', and the use of a community-like method to prepare and

TABLE 6.2   *The preferences of the European Commission in the 2000 IGC*

Issue area	Commission preferences
Re-weighting of Council voting weights	• the Commission was somewhat uninterested in the question, as 're-weighting seems to us to have extremely undramatic effects' (Petite, 2000, p. 65) • advocated simple dual majority • potentially lower the threshold for a majority
Size and reform of the Commission	• proposed two options: 20 with equal rotation or one member per member state • strengthened President and the individual accountability of Commissioners • strengthen the Commission by amending the enforcement procedure in the EC Treaty along the lines of the ECSC Treaty, where the Commission has much stronger authority in deciding whether a member state has failed to fulfill its treaty obligations
Size of the European Parliament and the extension of co-decision	• EP: upper limit of 700 members, let the EP allocate seats, and consider EU-wide lists for electing MEPs • the use of co-decision should be extended to all policies where QMV is used (including for CAP and fisheries policies)
The scope of EC competences	• extend the scope of Article 133 EC to all services, investment and intellectual property

$\rightarrow$

carry out treaty reform. The Commission would submit a draft treaty which would serve as the basis for negotiations in the IGC, where governments and the EP would negotiate changes.

The Council Secretariat – advocating the upper end of realism

While the Secretariat did not publish written opinions prior to the IGC as the other two institutions, and attempted to maintain the myth

$\rightarrow$

Issue area	Commission preferences

Reforms of other institutions	• ECJ
	  – set-up a reflection group on the future of the EU's justice system, which reported to the IGC
	  – make the legal system more effective by transferring a portion of cases to lower courts
	• creation of European Public Prosecutor to combat fraud
	• creation of Europe-wide political parties

Extension of QMV	• QMV should be the general rule, but allow for exceptions in five categories • QMV should be extended to trade policy, social policy, asylum and integration, cohesion policy, and certain tax matters (*Agence Europe*, no. 7833, 01.11.00)
Flexibility	• keep strict conditions for the use of flexibility, while removing the veto option • fix the minimum number of participants at one-third of member states • extend flexibility to the 2nd pillar
Other questions	• amend the way in which the treaties themselves are revised by creating a two-tier treaty split into a constitutional provisions and implementing provisions, thereby enabling the less fundamental provisions to be amended by the Council of Ministers with the assent of the European Parliament (European Commission, 1999b, pp. 7–8, 2000b; Petite, 2000; Europaudvalget, 2000c)

of its neutrality prior to the IGC, it is evident that the Secretariat had aggregate institutional interests and that key officials also had personal preferences that they pursued during the IGC. It is therefore possible to construct a preference profile for the Secretariat in the IGC based upon both interviews with Secretariat officials and other participants in the IGC, and from articles published by Secretariat officials prior to convening of the IGC.

On an aggregate level, the institutional interests of the Secretariat in the IGC were primarily to strengthen the Council vis-à-vis the

TABLE 6.3 *The preferences of the European Parliament in the 2000 IGC*

Issue area	European Parliament preferences
Re-weighting of Council voting weights	• called for a simple double majority system for QMV
Size and reform of the Commission	• allow the 2005–2010 Commission to consist of one member per member state, while after 2010 the size is capped at the President and twenty members
	• proposed reforms regarding the resignation of the Commission, including allowing the President of the Commission to dismiss individual Commissioners
	• wanted to allow the Commission President to ask the EP for a vote of confidence, and to appoint members of the college in consultation with member states
	• opposed to any weakening of the Commission's monopoly of initiation in the 1st pillar
Size of the European Parliament and the extension of co-decision	• wanted an upper limit of 700 for the EP based upon demography with a minimum of four seats, although transitional measures are envisioned for the 2004–2009 term where the number could exceed 700
	• proposed the creation of an EU-wide constituency that would elect 10 per cent of the members of the EP from 2009
	• co-decision should be made general rule except for constitutional and fundamental matters
	• called for strengthened EP role, particularly in budgetary matters and appointments, but also in international agreements and the common commercial policy
The scope of EC competences	• wanted to extend EC competences in external economic relations (Article 133 EC) to include all services and intellectual property rights
	• create specific legal bases for actions currently undertaken under Article 308 EC

$\rightarrow$

$\rightarrow$

Issue area	European Parliament preferences
Common foreign and security policy	• strengthen CFSP, including laying down a timetable for a common European policy on security and defence • create a Defence Ministers Council and merge the High Representative with the Commission for External Relations into a specially appointed Vice-President of the Commission • integrate WEU into the EU

Reforms of other institutions	• advocated that the Presidency should be held for periods of at least two years, but that different member states would hold the Presidency for different Council formations
	• divide the Council into executive and legislative parts
	• called for the introduction of Europe-wide political parties
	• ECJ
	  – proposed that the ECJ should consist of an odd number of judges equal to or greater than the number of member states
	  – allow the CFI to give preliminary rulings
	  – extend ECJ jurisdiction in 3rd pillar
	  – make it easier for individuals to raise cases before ECJ
	• creation of a European Public Prosecutor

Extension of QMV	• make QMV general rule except for constitutional matters
Flexibility	• reduce possibility for blocking while safe-guarding the single institutional framework • create a single chapter for the 2nd and 3rd pillars
Other questions	• strongly interested in incorporating the EU Charter into the treaties • called for a single legal personality for the Union • wanted a simplification and unification of the EU Treaties into two sections: a constitutional section comprised of institutional and compe-tence questions that is difficult to modify, and a second section of other areas • called for the revision of the treaty reform procedure • introduce openness in the Council in legislative matters

European Parliament and Commission. Additionally, as in previous IGCs, the Secretariat attempted to push for an outcome that was slightly more ambitious than what the member states would otherwise have agreed upon, but still within the zone of possible agreements.

As in past IGCs, the individual preferences of key officials in the Secretariat were very significant in determining which set of goals the Secretariat advocated. Participants in the IGC noted that the Secretariat had a 'big state' bias in many of the papers it drafted for the Presidency (Interview NAT-9), perhaps due to the fact that the key members of the staff in the IGC all came from big member states. Further, as the Secretariat has become increasingly an executive actor within foreign policy, it has developed an even more autonomous institutional identity (Christiansen, 2003).

Insiders also point out that newly appointed deputy Secretary-General Pierre de Boissieu's overriding goal is to transform the Secretariat into the 'new Commission' within a more intergovernmental EU (Interviews NAT-6, NAT-7). The head of the Secretariat's Legal Service, Piris, who also acted as the Legal Adviser to the IGC, also had several issues that he personally lobbied for during the IGC. Piris for example wanted to clarify the status of inter-institutional agreements, which are political declarations between the Council, Commission, and European Parliament (Galloway, 2001, p. 159; Interview NAT-4). Piris had also gone on the record as wanting to: extend the scope of Article 133 EC to include services and intellectual property (Piris, 1999, p. 574); extend QMV through the 'quasi-elimination' of unanimity (ibid., p. 582); and increase the weights of larger member states in the re-weighting of Council votes (ibid.).

Changes in the leadership resources of EU institutions since 1997

The material resources of EU institutions

In comparison to earlier IGCs, there were few material leadership resources that EU institutions could link with IGC outcomes due to the issues on the IGC agenda. Issues such as cohesion policies were not on the table, and there were few opportunities for the EP to link its creative exploitation of existing rules to the issues in the IGC.

The informational advantages of EU institutions

Looking first at the Commission and starting at the top of the institutional hierarchy, both of the top officials in the Commission that dealt with the 2000 IGC were relative novices. Newly appointed Commission President Prodi had no direct experience in IGC negotiations from within the Commission, although he had taken part in the European Council summits during the 1996–7 IGC as Italian Prime Minister. The Commissioner appointed to be responsible for the IGC was Michel Barnier, who had also taken part in the 1996–7 IGC at the political level as the French European Affairs Minister until June 1997. Both were not familiar with the lower-level, technical negotiations that are a vital forum in IGC negotiations for the Commission.

In the issues that were central for the Commission, Barnier had no direct policy experience with the EU's common trade policy. By appointing Barnier as Commissioner responsible for the IGC, it was then not formally or politically possible for the Commission to let their expert, Commissioner Lamy, take over the negotiations in trade policy in IGC negotiations at either the Foreign Minister or Preparatory Group level.

At the lower level, the Commission's IGC Task Force was also reduced from the ten members it had in the 1996–7 IGC to four members in the 2000 IGC, although the core of the group was the same as it had been in the 1996–7 IGC, ensuring a degree of consistency and expertise (Gray, 2001).

Turning to the EP, it had few if any informational advantages vis-à-vis governments. The size of the EP's Secretariat was unchanged since the 1996–7 IGC (Europa Kommissionen, 2001, p. 355). The EP appointed Elmar Brok and Dimitris Tsatsos as EP observers to the IGC. While Brok could draw on his experience in the 1996–7 IGC, he lacked the time to devote himself fully to the IGC, as he also acted as the chair of the EP's Foreign Affairs Committee (Interview EC-2). Tsatsos as a constitutional lawyer knew some of the issues, but lacked IGC experience or the necessary negotiating skills (Interview EC-2).

As for the staff of the Secretariat, the core of its staff had taken part in every IGC since 1985, giving it an institutional memory and experience unparalleled by any other actor in the IGC (Christiansen, 2002, p. 47, 2003; Galloway, 2001, pp. 38–9). The extremely competent core of Secretariat officials, including Keller-Noëllet, Galloway, Jacqué and Piris, also had extensive experience from daily EU policy-making in finding the centre of gravity of member state positions, and formulating acceptable compromises. However, the official that was directly responsible for Presidency–Secretariat relations was deputy

Secretary-General Pierre de Boissieu, who had been appointed at the Cologne European Council Summit in June 1999. But de Boissieu did have extensive experience with IGC negotiations given that he had been the French Permanent Representative in the 1996–7 IGC, and had been closely involved with the 1990–1 IGC as a civil servant in the French Foreign Ministry. Overall, the Secretariat A-grade staff had grown by 28 per cent since 1995, with 317 officials including temporary agents (General Secretariat of the Council, 2002).

The reputation of the EU institutions

The downfall of the Santer Commission in March 1999 left the reputation of the Commission in tatters. While newly appointed President Prodi attempted to rectify this situation by, for example, advocating the creation of a European Public Prosecutor in order to be seen as fighting fraud in the EU, the views of the Commission were widely seen to be far outside of the zone of possible agreements in the IGC. Prodi's strongly pro-integrative speech to the EP in July 1999 on the upcoming IGC contributed to the sidelining of the Commission in the IGC, as it was seen to be advocating 'politically difficult positions' (Christiansen, 2002; Galloway, 2001, p. 37; Interview NAT-4). This was particularly evident in issues such as the creation of a two-tiered treaty structure; an issue that despite repeated Commission attempts to put on the agenda was never seriously discussed in the IGC.

Another factor that crippled the Commission during the IGC were the neo-Gaullist views of President Chirac towards the role of the Commission. While pro-Commission member states such as Belgium often have let the Commission play a very important role in their Presidencies, Chirac was a strong advocate of the Gaullist vision of a *Europe des patries*, and he for example went out of his way in the Nice Summit to insult the Commission and attempt to prevent it from gaining influence (see above).

A somewhat mitigating factor in this respect was Barnier's appointment as the Commissioner in charge of the IGC, given his close relations with Chirac and influential position within Chirac's *RPR* party. Yet Barnier's close ties with Chirac had the opposite effect during the Portuguese Presidency, with the Portuguese State Secretary for European Affairs seeing Barnier as 'singing Chirac's tune' – a view that was shared by many other actors in the negotiations.

The EP was a more accepted participant in the 2000 IGC than in previous IGCs. This was primarily due to the constructive role that the EP had played in the 1996–7 IGC, but also was part of an attempt to avoid what one participant termed the 'absurdity' of repeating already held debates with the EP (Interview NAT-4). But France and the UK were still opposed to full EP involvement in the IGC, and ensured that the EP did not take part in the political-level negotiations in the IGC.

In general the reputation of the Council Secretariat had not changed since the previous IGC, with member states in general seeing the utility of using the Council Secretariat as a source of information and as an 'honest broker'. Additionally, key Secretariat officials such as Keller-Noëllet and Galloway had built up strong trust relationships with member state representatives both from their work in the daily Council decision-making and in previous IGCs. However, both deputy Secretary-General de Boissieu and the head of the Secretariat's Legal Service, Piris, were perceived by many national delegates to be political actors with personal agendas in the IGC (Interviews NAT-4, NAT-10, EC-2).

The opportunities for leadership created by the negotiating context

The role of EU institutions in the 2000 IGC

The Commission played in many respects the role of an unwanted guest in the 2000 IGC, with the added disadvantage of having an extreme policy position. Based upon historical precedent, the Commission had the right to put forward proposals in the IGC and was allowed to participate in all levels of the IGC, but it had no vote over the outcome of the IGC. The Commission was also drawn upon by Presidencies and individual delegations as a source of advice and information during the negotiations.

While the Commission had quite good contacts with the Finnish Presidency, and assisted it extensively, it had relatively poor relations with both the Portuguese and French Presidencies. Portuguese State Secretary for European Affairs, da Costa, saw the Commission as French dominated – especially Commission representative Barnier (see above). Relations with the French Presidency were if anything worse, with the Presidency for the most not drawing upon the expertise of the Commission in the drafting process. At the highest level, Chirac had a very confrontational relationship with both the Commission and in particular President Prodi.

The relatively weak role of the Commission in the negotiation of most of the issues in the IGC can be contrasted with the Commission's role in the negotiation of the reform of the EU's judicial system. Through clever institutional politics, the Commission convinced governments to set up a Working Party on the Future of the European Court of Justice in the spring of 1999, consisting of former members of the ECJ and CFI (Due, 2000). The Commission then provided the working party with a set of questions to discuss. After the working party was finished, the Commission convinced member states that the negotiation of the issue in the IGC should be done within the Friends of the Presidency Group, and that the Group should be composed of national legal counsellors together with a representative of the Commission and the Council Secretariat. This created a privileged institutional forum for Commission attempts to provide leadership in the issue.

Turning to look at the EP, while its role in the 2000 IGC was very weak, it marked a substantial improvement upon the past. By gaining an observer role with speaking rights in meetings of the Preparatory Group and Friends of the Presidency, the EP had finally managed to gain access to the actual IGC negotiating room – allowing it to present its opinions and engage in debates with governmental delegates. The EP was not allowed to attend formal ministerial meetings or those of heads of state and government within the European Council. The two EP delegates (Elmar Brok (EPP) and Dimitrios Tsatsos (PES)) took active part in the debates, and repeatedly presented EP viewpoints on major issues in the IGC. The President of the EP, Nicole Fontaine, also met with ministers and heads of government and state prior to their meetings in an exchange of opinions.

Article 48 EU mandates that the EP has to be consulted by the Council prior to the convening of an IGC, and the EP publishes an opinion on the IGC. However, as with the other EU institutions, the EP had no vote on the final outcome in the 2000 IGC – despite repeated calls by the EP for the outcome to be adopted using the assent procedure.

As in previous IGCs, the official mandate of the Council Secretariat was to play a secretarial function for the IGC and the Presidencies in charge of the negotiations. In the 2000 IGC, the Secretariat supported the Presidencies by drafting most of the Presidency texts for the IGC, together with the agenda and minutes of meetings, though often under strong guidance by the Presidencies (Interviews NAT-6, NAT-7, NAT-9). The Secretariat also provided assistance to the Presidencies by offering suggestions and ideas on how to reach acceptable agreements based upon its prior experience in IGCs and from daily EU policy-making, and from its close contacts with member state delegates prior to and during the IGC.

However, the Secretariat had relatively poor relations with the Portuguese Presidency, preventing it from successfully playing the role of trusted adviser and confidante in the negotiations as in previous IGCs. One of the main problems was that the Portuguese believed that de Boissieu was pursuing a pro-large state agenda, and they made it clear that they would not accept de Boissieu's amendments as had the Finnish (see below). The Portuguese even excluded de Boissieu from the coordinating meetings held between the Secretariat and the Presidency, and they chose instead to work closely with other Secretariat officials such as Galloway and Keller-Noëllet (Interview EC-8).

The Secretariat played an even more restricted role during the French Presidency. The main problem for the Secretariat was that the French Presidency was run from Paris, and not from the French Permanent Representation in Brussels (Christiansen, 2002, p. 48). A Presidency run from a national capital usually is more partial to national interests, whereas a Permanent Representation in Brussels is used to working within the EU framework, and in focusing upon common European interests. A Permanent Representation is therefore often more aware of what is acceptable among the other member states as they are used to deconstructing the Brussels diplomatic code, and is also more aware of the utility of using the Secretariat and/or Commission as a source of information and as a broker.

The Secretariat did have close relations with French Permanent Representative Vimont in Brussels. In issues where Vimont was responsible, the Secretariat was drawn on extensively (Gray and Stubb, 2001, p. 11; Interviews NAT-6, NAT-7, NAT-9). However, on most of the other issues, Paris attempted to control the negotiations and therefore for the most part did not draw upon the Council Secretariat for either assistance or guidance (Christiansen, 2002, p. 48; Interviews NAT-4, NAT-6, NAT-7). But deputy Secretary-General de Boissieu was allowed to play an influential role in the final days of the French Presidency owing to his personal relationship with Chirac. For example, on the last evening of the Nice Summit, de Boissieu was seen sitting on the left hand side of Chirac, 'writing' his script (Interview NAT-4; *Economist*, 16.12.00, p. 28).

The nature of the issues being negotiated

While the institutional questions of the re-weighting of votes and the composition of the Commission were relatively clear-cut, there were

several substantive issues on the IGC agenda that were highly technical and legally complex. For instance, revising Article 42 EC (social
security coordination) and Article 133 EC (common trade policy)
was legally complex, and national delegates were dependent upon
Secretariat and/or Commission expertise both in order to find out
what the existing legal status quo was together with the possible
implications of different revisions of the articles (Interview NAT-4;
NAT-9).

The number of issues and parties in the negotiations

The 2000 IGC was a relatively simple negotiating situation, with the
three issues in the institutional triangle the most salient points on the
agenda. However, when discussions turned to dossiers such as the
extension of QMV, there were many sub-points on the agenda,
making it very difficult to have a synoptic view of the state of play
across the issues. For example, for the 4 September Preparatory
Group meeting, the Presidency conducted a *tour de table* where
governments expressed their views regarding the transferal of *forty-
three* different provisions to QMV (CONF 4767/00). And as with the
1996–7 IGC, with fifteen governments and representatives from both
the Commission and EP at the table, it was difficult for negotiating
sessions to ever evolve beyond a mere airing of opinions, especially
when they were conducted as *tour de tables*. This complexity
increased the demand for behind-the-scenes leadership to find and
craft compromises.

The distribution and intensity of governmental preferences

The cleavages and potential compromises were relatively obvious in
the 2000 IGC (see Figure 6.1). Indeed, the basic contours of the
compromise between large and smaller member states had already
been included in the protocol attached to the Treaty of Amsterdam
(Protocol 11). There was therefore no strong demand for leadership to
find a solution.

Most of the key issues in the IGC were zero-sum, where one
government's gain was another's loss. Issues such as the re-weighting
of Council votes pitted member states directly against each other, with
the increase in the voting power of one member state decreasing the
voting power of other member states. Other issues such as the number
of Commissioners touched on delicate matters of national power and
prestige, with the appointment of a Commissioner being seen by

FIGURE 6.1 *Major cleavages in the 2000 IGC*

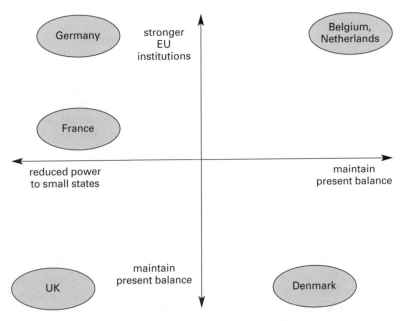

smaller member states as essential to ensure that their interests were protected in an EU increasingly dominated by the larger member states (Galloway, 2001, p. 46; Schout and Vanhoonacker, 2001). In such issues, the potential for EU institutions to gain influence through clever leadership strategies is, at least in theory, much lower. National delegates scrutinized proposals and their implications on these core issues in much more detail than they had in previous IGCs (Interview EC-5). But pulling in the other direction was the demand for leadership due to the strength of the cleavages, which when coupled with the demand for a solution in order to prepare for enlargement created a strong demand for leadership to *broker* a compromise deal.

Leadership by EU institutions

The above makes it clear that in contrast to previous IGCs, the opportunities for EU institutions to provide leadership were low in the 2000 IGC – owing to the roles that the institutions were allowed to play, the nature of the issues, and the simplicity of the negotiating situation. But were any of the EU institutions able to successfully exploit these limited possibilities?

Leadership by the European Commission

The only options open to the Commission to play an instrumental leader role were: offering expert advice to Presidencies, putting forward proposals in the IGC and attempting to broker deals.

Investigating first the importance of assisting Presidencies, the Commission had good contacts with the Finnish Presidency. The Finnish Presidency was assisted by the Commission in its attempts to introduce a categorization of different types of articles that could be transferred to QMV (Gray and Stubb, 2001, p. 16; Interview EC-5). However, in the subsequent negotiations this formula approach was abandoned in favour of a case-by-case method – and the final outcome was much closer to the lowest common denominator than would have been the case if the Commission's approach had been used (Gray and Stubb, 2001, p. 16). As was seen above, both the Portuguese and French Presidencies did not draw upon the Commission as a source of information, preventing the Commission from being able to shape the agenda in this manner.

In contrast, the Commission was very influential in the discussions on the reform of the EU's judicial system, where the agenda-setting phase took place within an expert working party set up by the Commission, and the actual negotiations took place in the Friends of the Presidency Group chaired by the Commission. The choice to have national legal experts instead of political representatives in the working party set the tone for the further negotiations, implying that they would be dealt with in a non-political and technical manner among what can be termed an empowered epistemic community (Haas, 1992; Sebenius, 1992). The national legal experts shared common beliefs and norms, and a common policy project relating to which type of reforms of the EU's judicial system were necessary. Given their strong institutional position in the negotiations, and the strong legitimacy of the expert opinions of former ECJ judges, it could be expected that the outcome of the working group would be accepted as the basis for discussions in the IGC.

The Commission was successful in garnering for itself an exclusive agenda-setting role in the working party, enabling it to table the set of questions that formed the basis of the discussions. The Commission also played a central role in the Friends of the Presidency Group, chairing the group and guiding the debates.

Being negotiated within the Friends Group had three effects. First, it privileged technical legal arguments, giving the Commission a comparative advantage in providing leadership given its extensive and authoritative expertise in dealing with EU law. Secondly, the

Commission succeeded in its attempts to restructure the rules of the game by creating a privileged institutional position for itself. Thirdly, and most significantly, the Commission could predict with reasonable certainty the negotiating outcome that would be reached by this epistemic community of legal experts, given that the group shared policy goals regarding the need to ensure the effective functioning of the EU's legal system post-enlargement. If the negotiations had been dealt with by political actors, agreement might not have been reached, as there were voices in several governments that were very critical of the ECJ's strong pro-integrative role, and therefore were not motivated to undertake the necessary reforms to ensure the effectiveness of the judicial system – even seeing paralysis of the legal system as being in line with their interests (Beach, 2001).

Therefore, by creating a coalition of empowered 'believers' (Sebenius, 1992, p. 354) in the Commission's preferred outcome, this created an advantageous shift in the zone of possible agreements for the Commission from what it otherwise would have been if the issue had been dealt with by political negotiators. The actual outcome did indeed reflect Commission preferences in most of the issues, although the Commission's proposed clarifications of Article 234 EC (preliminary references) were not adopted (European Commission, 2000c; Galloway, 2001; Gray and Stubb, 2001, pp. 17–18; Working Party, 2000). Yet while the reforms of the judicial system were negotiated at the technical level, the amendments they agreed upon were not, and 'may have a more significant impact on the development of the European Union than any of the other changes agreed in Nice' (Gray and Stubb, 2001, p. 17).

Turning to an investigation of Commission attempts to shape the agenda by submitting proposals, in the agenda-setting phase prior to the opening of the IGC, newly elected President Prodi attempted to broaden the IGC agenda by appointing a 'wise group' under the leadership of Jean-Luc Dehaene to comment on the agenda. The group presented its report in October 1999 (Dehaene, 1999). However, the report was well outside of what governments were interested in considering, including items such as the creation of a two-tiered treaty structure and questions relating to the European Security and Defence Policy (ESDP) (Interview NAT-4). The report did though give the Commission the opportunity to gauge the reaction of the member states to these ideas, and the Commission's subsequent submission to the Finnish Presidency was more restrained, although the Commission still argued for fairly broad IGC agenda (Dinan and Vanhoonacker, 2000–2001, pp. 2–3; European Commission, 1999b; Gray and Stubb, 2001, p. 9).

If we first look at one of the most salient issues on the agenda, the Commission's proposal for introducing a simple double majority voting system was supported by a majority of member states (CONF 4763/00; Dinan and Vanhoonacker, 2000–2001; European Commission, 2000a; Gray, 2001). The intention was to provide an objective formula that took into account the population of larger member states while also giving assurances to smaller member states through the use of a simple majority condition (Galloway, 2001, pp. 71–2). This proposal did not convince the French or Spanish and did not influence the final outcome, owing to French insistence on a simple re-weighting of votes that would preserve the illusion of Franco-German parity, and to poor negotiating tactics on the part of the Commission. Prodi for instance fell asleep more than once during the negotiation of the issue in European Council Summits (Interview NAT-4).

The basic problem for the Commission's proposals was that they were far outside of the zone of possible agreements, and the Commission to the consternation of national delegates kept trying to push its own hobby horses. For example, one of Barnier's pet projects was the creation of a European Public Prosecutor (CONF 4779/00), but the idea was from the start a non-starter despite repeated attempts by the Commission to push it (Interviews NAT-4, NAT-6, NAT-7; Gray, 2001). Another proposal that the Commission together with the EP continued advocating throughout the IGC was the idea to split the treaties into constitutional and legislative parts (CONF 4763/00). The proposal attracted little interest among governments, who feared the consequences that a comprehensive revision of the treaties could have – in effect it could be a Pandora's box that would reopen the complicated web of compromises and concessions built up over fifty years of integration. French Minister for European Affairs Moscovici in October 1999 declared that the proposal was both 'unrealistic' and 'tantamount to overloading the IGC boat' (*Agence Europe* No. 7582 28.10.99). Prodi had also put forward the idea of moving the High Representative for CFSP from the Secretariat to the Commission in an attempt to unify the EU's external representation – this was not even discussed in the IGC (*Agence Europe* No. 7812 04.10.00)!

Other Commission proposals were more successful. The Commission proposed changes to Article 7 TEU that would enable the EU to establish an 'early warning' procedure (CONF 4782/00). Article 7 TEU deals with sanctions against member states that breach basic democratic principles (Galloway, 2001, p. 153–4). The proposal formed a focal point for debates and was adopted in the final treaty in a modified form. Another Commission proposal dealt with

European political parties, with the Commission proposing the inclusion of a provision in Article 191 EC that opens for the EP or Council to create regulations governing political parties at EU level, which was included in the Treaty of Nice (CONF 4764/00) (Galloway, 2001, p. 126).

Finally, the Commission had few opportunities to provide leadership through brokerage. One of the basic problems for the Commission was its poor reputation. Another problem was that the Commission in the 2000 IGC did not have the trust of smaller member states (Gray, 2001). This was partially due to the downfall of the Santer Commission in 1999, and partially due to the suspicions of many smaller member states that top Commission officials were advocating pro-large member state outcomes. Finally, Commission President Prodi was widely perceived to be a relatively ineffectual leader both in daily EU policy-making and in the IGC negotiations.

Yet despite these weaknesses, the Commission was able to broker an important compromise in one of its main priorities – the common trade policy (Article 133 EC). The Commission had originally proposed an across-the-board transferral of all aspects of trade policy to QMV and EC competences, but this encountered resistance from especially France, supported by Austria, Denmark and Greece. Despite repeated attempts by the Commission to tailor its proposal to meet these objections, no agreement had been reached as delegates arrived in Nice. During the Nice Summit, the Commission together with the Finnish delegation took part in intense, behind-the-scenes negotiations. The main problem was getting the French on board, while also maximizing the extent of the transferral of competences as wanted by a majority of other delegations. Yet the complexity of the issue prevented other actors except the Secretariat from stepping in and formulating a compromise, as national experts in trade matters were not present in the Nice Summit (Interview EC-5). The Commission put forward two suggestions on the third day of the Summit that formed the core of the final proposal together with a legal formula provided by Piris that helped the French swallow the solution (CONF 4818/00; SN 526/00) (Interviews NAT-1, NAT-9, EC-15).

Leadership by the European Parliament

Attempts by the EP to provide leadership were weakened by the late arrival of a detailed EP position on the issues in the IGC. This had the effect that 'the Parliament struggled to stamp its authority on the agenda or the rationale behind each of the issues' (Gray and Stubb,

2001, p. 9). EP attempts to provide leadership were also not helped by the relative ineffectual Brok/Tsatsos team (see above).

During the IGC, the EP delegates were not actually 'involved' in the real negotiations but were merely kept informed (MEP in Neuhold, 2001, p. 6). Furthermore, the EP delegates did not take part in the political-level meetings, and were forced to rely upon speeches by the President of the EP before she was asked to leave the room. The EP tried repeatedly during the IGC to gain access to the political-level meetings, but was politely reminded that this was not part of the Helsinki mandate.

In the lower-level meetings, EP interventions were often out of synch with the thrust of the debates among governmental representatives. In a debate on flexibility for example, while most governmental interventions dealt with specific problems such as 'critical mass' and 'emergency brakes', the EP's intervention stated that the goal of flexibility was to push the integration process forward (Interview NAT-4).

There are few indications that the EP was able to either shape the agenda or broker compromises in the IGC. When we look at the priority areas for the EP, co-decision was not made the general rule for first pillar decision-making, nor was it extended to agriculture. EP powers were not extended in the budgetary provisions either, despite repeated attempts by the EP to remove the distinction between compulsory and non-compulsory expenditure. The EP, together with a majority of governments, was also not able to overcome British resistance to adopting the Charter of Fundamental Rights as a legally binding document (Deloche-Gaudez, 2001).

The only real evidence of EP leadership was in the debate on the post-Nice agenda that would lead to the European Convention in 2002–2003. Although German Foreign Minister Fischer was a key advocate of the post-Nice agenda, the EP also played a key role in advocating a break with the IGC method (Norman, 2003, pp. 24–5). As will be seen in Chapter 7, the European Convention proved to be a much more favourable forum for EP leadership.

Leadership by the Council Secretariat

The Secretariat attempted to use its institutional position to influence the IGC's agenda and outcome through the use of instrumental leadership strategies. During the Finnish Presidency that prepared the agenda of the IGC, the Secretariat drafted the Presidency's IGC report together with the Presidency. Deputy Secretary-General de Boissieu was able to significantly shift the content of the original

Finnish report away from what he perceived was a small state and pro-Commission agenda, for example by preventing the Finns from attempting to widen the IGC agenda along the lines advocated by the Commission (Interviews NAT-6, NAT-7, EC-5, NAT-4). The Secretariat also tabled a paper that argued that while flexibility should be on the agenda, other issues such as defence should be excluded (Interview NAT-6).

As was seen above, the Secretariat was sidelined by the Portuguese Presidency. Despite this handicap, the Secretariat did convince the Portuguese Presidency to take up the question of creating specific legal bases for policies that had until then been adopted using Article 308 EC (Interview NAT-4). The Secretariat was interested in creating specific legal bases to both simplify the treaties, and bolster the total number of articles that would be transferred to QMV. No government was pushing for this, and without Secretariat advocacy it would not have been on the agenda (Interviews NAT-6, NAT-7). The debates on the subject were also dependent upon the legal expertise of the Secretariat's Legal Services, as they had knowledge of the current situation in Article 308 EC that no government possessed. But the final outcome proved to be a disappointment. Only one new legal base was created on provisions on financial and technical cooperation with non-developing countries (Galloway, 2001, pp. 109–11).

The Secretariat was able to play a key leadership role in the debates on the extension of QMV and flexibility during the French Presidency, as the issue was run from the French Representation in Brussels. The Secretariat drafted all of the texts on flexibility without much input or guidance from the Presidency, as the French did not fully understand the complex implications of the issue (Interviews NAT-6, NAT-7, EC-5).

On the extension of QMV, the French Presidency and Secretariat churned out a number of drafts that attempted to find a compromise that took into account the sensibilities of all parties (Galloway, 2001, pp. 101–11). But the Presidency and Secretariat made a tactical mistake in the issue, as they produced new drafts with such rapidity that governments were unable to develop a position on one text before another hit the table (Gray and Stubb, 2001, p. 12). As a result, delegations started rejecting texts out of hand, and the final result was much closer to the lowest common denominator than either party would have liked to see (Interview EC-5).

While the overall contours of reforms to the flexibility provisions were agreed by national delegates prior to Biarritz, the Secretariat ensured that a final deal could be reached by placating the fears of sceptical governments (Stubb, 2002, pp. 118, 121). The Secretariat created a legal formula that 'ring fenced' the core areas of the Community, which made it easier for sceptical governments to accept the easing of requirements on the use of flexibility (Galloway, 2001, p. 134; Interview NAT-4; Schout and Vanhoonacker, 2001). Piris also prevented the creation of a single flexibility article applicable for all three pillars, arguing that it could raise legal problems given the differing natures of the pillars (Galloway, 2001, pp. 139–40; Stubb, 2002, p. 120).

The Secretariat had particular success with several of its pet projects in the final weeks of the IGC. At an informal lunch in the Preparatory Group in Val Duchesse on 25 November, the Secretariat put forward several items where 'member states rolled over and took them without debate' (Interview NAT-4; EC-8). There were two reasons for this acquiescence. First, the issues were perceived to be low salience. Secondly, national experts did not take part in the lunch, and were therefore unable to explain potential problems to delegates (Interviews NAT-6, NAT-7). Among the Secretariat proposals that were accepted were: provisions on the financial consequences of the expiry of the ECSC Treaty; a declaration on inter-institutional agreements; Eurojust cooperation; and reforms of the court of auditors.

Rare examples of successful Secretariat brokerage were on the common trade policy and venue for European Council in the Nice Summit. Piris produced a legal formula for Article 133(6) EC that made trade in services a Community competence, but that explicitly excluded the sensitive areas of culture and shipping (Galloway, 2001, pp. 106–9; Interviews NAT-4, EC-10). This compromise pleased both pro-integrative governments, and those such as France which had specific problems that needed to be dealt with. On the venue for European Councils, de Boissieu wrote the declaration that stated that all European Council summits after 2002 would be held in Brussels, enabling Belgium to accept being given fewer Council votes than the Netherlands (Galloway, 2001, pp. 82–3, 158; Gray and Stubb, 2001, p. 21; Interviews NAT-6, NAT-7).

The Secretariat had much less success in other issues. Some participants point out that the Secretariat's perceived large state bias became apparent in their advice to the French Presidency on how to handle the issue of the re-weighting of Council votes (Interviews NAT-6, NAT-7, NAT-9). The Secretariat allegedly suggested that the French keep the issue open until the final stage, as it would both prevent consensus forming around the Commission's simple double majority proposal, and would potentially put smaller governments under pressure in Nice, forcing them to accept a re-weighting that favoured larger member states (ibid.). Whether this strategy was chosen solely by the French, or was based upon a suggestion from the Secretariat, the result of the strategy was the messy horse-trade in Nice.

After the provisional text of the Treaty of Nice was finally agreed upon, the Secretariat was delegated the job of tidying up the treaty – a job that turned out to be quite significant as the provisional treaty text was highly ambiguous. One of the best examples of the impact of the Secretariat was in the redrafting of Article 66 EC, which deals with cooperation between departments of national administrations, and between these and the Commission in visa, asylum and immigration policies. At Nice the heads of state and government agreed to move the article to QMV, but did not decide whether co-decision should apply. The provisional Treaty of Nice merely stated that the mechanism for Article 67 EC should be used. However, governments overlooked the fact that Article 67 EC called for co-decision. In the process of tidying up the treaty, the Secretariat on its own initiative first put in a declaration that stated that the provision would switch to QMV in 2004 *without* co-decision, and then changed this to a legally binding protocol in the final treaty text (Interview NAT-1) (SN 533/00, SN 534/00, Treaty of Nice, OJ C 80 of 10 March 2001). While the Secretariat based these changes upon legal arguments, it is not difficult to see this as an example of the Secretariat's interests in strengthening the Council contra other EU institutions.

Concluding, the Secretariat was with a few notable exceptions less successful in its attempts to provide leadership than in the 1996–7 IGC. While much of the Treaty of Nice came 'from the Secretariat's kitchen' (Interview EC-5), the Secretariat's role was primarily one of ensuring the efficiency of the negotiations, and there were few examples where Secretariat leadership shifted outcomes on the distributive dimension from what they otherwise would have been. The lack of Secretariat success was due both to de Boissieu's assertive style during the Portuguese Presidency and to the position that the Paris-based French Presidency granted the Secretariat.

Conclusion

The 2000 IGC was in many respects a worst-case scenario for EU institutions – particularly during the French Presidency. Both the Secretariat and Commission had considerably weaker roles than in previous IGCs, and while the EP had a stronger role than in the past, it was not listened to. Both the nature of the issues being negotiated and the relative simplicity of the negotiating situation opened few

TABLE 6.4   *Conclusions – leadership in the 2000 IGC*

Issue area	*Outcome*
Re-weighting of Council voting weights	• strong 'leadership' by French Presidency, assisted by Secretariat, which brokered several compromises in Nice Summit
Size and reform of the Commission	• strong leadership by French Presidency together with other 'G-5' governments, with smaller member states acting as brakes
Extension of co-decision	• Germany acted as leader, naturally backed by EP
Other institutional reforms	• ECJ reforms – strong Commission leadership role • simplification – Commission and EP attempts to simplify treaties blocked by significant opposition among governments • Commission and EP had some success, together with Belgium and Germany, in influencing the so-called 'post-Nice' debates
Extension of QMV	• QMV extension – French Presidency provided leadership, abetted by Secretariat • common trade policy – Commission and Finland acted as leaders, assisted by Secretariat, with France, Denmark and Greece as brakes
Flexibility	• key Secretariat intervention by filling in the details and placating fears of sceptical governments

opportunities for the provision of leadership by EU institutions. Yet both the Secretariat and Commission were able to influence outcomes in the IGC, although arguably on minor points. How was this possible?

The Secretariat was in several instances able to exploit its institutional position in the drafting process to gain influence over outcomes. But the Secretariat had three problems in the IGC. First, the issues being debated opened few opportunities for it to translate its comparative informational advantages into the provision of leadership. Secondly, during the Portuguese Presidency the Secretariat's interventions were sometimes too partial to its own preferences. Thirdly, the French Presidency as a large-state Presidency attempted to provide all of the types of leadership to the IGC itself – with predictable results. Whether a well-functioning Secretariat together with a small state Presidency could have produced a 'nicer' outcome in Nice is debatable, but the Secretariat would have at least strongly advised against the antagonistic tactics used by the French that were very close to leading to a negotiating breakdown.

For the European Parliament, even having a foot inside the door marked a major advance from previous treaty reform negotiations, where it had to follow the negotiations from the sidelines. But there were few indications that the EP was able to successfully exploit this new-found seat to provide leadership.

The Commission also had a weak role, and was not helped by inept negotiating tactics, although the Commission was able to gain significant influence upon the negotiation of reforms to the EU's legal system through the clever use of institutional politics.

In spite of this picture of a lack of Commission and EP influence, it can also be argued that the Commission and EP were in many respects following a long-term strategy, and that many of the Commission's and EP's proposals from the 2000 IGC were aimed more at the next round of treaty reform (see the next chapter). If we look at the agenda and outcome of the Constitutional Treaty negotiations, many of the Commission's and EP's radical ideas have become reality, such as splitting the treaties into constitutional and policy parts.

In general, none of the EU institutions was able to gain significant influence upon the Treaty of Nice, with their influence primarily on the margins. This was due to the nature of the issues, the relative simplicity of the negotiating situation, and how the negotiations were conducted. The Commission and EP did though learn the institutional lessons of the 2000 IGC, and fought to change the rules of the game prior to the next IGC. As will be seen in the next chapter, they succeeded in their efforts during the Belgian Presidency in 2001 in securing a more privileged institutional forum for their efforts to play leadership roles in the European Convention.

Chapter 7

Negotiating the Constitutional Treaty

Introduction – the European Parliament comes of age

Frustrated with the lack of more radical reform in the 2000 IGC in the face of the internal and external challenges facing Europe on the eve of enlargement, a strong coalition of actors began calling for more fundamental reforms of the Union. This resulted in declarations in the Treaty of Nice that mandated that a new IGC would be held by 2004. This led to the Laeken Declaration in December 2001 that called for the creation of a Convention on the Future of Europe to prepare the agenda for the next IGC. This Convention was held from March 2002 to June 2003 amongst representatives from governments, national parliaments, the EP and the Commission.

Somewhat surprisingly to many observers, the Convention proved successful in agreeing upon a draft Treaty establishing a Constitution for Europe (European Communities 2003). Within the Convention, EU institutions had stronger positions from which to provide leadership, leading to an outcome that was both more ambitious and simpler than it would have been if it had been negotiated by an IGC. After the Convention, a strong coalition of core governments signalled that they wanted the IGC to accept the Convention's text more-or-less *as is*. This then relegated the subsequent IGC to being a tidying-up exercise with the exception of a handful of contentious institutional issues in which several governments had a credible veto threat of the whole treaty if their demands were not accommodated.

This chapter investigates the impact of the radical change in how treaty reform is conducted. While the substantive negotiations of previous treaty reforms took place within the actual intergovernmental conference (see Chapters 3 to 6), the real negotiation of the Constitutional Treaty took place within the Convention, and the subsequent IGC was a 'rubber stamping' exercise with the exception of a half dozen sensitive institutional issues.

The findings highlight the importance of this shift to a context where the Commission and EP had many opportunities to provide leadership. The chapter first reviews what EU institutions wanted in the negotiations, and the leadership resources that they possessed. Thereafter the chapter discusses the impact of the shift of the negotiating context from the IGC to the Convention on the ability of EU institutions to provide leadership. Finally, the chapter clearly shows the impact of the choice of leadership strategy, for despite having similar positions the EP succeeded in providing leadership, while the Commission played itself out of influence through a combination of conflicting and extreme positions.

The course of the negotiation of the Constitutional Treaty

The agenda-setting phase – from Humboldt to Laeken

The magniloquently named debate on the 'Future of Europe' was sparked by a speech by German Foreign Minister Joschka Fischer on 12 May 2000, halfway through the 2000 IGC. Speaking in a personal capacity at Humboldt University in Berlin, Fischer shared his thoughts on how to move the integration process forward (Fischer, 2000). He argued that it would be increasingly difficult for a Union of thirty members to work, but that further movement forward was not possible within the existing framework. Fischer therefore called for the drafting of a constitution that would involve a more fundamental reform of the Union's institutional set-up, including 'full parliamentarization' through the creation of two European parliaments. The first chamber would include MEPs who would also have national seats. The second chamber would be a European senate, with directly elected senators from each member state. Echoing demands from the German *Länder*, Fischer saw the need for a clearer cut division of competences, and envisioned the creation of a 'lean European Federation' – stronger in the areas of its competences and understandable to citizens, but also with a strong role for nation-states.

Fischer's remarks were subsequently commented on by many heads of state and government, including French President Chirac and UK Prime Minister Blair. Chirac echoed the call for the creation of a constitution for Europe, where the Union would be a 'world power' with strong institutions, but his vision was less federal than Fischer's (Norman, 2003, pp. 12–13). Blair's vision was even more nation-state oriented, and called for the strengthening of the European Council and upgrading foreign and JHA policies (Blair,

2000). Blair did not want a constitution, but merely a 'statement of principles'.

As the 2000 IGC ground to a close, several unsatisfied governments pressed for another round of treaty reform. Under pressure from the German *Länder*, German Prime Minister Schroeder called for a future IGC to look at the question of the division of competences between the Union and the national and regional levels (Galloway, 2001, pp. 169–74; Ludlow, 2002, p. 51). Secondly, several governments wanted to adopt the Charter on Fundamental Rights that had been drafted by a Convention parallel with the IGC 2000 as a legally binding document, but were blocked by a British/Danish veto (Galloway, 2001, p. 174). Finally, two issues were on the agenda in an attempt to democratically legitimize the Union: the question of the simplification of the treaties to allow citizens to actually understand the treaties; and an increased role for national parliaments in European decision-making.

These demands led to the adoption of Declaration 23 on the future of the Union attached to the Treaty of Nice. The declaration addressed the four questions of the division of competences, the legal status of the Charter, the simplification of the treaties, and the role of national parliaments. An IGC was scheduled to be convened in 2004, prior to which the Swedish and Belgian Presidencies were to encourage 'wide-ranging discussions' in cooperation with the Commission and EP. The Belgian Presidency was entrusted with negotiating a declaration in December 2001 for the continuation of the process.

After lying relatively dormant during the Swedish Presidency in the spring of 2001, the debate was pushed energetically by the Belgians during their Presidency (Ludlow, 2002, pp. 53–74; Norman, 2003, p. 20). The debate resulted in the adoption of the Laeken Declaration at the Laeken European Council in December 2001 (European Council, 2001).

Beyond fleshing out the four points of the Nice declaration, the debate on the Declaration centred on finding a new method for preparing the coming IGC. After the failings of the traditional IGC method of using unanimity and concluding in a final make-or-break summit became all too apparent in Nice, a core of key actors said 'never again' (Closa, 2004a; Ludlow, 2002, p. 52). At the same time, the parallel Convention on the Charter on Fundamental Rights in 2000 was widely perceived to have been relatively successful. Pushed by federalist-oriented governments, together with the Commission and the EP, the Laeken European Council in December 2001 decided that a European Convention would be used to prepare the agenda of the next IGC (Jonsson and Hegeland, 2003; European

Parliament, 2000y, 2001b; Interview EC-16; Ludlow, 2002, pp. 57, 59; Norman, 2003, pp. 24–5).

Yet more sceptical governments also installed a range of institutional 'safeguards' to ensure that a possible federalist majority in the Convention did not 'run riot' (Ludlow, 2002, p. 59). Ministers ensured that national delegates outnumbered EU institutional delegates, and that the Convention would only produce 'options' instead of a ready-made constitution. Further, after the Convention, the Laeken Declaration envisioned a six-month 'cooling-off' period in order to prevent the Convention's text from achieving unstoppable momentum.

The European Convention – an attempt at democratizing treaty reform

The mandate of the European Convention as laid out in the Laeken Declaration called for the creation of a Convention composed of representatives of each national governments and two from the European Commission, 16 MEPs, and two national parliamentarians from each member state, along with governmental representatives and national parliamentarians from the accession states. There were also to be an equal number of alternates, but when the Convention started the alternates took part as full members.

After intense negotiations, it was decided that the Convention would be chaired by former French President Valery Giscard d'Estaing, assisted by vice-chairmen Giuliano Amato and Jean-Luc Dehaene (Ludlow, 2002, pp. 67–70). Representatives of each of the groupings were to form the Praesidium, which was envisioned to play a steering role similar to the EU Presidency in IGC negotiations. The Convention Secretariat was to be provided by seconded officials from the secretariats of the Commission, Council and EP.

The mandate for the Convention was relatively modest, namely, 'to consider the key issues arising for the Union's future development and try to identify the various possible responses' (European Council, 2001, p. 24). However, once the Convention started this modest goal was replaced by the much more ambitious goal of replacing the existing EU Treaties with a single, more effective and simplified Constitutional Treaty (Closa, 2004a; 2004b, pp. 186–7; Norman, 2003). It was hoped by many of the members of the Convention, the so-called 'conventionnels', that this new Constitution would then be accepted as is by national governments in the following IGC.

There were no formal voting procedures in the Convention. The rules of procedure stated that the final product of the Convention shall be adopted by consensus (CONV 9/02) but there were no votes held in the Convention plenary, and there were significant disagreements regarding the final outcome within the plenary, which resulted in a minority text being produced (CONF 773/03). However, a sizable majority of members indicated that they supported the final draft on the final day of the Convention plenary. Within the steering Praesidium, decisions on questions such as tabling draft texts were based upon consensus, although serious disagreements within the Praesidium did erupt during the final process, and some members were opposed to some of the final texts distributed by the Praesidium (see below).

The work of the Convention was divided into three phases: a listening phase that stretched from the start to the summer of 2002; a study phase during which working groups deliberated in the fall of 2002; and the final deliberation phase, which lasted from early January 2003 to the final sessions in June 2003.

After the initial ceremonial plenary meeting on 28 February 2002, six plenary meetings were held during the listening phase. Topics for plenary meetings included the roles of national parliaments, the division of competences, and more effective EU external action. Each debate was based on analytical papers drafted by the Convention Secretariat.

Debates in the Convention revealed two overall cleavages. One was the supranationalist/intergovernmentalist cleavage, and the other was the large/smaller member state cleavage on institutional issues that had developed during the 1990s.

During the summer of 2002, it was decided to create working groups that would produce reports, allowing negotiations to take place in smaller groupings that were more amiable to debate and discussion. Six working groups were originally created, but after further discussions four were added to the number. The ten working groups dealt with:

1 subsidiarity,
2 the Charter,
3 legal personality of the Union,
4 the role of national parliaments,
5 complementary competences,
6 economic governance,
7 external action,
8 defence,
9 simplification of the treaties, and
10 freedom, security and justice.

An eleventh group on Social Europe was created in late autumn 2002 after intense pressure from socialist and green conventionnels (Norman, 2003, pp. 125–7). Each working group was chaired by a member of the Praesidium. The groups drafted a report to the plenary after a series of meetings and hearings that summarized the areas of consensus achieved, and possible proposals and options to move forward. Notably, no working group was set up to discuss institutional questions.

During the autumn of 2002, several governments including France and Germany chose to replace their representatives with their foreign ministers. But while this illustrated that the Convention was not just a talking forum, and was something to be taken seriously by governments, the tactic backfired, as none of the foreign ministers spent enough time in Brussels to make an impact (Jonsson and Hegeland, 2003; Norman, 2003, pp. 155–9). In contrast, the UK kept its junior ministerial appointment, Peter Hain. In all accounts Hain is seen as very active *and* influential in the debates, with some participants stating that Hain was 'everywhere' (Interview NAT-19; Jonsson and Hegeland, 2003, p. 22; Menon, 2003; Norman, 2003, p. 55)

The Praesidium tabled a skeleton text of the draft Constitutional Treaty in October 2002 (CONV 369/03). The text was drafted within the Convention Secretariat, under the guidance of chairman Giscard d'Estaing. The draft outlined a three-part treaty, with an institutional part, a section outlining Union policies, and a final section of general and final provisions. The draft included proposed brief texts for some of the first 46 articles in the institutional section. The articles set out briefly the definition and objectives of a Union, including proposed names for the Union ranging from United States of Europe to the European Community. Innovations included stating that: the Union would administer common competences 'on a federal basis' (draft Article 1); the Union had a single legal personality (draft Article 4); the conferral principle that competences not conferred on the Union rest with member states (draft Article 8); the pillar structure would be removed (draft Article 14), and legislative debates in the Council would be public (draft Article 36). Several of Giscard's own personal priorities were controversially included in the draft, including a Congress of Peoples of Europe (draft Article 19).

The plenary welcomed the skeleton text, with key EP representatives especially excited (CONV 378/02 and verbatim summary). But the cleavage on the balance of power between the supranational Community and governments was very apparent in the debates on the draft.

Another event in the autumn and winter of 2002 was the tabling of several 'freelance' constitutions by prominent members of the EP delegation, including Elmar Brok and Andrew Duff, and by the Commission in December (see below in the section on Commission and EP leadership for more).

The reports from working groups were presented to the plenary and debated in the autumn and winter of 2002/2003. The reports were not intended to be final conclusions, but merely a basis for discussions and a source of inspiration for the Convention Secretariat when producing draft texts.

The final deliberation phase was kick-started by a key Franco-German proposal on institutions in January 2003 (CONV 489/03). The proposal attempted to bridge the gap between the German position of strengthening the Union through stronger supranational institutions, and the French goal of a strengthened government-based Union. The text spoke of creating a long-term Union President heading a stronger European Council, the creation of a foreign minister sitting in both the Council and Commission, majority voting in most foreign policy matters, a Commission President elected by the EP, and the extension of parliamentary co-decision.

The proposal met with strong negative reactions from many conventionnels (*Agence Europe*, 16.01.03, pp. 5–6; 17.01.03, p. 4; 18.01.03, p. 4; 21.01.03, p. 4; *Economist*, 18.01.03, pp. 27–8). MEPs were especially vehement in their comments, seeing for example the creation of a permanent President of the European Council as a strongly intergovernmentalist element that would in the words of Elmar Brok 'be the beginning of the end of Community Europe' (*Agence Europe*, 16.01.03, p. 5). Yet the Franco-German proposal set the parameters for further debates on institutional questions (Norman, 2003, p. 180). The proposal was then echoed in a more intergovernmentalist British–Spanish paper in February (CONV 591/03).

But the small-larger member state cleavage was also provoked by the Franco-German proposal, and the draft texts later prepared by Giscard and the Convention Secretariat. These concerns led to the production of a paper from sixteen smaller governments dated 28 March 2003 that called for the preservation of the rotating Presidency, keeping one Commissioner per member state, and in general reinforcing the Community method (CONV 646/03).

By early 2003 there was broad support in the Convention for an extension of co-decision and QMV, and maintaining the general institutional balance between EU institutions and member states (Norman, 2003, p. 181). Another development in early 2003 was the decision to create a team of legal experts drawn from the secretariats of the Commission, Council and EP to make so-called 'technical adjustments' to the policy section of the draft Constitutional Treaty – what would become part III (CONV 529/03). While the overall structure of the EU Treaties and the institutions would be dramatically overhauled, the actual policy sections of the existing treaties would be merely reordered and transposed into the Constitutional Treaty without significant revisions.

The drafting of articles for part I and the general and final provisions took place in two stages. First, draft texts that fleshed out the components of the October skeleton draft were tabled from February to April. After debates in the plenary and a flood of proposed amendments from conventionnels, the Convention Secretariat and chairmen drafted a third generation of texts that incorporated changes backed by strong majorities in Convention.

The first set of draft texts for part I dealt with the first 16 articles on the Union's values, objectives and competences (CONV 528/03). The text kept the controversial reference to federalism from the original skeleton draft. On the issue of competences, the text stated that the Union shall act within the competences conferred upon it *by the Constitution* (draft Article 8). Draft Article 11 listed the areas where the Union had exclusive competence, including *all* aspects of the common commercial policy. The draft also enshrined the supremacy principle established by the ECJ in the early 1960s (draft Article 9). Reactions to the draft texts ranged from very positive from MEPs to strong opposition from French representatives on the issue of the common commercial policy, and the UK objected to the articles on competences and the use of the 'F-word' (Norman, 2003, pp. 198–201). The draft was then the subject of hundreds of proposed amendments (see CONV 574/03).

The next set of draft articles were on the proposed protocol on subsidiarity and national parliaments (CONV 579/03), which built upon working group reports (CONV 286/02 and 353/02). The protocol called for the creation of a 'yellow card' system, where one-third of the Union's national parliaments could ask the Commission to review a proposal if they saw that it did not comply with the subsidiarity principle established in the Treaty of Maastricht. The principle states that actions should be taken at the level where results can best be achieved. However, the Commission in the protocol was *not obliged* to withdraw the proposal.

Texts on the Union's instruments were tabled by the Praesidium on 26 February 2003 (CONV 571/03). Building on the consensus of the working group on simplification, the text called for: the re-designation of Union legal acts from Regulations, Directives and so on to European Laws and framework laws (draft Article 24); using co-decision as a general rule (draft Article 25); and the delegation of powers to the Commission to enact 'delegated regulations' (draft Article 27) (see Norman, 2003, pp. 203–4). The texts were welcomed by the plenary, although many minor amendments were proposed (see CONV 609/1/03).

Important texts were produced in March 2003 on the Union's finances (CONV 602/03) and the so-called democratic life of the Union (CONV 650/03), which related to issues of transparency, political participation and the European Ombudsman. On finances, the major innovation was increasing the power of the EP in the budgetary procedure, both as regards giving the EP the final say, and by extending EP powers to all of the budget, including so-called 'compulsory expenditure', which deals primarily with CAP spending. This was strongly opposed to by a coalition of governments led by France who feared that the EP would push for cutting agricultural spending (see CONV 643/03; Norman, 2003, pp. 211–12). More complex and technical issues relating to the budgetary procedure, along with the system of Union revenues (own resources) were delegated to two discussion circles in March (CONV 612/03, 654/03).

The draft general and final provisions were presented on 4 April (CONV 647/03). Important and controversial clauses were the revision clauses (draft Article F), which stated that existing procedures for IGCs (Article 48 EU) should be kept, but that future IGCs should be preceded by conventions. Not surprisingly, MEPs tabled amendments suggesting that the EP should have a stronger role in IGCs, and they were supported by many other conventionnels (CONV 673/03). The Praesidium also toyed with the idea of allowing the Constitutional Treaty to enter into force before all member states had ratified it, but the draft text only suggested that the European Council would 'take up the issue' if four-fifths of the member states had ratified and one or more members were having difficulties. However, as the Praesidium was unable to finish the drafting of part IV by the June deadline, the proposal did not make it into the final Convention text (Norman, 2003, p. 217).

Most of the elements of the draft Constitutional Treaty had been agreed by April. Consensus had been reached on issues such as: clarifying and categorizing Union competences; incorporating the Charter as a legally binding document; simplifying and consolidating the Union's legal instruments; giving national parliaments a stronger role; granting the Union a single legal personality; and replacing the pillar structure with a single treaty structure with special exceptions for sensitive areas of the former second and third pillars. But the sensitive debates on institutional questions and foreign policy loomed on the horizon.

The institutional debate had been postponed by Giscard until April. Giscard had wanted to grant governments the opportunity to debate institutional questions prior to his tabling of draft texts in the Praesidium. Giscard had planned to do this at the March European Council Summit, but the Iraq crisis/war intervened, and the debate was postponed to the Athens Summit on 16 April 2003 (Interview EC-23). On the institutional question, key questions were: how leadership would be provided in the European Council and Council of Ministers; what the size of the Commission and the method for appointing the Commission President should be; what powers were to be given to the foreign minister, and the degree to which he/she would operate within the Commission; and other questions such as whether a Congress of Peoples should be created.

Giscard's draft institutional articles were given to the Praesidium for approval on 22 April 2003 (the texts are reproduced in Norman, 2003, pp. 343–8). The text was close to the Franco-German and British–Spanish proposals. Giscard called for the creation of a strong President of European Council that would 'prepare, chair and drive', and would be supported by a powerful cabinet (draft Article 15a). The vice-president would chair the Council, replacing the rotating Presidency (draft Article 17a). The draft also called for the creation of a Legislative Council, and the creation of a foreign minister that had a seat both in the Council and in the Commission, but was closest to the Council (draft Articles 17a, 19). The draft called for the creation of a system of simple dual majority based upon 50 per cent of member states representing 60 per cent of the Union's population (draft Article 17b). The idea of a Congress of Peoples popped up again, although by titling it 'Article X to be inserted into the title on the Union's democratic life', it looked like the article was a negotiating ploy that could be jettisoned when opportune. Finally, on the size of the Commission, Giscard's draft echoed earlier French proposals for a small Commission (see Chapter 6), but it also gave the EP the ability to approve by a three-fifth majority a candidate for Commission President that had been chosen by the European Council (Article 18a).

The strong negative reaction within the Praesidium towards Giscard's draft will be discussed in more detail below. Here it is suffice to say that the MEP and Commission representatives in the Praesidium succeeded in removing the most intergovernmental elements from the draft texts approved by the Praesidium and put to the plenary on 23 April 2003 (CONV 691/03), including weakening the European Council President and reintroducing the rotating Presidency of the Council. The Spanish governmental representative in the Praesidium complained about the changes to the Nice compromise on voting weights, but only succeeded in getting the objection mentioned in the introductory text of the proposal (Norman, 2003, p. 230; CONV 691:03, p. 1). Not surprisingly, the Congress of Peoples was shot down, once again.

The draft institutional text generated a plethora of proposed amendments from conventionnels, many of which argued for the preservation of the status quo on points such as the rotating Presidency and size of the Commission (see CONV 709/03). But most also agreed that the text was 'negotiable', although the smaller governments were uneasy about certain elements (Norman, 2003, pp. 240–1).

On foreign and security matters, the split into what US Secretary of Defense Rumsfeld had termed 'old' and 'new' Europe on the Iraq issue spilled over into the Convention, and made reform more acute in order to make the Union's foreign policy articles more effective, as well as created strong demands for more flexibility in Union foreign policy (Norman, 2003, p. 186). The external action articles produced for the plenary on 24 April 2003 were based upon the reports of the working groups on external action and defence (CONV 459/02, 461/02). The draft articles called for the creation of a 'double-hatted' Minister of Foreign Affairs, with responsibilities both in the Council and in the Commission. In foreign and security policy, decision-making would be by unanimity, with the option that the European Council can unanimously decide to allow majority voting in specific areas, and abstention is also possible. Flexible cooperation was made possible in security and defence, including the possible creation of a mutual defence clause for participating governments (draft Articles 20–21). The texts on the common commercial policy were relatively moderate, and did call for QMV in all areas of external negotiations as wanted by a majority in both the working group and plenary, although the text kept the categorization of trade in services as an exclusive Union competence despite French protests (see comments, CONV 685/03, pp. 53–4).

After intense pressure from the UK, the final articles on CFSP shifted towards the UK position. For example, the clause in the April draft article that stated that QMV would be used in joint proposals from the foreign minister and Commission was deleted due to British fears of Commission involvement in foreign policy (Norman, 2003, pp. 255–6).

After a three-day Praesidium meeting held on 21 to 24 May 2003, the third generation of Praesidium draft texts were tabled in late May in the form of revised parts I to IV (CONV 724 to 727/03). Significantly, the section on the institutions in part I was unchanged from the April draft owing to splits within the Praesidium on whether to keep the Nice compromise or not (Norman, 2003, p. 248). Important changes to part I included: the removal of the 'F-word' from the first article; opening for the possibility for creating European taxes or other new forms of revenue (draft Article I-53); and giving the multi-annual financial framework a treaty base (draft Article I-54). The Charter was to be attached to the Constitutional Treaty as part II, although the UK was still concerned about the impact of the Charter on its legal system.

Both Poland and Spain made their concerns regarding the revision of the Nice compromise known in Convention. In early 2003, then Spanish representative Palacio tabled an amendment to the provisions on qualified majority voting that called for keeping the Nice formula, which was echoed by other conventionnels, including the UK government representative (CONV 709/03). After Palacio was replaced by Dastis in March as the representative of the Spanish government, he clearly stated in both the 15 May plenary and the 21–4 May Praesidium meeting that Spain could not accept a revision of the Nice compromise, and that any revision would lead to a 'long and difficult Intergovernmental Conference' (Norman, 2003, p. 262; Interview NAT-26). Dastis succeeded in mobilizing the support of nine governments for a proposal against tampering with the Nice compromise (CONV 766/03).

But Giscard, backed by a strong majority in the plenary, pushed for revising Nice. Giscard stated that 'If we stick with Nice, the constitutional part of the Convention is pointless' (Norman, 2003, p. 271). In the revised institutional draft of 31 May 2003, the simple double majority proposal was kept despite Polish and Spanish protests (CONV 770/03).

As the Convention went into its final weeks in June 2003, the two key questions were whether the Nice compromise on institutions would be kept, and whether the UK would stay on board. First, a broad majority in the plenary, led by the triumvirate chairmen pushed for the revision of Nice that made its way into the final draft Constitutional Treaty (Brown, 2003; Interview EC-23; Norman, 2003, pp. 290–3). Secondly, the UK started clearly signalling that it had 'red-lines' on issues such as the 'F-word', along with the introduction of majority voting on foreign, tax and social policy (*Guardian*, 28.05.03; *Le Monde*, 30.05.03, p. 4; Menon, 2003; Norman, 2003, pp. 269–71). While the final draft

Constitutional Treaty did open for majority voting, the word 'federal' was kept out.

In the final days of the Convention, national and European parliamentarians organized along party lines attempted to push the draft towards a slightly more pro-integrative outcome, including proposals for making treaty revision easier and making QMV the general rule in *all* policy areas (*EU Observer*, 12.06.03; Halligan, 2003; Norman, 2003, pp. 290–3). The final texts did not make QMV the general rule nor was treaty revision made easier. But to please the pro-integrative majority in the Convention, Giscard introduced a *passerelle* (general bridging clause), whereby the Council could agree by unanimity to transfer a policy area to qualified majority voting (CONV 797/03, 802/03, 811/03). The final draft landed between the large government position by creating a permanent President of the European Council, and the smaller government position by keeping a form of rotating Presidency for the Council and introducing an equal rotation within a downsized Commission.

After governmental representatives from Poland, Spain and the UK laid down their swords in the Convention's final days, choosing instead to fight for their red-lines in the coming IGC, the Convention accepted the final draft Constitutional Treaty to the sounds of Beethoven's 'Ode to Joy' echoing through the EP's plenary room (*Agence Europe*, 14.06.03, pp. 3–6; *Financial Times*, 16.06.03; *Guardian*, 19.06:03; Interviews NAT-24, NAT-25, EC-19; *Le Monde*, 15–16.06.03, p. 2). The final text was then approved by the Thessaloniki European Council Summit as a 'good starting point' for the IGC (*Agence Europe*, 21.06.03, pp. 3–4; European Council, 2003, p. 2). Yet in reality, with the exception of the handful of sensitive Nice-related issues and the British 'red-line' issues, the IGC would in effect merely accept a tidied-up version of the Convention's text (Interviews NAT-17, NAT-26, EC-19).

The 2003–4 IGC – from the Italian job to a final deal

The IGC 2003–4 was convened by the Italian Presidency on 4 October 2003. The IGC was conducted among governmental representatives from the then 15 member states and 10 acceding states, along with observers from the three candidate states (Bulgaria, Romania and Turkey), two observers from the European Parliament, and the European Commission as a non-voting participant.

The Italian Presidency planned for the IGC to be concluded in December 2003 at the Brussels European Council Summit meeting, and then after translation to all Union languages and a judicial cleaning-up, the Constitutional Treaty was planned to be signed in a pompous ceremony in Rome in May 2004.

In contrast with previous IGCs, most of the negotiations in the IGC 2003–4 were held at the political levels of Foreign Ministers or heads of state and government. The Italian Presidency, backed by a German-led coalition of the six founding member states, used the draft Constitutional Treaty as the basic text for the IGC, and only tolerated serious negotiations on issues where governments were prepared to veto the whole treaty (*Agence Europe*, 09.09.03, p. 5, 03.10.03, pp. 6–10, 07.10.03, pp. 5–7; *FT* 03.10.03, p. 3, 04.10.03, p. 1; Interviews EC-19, EC-22, NAT-17, NAT-26; *Le Monde*, 04.10.03, p. 6). In order to clean up the draft Constitutional Treaty in relation to points of law, the Italian Presidency created a working group of legal experts chaired by the head of the Council Secretariat's Legal Services, Jean-Claude Piris. A 'Focal Points' group of senior officials was later created to prepare the ministerial meetings in the IGC.

Debates on the IGC only took place in a handful of contentious issues, primarily related to the size of the Commission and the re-weighting of Council votes. Smaller governments were strongly interested in keeping 'their' Commissioner and the rotating Presidency (*Agence Europe*, 9.09.03, p. 5; *FT*, 03.10.03, p. 3; *EU Observer*, 24.09.03), while Poland and Spain wanted to go back to the Nice compromise on Council voting weights, which disproportionally favoured them (*Agence Europe*, 01.10.03, p. 5, 03.10.05, pp. 6–10; European Parliament IGC Monitoring Group; *Le Monde*, 04.10.03:6). The UK was concerned about the extension of majority voting in several sensitive issues, including taxation and foreign policy (*Agence Europe*, 03.10.05, pp. 6–10; *Le Monde* ,11.09.03, p. 7).

Most issues on the IGC agenda were minor second-order issues dealing with tidying up the draft Constitutional Treaty text, for example by fleshing out the incomplete text from the Convention on matters such as the powers and position of the Foreign Minister, and the formations and form of Presidency for the Council (Interview EC-26). The negotiation of these issues was not contentious, and took place in a problem-solving environment. Another cluster of issues dealt with removing unwanted EP 'fingerprints' from the text. This was especially evident as regards the budgetary powers of the EP, where ECOFIN ministers attempted to reduce EP powers in October and November.

During the first two months of the IGC, the Italian Foreign Ministry together with the Council Secretariat guided the negotiations effectively on the minor points (Interview EC-19, EC-26). The idea of creating a Legislative Council was the first element of the

Convention's text that was removed in the IGC (CIG 1/03; Federal Trust, 2003a, p. 3; Interviews NAT-26, EC-22). Parallel with the political meetings, the Piris group undertook the legal 'tidying up', but the group did not deal with political questions (Interview EC-22). The group concluded its work in November with the production of a revised Constitutional Treaty, where minor inconsistencies and repetitions were removed (CIG 51/03).

In what was planned to be the IGC end-game, the Italian Presidency tabled a compromise proposal on most of the minor issues prior to an informal Foreign Minister conclave meeting to be held on 28–9 November 2003 (CIG 52/1/03 REV 1). The Naples conclave tied up agreement in most of the minor issues (*EU Observer*, 29.10.03; Ludlow, 2004b), which were then laid down as draft treaty text by the Presidency (CIG 60/03 ADD 1). But the handful of contentious institutional issues was bypassed, with the strategy of the Italian Presidency being to put governments under pressure in the final European Council Summit on 12–13 December 2003.

There were no real negotiations during the Italian Presidency on the contentious issues (*Agence Europe*, 17.10.03, pp. 4–6; Interview EC-26). Luxembourg Prime Minister Juncker clearly saw the danger with the Italian strategy when he stated that 'What particularly worries me is that meeting after meeting, the different positions become even more rigid because of the repetition' (*Economist*, 20.12.00, pp. 71–3). Positions hardened in the week prior to the Summit, with France and Germany warning that they wanted to keep the Convention text, and that they would go forward with ad hoc cooperation if the text was not approved by the IGC, whereas both Spain and Poland had backed themselves into a corner and were unable to step down on their insistence that the Nice compromise on vote re-weighting should be preserved (*EU Observer*, 13.12.03; *FT*, 10.12.03; *The Observer*, 14.12.03, pp. 16–17; *Süddeutsche Zeitung*, 09.12.03).

Italian Prime Minister Berlusconi took over the reigns of the Presidency in the final two weeks, utilizing Rome-based officials who had not followed the IGC, and he decided to *not* utilize the Council Secretariat as a source of advice and assistance (Interview EC-22). Berlusconi did not produce different compromise options for leaders prior to the Summit, and instead chose to keep a 'secret solution in his pocket' (Ludlow, 2004b). The Presidency paper only listed a summary of positions on the contentious issues prior to Brussels (CIG 60/03 ADD 2).

As the heads of state and government arrived in Brussels, the Italian Presidency had no game plan (Ludlow, 2004b). At a working lunch held as the summit started, Berlusconi decided to initiate discussion of IGC matters by proposing to talk about 'women and football' (Economist, 12.20.03, pp. 71–3; Ludlow, 2004b; *The Observer*, 14.12.03, pp. 16–17), managing to insult Polish Prime Minister Miller and German Chancellor Schröeder in the process, not to mention the women present.

In confessionals held by the Presidency in the afternoon with delegations, the Italian Presidency did not even have a schedule for meetings, forcing delegates to hang around for hours waiting (Interview NAT-21). A scheduled 6 pm plenary meeting started at 6.30 and lasted only 45 minutes, in which Berlusconi offered no compromise solutions or suggestions to move forward (Ludlow 2004b). After another wave of confessionals that lasted until 1.30 am, it became increasingly clear that neither side would compromise on the question of the re-weighting of votes (Ludlow, 2004b).

After Berlusconi did not even show up to lead further meetings on Saturday morning, the Italian Foreign Minister took over the confessionals (Ludlow, 2004b). At 11 am, Italy convened a small ad hoc group of 'friends of the Presidency' numbering Denmark, Greece, Hungary, the Netherlands and the UK. The group was asked to find a compromise (Interview NAT-21). Compromises that were floated included retaining the Nice formula while giving Germany two extra Council votes, deferring a change until 2014, and raising the blocking thresholds (*Independent*, 15.12.03, p. 10). Parallel with this, French President Chirac and German Chancellor Schröder began holding bilateral meetings, where France met with Spain, and Germany with the Polish. After the two leaders saw that there was no way forward they met with Blair, and the three then asked Berlusconi to close the summit in a dignified way instead of letting it degenerate into a Nice-like brawl (*Independent*, 15.12.03, p. 10; Interview NAT-17; Ludlow, 2004b).

The collapse of the IGC talks in the Brussels European Council Summit of 12–13 December 2003 clearly illustrated the importance of leadership, or more correctly the lack of it in an EU of 25. There are conflicting accounts of reasons for breakdown, with many pointing to Berlusconi as the culprit. But behind his handling of the negotiations were fundamental disagreements on the key institutional questions that had not been reconciled prior to the Summit (Economist, 12.20.03, pp. 71–3; Interviews NAT-26, EC-26).

After the Christmas break, the Irish Presidency took up the baton and started quiet consultations with other governments to see whether the pieces could be picked up after the Italian job (*EU Observer*, 19.01.04, 21.01.04; Irish Presidency, 2004; Interview EC-26). The Irish Presidency worked closely with the Council Secretariat (Interview EC-22, EC-26).

After a series of meetings with governments, and especially after the newly elected Spanish government and the Polish government sent signals that they could agree a compromise in February and early March (*EU Observer*, 17.03.04, 19.03.04), the Irish Presidency suggested to the March 2004 European Council Summit that the IGC should be relaunched, with the Irish assessment of the state of play being that agreement was possible by June (Interview EC-26; *Irish Times*, 25.03.04, 26.03.04; see CIG 70/04).

The Irish Presidency produced a series of papers for ministerial meetings in May and June that further cleared up several minor issues (CIG 79/04, 80/04, 81/04), including opening for the possibility of future further reforms of the Council Presidency (draft Article I-23, CIG 79/04), weakening the powers of the European Public Prosecutor and strengthening the veto option in CFSP because of British concerns (draft Article III-175, III-201(2), CIG 80/04), and narrowed the scope of possible QMV in taxation (draft Article III-62(2)), social security (III-21), and in the common commercial policy (draft Article 217(7), CIG 80/04).

On the main sensitive institutional issues, the Irish Presidency in April and May continued with its quiet consultations, attempting to find possible compromises (Interview EC-26). The Irish Presidency did not allow the negotiations to degenerate into a repetition of positions, but sought to narrow the parameters for compromise by testing different draft compromise texts with key delegations (ibid.). Besides the Nice-related issues, the issue of economic governance came to the fore in the spring of 2004. After France and Germany succeeded in blocking an attempt by the Commission to get the Council to use the excessive deficit procedure against them in November 2003, France and Germany were interested in weakening the provisions in the Convention text on the Commission's role. While the Convention text called for the Commission to make a formal 'proposal' to the Council on whether an excessive deficit exists, the final text ended with the Commission tabling a mere 'recommendation' (Compare Article III-76, European Communities, 2003 and same article in CIG 86/04; see also *FT*, 14.06.04; Grevi, 2004, p. 10; Interview EC-26).

The EU leaders arriving in Brussels for the final Summit were more determined to reach agreement after the poor results in the EP elections held on 10–13 June 2004, which saw both low turnout and victory for Eurosceptics in many countries (*FT*, 15.06.04, p. 1). In the final tinkering on the issue of re-weighting of votes, additional thresholds were introduced along with numerous qualifications to the simple double majority principle. For example, to prevent Germany together with two other large states from forming a blocking minority, the final article states that a blocking minority must encompass at least four states (Article I-24). Despite protests from the smaller states, it was clear in the spring of 2004 that the solution on the size of the Commission would be a reduced Commission (Interview EC-22). The Irish Presidency landed on the size of two-thirds of member states, which proved to be digestible by all.

Owing to careful preparations from the Irish Presidency, the parameters for a compromise agreement were already set, and when the final text landed on the table at 10.30 pm on 18 June, the text was met with a mere nod of approval (Interview EC-26). Three years of debate on the future of Europe ended almost in silence, and the press was more interested in the battle over the appointment of the next Commission President than in the new Constitutional Treaty (see Table 7.1).

What did EU institutions want in the Constitutional Treaty negotiations?

The Commission – another go at a more effective enlarged Union

The basic position of the Commission throughout the negotiations was to fight for a simpler and stronger Europe, making the Community method the basic rule in all policy areas – even for future treaty reforms.

In the Commission opinion from May 2002, and later in its opinion for the IGC, the Commission trumpeted well-worn positions, such as making QMV and co-decision the general rule, and removing the pillar structure of the treaties (European Commission, 2002a, 2003). The Commission argued further that its role in economic governance should be strengthened (ibid.). The Commission wanted the EU Charter to be incorporated into the treaties as a legally binding document.

In decision-making, the Commission reiterated its past proposal for a simple double majority voting system in the Council. Finally, the Commission was interested in safeguarding its own institutional prerogatives, and for example argued that a possible foreign minister should be a joint post between the Council and Commission, and not be a Council operative within the Commission.

But the Commission had conflicting positions on many issues, and on several issues flopped back and forth. On the issue of the size of the Commission, the Commission went from supporting a smaller

TABLE 7.1   *The outcome of the Constitutional negotiations – A Treaty establishing a Constitution for Europe*

Issue area	Outcome
Treaty structure	• replaces existing EU Treaties with a single Union, where the pillar structure is replaced by a single pillar with special provisions for foreign, security and defence policies, along with certain aspects of the area of freedom, security and justice • Charter of Fundamental Rights incorporated as a legally binding text • clarification of Union competences, and simplified set of legal instruments • the Union is given a single legal personality
Institutional changes	• creation of Union Foreign Minister, merging the tasks of the High Representative and the Commissioner for External Affairs. The minister is assisted by a new European External Action Service • Commission size to be reduced to two-thirds of the number of member states in 2014 • European Council established as separate institution, chaired by a permanent President appointed to two-and-a-half year terms • six-month rotation of Presidency preserved within a form of team Presidency held by three governments • Council voting procedure changed to a simple double majority with a majority being 55 per cent of the states representing 65 per cent of the Union's population, although it must also represent at least 15 member states. Blocking minority must consist of at least four states

$\rightarrow$

Commission back to supporting one Commissioner per member state (European Commission, 2003; Norman, 2003, p. 266). The disastrous conflicting Commission positions became apparent when the Commission on the same day in December 2002 tabled a proposal calling for a radical federalized Europe, and a set of more pragmatic solutions. See below for more.

→	
Issue area	*Outcome*
Institutional changes (*continued*)	• adoption of a general *passerelle* clause, allowing for a unanimous decision by the European Council to transfer a policy area in Part III to QMV • increased transparency of Union law-making • increased role of national parliaments in law-making, for example by allowing one-third to raise objections to the breach of the subsidiarity principle by a Commission proposal • allows the Council to create by unanimity a European Public Prosecutor to combat crimes affecting the financial interests of the Union
Extension of QMV and co-decision	• co-decision extended to most Union law-making, and the EP is given increased powers in the budgetary procedure, including for agricultural spending • QMV made general rule, with exceptions in several issues, including taxation and foreign policy
External action	• compilation of existing texts into single chapter • increased the possibility of 'permanent structured cooperation' in field of defence, enabling group of states to cooperate more closely

Source: Treaty establishing a Constitution for Europe, C16 8712/04 Rev 2, Brussels, 29 October 2004.

The European Parliament – for the creation of a European Constitution

The EP in its resolution prior to the start of the Convention called for the drafting of a European Constitution with a single pillar structure including CFSP and the remaining third pillar issues (European

Parliament, 2001). The EP called for the consolidation of all areas of external affairs into a single chapter, and for the creation of a single legal personality of Union. The former third pillar issues relating to justice and home affairs were to be transferred to a genuine area of freedom, security and justice, where the Community method would be the rule. The EP wanted to establish a European Public Prosecutor, and also advocated the simplification of legislative procedures. Finally, the EP argued for an increase in its own powers, especially in the budgetary procedure and as regards election of the Commission President (European Parliament, 2001).

During the Convention, prominent MEP representatives had quite differing views, ranging from Duff's strongly federal vision of Europe in his 'Model Constitution for a Federal Union of Europe' (CONV 234/02) to Eurosceptical Jens Peter Bonde's vision of a more intergovernmental and restrained Union. But as the Convention progressed, most MEP representatives, including Duff, converged around a more pragmatic vision of a Constitutional Treaty, although they fought against the strengthening of the intergovernmental elements of the Union, including the creation of a strong European Council President. For more, see below in the section on leadership of the EP.

During the IGC 2003–4, the main goal of the EP was to preserve the Convention's draft as is (European Parliament, 2003b). In particular, the EP was interested in preserving its new-found powers in the budgetary procedure, and the simple double majority system for Council voting (*Agence Europe*, 24.05.04).

The Council Secretariat – tidying up the Constitutional Treaty

The Council Secretariat did not take part in the Convention, and as such did not have views on the issues. However there were certain issues that were of concern to the Secretariat, such as merging the High Representative with the Commissioner for external affairs – something that High Representative Solana did not approve of (Interview NAT-21).

In the IGC, head of Legal Services Jean-Claude Piris was not satisfied with certain elements ranging from details such as the use of roman numerals for the four parts of the Constitutional Treaty prior to the article number, to concerns about the practicality of the Legislative Council (Interviews EC-16, EC-22).

Changes in the leadership resources of the EU institutions since 2000

The material resources of the EU institutions

There were few relevant material resources available to the EU institutions during the Constitutional Treaty negotiations. Budgetary concessions were a potential option that could be used to secure Polish and Spanish acceptance of a final compromise during the IGC, but this was never a realistic option. Any *increase* of structural fund spending post-enlargement was simply not a realistic option, although the preservation of veto power for structural fund spending was an important element in Spanish acceptance of the final deal. During the IGC, France and Germany attempted to link the conclusion of the IGC with the coming negotiation of the financial perspective, with the prospect being that if Spain and Poland did not compromise, France and Germany would fight for drastic cuts in structural spending (*Agence Europe*, 08.10.03, p. 6). But the Commission explicitly denied that there was any link, and stated that were would be no financial 'blackmail' that would be used against Poland and Spain.

The informational advantages of the EU institutions

The Commission enjoyed strong informational advantages in the Convention vis-à-vis other actors, especially national parliamentarians, but on some issues even governmental representatives. The informational advantages of the Commission were particularly evident vis-à-vis national parliamentarians, who did not have experience dealing with EU matters nor have the back-up of the Commission civil service or a national government (Interviews EC-10, EC-12, EC-16, NAT-26; Norman, 2003, pp. 31–2, 49). Governmental representatives could draw on national ministries, but only the largest governments could compete with the Commission as regards EU expertise (Interviews NAT-12, NAT-25). Within the Praesidium, the two Commission representatives had twelve officials provided to assist them (Norman, 2003, pp. 202, 267).

If we canvass the topics dealt with in the negotiations, the only issue in which the Commission did not have substantive and legal expertise was in aspects of foreign and defence policy that have traditionally been the remit of national governments. And in general, Convention participants agreed that the Commission was a useful and often vital source of substantive and legal expertise (Interviews NAT-15, NAT-17, EC-23; also Norman, 2003, pp. 31–2, 202, 267). Commissioner

Vitorino, as Commissioner for Justice and Home Affairs (JHA), was for example able to speak with considerable weight in the sensitive aspects of JHA relating to cooperation in criminal matters, and issues relating to the possible incorporation of the EU Charter into the final treaty (Interviews NAT-15, EC-23, Norman, 2003, p. 31–2).

Another advantage of the Commission was the depth of knowledge and experience with treaty reform negotiations that it had acquired, especially at the civil servant level. In the 1996–7 and 2000 IGCs, and in the European Convention, the Commission created a task force of officials to back up the Commission representatives. Many of these officials had dealt with several treaty reform negotiations, giving them strong comparative advantages vis-à-vis national civil servants who, because of frequent rotations in national foreign ministries or because they were from acceding countries, were often working on their first treaty reform negotiations. At the highest level, Commission representative Vitorino took part in the EU Charter negotiations, while Commissioner for Regional Policy and Institutional Reform Barnier was the Commission's representative in the 2000 IGC – giving both Commissioners first-hand experience with treaty reform negotiations.

Members of the EP delegation lacked the infrastructural backing that the Commission representatives enjoyed. MEPs were for the most left on their own regarding gathering and processing information in the Convention, although some MEPs utilized the resources of their respective national Permanent Representations to the EU (Interviews EC-12, EC-13). Despite some MEPs closely following work in IGCs during the 1990s, and having observer status in past IGCs, the Convention were the first real treaty reform negotiations that most MEPs were a party to. But MEPs such as Duff and Brok knew the issues thoroughly through their work on the EP Constitutional Affairs Committee, and Brok had also followed two IGCs as EP representative. Further, MEPs were used to working in a European-level parliamentary-like environment, and as will be seen below, were especially skilful at building coalitions behind the scenes (Interview NAT-25; Jonsson and Hegeland, 2003).

The Council Secretariat did not directly take part in the Convention, but in the IGC the Secretariat enjoyed its traditional comparative advantages. With a small task force headed by Jean-Claude Piris, ably assisted by veteran Max Keller-Noëllet and six other officials, the Secretariat was in experienced hands (Interview NAT-17, EC-22). Further, during the legal 'tidying up' of the Constitutional Treaty during the IGC, the use of legal French was a challenge for many acceding countries, making them more dependent upon the assistance and expertise of the Council Secretariat (Interview NAT-16).

The reputation of the EU institutions

In contrast to past rounds of treaty reform, during the Convention both the Commission and EP were legitimate participants. The Commission had a 'fund of goodwill' and many natural allies at the start of the Convention (Norman, 2003, p. 161). The Commission was also seen by many participants as a source of technical expertise and advice, especially among officials from the acceding states owing to their close relations with the Commission during the accession process (Interview EC-12, NAT-24). But by trumpeting 'blue sky' proposals such as Penelope during the Convention (see below on Penelope), the Commission upset even traditional allies (Interview EC-13, NAT-24). And its failings during the Convention haunted the Commission during the IGC (Interview NAT-26).

MEPs were not seen as a source of expertise by other members of the Convention, but they did have the substantial benefit of being directly elected, and therefore had a source of democratic legitimacy that the Commission did not enjoy. Given that the Convention's text formed the default option during the IGC, the EP had a stronger claim to play a role in the IGC than in the past (Interview NAT-26). But after Elmar Brok replaced de Vigo as EP representative in the IGC in November, the EP was being represented by two Germans (Hänsch and Brok) – something that came across quite badly in the IGC negotiating room (Interview NAT-17).

The Council Secretariat was not an accepted participant in the Convention, but was seen as a trusted impartial assistant by governments during the IGC (Interview NAT-16, NAT-17, NAT-19).

The opportunities for leadership created by the negotiating context

The role of the EU institutions in the European Convention and 2003–4 IGC

While the Commission also enjoyed a privileged position in the preparatory phase of the EMU IGC (see Chapter 4), the Commission and the EP had much stronger roles in the Convention which drafted most of the Constitutional Treaty than they have had in past rounds of treaty reform. Both the Commission and EP were full parties to the

Convention negotiations, and had a say within the Praesidium and the plenary assembly. The Council Secretariat had no direct role in the Convention, although some of its officials took part in the expert hearings held by working groups. The Convention Secretariat, which had the role normally played by the Council Secretariat comprised seconded officials from the secretariats of the Commission, Council and EP.

The Commission was represented by two Commissioners in the plenary, and enjoyed two seats in the Praesidium. The EP was represented by 16 MEPs, with 16 alternates who fully took part in the negotiations. The EP also had two seats on the Praesidium.

The Praesidium played a role comparable to that of the Presidency in IGC negotiations, controlling the agenda and drafting texts. The seats on the Praesidium gave both the Commission and EP significant opportunities to guide the negotiations in their favoured direction by having a say in how the negotiations are conducted, and what texts were put before the plenary. Both the Commission and EP representatives were 'first-tier' members of the Praesidium, whereas certain other representatives such as national parliamentarian Gisela Stuart were sometimes not listened to (Interview NAT-21; see Stuart 2003, for a confirmation of this). Further, Praesidium members were chosen to chair the working groups, giving them significant opportunities to shape the emerging agenda of the Convention.

Voting procedures were not clear in the plenary or Praesidium. It was stated in the Convention rules of procedure that the final product of the Convention should be adopted using consensus (CONV 9/02) – but there were no votes held in the Convention plenary, and there appears to have been significant disagreements regarding the final outcome within the plenary, with a minority text even produced by Eurosceptics (CONV 773/03). But on the final day of the Convention plenary, a sizable majority of members indicated that they supported the final draft.

In the IGC, the Commission was a participant, while the EP was only an observer. The Council Secretariat played its usual role in the IGC 2003–4, assisting Presidencies that were willing to draw upon it in producing alternative solutions and probing for consensus (Interviews NAT-17, EC-26). The Council Secretariat drafted most of the texts for the Italian Presidency, and all of the texts for the Irish (Interview EC-26).

During the IGC head of the Council Secretariat's Legal Services Piris chaired the group of legal experts during the IGC that attempted to legally tidy up the final Constitutional Treaty. Yet by giving Piris the chair, the Italian Presidency attempted to signal that the process was to be a technical and not political exercise. The mandate of the group was also restrictive, being intended to be merely a legal and technical clarification exercise and not a political negotiation (CIG 4/1/03, 42/03, 43/03).

The nature of the issues being negotiated

The topics on the agenda of the Convention were divided into eleven main categories by the Praesidium and plenary. Topics such as the simplification of the treaties, legal personality, and competence issues were highly complex both legally and substantively, requiring detailed knowledge of the existing *acquis communautaire* and the functioning of Union decision-making. Issues regarding the exact form of the incorporation of the Charter were dealt with mainly by expert actors (Interviews NAT-15, EC-15). The simplification of budgetary rules was also very technical, and the Commission was for example represented in the discussion circle on the issue by a senior official from DG Budget (Interview EC-14). In these types of issues we should expect that expert actors would have more discretion to shape discussions and outcomes.

The number of issues and parties in the negotiations

The negotiating situation in the Convention was incredibly complex. Hundreds of salient issues were being negotiated among the 204 delegates and 3 chairmen in the Convention, that was composed of one representative from each of the 15 EU governments and 13 candidate countries along with two from each national parliament, 16 MEPs, and two Commissioners, along with an equal number of alternatives. This large number made it impossible for any one actor to have a synoptic view of the negotiations, and also preventing any real negotiations in the plenary.

In order to manage this complexity, working groups were for example set up to discuss and debate issues relating to a single theme. The drafting of the single official negotiating text was undertaken by the Convention Secretariat, under leadership of the Convention chairmen. Conventionnels were invited to submit amendments to the texts after their presentation, which led to thousands of amendments, but Giscard and the Convention Secretariat had the final say over whether they would be incorporated into the draft to be sent to the Praesidium for approval.

The IGC was a simpler negotiating situation, as there were only a handful of salient issues being negotiated among 25 governmental representatives. During the Italian Presidency, negotiations were merely *tour de tables* where parties reiterated their national positions, as real negoatiations were not feasible with 25 governments sitting at the table. The Irish Presidency therefore used bilateral meeting to find zones of consensus instead of plenary sessions (Interview EC-26).

The distribution and intensity of governmental preferences

There were two overall cleavages among governments in the Convention and IGC 2003–2004: a supranationalist/intergovernmentalist cleavage; and a large/smaller member state cleavage (see European Parliament IGC Monitoring Group, 2003 and Norman, 2003). While agreement was often difficult to reach owing to political factors, zones of agreement did exist on most issues (see Figure 7.1 below). As the Convention's draft text had to be accepted by governments in the IGC, the views of governments were also important in the Convention (Interview NAT-25; Norman, 2003).

In the Convention, the integrationist/intergovernmentalist cleavage was most evident on issues such as whether to increase Union competences and extend QMV and co-decision to all policy areas, including

FIGURE 7.1   *Major cleavages in the Constitutional Treaty negotiations*

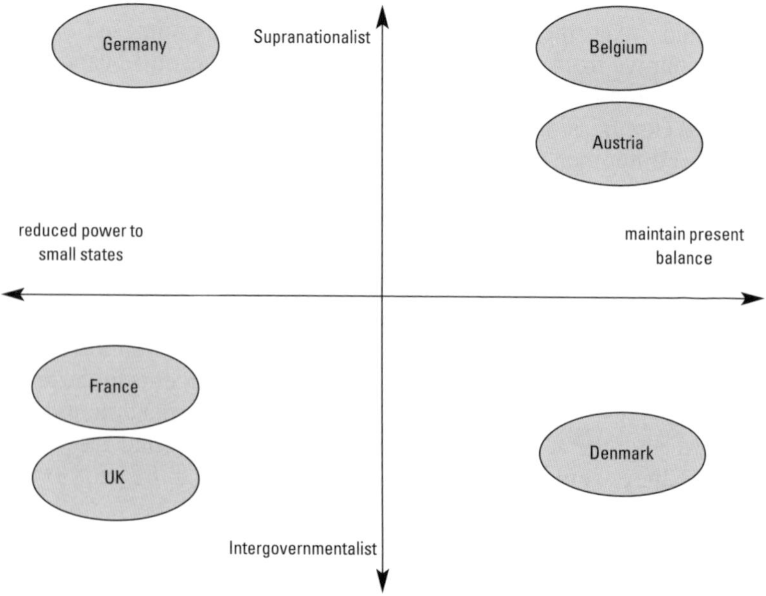

foreign policy, together with whether to create new supranational institutions such as a European Public Prosecutor (Norman, 2003, pp. 170–1, 198–201, 243). Belgium and Germany were amongst the key governmental advocates of more integration, whereas France and the UK were central proponents of more intergovernmental solutions (Interview NAT-25; Ludlow, 2004b; Menon, 2003; Norman, 2003, pp. 198–201). During the IGC, this cleavage manifested itself in the question of whether the Convention's draft should be amended or not, with supranationalists defending the text, and intergovernmentalists wanting to chip away integrative elements of the draft.

The smaller/larger government cleavage that developed during the 2000 IGC re-emerged in the spring of 2003 within the Convention and carried over into the IGC. Under Austrian/Finnish leadership, a coalition of smaller governments actively attempted to prevent the creation of a strong European Council President – a post they feared would be subservient to the interests of the larger governments – and the reduction of their weight in Union decision-making by for example losing 'their' Commissioner.

Another cleavage that developed during the Convention and IGC was whether the Nice institutional compromise should be revised or not, with the major 'losers' vehemently contesting any revision of the Nice formula on Council voting weights, whereas the major 'winner', Germany, argued for adopting the Convention text without amendment.

As the European Convention was in effect renegotiating the EU Treaties and replacing them with a simpler Constitutional Treaty, there were many politically sensitive issues being raised. Among these were questions of extending EU competences, particularly in the fields of social policy and defence, and the creation of a European Council President. In many of these institutional issues, the basic question was whether authority should rest with the Commission or the Council. Finally, the key institutional questions of the Nice compromise, such as re-weighting of Council votes became life-or-death matters, as politicians increasingly backed themselves into corners. In these sensitive issues, we would expect much lower levels of influence for EU institutions.

Leadership by EU institutions in the Constitutional negotiations

Were any of the EU institutions able to translate their positions into actual influence over the final Constitutional Treaty through the provision of leadership? The answer regarding the European Commission is basically 'No'. While the Commission had a very advantageous position at the start of the Convention, and Prodi promised that the Commission would 'provide its full and enthusiastic contribution, drawing on all its own experience and expertise' (CONV 04/02), the Commission played itself out of the negotiations through a combination of contradictory and extreme positions. For the Council Secretariat the answer is also 'No' as regards the Convention, as they had no role, but during the IGC they played a key behind-the-scenes role during the Irish Presidency, assisting the Irish in finding a solution where the Italians failed.

In contrast, the EP was the driving force of the Convention in most issues, with the EP's coalition-building leading to a more ambitious and simple Constitutional Treaty than would otherwise have been agreed by governmental representatives left to themselves. During the IGC, the EP played the role of being the Convention's 'cheerleader', although the survival of the Convention's text more or less intact in the IGC was more due to the insistence of a German-led coalition than the EP.

Leadership by the European Commission

The Commission was active in setting the agenda for the Convention, and in ensuring that a Convention was used to prepare the IGC instead of using more traditional methods (Interview EC-16; Ludlow, 2004a). Together with the Belgian Presidency, the Commission shaped the Laeken conclusions that laid down a series of points to be discussed by the Convention, including several issues that were in the Commission Opinion in the 2000 IGC (see European Commission, 2000a; European Council, 2001; Ludlow, 2004a; Interview EC-16).

In the Convention itself, the Commission had a considerable impact when it played a low-profile and realistic role, enabling it to shape the agenda to reflect its own priorities. But the Commission often played itself out of the picture by not adopting coherent positions in the college, and by pursuing poorly planned and uncoordinated strategies.

The overall strategy of the Commission vacillated between supporting realistic positions close to the centre of gravity and advocating much more radical pro-integrative/federalist positions (Interviews EC-11, EC-16; Norman, 2003, p. 162). This dichotomy reflected tensions within the Commission, for example between the two Commission representatives and the college of Commissioners, and between the Commission task force and the representatives on whether to push for an extremely ambitious, blue-sky outcome, or to be more moderate and go for an ambitious but realistic outcome Interviews EC-11, EC-16, EC-23, NAT-21, NAT-24, NAT-25; Norman, 2003, pp. 161–9, 176). Further, the Commission did surprisingly little to prepare itself for the Convention (Interview EC-11), and was only able to table a fleshed-out proposal in December 2002 – over seven months *after* the Convention started (European Commission, 2002b; Norman, 2003, p. 162)!

In issues where the Commission intervened with well-organized and realistic positions, it was able to exploit its position in the Convention to gain influence. One example was the negotiation of the issue of incorporating the EU Charter of Fundamental Rights into the Constitutional Treaty as a legally binding document – something that the Commission was strongly interested in achieving. Commissioner Vitorino secured the chair of the working group on the Charter that was created in the autumn of 2002 in the Convention. Vitorino chaired the group brilliantly, employing his considerable expertise in the issue and careful chairmanship to secure an outcome in the working group that ensured that the Charter would be incorporated into the Constitutional Treaty as a legally binding document, while also taking on board British and Irish concerns (Interviews EC-11, EC-14, Norman, 2003, pp. 85–9). In the final weeks of the Convention, Vitorino also worked behind the scenes to secure an explanatory declaration on the impact of the Charter on national law that satisfied UK concerns (Norman, 2003, p. 258). By taking into account British and Irish concerns, Commission interventions ensured that the final outcome survived the IGC 2003–4.

Another example of Commission success was in the issue of public health, which was also a priority for the Commission. The Commission appointed Commission Secretary-General O'Sullivan as its representative to the working group on Social Europe. He presented a clear and moderate case in the group based upon his considerable expertise, and succeeded in putting the issue of public health on the agenda, and shaped the final report of the group (Interview EC-13, EC-15, NAT-25). O'Sullivan argued that the EU should have competence under Article 152 EC to deal with cross-border issues of public health, and especially problems such as communicable diseases and bio-terrorism (WD 37, WG XI). Although the wording in the draft Constitutional Treaty on public health was not exactly the same as the Commission-inspired working group conclusions, Commission interventions persuaded sceptics to accept Union competences in public health by showing what the Commission intended to do with new competences, and, just as importantly, what it did not intend to do (Interview EC-13) (see III-179).

Finally, the Commission was able to exploit its seats in the Praesidium in several instances, often in concert with the European Parliamentary representatives. For example, in Praesidium meetings on 22–3 April 2003, the Commission and EP representatives in the Praesidium threatened to veto chairman Giscard d'Estaing's draft texts on institutional issues, including the creation of a strong European Council President and Congress of Peoples (*EU Observer*, 24 April 2003; 25 April 2003; Interview EC-23). The Commission complained publicly that Giscard's draft ran counter to 'orientations of the debate in the Convention and its working groups' (Norman, 2003, p. 228). This forced the chairman to remove the most intergovernmental elements of his proposals in the draft, including provisions calling for a strong institutional backup for the President of the European Council, and calling the European Council the Union's 'highest authority' (Interview EC-23; Norman, 2003, pp. 229–35). The Praesidium then approved the revised draft, which was sent to the plenary (CONV 691/03)

Yet these few examples of success were overshadowed by the uncoordinated and extreme positions and strategies of the Commission in most issues. This was vividly displayed in December 2002 when the Commission tabled both a relatively realistic and operational opinion together with a radical draft treaty that was code-named 'Penelope' (European Commission, 2002b, 2002c). The official opinion was produced by the two Commission representatives to the Convention, and was a pragmatic document calling for increased co-decision and QMV, and a strengthened Commission role in certain policies, including locating the EU foreign minister solely within the Commission. The competing 178-page Penelope paper was produced by a team of Commission civil servants directly under the authority of Commission President Prodi, and according to inside sources, it was kept secret from the two Commission representatives until *after* it was published (Interview EC-16). The Penelope document was ill-received in the Convention due to its radical nature, which included proposals for a form of European government based upon the Commission, and called for majority voting for future treaty reform and foreign policy (Interviews NAT-24, NAT-25, EC-16, EC-23; Norman, 2003, pp. 161–9, 265–8)! Yet Penelope bound Commission representatives in further discussions, and the internal disagreements and conflicting positions led to the Commission going 'missing in action' in the important final months of the Convention (Interview EC-23; Norman, 2003, pp. 265–8).

After the Convention concluded, Prodi advocated reopening the Convention's text (*Agence Europe*, 17.06.03, pp. 4, 8; 18.09.03, p. 5). This was surprising given that the Commission had a much weaker role in the IGC than in the Convention. The Commission had shifted to advocating one Commissioner per member state in the spring of 2003 in a bid to gain the support of smaller governments (ibid.), and fought for this position unsuccessfully during the IGC. On other issues, the Commission for example found itself fighting an unsuccessful rearguard action to protect its powers in the economic governance provisions of the Convention's draft, especially as regards its role in euro-zone rules relating to the EMU's excessive deficit procedure (Grevi, 2004, p. 10; *FT*, 14.06.04; Interview EC-26; *EU Observer*, 15.06.04). The final text weakened the Commission role in the excessive deficit procedure.

Leadership by the European Parliament

The EP succeeded in pushing the final Constitutional Treaty in a more pro-integrative direction than would have been the case had the treaty been drafted by an IGC. The EP enjoyed a strong position in the Convention, and exploited this to become one of the key driving forces of the negotiations. MEPs were particularly successful when they were able to coordinate their positions around ambitious but realistic outcomes, and formed large coalitions often organized along political party lines (Interview NAT-24; Hughes, Sasa and Gorden, 2003; Maurer, 2003, p. 184; Norman, 2003).

But there were also certain issues that were 'no-go' areas for the EP, and governments rebuffed attempts by MEPs to influence outcomes in foreign and defence policies, together with certain institutional issues such as ratification rules for the Constitutional Treaty. Yet despite this, the 'fingerprints' of the EP are scattered throughout the Constitutional Treaty, and it in many ways reads like an updated and lengthened version of the EP's Draft Treaty establishing the European Union from 1984 (see European Parliament, 1984, also Chapter 3).

There were few signs at the start of the Convention that the EP would play a guiding role. In past rounds of treaty reform, the EP had strongly advocated extremely pro-integrative positions. Echoing the past, EP resolutions and reports on the coming Convention took very ambitious positions, including calls for the full incorporation of CFSP and JHA into the Community pillar, the creation of a European Public Prosecutor, the revision of the Nice compromise on the institutional issues, and increased powers to the EP by extending co-decision to all policies, including the budget (European Parliament, 2001a, 2001b). In the first half year of the Convention, three central MEPs tabled draft constitutions, with Andrew Duff's contribution for example being a short and strongly federalist vision of a 'Federal Union of Europe' (see CONV 234/02).

Yet in the autumn of 2002, key MEPs started to shift tactics from past extremes towards more pragmatic coalition-building around ambitious but realistic positions (Jonsson and Hegeland, 2003, p. 37; Norman, 2003, p. 278). MEPs even signalled in the final months of the Convention that they could live with a long-term president of the European Council in return for the ability of the EP to elect the Commission president (Norman, 2003, p. 278). After the last plenary session, MEP Duff signalled this new pragmatism when he said that the 'result is not perfect . . . But what we have is, frankly, the best we could get' (*Agence Europe*, 14.06.03, p. 4).

MEPs held many coordination meetings mostly along party lines, and operated well in the plenary debates, with good interventions and the pooling of speaking time within party groupings (Interviews NAT-15, NAT-24; Jonsson and Hegeland, 2003, pp. 34–5). And when MEPs were able to build large coalitions, these had a significant impact, as proposals with many signatures were often taken more seriously by the Praesidium (Norman, 2003, p. 247). Within the Praesidium, especially EP representative de Vigo played a key role, with a central participant stating in an interview that de Vigo skillfully advanced EP interests while also having a good sense for what the 'market would bear' (Interview EC-23).

Looking at the draft Constitutional Treaty, the final document is littered with examples of EP influence. The concept of a 'constitution' was strongly advocated by the EP (Interviews Nat-17, Nat-24). Due to the success of EP leadership strategies, the draft Constitutional Treaty also significantly strengthened the powers of the EP in Union decision-making. On the issue of expanding EP powers in the budgetary powers to also include 'compulsory expenditure' (i.e. CAP spending), France and Ireland were the most prominent objectors, but the EP succeeded in extending EP budgetary powers in the final text to all areas of the budget; first in the Simplification Working Group and then through drafting assistance by de Vigo in the Praesidium (Interviews NAT-24, EC-23) (see Article III-310 in the draft Constitutional Treaty).

The EP also rallied for an extension of the co-decision procedure and QMV to all policy areas of the Union. While the final text kept unanimity in several 'red-line' areas, the final outcome was significantly influenced by the EP representatives (Interviews NAT-21,

EC-23; Norman, 2003, p. 366). For example, to please MEPs and other pro-integrative actors, the final Convention text included in Article I-24 a general bridging clause (*passerelle*) that allowed the European Council to transfer a policy area in Part III to QMV by a unanimous vote (Interviews NAT-21, EC-23; Norman 2003:366). The *passerelle* survived the IGC, although it was moved to part IV (Article IV-7a).

The EP together with the Commission was also able to kill the most intergovernmentalist elements of Giscard's institutional ideas, including the strong European Council President (Interview EC-23; Norman, 2003, pp. 150, 279). Further, in the key debates on institutional issues in late April in the Praesidium, EP representatives were able to pressure Giscard to upgrade the role of the EP in the appointment of the Commission president (Norman, 2003, p. 234). And in the dying days of the Convention, MEPs built a coalition of like-minded members that succeeded in ensuring that the draft Constitutional Treaty revised the Nice compromise on institutional issues, including the controversial simple double majority rule for Council voting that was a direct cause of the breakdown of IGC negotiations in December 2003 (Norman, 2003, pp. 280–96; Ludlow, 2004b; Brown, 2003).

During the IGC, the EP acted as the Convention 'cheerleader', and argued that the IGC should 'avoid negotiations on the fundamental decisions reached by the Convention' (European Parliament, 2003b; Interview NAT-21, NAT-26; *Agence Europe*, 11.09.03, p. 7). MEPs were especially concerned about the provisions on their budgetary powers as governments attempted to remove the EP's 'final say' over the budget in the Convention text, and reduce EP powers over 'compulsory expenditure' (European Parliament, 2003c; Interviews EC-19, NAT-21; *EU Observer*, 25.11.03; 28.11.03, 09.12.03). While the Convention's Article III-310 granted the EP the final say over the budget, allowing it to confirm amendments opposed by the Council, the IGC whittled away at these powers. The final outcome was agreed at the Naples meeting in December, which allowed the Council to reject EP amendments by asking the Commission to table a new budget (CIG 60/03 Add 1). The EP even raised the possibility of rejecting the final Constitutional Treaty and mobilizing a campaign against it if its new-found powers in the budget were taken away, but the final text did not grant the EP the final say, although the EP's budgetary powers are extended to the whole of the budget, including agricultural expenditure (*EU Observer*, 25.11.03, 09.12.03, 23.04.04; Grevi, 2004).

Leadership by the Council Secretariat

The Council Secretariat played a key role in the IGC, facilitating compromise and assisting governments in the technical cleaning-up of the Convention's draft text. But as most of the real negotiations during the IGC were held at the highest political levels, the Council Secretariat mostly provided leadership that ensured the efficiency of the negotiations, and it had few opportunities to shift outcomes closer to its own position, as the Secretariat is more effective at the technical and ambassadorial levels.

The Council Secretariat signalled that it viewed the IGC as a technical exercise by appointing head of Legal Services Jean-Claude Piris to head its IGC team instead of Keller-Noëllet (Interview EC-19). Piris also actively attempted to downplay the political nature of the legal experts working group that he chaired (ibid.).

Looking first at the Secretariat's impact in the legal experts working group, there are few indications that Piris provided more than technical leadership that improved the efficiency of the negotiations. All of the discussions used the draft text produced by the Council Secretariat (CIG 04/03), but there is no evidence that the Secretariat inserted unwanted elements into the text. In an attempt to ensure legal continuity, and to iterate that the Union is not a tabula rasa but builds on fifty years of treaty-making, the Council Secretariat suggested in CIG 04/03 that a paragraph be inserted into the preamble about past EU Treaties (Interview EC-22). This made its way into the final text. But there is no evidence that Piris succeeded in pushing the group in issues where he had strong views. The best example was the issue involving the numbering of the Convention's draft into four parts using roman numerals, followed by an article number. Piris was concerned that when article numbers were read aloud, that Article I-45 would sound like 145, which then could be confused with Article III-145 (Interview EC-22; NAT-19). But changing the numbering of the parts involved sensitive questions relating to the Charter, and the UK was strongly interested in keeping the Charter as a separate part of the treaty (ibid.). Piris did not succeed in overcoming British objections.

In the actual IGC, the Council Secretariat did play a role in the Italian Presidency prior to the final Brussels Summit. The Italians drew upon the Secretariat, but relations were not close, and the Secretariat did not agree with the way in which the Italians handled the negotiations (Interviews NAT-19, NAT-21, NAT-26, EC-19, EC-26). The Secretariat was particularly concerned about the lack of papers being advanced on the key institutional issues, which were not seriously discussed prior to the Brussels Summit (Interview EC-26). The Secretariat did though draft papers and texts for the Italians on minor issues which were then approved by the Presidency for circulation (Interview EC-19, EC-26). For example, the Italian Presidency prior to Naples proposed going further than the weak Convention text on the issue of the Union acceding to the ECHR that stated that the Union 'shall seek accession', and instead wrote that the Union 'shall accede' (CG 52/1/03 Rev 1). The Council Secretariat was aware that this raised problems for several delegations, and after discussions with several delegations, they drafted a protocol to explain the conditions for accession (Interview EC-22) (see protocol on the ECHR in CG 73/04 p. 112).

When Berlusconi took over the handling of the Italian Presidency in the run-up to Brussels, he did not use the Council Secretariat – with predictable results (Interview EC-19, EC-22, EC-26). According to participants, Piris had a range of possible compromise solutions prepared for the Summit, but Berlusconi did not listen to him (Interview EC-22, NAT-16).

The Irish Presidency handled the negotiations differently, and worked very closely with the Council Secretariat (Interviews EC-19, EC-22, EC-26). The Council Secretariat was fully associated with the Irish Presidency at all levels (Interviews EC-22, EC-26). The Secretariat was kept informed of results of the bilateral meetings held by Irish Taoiseach Ahern with his colleagues. At the focal point level, the Council Secretariat took part in all of the meetings, and discussed with the Presidency both the outcome and ways forward. There was a mutual dialogue, where the Secretariat offered ideas and advice to the Irish Presidency on how the negotiations should be managed, and the state of play and possible compromises (Interview EC-26). The Secretariat drafted all of the texts for the Irish, though under their guidance (ibid.).

The overall strategy agreed upon between the Irish and the Council Secretariat was to gradually narrow the parameters for agreement by testing compromises with different parties, and then tabling papers on the sensitive issues (ibid.). For example, after bilateral meetings between the Irish and Polish prime ministers, where Poland indicated that they would not accept a re-weighting of votes that did not incorporate an Ioannina-like agreement on blocking thresholds, the Council Secretariat produced a Draft Decision on implementing the new majority rules that stated that if a minority slightly smaller than a formal blocking minority was against a proposal, the Council would attempt to reach 'a satisfactory solution' (CIG 83/04, pp. 8–9; ibid.). This enabled Poland to accept the final outcome. Other actors also accepted it as the outcome after the Council Secretariat pointed out that the rules were not legally binding. The Secretariat also copied the Ioannina agreements insertion of a reference to the Council rules of procedure that stated that a simple majority can stop the Council's attempts to find a 'satisfactory solution' by calling for a vote.

TABLE 7.2   *Conclusions – leadership in the Constitutional Treaty negotiations*

Issue-area	*Outcome*
Treaty structure	• removal of pillar structure – idea broadly supported, with intergovernmentalist governments acting as brakes • Charter – Commission leadership • simplification – EP leadership
Institutional changes	• Union Foreign Minister – idea broadly supported within both Convention and IGC • size of Commission – Compromise found by Irish Presidency and Council Secretariat • European Council President – leadership provided by larger governments, with Commission and EP acting as brakes on more intergovernmental powers • Council Presidency – leadership provided by smaller governments • Council voting procedure – German leadership in pushing for revision, with Poland and Spain acting as brakes. Compromise found by Irish Presidency and Council Secretariat • *passerelle* – provision inserted by Giscard due to pressure from EP-led coalition • role of national parliaments – leadership by national parliaments • European Public Prosecutor – strong EP leadership role, although governmental concerns led to weak provisions
Extension of QMV and co-decision	• co-decision extended – EP leadership role • QMV made general rule – EP leadership role, with the UK acting as a brake
External action	• defence – Leadership provided by France, Germany and UK

Conclusion

Table 7.2 illustrates which actors were most influential in the issues during the Constitutional Treaty negotiations. As the real substantive negotiations of the Constitutional Treaty took place within the preparatory Convention where the Commission and EP had privileged positions, both institutions had many opportunities to push the final outcome closer to their own positions. But despite having a strong position, the Commission's strategy clearly showed the importance of choosing appropriate leadership strategies. Without a clear line and with poorly prepared and extreme positions, the Commission foundered in the water during the Convention. Notable exceptions included the Charter, where the Commission assisted in finding an outcome that was acceptable to both those that wanted it to be included, and took account of UK fears of its impact upon their domestic legal system. In contrast, after key MEPs lowered their ambitions and actively attempted to build large coalitions around ambitious but realistic positions, the EP became the driving force during the Convention, and the final Convention text is strewn with EP 'fingerprints'. Issues such as creating a simplified and unified Constitutional Treaty, and the extension of co-decision and QMV were driven by the EP.

During the following IGC, only a handful of contentious issues were seriously negotiated among goverments, as a core group of governments led by Germany wanted to adopt the Convention's text as is. Therefore, most of the issues on the agenda dealt with mere clarifications of the Convention's draft Constitutional Treaty. But in the sensitive Nice-related issues that led to the suspension of the IGC in the December 2003 Brussels Summit, the Irish Presidency was able to forge consensus through discrete behind-the-scenes negotiations, ably assisted by the Council Secretariat. Issues such as creating a simplified and unified Constitutional Treaty, and the extension of co-decision and QMV were driven by the EP.

Chapter 8

Negotiating the Fifth Enlargement

Introduction

'Today we succeeded in fulfilling the aim, which generations of Europeans have fought for. In 1989 brave and visionary people tore down the Berlin Wall. They would no longer tolerate the forced division of Europe. Today, we have delivered on their hopes. We have decided to heal our continent. We have decided to create One Europe.' (Danish Prime Minister Anders Fogh Rasmussen on the conclusion of the Eastern enlargement negotiations in Copenhagen, 13 December 2002)

These self-congratulatory words concluded the negotiation of the largest enlargement in the history of the EU. From the original six in 1951, the EU expanded in May 2004 to encompass twenty-five states with a total population of over 450 million citizens, including eight countries in Central and Eastern Europe, together with Cyprus and Malta.

Negotiating the fifth enlargement was one of the greatest challenges that the EU has ever faced. First, the sheer number of countries being admitted created a strong demand for fundamental reforms of the EU institutions that were designed for a community of six. Secondly, the candidate countries in the enlargement negotiations were relatively poor, with a real GDP/capita of about 40 per cent of the EU average, with much larger agricultural sectors than present EU member states (Eurostat, 2003 – corrected for purchasing power). These differences posed serious problems for some internal EU policies, such as the Common Agricultural Policy (CAP).

Previous chapters examined the roles of EU institutions in IGCs on major treaty reform. The fifth enlargement negotiations were also conducted as an IGC, but held between EU member states and the candidate state. Like IGCs on major treaty reform, EU institutions have few formal powers in enlargement negotiations. But unlike in treaty reform, the Commission played a key role in the *actual* negotiations with candidates by both drafting proposals for negotiating positions for the EU, dealing with the day-to-day negotiations with the candidates, and monitoring their progress in implementing the EU's *acquis communautaire*. The EP was also slightly better off in enlargement negotiations than in IGCs, having the power of assent over the final outcome. The Council Secretariat had a smaller role in the enlargement negotiations, but still provided assistance to both Presidencies and member state delegations. Further, the enlargement negotiations had an internal aspect, where key reforms of existing EU policies were necessary. In these internal negotiations, EU institutions had strong treaty-based powers.

Were any of the EU institutions able to provide leadership in either the external or internal aspects of the fifth enlargement negotiations? If so, when were they able to provide leadership and why? The following will investigate these questions by focusing on the key issues in the enlargement negotiations, including the internal debates on:

- the decision to enlarge the EU;
- the debate on the number of candidates and the criteria to evaluate them by;
- the internal discussions on the reform of the CAP, structural funds, and the budget; and
- the external negotiations with the candidates on the terms, timing and conditions of entry.

The chapter will first detail the course of the enlargement negotiations. It will then review what the three institutions wanted in the negotiations. The chapter then turns to look at the leadership resources available to the three EU institutions, and how the negotiating context and their conduct in the negotiations affected their ability to translate these resources into influence over outcomes.

The course of the negotiation of the fifth enlargement

From Berlin to Luxembourg – deciding whether and when to open the negotiations

The fall of the Berlin Wall in 1989, and the dramatic changes in Central and Eastern Europe in its aftermath, posed an enormous challenge for the EU. The basic question in the early 1990s was whether the EU could and should enlarge in Central and Eastern Europe. The size of the task was daunting.

The first steps towards enlargement were taken within the context of the PHARE program that provided aid and assistance to Central and Eastern Europe, and the negotiation of Association or Europe Agreements with the Czech Republic, Hungary and Poland in 1990–1991 (Beach, 1998; Friis, 1997; Niemann, 1998). While the PHARE program started as food aid and technical assistance, it gradually became to be an integral part of the EU's pre-accession strategy (Niemann, 1998). In the first Europe Agreements, the EU acknowledged that the three countries wanted to join the EU, but governments opposing enlargement were able to prevent the inclusion of more formal membership clauses in the final agreements (Torreblanca, 2001, pp. 150, 151–2, 179).

Two more years would pass before the EU officially acknowledged in the Copenhagen Summit conclusions in 1993 that 'the associated countries in central and eastern Europe that so desire shall become members of the European Union. Accession will take place as soon as an associated country is able to assume the obligations of membership by satisfying the economic and political conditions required' (European Council, 1993, p. 6). The Copenhagen conclusions also listed the now famous basic conditions for enlargement, including the existence of political democracy, a functioning market economy, and the ability to take on the obligations of membership.

The first applications for EU membership were submitted by Hungary and Poland in the spring of 1994, with further applications in 1995 and 1996 from eight other countries in Central and Eastern Europe. The applications triggered the Council to start the enlargement procedure under Article O TEU (now Article 49 EU). In the Corfu European Council Summit conclusions from June 1994, the Commission and the Presidency were asked to prepare a strategy for the accession process.

During the German Presidency in the second half of 1994, the Commission tabled a paper proposing that the Commission should both prepare a white paper that would set out a program for the candidates to meet the obligations of the Internal Market, and a paper that would study the impact of enlargement on the EU's common policies (European Commission, 1994a). In a second paper, the Commission argued that the pre-accession strategy should be enhanced and expanded (European Commission, 1994b). The Essen Summit conclusions endorsed the proposals of the Commission by strengthening the pre-accession strategy, and asking the Commission to prepare both a white paper and the study on the impact of enlargement.

The Commission published its White Paper in May 1995, which detailed key parts of EU legislation for the candidate countries to implement prior to accession, but it did not mention a timetable for enlargement (European Commission, 1995a). The Cannes European Council in June approved the Commission's White Paper.

The key internal debates among the EU countries dealt with when (and whether) the EU should open enlargement negotiations, together with the number of candidates that should be included in the first round. This debate heated up in the second half of 1995 during the Spanish Presidency. While the opposition to opening negotiations was primarily behind the scenes, given that it was difficult to publicly oppose enlargement (Schimmelfennig, 2001), there was much public debate on numbers. Despite the debate on numbers being contingent upon the opinions of the Commission that were scheduled to be published in July 1997 in the Agenda 2000 package, prior to the Madrid Summit in December 1995, Helmut Kohl publicly suggested that the EU should open negotiations with Poland, Hungary and the Czech Republic six months after the 1996–7 IGC was concluded (Baun, 2000, p. 69). The Nordics argued the case of the Baltic states, while France championed Romania (Baun, 2000, pp. 69–70).

The Commission's first opinion on the applications for membership was included in the Agenda 2000 paper published in July 1997 (European Commission, 1997) (see below for more). It stated that Cyprus, the Czech Republic, Estonia, Hungary, Poland, and Slovenia would meet the economic and political criteria in the medium-term, and recommended opening negotiations with the five Central and Eastern European countries together with Cyprus – the so-called 5+1 formula. Many governments criticized the Commission stance, either arguing like Denmark, Italy and Sweden that negotiations should be opened with all ten applicants, or as Germany did in favour of a more limited first wave (Baun, 2000, pp. 89–90; Friis, 1998, pp. 6–7). These debates continued until the Luxembourg Summit in December 1997, which settled the question by stating that the EU would only open negotiations with the 5+1 countries, but that the Commission would also conduct individual screenings of the other candidates, supplemented by further strengthening of the pre-accession strategy (European Council, 1997b).

Negotiations opened with the 5+1 countries in March 1998, but the start of real substantive external negotiations with the candidates would have to wait until the EU had put its own house in order by reforming key internal policies that were being negotiated in the Agenda 2000 package.

The internal debate – negotiating Agenda 2000 from Luxembourg to Berlin

The Commission also outlined in its Agenda 2000 package proposals for reforms of the CAP, the structural and cohesion funds, and the future financial framework for the Union for the period 2000–6. These sensitive issues pitted the net beneficiary governments – the so-called 'cohesion' states and France – directly against the net contributors to the budget, including Germany and the Netherlands.

The net contributors believed that fundamental reforms of expenditure-heavy policies was necessary prior to enlargement in order to ensure that the size of the EU budget did not increase, whereas net beneficiaries such as France and the cohesion countries were concerned about the domestic impact of major reforms of the CAP and structural funds. But Germany was split, for while it on the one hand wanted significant reforms of expenditure-heavy policies given its net contributor status, on the other hand, given the structure of German agriculture, it was against a significant reform of the CAP through price cuts (Ackrill, 2000, p. 346).

The Commission tried to square the circle by freezing the EU budget and reforming expenditure-heavy programs in its Agenda 2000 report. The package was later fleshed out in formal legislative proposals tabled in March 1998 (see *Bulletin of the EU*, 3/1998). The basic outlines of the proposals were relatively modest reforms of the CAP and structural funds, together with a suggested financial framework for the 2000–6 budget period that enabled enlargement to take place *within* the existing budgetary ceiling of 1.27 per cent GNP of the EU (see Table 8.1). The proposed reforms to the structural policies dealt with consolidating the number of programs and in general refocusing funds on the poorest regions of the EU.

The CAP proposals were a continuation of the MacSharry reforms of 1992, where the main aim had been to bring the CAP in line with GATT/WTO rules. The Commission proposals argued for a slight 'de-coupling' of price and production supports from payments to farmers, meaning that cuts in prices would not be fully compensated with direct payments. The Commission also suggested that direct payments should be reduced over time ('degressivity'). Further, the Commission argued for cuts in support prices to bring them closer to world prices, that funding for rural developmental should be increased, and environmental protection measures should be strengthened. The Commission proposed that farmers in the accession states would *not* be eligible for direct income payments. But the proposal would also lead to a real increase in the size of the EU's overall budget (Serger, 2001, p. 112).

While internal talks at the technical level continued throughout 1998, the political-level negotiations were stalled pending the results of the German elections held in September 1998. As the Cardiff Summit in June 1998 had fixed the deadline for the conclusion of the Agenda 2000 negotiations as March 1999, discussions began in earnest after the new German SPD-led government was formed on exactly how to square the circle by preventing an increase in the EU budget *and* minimizing the impact of reforms of the CAP and structural funds for the net beneficiaries. In December 1998 a large majority of countries agreed upon a 'stabilization' of the EU budget, including CAP spending (Serger, 2001, p. 112).

The incoming German Presidency in the first half of 1999, which took charge of chairing the Agenda 2000 negotiations, tabled a detailed 'negotiating box' package in early January to enable delegations to examine the details of the pre-draft of conclusions prior to arriving in the Berlin Summit in March 1999. But much work remained, especially as regards the CAP, which not surprisingly proved to be the toughest nut to crack.

As will be discussed further below, the Commission's proposals were significantly changed in meetings prior to Berlin in the Agricultural Council and among Heads of State and Government (see Serger, 2001 for more). Finance Ministers in February 1999 agreed that CAP spending should be limited to then current levels, which was a substantial departure from the Commission's proposals that called for a substantial increase in spending due to increased direct payments (Serger, 2001, p. 114). While the subsequent informal European Council Summit in Petersberg in late February did not endorse this position, it was clear that CAP costs would be reduced in relation to the original Commission proposal (ibid., p. 115). A first agreement was reached in multiple marathon sessions of the Agricultural Council in late February and early March, after which the Heads of State and Government further tinkered with the deal, leading to a final agreement in Berlin in March (ibid., pp. 119–24).

To save money, the final Berlin agreement reduced the size of the proposed price cuts in order to lower the direct payment funds necessary to compensate – in effect a less ambitious reform to save money (ibid., p. 121; see above Table 8.1). The de-coupling principle was also removed. Plans that direct payments should be reduced over time ('degressivity') were also shelved, and the dairy reform was postponed. But proponents of reform also secured a sentence in the conclusions that stated that the European Council invited the

TABLE 8.1 *Internal reforms of EU policies and the package offered to the candidates*

	Agenda 2000 proposal (July 1997)	*Final outcome in Berlin (March 1999)*	*Commission proposals (January 2002)*	*Final outcome in Copenhagen (December 2002)*
Common Agricultural Policy				
Level of support prices	• reduce by 20% for arable crops, 30% for beef, and 10 % for dairy products	• reduction for arable crops 15%, 20% for beef, and 15% for dairy products (cuts for dairy to start in 2005/6)	n/a	• further reductions possible in mid-term review scheduled for 2003
Quotas		• increase dairy quota by 2.4%		
Direct income payments	• 50% compensation for arable crops, 80% for beef, and 70% for dairy products	• slight increase in level of compensation for beef	n/a	• further reforms possible in mid-term review scheduled for 2002–3
	• ceiling for amount to individual farmer	• no mandatory ceiling, but up to MS discretion		n/a
	• no national co-financing	• unchanged	• allow new MS to co-finance direct payments by using national funds to 'top up'	• allow national co-financing by new MS up to level of existing MS
	• no payments to farmers in new member states	• unchanged	• step-wise introduction over 10 yrs 25% (2004) 30% (2005) 35% (2006)	• same, but with ability to 'top-up' nationally
Structural and Cohesion policies				
Number of objectives	• from 7 to 3	• unchanged	• unchanged	• unchanged
Eligibility for programmes	• reduce to below 40% of population	• reduce to 38%	• more funding in objective 1	• unchanged

Level of spending	• 45 billion for the new members in period 2000–6	• 45 billion for new members	• 25.5 billion for 2004–6 for 10 new members • increase amount of funds given through Cohesion Fund	• 21.7 billion for 2004–6 for 10 new members
Total level of funds per member state	• limit of 4% of national GDP	• unchanged	• unchanged	• unchanged
Financial Framework Funds for enlargement	• 41.2 billion (payment appropriations)	• 42.59 billion total in commitment appropriations 45.4 billion in payment appropriations	• 40.16 billion total in commitment appropriations	• 40.85 billion total in commitment appropriations
New member state contributions to budget	• not decided	• not decided	• full contributions offset by 800 million/year from 2004–6 to compensate	• postponed date from January 1 to May 1 2004 • introduced additional budgetary compensations (Schengen facility and compensation)
Size of overall budget	• cap at 1.27% • appropriations for *payments* 1.24% – 2000 1.24% – 2001 1.22% – 2002–6	• cap at 1.27% • appropriations for *payments* 1.13% – 2000 1.12% – 2001 1.14% – 2002 1.15% – 2003 1.11% – 2004 1.09% – 2005–6	• cap at 1.27%	• cap at 1.27%

Sources: European Commission, 1997; COM (98) 131 and 158; European Council, 1999a; and Serger, 2001, p. 125; Treaty of Accession, *Official Journal* L 236, 23.9.03.

Commission to submit a report on developments in agricultural expenditure that 'if necessary' can be accompanied by proposals for reform (European Council, 1999a, para. 21). The possibility of a mid-term review kept the issue of CAP reform on the agenda, and led the Commission to table proposals for reform in mid-2002 that led to the 2003 mid-term review reforms (see Daugbjerg and Swinbank, 2004). The sum available for enlargement was to be 42.59 billion in commitment appropriations. Further, the size of the overall budget was significantly reduced in comparison to the Commission's proposal (see Table 8.1).

Negotiating the final deal – from Berlin to Copenhagen

Once the necessary internal reforms for enlargement were solved in Berlin, substantive external negotiations on the terms of entry for the candidates could begin. During the Finnish Presidency, the debate on numbers resurfaced after the Commission's Regular Report in October 1999 recommended opening accession negotiations with all ten of the Central and Eastern European applicants (see below for why the Commission changed its views). The Helsinki Summit endorsed the Commission's recommendation, and negotiations were subsequently opened with the five new countries in the so-called 'Helsinki group' and Malta in February 2000.

The subject matter of the negotiations with the candidates was in effect the entire *acquis*, which was divided into thirty-one chapters to be negoatiated after 1998. The first stage of the negotiations was a multilateral screening process, where the Commission and all of the applicants undertook a chapter-by-chapter examination of the *acquis*. The second stage of negotiations was bilateral negotiations between the Commission and the candidate, where the Commission examined the transposition and implementation status of directives in each of the chapters to the candidates state. The final stage was the substantive bilateral negotiations between EU governments represented by the Presidency and the candidate. These negotiations dealt with transitional periods, the financial package, and dates of entry.

The EU's basic negotiating position vis-à-vis the candidates was that they had to accept and faithfully implement the whole of the *acquis* from day one of membership, but as this was a very unrealistic goal the negotiations dealt with granting candidate countries transitional periods for the implementation of certain limited areas of the *acquis*. Examples include the implementation of costly aspects of the EU's environmental *acquis*, such as drinking water requirements that would require investments far in excess of the capabilities of most of the candidates. The EU was adamant in the negotiations that no permanent exemptions would be granted, in contrast to previous enlargements, but that transitional periods were to be limited both in time and scope. Therefore the basic question was how generous the EU would be in granting transitional periods given to the candidates.

As had so often happened in the course of the enlargement negotiations, the negotiations with the candidates were again put on the back burner as the EU turned inwards to focus on internal reforms – this time in the IGC 2000 (see Chapter 6). But the Commission did publish a road map in its Enlargement Strategy Paper in November 2000 that detailed when member states should agree upon common positions, when chapters should be closed and when the negotiations should be concluded (European Commission, 2000d). The Commission proposed that chapters with the greatest budgetary implications (CAP, structural funds, and budgetary issues) and the institutional chapter should be saved until the final stage of the negotiations. The Nice Summit accepted the road map, and stated that the EU should be 'in a position to welcome those new member states which are ready as from the end of 2002 in the hope that they will be able to take part in the next European Parliament elections' (European Council, 2000b).

It was then during the Swedish Presidency in the first half of 2001 that enlargement negotiations returned to the top of the EU's agenda (Friis and Jarosz-Friis, 2002, p. 23). Both the Swedish and subsequent Belgian Presidencies moved the negotiations forward in 2001, and concluded many of the simpler chapters (see Ludlow, 2004a).

The final phase of the negotiations started after the Laeken Summit in December 2001. In the Laeken Conclusions the EU listed the ten candidate countries with which negotiations could be concluded in 2002 – all but Bulgaria and Romania. As the final stage of the negotiations started, the EU had provisionally closed 20 to 25 chapters with all ten of the candidates, with most of the remaining issues dealing with sensitive budget-related questions. The Spanish Presidency focused upon these difficult issues.

The Commission submitted a memorandum in January 2002 on the financial framework for 2004–6 that drew the contours for the final internal debates on the budget (Avery, 2004; Ludlow, 2004) (see SEC (2002) 102). As the Commission proposed that the ten candidates should join the EU on 1 January 2004, whereas the Berlin agreement was based upon the presumption that only six candidates would join in 2002, the delay of two years enabled the Commission to argue that enlargement with ten instead of the planned six would not increase the total costs of enlargement for the budgetary period 2000–6.

The Commission also tabled a paper proposing an EU mandate in the agricultural chapter, which suggested that farmers in the new member states should be eligible for direct payments, but that these funds would be phased in over time, and that the new member states would be able to 'top up' with national funds in order to match levels of support in existing member states (SEC (2002) 95). This had not been agreed in the Berlin conclusions in 1999 (see Table 8.1).

Unfortunately for the Spanish Presidency, internal negotiations on the financial chapters stalled as the EU once again waited on the outcome of a German election, this time in September 2002. The plan had otherwise been that by June 2002 the EU would have agreed common positions on all of the chapters of the negotiations, which would have enabled the Spanish Presidency to negotiate on these issues with the candidates (Avery, 2004).

The incoming Danish Presidency had the stated goal of completing the circle started in Copenhagen in 1993. The strategy of the Presidency was to clarify all of the technical issues prior to an informal European Council Summit to be held in October 2002 in Brussels, which would then give the Presidency a mandate for the budget-related chapters that would allow it to conclude the negotiations with the candiates by December. The Commission tabled its annual report on the progress made by the candidates on 9 October 2002, suggesting that negotiations could be closed with the ten countries, as they all had made sufficient progress (European Commission, 2002d).

But the internal negotiations on the EU mandate made little headway until the informal European Council summit in Brussels, where a common EU position was agreed on the expenditure-heavy chapters. The intense bilateral activity between Chirac and Schröder that had started in August finally bore fruit only hours before the Brussels Summit was scheduled to open. Based upon a French draft, the two leaders together with one senior aide each stitched together a compromise that bridged the gap between the positions of the net contributors and beneficiaries (Ludlow, 2004a, pp. 196–7, 202).

Germany ensured that there would be a limit on expenditure, including CAP, in the next budgetary period (2007–13) that would de facto lead to degressivity in CAP spending, whereas France was promised that CAP spending levels would be maintained until 2006, and that spending caps post 2006 would also affect other policies. Germany also accepted the phasing-in of direct payments to farmers in the candidate states from 2004, while France accepted the introduction of co-financing within CAP in the accession states.

The Franco-German deal formed the core of the Brussels agreement, but the Commission text on cuts in other policy areas, notably the structural funds, was removed. The level of structural funds was reduced from the Commission proposal (from €25.6 billion to €23 billion). The European Council also accepted the use of temporary budgetary compensations to ensure that new members would not be net contributors, but kept the total commitments for enlargement well below the Berlin ceiling (€39.23 billion for 2004–2006) (see Table 8.1). Safeguard and monitoring clauses were introduced based upon Commission proposals, but were strengthened and extended beyond merely Internal Market-related areas to include all cross-border activity to placate Dutch concerns (Ludlow, 2004a, pp. 195–6).

One key issue that risked upsetting the Brussels agreement was pending CAP reform. The Commission had in July 2002 tabled proposals for a mid-term review of CAP for 2003 that risked upsetting the budgetary decisions to be taken in Brussels (Ludlow, 2004a, pp. 127–32). For example, proponents of CAP reform feared that if they agreed in Brussels to, for example, introduce direct payments in the accession states, this could freeze the CAP in its present form, preventing further reforms in the future. A crucial compromise was proposed by Belgium that decoupled the two issues by introducing quite ambiguous wording on whether a mid-term review in 2003 could affect CAP spending for the 2000–2006 period, satisfying both proponents and opponents of CAP reform (Ludlow, 2004, pp. 196–202).

While the candidates welcomed the Brussels conclusions as a step to concluding negotiations by December, they felt the financial package was too miserly and that the EU should at least make available the funds agreed in Berlin (Ludlow, 2004a, p. 229; *AE*, 8329, 28–29.10.02, p. 10, *AE*, 8342, 18–19.11.02, p. 5). But both the Danish Presidency and the Commission stressed that there would be 'real negotiations' after Brussels (Ludlow, 2004, p. 226), that financial concessions could be given as long as they did not have 'great financial repercussions', and that transitional periods could be reviewed in order to give further concessions (*AE*, 8329, 28–29.10.02, p. 10).

After a series of bilateral negotiations with the candidates, the Danish Presidency tabled what it termed a final compromise package in late November to the candidates, which contained an additional €1.3 billion in relation to the Brussels agreement (*AE*, 8349, 28.11.02, p. 10). In a major breach of Presidency etiquette, the package had not been accepted by the other fourteen EU governments, and Germany in particular thought that the new offer was too generous (Ludlow, 2004a, pp. 239–43; *AE*, 8349, 28.11.02, p. 10, 8352, 2–3.12.02, p. 9).

While many governments were upset about the move, they did retro-spectively approve the Presidency package in early December. The candidates in contrast did not see the financial concession as enough, especially regarding the CAP and budgetary compensations, drawing the lines for battle for Copenhagen (*AE*, 8353, 4.12.02, p. 11).

An issue that loomed over the negotiations throughout 2001–2 was the issue of Turkish membership. Turkish membership had been linked by the Turks with a solution on the development of the EU's ability to utilize NATO assets in EU military operations, where the EU was strongly interested in a deal to enable the deployment of an EU force to Macedonia (Ludlow, 2004a, p. 249). Behind-the-scenes negotiations led to two deals in December 2002. First, the EU agreed that accession negotiations with Turkey could be opened 'without delay' if the EU in December 2004 believed that Turkey had made satisfying progress in meeting the Copenhagen criteria. This opening paved the way for a deal within NATO that resolved the question of the EU's use of NATO assets (Ludlow, 2004, pp. 312–13).

At the Copenhagen Summit, the negotiations focused on pressuring Poland to accept the EU's offer of slightly increased concessions, often without a mandate from the other EU governments, the Presidency was able to conclude a deal at 7.15 pm on Friday, 13 December 2002. The final package increased the amount of funds available to enlargement, especially through forms of budgetary compensations. Enlargement with ten new members was a reality (for a detailed description of the Summit, see Ludlow, 2004a).

What did the EU institutions want in the fifth enlargement negotiations?

The European Commission

Enlargement posed a considerable challenge for the Commission. On the one hand, it had manifest political interests in widening the EU as a political vision for a stable and democratic Europe; also, enlarge-ment in the past has gone hand in hand with deepening of the Union. On the other hand, the sheer enormity of the project and the risks that it raised for the internal coherence of the EU and the proper imple-mentation of the *acquis,* together with the necessity for reforms of key EU policies like the CAP, raised many dilemmas for the Commission.

Looking first at the Commission's preferences on the external side of the enlargement negotiations, enlargement differs from other external EU negotiations in that it is not a negotiation of 'us versus them', but between the 'future us' (Avery, 1995; Cameron, 2000, p. 14). The Commission therefore had to take into consideration future relations between the new and existing members in the enlarged EU, and what would work in the future enlarged EU (Avery, 1995, p. 2).

The Commission was split internally throughout the process on the questions of whether the EU should expand eastwards, and later on the terms of entry. At the highest level, President Jacques Delors did not want to commit the EU to promises of membership for the CEE countries, as he was unsure whether the transition would last, and whether the EU could agree the fundamental institutional reforms that he thought were necessary to enlarge further (Friis, 1997, pp. 253–4; Torreblanca, 2001, pp. 54, 103; Landau, 2004). The Commissioner in charge of relations with the countries of Central and Eastern Europe, Frans Andriessen (until 1993), was though more favourable (Torreblanca, 2001, p. 105). After Andriessen, Commissioner for External Relations Leon Brittan (1993–5) strongly supported membership (Grilli, 1993, p. 320), but was followed by van den Broek (1995–9), who was much more sceptical, reflecting broader attitudes throughout the Santer Commission in 1995–9 (Ludlow, 2004, p. 23). The relatively cautious attitudes of the Santer Commission were overturned in 1999 by the enthusiastic support of enlargement within the Prodi Commission, and especially Gunter Verheugen in the newly created post of Commissioner for Enlargement in the new DG Enlargement (Ludlow, 2004, pp. 33–4, 136).

When the debates turned from the question of whether to enlarge to the terms of entry and the number of states with which negotiations should be opened, the Commission was faced with the dilemma of protecting the *acquis* versus ensuring that enlargement took place, and that all candidates were treated equally. There were though large differences within the Commission, with sectoral DGs often arguing for strong protection of 'their' part of the *acquis*, while the Enlargement DG created in 1999 attempted to create a compromise which satisfied sectoral DGs while also ensuring that enlargement took place (Interviews EC-20, EC-21).

The Commission as the guardian of the treaties was obliged to ensure that enlargement did not endanger the *acquis*. The Commission was also afraid that if the EU was too generous in offering transitional periods, this would create similar demands for protection from industries and governments in existing member states (Landau , 2004). Therefore the Commission's basic position on the terms of entry was to ensure that few transitional periods were given, especially as regards the Internal Market, and that those that were given were limited both in time and scope. Further, the Commission argued for strict conditions for entry in order to ensure that acceding states were ready to lift the burdens of membership, and in contrast to earlier enlargements it wanted to verify that the *acquis* was in fact implemented *prior* to accession. Regarding numbers, the Commission's position was that negotiations should only be opened with those member states that had made demonstrable progress in fulfilling the EU's conditions.

On the internal aspects of enlargement, while the Commission had been pushing for CAP reform since the early 1990s (Mayhew, 1998, pp. 278–81), it was afraid that if it linked these reforms too closely with enlargement, it could risk that its strategy would backfire, and that the enlargement process itself could be held hostage if far-reaching reforms were not agreed (Interview EC-20). The basic Commission position on the CAP was to further the MacSharry reforms of 1992 by cutting support prices, decoupling income support from price cuts, and renationalizing parts of the CAP to cut costs.

On other internal issues, the Commission argued for reforms that would hinder the explosion of the EU budget post-enlargement. For example, it wanted to re-focus the structural and cohesion funds upon the poorest regions. On the size of the budget, the Commission was concerned about reopening the fierce debates from the early 1990s on the budgetary ceiling, and therefore it chose to advocate maintaining the current 1.27 per cent ceiling in the 2000–6 financial framework.

The European Parliament

It is necessary to be cautious when speaking of the 'preferences' of the EP as a whole regarding enlargement, as it is composed of many different parties with opposing views, and the EP was also sometimes split along national lines. Further, many of the reports and papers published by the EP were the product of committees, where MEPs were sometimes more motivated by sectoral interests than the general institutional interests of the EP as a whole (Peterson, 1999, p. 58).

The EP was quite sceptical about enlargement in the early 1990s, and a general condition for a majority of MEPs throughout the process was that they did not want enlargement *before* significant institutional and policy reforms had been undertaken (Harris, 2000, pp. 26, 29; European Parliament, 1993, 1997a, 1999a; Torreblanca, 2001, p. 126). Further, the EP was concerned about the potential costs of enlargement, and therefore advocated far-reaching reforms of both the CAP and structural funds, but it also advocated increasing the budgetary ceiling beyond 1.27 per cent GNP (European Parliament, 1996y).

The EP later became the strongest proponent of enlargement, as it was seen as a politically popular cause that it could champion; it was also felt that widening would go hand in hand with further deepening (treaty reform). By 2002 the EP saw enlargement as the greatest political priority of the EU (Bailer and Schneider, 2000; Ludlow, 2004a, pp. 64–6). In the debate on numbers, the EP advocated opening negotiations with all of the candidates by 1998 (the so-called 'regatta' model) (Bailer and Schneider, 2000b, pp. 28, 32; European Parliament, 1996x).

The Council Secretariat

The Secretariat did not have strong preferences on any of the issues in the enlargement process, and only focused upon helping Presidencies and governments in the Council in achieving their own goals (Interview EC-17). The Secretariat basically saw itself as an honest broker that attempted to translate often vague ideas and proposals into legal text (Interview EC-18).

The leadership resources of the EU institutions

The material leadership resources of EU institutions

The Commission had some material leadership resources in the internal aspects of the enlargement process. As the Agenda 2000 negotiations dealt with first pillar issues, they were conducted using the Community method, giving the Commission the ability to link issues in daily EU policy-making with the enlargement negotiations. But at the end of the day, it was governments that had to agree upon the final reforms, so the ability of the Commission to exploit its monopoly on initiation was limited. And in the actual enlargement negotiations with the candidates, the Commission had no say over the final outcome.

The EP did possess certain material resources in the enlargement negotiations. First, in the internal reform negotiations such as Agenda 2000 that took place using the Community method, the EP had significant power over the final outcome, especially on issues that were negotiated using the co-decision procedure. The financial framework for 2000–6 was adopted through an Inter-Institutional Agreement, granting the EP veto power (see 1999/C 172/01). In the actual enlargement negotiations, the EP also had gained in the SEA in 1985 the power of assent over final accession treaties (Article 49 EU).

The Council Secretariat had no relevant material leadership resources.

The informational advantages of EU institutions

The Commission did have strong comparative informational advantages. By being the 'guardian of the treaties', the Commission possessed detailed knowledge of the over 80,000 pages of detailed and technical EU legislation (Interview EC-18). Further, during the enlargement negotiations, the Commission was delegated the functions of monitoring how the candidate countries implemented the *acquis*, as well as the overall pre-accession strategy to prepare the candidates for membership. This role gave the Commission privileged information both on the detailed content of the *acquis*, the progress made by candidates in different chapters of the *acquis* – and in particular whether the demands for transitional periods in the candidates were valid or not – and what the preferences of the candidates were (Interview EC-17, EC-18). Finally, in comparison to IGCs on major treaty reform, the Commission devoted many resources to enlargement. In the later phases of the negotiations, over 300 Commission officials dealt directly with enlargement, and they drew directly on expertise throughout the Commission in informal talks and the presentation of internal non-papers (Landau, 2004).

Turning to informational advantages of the EP, although the Secretary-General of the EP in 1997 created a task force of six officials to collect documentation relating to enlargement, later expanded to thirteen officials, and expanded the number of staff servicing MEPs both in Joint Parliamentary Committees and in EP committees (Priestley, personal communication; Harris, 2000, p. 34), the EP never possessed comparative informational advantages vis-à-vis governments. EP committees attempted to monitor the enlargement process closely, but did not take direct part in the negotiations, and did not possess the specialized expertise on substantive issues that the Commission and the foreign ministries of the largest EU member states had.

The EP did gain some information on the preferences of the candidates through its biannual meetings in both Joint Parliamentary Committees with the candidate countries, and the President of the EP with the presidents of the parliaments of the candidates. The Joint Parliamentary Committees existed for all of the Central and Eastern European candidates, and for Cyprus, Malta and Turkey. The Committees were composed of delegates from the EP and candidate national parliaments, together with representatives of the Commission and the Presidency. The Committees meetings were concluded with joint declarations and recommendations.

The Secretariat had very few informational resources in comparison to the Commission or most member state governments. The Enlargement Division of the Secretariat had only six A-level officials in total, split into three units (Interview EC-18) with which to cover negotiations on thirty-one chapters among twelve candidate countries!

The reputation of the EU institutions

The Commission in the EFTA enlargement negotiations in the early to mid-1990s was seen to be more neutral than the Presidencies involved (Avery, 1995, p. 3). In relations with the candidates, the Santer Commission had been relatively cautious, but this changed with the appointment by Prodi in 1999 of Gunter Verheugen, who quickly came to be trusted by the candidates to both listen and take account of their interests (Interview NAT-20). The EP had increasing clout in the later part of the 1990s, and was widely seen by governments in both the EU and the candidate states as the 'champion' of enlargement (Bailer and Schneider, 2000). While the Secretariat was widely seen throughout the period as a trusted assistant to governments, governments in general perceived the Commission to be a more useful assistant than the Secretariat in most questions.

Opportunities for leadership opened by the negotiation context

The role of EU institutions in the enlargement negotiations

The external negotiations with candidates are conducted as an intergovernmental conference (IGC) between the EU member states and the applicants, as accession requires the revision of the treaties (see Chapter 1). Both the Commission and the EP do not have strong *formal* roles in the external enlargement negotiations. But in reality, the Commission was delegated an integral role in the enlargement process, whereas the EP primarily played the part of the 'conscience' of the Union, admonishing governments in its plenary resolutions for not moving fast enough and not undertaking what it viewed as necessary reforms of the Union.

In the external negotiations with the candidates, the Commission was delegated responsibility for:

- monitoring the progress of the candidates in implementing the different sections of the *acquis*;
- administering aid and assistance through the pre-accession programs;
- preparing the draft common negotiating positions for the Council of Ministers; and
- assessing the requests of candidates for transitional periods. (Avery, 1995, p. 2; Cameron, 2000; Landau, 2004; Interview EC-20, EC-21)

The Commission also played a key role of assisting Presidencies in the external negotiations by, for example, assessing the validity of demands by candidates for transition periods.

In the internal negotiations on the Agenda 2000 package of reforms of EU policies, the Commission had a strong formal agenda-setting role, and was intimately involved in the negotiations both as an assistant to the Presidencies, and as a political actor attempting to drive the process forward. The Presidency and governments also often asked the Commission to draw up background papers and proposals on various aspects of the negotiation process, such as when the Council agreed in 1995 to the Commission's suggestion that the Commission draft a paper studying the impact of enlargement on the budget and other EU policies – what was to become Agenda 2000.

The EP had a much weaker role than the Commission in the external negotiations with the candidates. The EP's actual involvement in the process was primarily through the meetings of the Joint Parliamentary Committees, and between the President of the EP with the presidents of the candidate states. In contrast, the EP did have a role in the internal reform process, being closely involved in the negotiation of the Agenda 2000 package.

The Council Secretariat played its usual assisting role both in internal Council decision-making and in the external negotiations as an assistant to the Council and Presidency. The Secretariat drafted common proposals based upon Commission proposals for Presidencies, and helped broker deals in the Council (Interview EC-18).

The nature of the issues being negotiated

When discussions turned from broad questions and turned towards the specifics, matters became very complex and technical. This was especially true in the external negotiations with the candidates, where the EU had to plough through over 80,000 pages of legislation in the attempt to determine where transitional periods could be granted to the candidates. In the final six months of the negotiations, the negotiations were close to an information overload, with 300 official documents being produced together with over 8,000 pages of meetings documentation, and over 500 conference documents (Interview EC-18).

The number of issues and parties in the negotiations

The external negotiation with the candidates was an immensely complex process, where the EU was negotiating with first six, then later twelve countries on thirty-one different chapters of the *acquis*. The maximum number of countries that the EU had previously negotiated with had been the four in the 1995 EFTA enlargement. Secondly, the *acquis* had grown significantly through the 1990s, with many new areas of legislation that had not been dealt with in previous enlargements. Within each of the chapters were numerous issues, and the sheer complexity of the negotiating situation can be illustrated by the fact that the final Accession Treaty contains an estimated 322 transitional measures in seventeen different chapters and spans over 5,000 pages (Avery, 2004; Treaty of Accession, *Official Journal* L 236, 23.9.03, p. 20).

The distribution and intensity of governmental preferences

An overreaching pro-enlargement versus sceptic/opponent cleavage existed among the EU member states, but this cleavage was often disturbed by specific national concerns. For example, despite Germany being a major proponent of enlargement, it was also strongly concerned about the free movement of workers from the accession states. The Netherlands switched camps in mid-2002, and was close to braking the process during the enlargement end-game, where Dutch ministers argued for strict budgetary discipline and for much stricter safeguard clauses (Ludlow, 2004, pp. 164–9). A second cleavage dealt with the number of candidates with which negotiations should be opened, with Germany the most prominent supporter of a limited enlargement, whereas the Nordics and the UK wanted a more inclusive process including all ten candidate countries in Central and Eastern Europe.

The internal negotiations on reforms of existing policies within Agenda 2000 was also affected by one overreaching cleavage. The basic cleavage was between net contributors and net beneficiaries, pitting Germany, the Netherlands, the UK and Sweden against France and the 'cohesion' states. But even here there were complexities, especially as regards the CAP (Serger, 2001, pp. 41–101). Germany for instance was strongly interested in reducing the EU budget, but opposed CAP reform that led to substantial price cuts (ibid.).

During the early 1990s, the question of whether the EU should expand eastwards was a political issue that was intensely debated at the highest level within the EU, although as it increasingly became politically correct to support enlargement, arguments against enlargement had to be cloaked in more technical terms (Schimmelfennig, 2001). Other issues later in the process that were debated at the highest level dealt with both the number of candidates that should be accepted, and general questions such as the scope of reforms to the CAP, structural funds and the budget. Many of the internal reform issues were also politically sensitive – especially CAP reform, where even the smallest change could have far-reaching effects for national farmers. Although CAP reform is immensely complex, and governments were often dependent upon calculations provided by the Commission on the effects of different options, the issue was also so sensitive that governments mobilized the resources necessary to keep it firmly under their control.

Leadership by EU institutions in the Eastern Enlargement negotiations

Leadership by the European Commission

Despite playing a key role in both the internal and external negotiations, it is surprisingly difficult to find the 'fingerprints' of the Commission on the final outcomes. Perhaps the only true mark of the Commission on the process was its role in sustaining the process, facilitating compromise, and ensuring that the enlargement negotiations did not reach an impasse. In the Iberian enlargement for example, France and Italy blocked Spanish accession for several years until a satisfactory solution could be found regarding agricultural imports. Similar blockages could easily have occurred regarding the conditions for entry of the candidates if the Commission or EU governments had been stricter in their interpretation, or if the Commission or EU governments had insisted on more far-reaching reforms of either EU policies such as the CAP, or institutional reform, prior to enlargement.

The debate within the Commission on leadership strategy was split between advocates of 'glorious' or 'blue sky' proposals, and those that argued that the Commission's basic role was to get the job done by producing realistic compromises that took into account interests of both EU and candidate countries (Interview EC-20). The pragmatic approach won out, with multiple instances where the Commission denied linking positions that it otherwise was interested in (for example CAP reform) with enlargement.

Looking chronologically at the provision of leadership by the Commission in the negotiations, the Commission did play a role in pressuring EU governments to decide to offer membership to several countries in Central and Eastern Europe. Contrary to what a majority of member states wanted, the Commission attempted to insert into the draft negotiating mandate of the Europe Agreements a reference to membership (Torreblanca, 2001, p. 97). The reference was cut out of the final negotiating mandate by the Council, but a confidential provision was inserted that did grant the Commission the ability to offer a non-binding reference to membership during the course of the negotiations (ibid, pp. 98, 105–6, 147). The Commission in the final stage then inserted a sentence that recognized that Poland, Hungary and Czechoslovakia had EU membership as a goal (Beach, 1998, p. 37; Friis, 1997, pp. 259–60).

Prior to the Lisbon European Council Summit in June 1992, the Commission submitted a report on the criteria and conditions for the accession of new members in which it proposed 'a strategy of opening negotiations soon with those countries which are ready and able to join' (European Commission, 1992, p. 8). The report with the reference to membership and conditions was attached without discussion to the Lisbon Conclusions, and was barely discussed by governments prior to the Edinburgh Summit in December 1992, or the Copenhagen Summit (Mayhew, 1998, pp. 25–7; Interview EC–17), where both the overall goal of membership of the Central and Eastern European countries was publicly raised, and the now famous Copenhagen criteria were drawn directly from the Commission's report (European Council, 1993).

After Copenhagen, the Commission was delegated the task of drafting more elaborate criteria, along with a list of legislation that should be implemented by the candidates (Smith, 2003, p. 115). Surprisingly, the EU in the early 1990s had no description of the *acquis* that could be given to the candidates. A team within the Commission, drawn mainly from the Internal Market DG, drew up the White Paper that described the *acquis* (see European Commission, 1995a). On the conditions for membership, the Commission took a pragmatic approach that ensured that both the concerns of the sceptics were satisfied, while also not creating insurmountable barriers. For example, in the Agenda 2000 opinion on the progress of the candidates, many deficiencies were listed, but the opinion also stated that they could be ready for membership in the medium term (European Commission, 1997; Ludlow, 2004a, pp. 24–5).

The next major decision in the enlargement process was the question of numbers. The Commission's proposal for the 5+1 formula included in the Agenda 2000 paper was accepted by the European Council at the Luxembourg Summit in December 1997. But the formula proposed by the Commission was merely a compromise between proponents of a small enlargement and those wanting a more inclusive enlargement process with up to ten countries. Further, while the Luxembourg Presidency used the Commission's 5+1 formula, it also accepted a Danish/Swedish idea of individual screening of *all* of the applicants within a *single* accession process. Finally, only two years after Luxembourg, the Commission had changed its stance owing to events, arguing in its October 1999 Regular Report that there were few objective differences between the candidates, especially as slow-progressing Poland for political reasons had to be in the first wave (Interview EC-20). Therefore the Commission proposed that the EU should open negotiations with all of the applicants with the exception of Turkey (Bailer and Schneider, 2000, pp. 28–30; European Commission, 1999a).

The next major set of issues in the negotiations were the internal reforms necessary for enlargement. As the institutional reforms through treaty revision are dealt with in Chapters 5 to 7, the following will deal solely with the provision of leadership by the Commission in the negotiation of three key policy areas – the CAP, structural funds and the budget.

Looking at the three issues, while the Commission tabled the legislative proposals that served as the basis for Council negotiations, it is surprisingly difficult to find instances where Commission leadership shifted outcomes on the distributive dimension. The major impact of the Commission was perhaps more of a 'non-decision', in that the Commission actively sought to *not* link enlargement with more fundamental reforms of the CAP and other sensitive policy-areas – something which would have endangered the enlargement process. While this had the effect of diluting the internal reforms that were agreed upon in Berlin, it ensured that the enlargement negotiations were not hijacked by national special interests. In the Agenda 2000 report, the Commission repeatedly stated that reform of the CAP was necessary *irrespective* of enlargement, and when the Commission listed the reasons for reform, enlargement was placed last (European Commission, 1997).

The basic outline of the proposals on CAP that the Commission contained in the Agenda 2000 report, and then fleshed out as formal legislative proposals in March 1998, was a continuation of the MacSharry reforms in an attempt to bring the CAP in line with GATT/WTO rules while also cutting costs by decoupling direct payments from price cuts. Comparing the Commission's proposals with the Berlin agreement, there are few differences, which on the face of it could lead us to suggest that the Commission had significant influence upon the CAP outcome (see Table 8.1). While Berlin diluted the size of the price cuts proposed by the Commission, it maintained the reforms in two of the three areas suggested by the Commission. But key elements of the Commission proposals, such as the partial decoupling of price cuts with increases in direct payments, were removed by governments (Serger, 2001, pp. 146–58).

In the negotiations on the EU's common position in the agricultural chapter in 2002, there are indications that the Commission played a more significant role. The Commission's January 2002 proposal for a draft EU common position introduced elements of CAP reform for the candidates that would have been patently unacceptable for EU governments if the Commission had suggested that the reforms were also applicable in existing member states, especially regarding the introduction of national co-financing (SEC 2002 95 final). Further, the Berlin agreement did *not* extend direct payments to farmers in the accession states, and was therefore not calculated in the financial framework agreed in Berlin. But the Commission in its talks with the candidates found that the candidates regarded this as highly unfair, and the Commission decided to break with Berlin and propose that direct payments be gradually introduced in the accession states (Ludlow, 2004a, pp. 68–9) (see Table 8.1). After Verheugen sounded out the Polish Prime Minister on what levels he could accept, the Commission proposed a schedule that started at 25 per cent in 2004 and increased to 100 per cent by 2013 (Ludlow, 2004, p. 69).

This proposal provoked strong reactions from net contributors such as the Netherlands, Germany, Sweden and Denmark, who argued that it went against the Berlin agreement, while CAP advocates like France supported the move as a way to ensure that direct payments were kept in place after the forthcoming mid-term review (*EU Observer*, 19.03.02; Ludlow, 2004a, pp. 72–6). A compromise was then reached in Brussels that kept the options open for further negotiations on CAP reform (the mid-term review), while also agreeing upon the main elements of the Commission proposal, including the extension of direct payments and the introduction of national co-financing in the candidate states. The Commission succeeded in formulating a position that proved acceptable to both the candidates and existing EU governments (Interview NAT-15).

The Commission also played a key leadership role in the internal budget negotiations. For example, instead of reopening the budget debate that has so often plagued the EU, the Commission simply decided to extend the financial agreement reached in 1992 to the next budgetary period by keeping the 1.27 per cent GNP ceiling. Another key decision taken by the Commission was to focus only upon the 2000–6 budgetary period, and not upon the longer-term budgetary consequences of enlargement. This ensured that there was a 'firewall' between the actual accession negotiations and the longer-term costs of enlargement, although this wall was breached at the end when plans were agreed that provided for a ten-year transition period for direct payments (Interview EC-20).

In the debates on the EU's common position on the budget, the Commission's position paper from January 2002 proved influential (SEC (2002) 102 final), and in the words of Avery, it set the parameters for the agreement reached (Avery, 2004). While governments did knock off several billion euro in the common position agreed in Brussels, the Danish Presidency together with the Commission gave most of the funds back in the final stage through different forms of budgetary compensations (Interview EC-21, NAT-20; Ludlow, 2004a, pp. 303–5).

One key budgetary problem was that due to the different payment horizons of EU funds, several of the candidates would be net contributors in the first year of membership. The problem was spotted by the Commission in early 2002, and one idea for solving the problem that was analysed within the Commission was the suggestion to postpone the date for enlargement by several months (Interview EC-20, EC-21). This would ensure that the new member states would pay lower budgetary contributions for 2004 whereas they would receive full benefits. The Commission discussed the idea with the Danish Presidency, which then in close association with the Commission formulated the final outcome of postponing enlargement until 1 May 2004 (Interview NAT-20; Avery, 2004).

The Commission also had a significant impact in the decisions on the granting of transitional periods, as it was the only actor in many technical areas that could realistically determine the reality of the demands for transitional measures from candidates (Interview NAT-15). Two key linked issues which could have derailed the enlargement process were the questions of limiting the free movement of workers from the candidate states to the EU, and restrictions on the ability of EU citizens to buy certain types of property in the candidate states. Both issues were politically sensitive, and no agreement could have led on the EU side to non-ratification of the Accession Treaty in national parliaments, and failed referendums on membership in the candidates. While the Commission's own position was for a liberal solution, and it, for example, published a study in March 2001 that showed that the costs of free movement of workers would have low costs for existing members in an attempt to defuse the arguments of the opponents (European Commission, 2001) – the Commission tabled a necessary and well-timed compromise in 2001 that removed this potential roadblock (Interview EC-20). The Commission's proposed draft common position in April 2001 stated that current member states could introduce an up to seven-year transitional period. EU governments then accepted that the candidates were granted transitional periods on the sale of agricultural land and second homes (Interview NAT-15, EC-20).

The Commission played a key role in assisting the Danish Presidency in the final months of the enlargement negotiations (Ludlow, 2004a, pp. 93, 224–43; Interview NAT-20). A small team from the Commission assisted the Presidency by drafting fiches and reports, and by providing suggestions on the overall conduct of the end-game, and on the bottom lines of the candidates (Interview EC-21; Ludlow, 2004a, pp. 119, 126). Commission proposals solved key problems, such as the introduction of safeguard clauses that assuaged sceptics (both within and outside of the Commission!), and ideas for increasing the budgetary compensations granted the candidates (Interview NAT-20; Ludlow, 2004a, pp. 134–40). The Commission also played a key role in the drafting of the final budgetary package, and provided key ideas such as allowing the candidates to 'cross-subsidize' direct payments with funds from rural development programs (Interview EC-21). Another area where the Commission played a key role was quietly brokering deals in sensitive bilateral issues, such as the Temelin nuclear plant in the Czech Republic (Interview NAT-20, EC-21). But as the Commission team worked intimately with the Danish Presidency in the crucial behind-the-scenes negotiations in the final stage, it is very difficult to detect the paternity of most of the key ideas, proposals and compromises.

In general though, the Commission's major influence in the enlargement negotiations was to ensure that enlargement took place. The Commission played a key role in preparing the candidates for membership through the pre-accession strategy, which was a job that no other actor could lift (Interview EC-21). The Commission assisted the candidates in implementing the *acquis* in the pre-accession framework, developed draft common positions for the EU based upon its knowledge of the workings of the *acquis* and discussions with both the candidates and EU member states, and provided information and assistance to member states and the Presidencies in finding acceptable compromises.

The overall importance of the Commission in the process can be best summarized by looking at its role in the publication of the so-called Road Map in mid-2000. Throughout 1998 and 1999, proponents of enlargement had been trying to fix a date for enlargement. With the tacit support of several member states, the Commission decided to draw up a detailed timetable for the conduct of the negotiations, but that did not contain a fixed date for the conclusion of the negotiations (European, 2000d; Interview EC-20; Ludlow, 2004a, pp. 43–6). The French Presidency did not view the issue as a high priority. Yet the Council of Ministers adopted the Commission's timetable in December, and it was then endorsed by the Nice Summit, although the Heads of State and Government went further than the Commission by inserting a date for the conclusion – December 2002.

The Road Map then gave discipline to the process, as the EU often works best when there are firm deadlines, and made it difficult for opponents to slow the process down (Interview EC-20). Further, as the proposal came from the Commission, which was intensely monitoring the progress of the candidates in implementing the *acquis*, the proposal had a much greater impact than if it had come from a member state. The Road Map then had the effect of becoming a source of competition between Presidencies in how many chapters they succeeded in opening and closing (Ludlow, 2004a, p. 59).

Concluding, the Commission's overall influence upon the process can be best seen in the fact that the negotiations were successfully concluded in December 2002, and that all of the candidates accepted the final Accession Treaty in their referendums in 2003. By helping steer the process between intractable internal debates on EU policies such as the CAP by proposing only relatively modest and incremental reforms, and away from an Accession Treaty that would have been rejected in referendums by taking note of the interests of the candidates and acting as an honest broker, the Commission achieved its overall objective – an enlargement with ten new members on 1 May 2004. Commission leadership was mostly on the efficiency dimension, and was most successful in technical and complicated issues, and when the Commission brokered compromises that bridged the interests of the candidates and existing member states.

Leadership by the European Parliament

While the EP became an increasingly significant political actor in the 1990s, there is little evidence that it had a significant direct impact in the enlargement process (Ludlow, 2004a, pp. 64–6; Interview NAT-17). Perhaps the main impact of the EP was to act as the 'conscience' of the EU by attempting to 'shame' the member states into enlargement (Bailer and Schneider, 2000; Schimmelfennig, 2001). This moral leadership strengthened the resolve of governments to enlarge the EU (Interview NAT-20).

EP positions on internal issues such as the size of the budget and institutional reform were incompatible with a fast enlargement process. If the EU had attempted to undertake major institutional or policy reform along the lines advocated by the EP *prior* to enlargement, the EU would simply not have been able to conclude the negotiations in Copenhagen.

And the most important leadership resource available to the EP – the threat of a veto – was simply not perceived by governments to be credible. As the EP was more pro-enlargement than most member states, it was not seen as likely that it would block enlargement, no matter how distasteful the final agreement was (Bailer and Schneider, 2000). Therefore despite repeated attempts to play this card by the EP, governments never took it seriously.

Leadership by the Council Secretariat

The Secretariat itself played a much more subdued role in the fifth enlargement negotiation. It was responsible for assisting Presidencies, and had a 'tidying up' function in translating Commission draft common positions into common positions and in drafting the final Accession Treaty, but it also had a more political function of facilitating compromise through informal discussions and providing compromise proposals (Interview EC-18). The Danish Presidency drew upon the Secretariat prior to the Brussels Summit in October 2002, especially as regards the institutional chapter and in the drafting of the annotated agenda for the Summit (Interview EC-18; Ludlow, 2004a, p. 180). But there are few examples of Secretariat leadership that went beyond assistance, and participants in the negotiations within the Commission and Danish Presidency confirmed that the Secretariat played only a minor role in the enlargement endgame (Interview EC-21, NAT-20).

Although it was not strictly related to the actual enlargement negotiations, head of the Secretariat Javier Solana and his *chef de cabinet* Alberto Navarro played a key role in solving an important impasse in the issue of Turkish membership and the ability of the EU to loan NATO assets (Ludlow, 2004a, pp. 148–51, 186, 214–15, 263–8). Solana first assisted the Greek Presidency in the second half of 2002

TABLE 8.2   *Conclusions – leadership in the fifth enlargement negotiations*

Issue area	Outcome
Overall	• key Commission leadership role – sustained the process by administering the pre-accession process, assisting and monitoring the adoption of the acquis by the candidates, providing the Road Map timeline, and providing assistance to Presidencies
Decision to enlarge EU	• Commission instrumental in starting the enlargement process, but became more sceptical in mid-1990s. After 1999 the Commission together with the EP acted as the 'champions' of enlargement, together with the Nordics, UK and Germany
Number of candidates	• the Commission proposed a compromise on numbers in 1997, but final agreement based upon suggestion of Nordics for a more inclusive approach
	• events led to a revision of Commission position in 1999, after which it was decided to open negotiations with all candidates except Turkey
Criteria for entry	• Commission drafted criteria that satisfied sceptics while also ensuring that enlargement was possible

$\rightarrow$

in drafting a plan of action (Denmark, due to its opt-out on CFSP matters with defence implications, relinquished the chair to the next Presidency, Greece) (ibid., pp. 148–51). Then Solana and his team acted as brokers based upon a mandate given by the Council in behind-the-scenes negotiations between Turkey and the EU governments that helped to secure an EU-NATO agreement reached in December that ensured that Turkey acquiesced in the EU borrowing NATO assets for the military mission to Macedonia (ibid., pp. 314–16). However, the key to the Turkish acquiescence was the pledge by the European Council in Copenhagen to review the Turkish application in 2004, which was a deal that was reached at the highest level (ibid., pp. 310–13).

→

Issue area	*Outcome*
Terms of entry	• Commission played a key leadership role in the granting of transitional periods, acting as an 'honest broker' between demands by the candidates and those of EU governments • negotiations on expenditure-heavy chapters in 2002 led by Danish Presidency and Commission, assisted by key Franco-German deal in October on main points of the financial package • CAP – Commission proposal in January 2002 influenced final outcome, with the introduction of direct payments in the accession states, and forms of national co-financing due to the Commission • Budget – Commission proposal in January 2002 shaped contours of final budgetary deal, though it was affected by Franco-German deal in October
Internal Reforms	• Commission leadership primarily in the form of the 'non-decision' to not undertake far-reaching internal reforms in connection with enlargement, both as regards the EU budget and CAP reform • internal reform negotiations were driven by France and Germany

Conclusions

The fifth enlargement of the EU was the most complex external nego-tiation ever undertaken by the EU. The Commission played a key guiding role in ensuring that an agreement was reached that was acceptable to both EU governments and the candidate countries. In comparison to IGCs on major treaty reform, the Commission had a much stronger leadership role, and the final agreement was arguably closer to what neo-functionalists have called an 'upgrading of common interests' than the lowest common denominator, which might have been the outcome had the Commission not played as forceful a leadership role. Based upon the often miserly offers tabled by governments, we can easily imagine that in the absence of the Commission, the final offer to the candidates might have been unac-ceptable to the candidates.

The role and impact of the EP was similar to what we have seen in previous chapters in IGC negotiations, where the EP was relegated to shouting its extreme views from the sidelines. In contrast, the Commission played in many respects the role of ensuring the effi-ciency of negotiations that the Council Secretariat had enjoyed in IGCs in the 1990s (see Chapters 4 and 5).

When we look at the overall strategies used by each of the actors, it appears that the Commission's relatively low-profile and incre-mental strategy of assisting EU member states, tabling modest reform proposals that postponed major internal reforms until after enlarge-ment, and gently pushing the negotiations forward was more success-ful than the EP's highly political strategy of admonishing member states for their lack of ambition both as regards internal reform and the size and timeline for enlargement.

The Commission's strategy of first securing enlargement and *then* embarking upon more fundamental reforms of internal policies and institutions was partially successful in the mid-term review of the CAP in mid-2003 (Daugbjerg and Swinbank, 2004), but whether it will work in an EU-25 is more debatable, as major reforms will become increasingly difficult to adopt.

Chapter 9

Conclusions

'. . . the Community is a little bit like a stage-coach drawn by twelve horses some of which have got harnessed in the wrong way round; it's only the chap with the whip who makes them run at all and the chap with the whip is the Commission.' (Interviewee in Fiedler, 2000, p. 84)

Introduction

The core debate in studies of the EU is whether governments are in control of the integration process. Intergovernmentalists argue that governments are firmly in control of the process, whereas supranationalists contend that EU institutions have acted as the motor, pushing the EU along the road towards the ever closer union envisioned in the Treaty of Rome. This book recasts the debate on the dynamics of integration by going beyond this dichotomy to explain when and why EU institutions matter, and equally important, when they *do not* matter.

The basic argument is that EU institutions matter in even the most intergovernmental forums of the EU, but that their influence is contingent upon the negotiating context and whether they use appropriate leadership strategies. While governments dictate the broad parameters of agreement, leadership by EU institutions can be very important in overcoming bargaining impediments and in ensuring that mutually acceptable agreements are reached. But by providing leadership EU institutions are also able to influence the contents of final agreements. Governments are therefore not even fully in control of the most intergovernmental forums of the EU – IGCs on treaty reform and enlargement.

A leadership model of European integration based upon rational choice institutionalism and negotiation theory was developed in Chapter 2. This model served as the theoretical baseline for Chapters 3 to 8, which looked at treaty reform negotiations from 1985 until 2004, and the negotiation of the fifth enlargement concluded in 2002. Based upon hard primary sources, including governmental archives in Sweden and another member state, and a series of interviews with participants, the chapters proved that EU institutions mattered in the EU's most intergovernmental forums.

In this concluding chapter, I will first discuss in more detail the empirical and theoretical findings of the book, relating them to existing findings in the literature, and then look at their democratic implications. The chapter concludes with a discussion of the implications of these findings for the future development of the EU.

The dynamics of European integration

This book developed a leadership theory of European integration that detailed when and why EU institutions matter and do not matter. The theory argues that EU institutions can provide leadership in the grand intergovernmental negotiations of European integration, helping governments overcome bargaining impediments that could potentially lead to sub-optimal outcomes. But the successful provision of leadership by EU institutions is contingent upon the specific negotiating context and whether the institution plays its hand well in the negotiations.

Based upon rational choice institutionalism and negotiation theory, the leadership model contends that EU institutions can be thought of primarily as informal entrepreneurs (Young, 1991). EU institutions possess leadership resources that can grant them advantages in providing leadership. While EU institutions usually do not have material leadership resources, they often do have substantial comparative informational advantages vis-à-vis governments. Further, a reputation for the provision of leadership in a manner that is broadly acceptable to governments is also a leadership resource.

The impact of the negotiating context

The importance of different negotiating contexts can be illustrated by comparing the opportunities available for EU institutions to provide leadership in the 2000 IGC and the European Convention in 2002–3. In the 2000 IGC, there were only a handful of politically sensitive issues on the agenda, and EU institutions had very weak institutional positions, granting them few opportunities to provide leadership. In contrast, the European Convention had hundreds of technical and low-salience issues on the agenda, and both the Commission and the EP had very strong institutional positions that could serve as platforms for their leadership attempts.

Looking at the findings of the book, four aspects of the negotiating context are important in determining whether EU institutions have opportunities to provide leadership. First and most importantly, when EU institutions possess privileged institutional positions such as a monopoly on drafting treaty texts, they have more opportunities to provide leadership. In the case studies, the institutional position of the EU institution was strongly correlated with the opportunities available to provide leadership. In the 1985 IGC, the Commission enjoyed both a central agenda-setting role and played a key part in the behind-the-scenes drafting process. These roles offered the Commission numerous opportunities to provide leadership in the negotiations. Similarly, the Commission had a central role in both the internal and external aspects of the enlargement negotiations. Most significant were the Commission's role of monitoring the progress of the candidates in implementing the *acquis* and the preparation of draft common positions for the Council.

The Council Secretariat had a very central position in the drafting process in both the PU IGC in 1990–1, and in the 1996–7 IGC. By having the power of the pen, the Secretariat was able to assist governments in finding mutually acceptable outcomes, while also subtly skewing outcomes closer to its own preferences. Finally, the European Convention negotiations in 2002–3 dramatically illustrated the impact of changes in the institutional set-up, with the EP gaining a strong position to attempt to provide leadership.

When EU institutions do not have strong institutional positions, there is often little they can do to provide leadership. This was illustrated in the 2000 IGC, when the French Presidency cut both the Commission and the Council Secretariat out of the negotiations, and in the 2003–4 IGC when the Italian Presidency fatefully decided at the Brussels Summit of December 2003 to *not* utilize the Council Secretariat.

Therefore, 'institutional politics', or actions to gain privileged institutional positions both prior to and during intergovernmental negotiations, are often critical to the ability of EU institutions to provide leadership, underlining the point that if one cannot 'win' in the game, the best strategy is often to redefine the rules of the game themselves (Sebenius, 1992).

Secondly, EU institutions possessing comparative informational advantages are better able to provide leadership in technical and complex issues. In the 1985 IGC, the Commission was able to mobilize its comparative informational advantages in complex and technical issues relating to the Internal Market, whereas it had few advantages in issues such as foreign policy. In the PU IGC in 1990–1, the Council

Secretariat was able to exploit its legal expertise to draft a formula for the structure of the Treaty on European Union. In the 1996–7 IGC, flexibility proved to be a very complex issue, granting the Council Secretariat an opportunity to create a focal point around which governmental preferences converged. In the enlargement negotiations, the vast majority of issues were highly technical, and the negotiation of them with the candidates was more or less delegated to the Commission. In contrast, in simple issues in treaty reform negotiations such as the weighting of Council votes or the number of Commissioners, EU institutions had no comparative informational advantages that they could exploit to provide leadership.

Thirdly, as the complexity of a given negotiating situation increases, the demand for leadership increases, and this can be provided by EU institutions. As the number of parties and issues increases, it becomes increasingly difficult for the parties themselves to identify possible agreements and then agree upon a mutually acceptable outcome. This creates a demand for leadership, which can be provided by either one of the parties, or a third party such as the Council Secretariat. The impact of complexity can best be illustrated by looking at the differences between the 1985 IGC and the European Convention negotiations in 2002–3. While the 12 delegations in the 1985 IGC were able to sit around a single table, the 207 parties in the European Convention were only able to fit into a plenary meeting room in the EP building. The 1985 IGC dealt with only around 30 different salient issues, whereas the European Convention in effect was renegotiating the entire body of EU Treaties. Thousands of amendments to the Presidium's drafts were tabled in the Convention, together with hundreds of other proposals from representatives. Comparing the two negotiations, the demand for leadership was relatively low in the 1985 IGC, whereas strong leadership was vital in the Convention in order to avoid sheer chaos.

Finally, the distribution and intensity of governmental preferences matter. Chapter 2 detailed four ways in which governmental preferences could affect the ability of EU institutions to provide leadership. When governments hold strong and irreconcilable positions, there is little that EU institutions can do to push governments towards agreement. This was best seen by the inability of EU institutions to push governments towards agreement in the sensitive institutional issues in the 1996–7 IGC. Governments were strongly split along a small/large axis, and they had few incentives to concede as agreement on the issues was not vital at the time.

But when governments have unclear preferences, EU institutions can potentially step in and create a focal point around which governmental preferences can converge. Again in the 1996–7 IGC, governments had unclear preferences on the flexibility issue, creating an opportunity to create a focal point which the Council Secretariat seized with its December 1996 non-paper that effectively defined the further debates on flexibility in the IGC. Governments generally had less clear preferences early in the negotiations, granting EU institutions more opportunities to provide leadership in these early phases than later in the negotiations.

Further, related to the 'high/low politics' and 'politicization' conjectures in integration theory (Hoffmann, 1966; Lindberg, 1966; Schmitter, 1970), when issues are highly political salient, governments have incentives to mobilize the necessary resources to reduce bargaining costs, whereas in lower salience issues we should expect greater opportunities for EU institutions to provide leadership. Looking across the cases, the political salience of an issue is correlated with Commission leadership. In low-salience economic issues, such as Internal Market-related dossiers, the Commission had many opportunities to provide leadership, whereas it was mostly excluded from debates in sensitive foreign policy-related dossiers. One exception was in the sensitive budget-related questions in the enlargement negotiations, where governments entrusted the Commission to assist Presidencies in providing behind-the-scenes and on-the-spot leadership on the technical budgetary questions.

In contrast, leadership by the Council Secretariat does not appear to vary according to political salience, which can possibly be explained by the high degree of trust among governments that the Secretariat will attempt to act impartially in even the most sensitive issues. The Secretariat, for example, brokered a deal on the High Representative for CFSP in the 1996–7 IGC, and was entrusted with finding a legal formula for the framework of the Treaties in the PU IGC. Further, the Secretariat played a key role in the negotiation of the high-profile issue of flexibility in both the 1996–7 and 2000 IGCs.

Fourthly, there is an increased demand for leadership when there is a strong demand for agreement and a zone of possible agreements exist, but governments have difficulties choosing a specific solution. In the enlargement negotiations, the self-imposed deadline to conclude the negotiations by December 2002 in Copenhagen created a strong demand for leadership, which was provided by the Commission and the Danish Presidency, assisted by the Franco-German tandem on the sensitive budget-related questions. There was also a strong demand for leadership in the 2000 IGC to reconcile the strong opposing positions, but this was provided somewhat partially by the French Presidency.

FIGURE 9.1   *The possibilities for providing leadership opened by changes in the negotiating context*

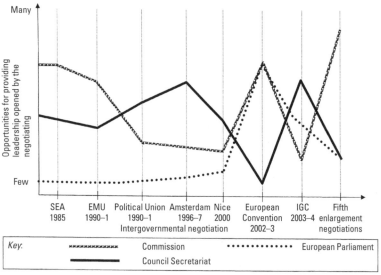

Concluding, the opportunities for EU institutions to provide leadership have varied substantially over time. These possibilities are depicted heuristically in Figure 9.1, where the specific points in the figure are merely intended to be illustrative. The figure depicts a composite measure of the impact of the negotiating context for the range of opportunities available for EU institutions to provide leadership across all of the issues in the specific intergovernmental negotiation.

The choice of leadership strategy

The negotiating context determines the *opportunities* that EU institutions have to provide leadership, or to use a metaphor, the cards that the EU institution holds during the negotiation. But to have an impact upon the negotiations, the institution must then successfully provide leadership, or play their hand skillfully. The model describes two types of leadership strategies: agenda-shaping and brokerage. Agenda-shaping relates to a variety of actions aimed at putting new issues on the agenda, removing issues, and manipulating the content of existing issues. Brokerage involved EU institutions utilizing their informational advantages to help governments find a mutually acceptable outcome. Strategies could either be relatively low-profile and instrumental, aimed at improving the efficiency of negotiations, or also aimed at shifting outcomes through higher-profile strategies (distributive dimension).

What types of strategies were most effective for the three institutions? Looking first at the Commission, as illustrated in Figure 9.1, the Commission had a strong position from which to provide leadership in the 1985 IGC. The Commission played its cards skillfully, tabling ambitious but realistic proposals in the issues, and worked quietly behind the scenes in drafting texts. The Commission used similar low-profile strategies in the agenda-setting phase of the EMU IGC, with Delors playing a careful brokering role in the Delors Committee that ensured that a unanimous report was achieved. In the fifth enlargement negotiations, the Commission from 1999 chose a pragmatic strategy of quietly brokering compromises on issues before they became problems, offering technical assistance to Presidencies, and downplaying the links between far-reaching internal reforms and enlargement. The low-profile leadership by the Commission ensured that the enlargement process did not stall, and that a mutually acceptable deal was reached in December 2002. In these cases, Commission leadership most affected the efficiency dimension, although the Commission in, for example, the 1985 IGC did affect the distributive dimension by ensuring an agreement with a broader and more ambitious scope than otherwise would have been agreed upon. These findings echo Dinan, who states that when the Commission has modest goals, and puts forward proposals that are at the highest realistic common denominator, the Commission can be influential (Dinan, 2000, pp. 261, 267).

When the Commission misjudges its proper role and adopts higher-profile political leadership strategies, it usually fails spectacularly. The best example of this was the PU IGC in 1990–1, where Delors surprisingly pulled the Commission out of the behind-the-scenes drafting group in which Emile Noël had been so influential in the 1985 IGC. The Delors Commission threw off its cloak and attempted to play the role of the 'Champion of Europe', but was rebuffed by governments. This was most evident when Delors backed the ill-fated Dutch draft treaty, after which the Commission was increasingly isolated, and was forced to adopt the EP's tactic of shouting from the sidelines.

While the Santer Commission appeared to have learned from Delors' mistakes by adopting a 'less action but better action' strategy, the opinion of the Commission prior to the 1996–7 IGC was still very ambitious (see Chapter 5). The Prodi Commission in the 2000 IGC also adopted a highly ambitious position that was far outside of any realistic zone of agreement (see Chapter 6). A significant problem for the Commission in comparison to the Council Secretariat is that most of the Commissioners appointed are high-level national politicians, which can result in them misunderstanding the type of leadership that the Commission can successfully provide in *intergovernmental* negotiations. Commissioners tend to think of themselves as political actors in their own right instead of lower-profile civil servants that can assist governments, and in limited cases, provide them with more imaginative proposals and ideas.

Further, the skill with which leadership attempts are attempted also matters. The Delors/Noël team was very skilful in the 1985 IGC, with Delors an effective player at the political level, and Noël extremely efficient behind the scenes. The Commission was especially ineffective during the Prodi Commission. Observers recount for example that Prodi fell asleep at the negotiating table several times during the 2000 IGC, which is not the most effective negotiating tactic under most circumstances (Interview NAT-4). In the European Convention in 2002–3, the now infamous 'Penelope' debacle in December 2002 also illustrated how not to provide leadership (see Chapter 7). By tabling two different positions on the same day – a moderate list of suggestions and the federal Penelope draft treaty – the Commission effectively played itself out of the Convention.

The EP had since the early 1980s been a bystander in intergovernmental negotiations outside of the negotiating room, and not helped by the radical nature of its positions, which were so far outside of the zone of possible agreements that they were usually irrelevant for debates on most issues. The best example was the Draft Treaty on European Union (DTEU) prepared prior to the 1985 IGC, which called for the creation of a federal European Union at a time when many governments thought a modest reintroduction of majority voting was radical. In contrast, when the EP has adopted more pragmatic positions and sought to build consensus for these, it has significant success. In the European Convention, while many of the early proposals of MEPs were federalist in nature, MEPs such as Duff and Brok were very effective during the final months of the Convention in building consensus on ambitious but realistic positions – realistic at least for a majority in the Convention, if not governments. This 'getting more through less' strategy proved to be quite effective for the EP in the European Convention.

Another strategy that the EP has used with success is exploiting the discretion it has in the interpretation of rules in daily policy-making to create *de facto* powers for itself. This has made it easier for governments to accept the entrenchment of these already established practices in the treaty. But as principal-agent theory teaches us, governments will learn about rule exploitation, and when governments delegate further powers to the EP they will design the rules with less room for discretion for the EP (Hix, 2002; Stacey, 2003).

Ironically, given the lack of success of EP attempts at leadership prior to the European Convention, the EP has been the major institutional winner in the treaty reform negotiations since 1985. But the dramatic increase in EP powers has for the most part *not* been due to skilful leadership by the EP, but has been the result of German pressure. Germany has since reunification in 1990 seen an increase in the powers of the EP as a relatively innocuous means of increasing German power relative to France and other member states. While France and Germany had the same number of MEPs prior to reunification, reflecting the near parity in population, Germany received nineteen extra MEPs afterwards to reflect the increase of German population. But Germany was not compensated accordingly in the Council. By supporting increased power to the EP, Germany can argue that it supports increased democracy in the EU (which they do), but an underlying motive is to strengthen the decision-taking institution in which Germany has greatest relative power.

The Council Secretariat has proved to be the penultimate 'entrepreneurial leader' in several treaty reform negotiations (Young, 1999, p. 807), facilitating compromise through its low-profile and behind-the-scenes assistance to governments and Presidencies. It is no coincidence that the role of the Council Secretariat is all but unexplored in the literature on the EU (for exceptions, see Beach, 2004 and Christiansen, 2002). The Secretariat is quite pragmatic in its views in contrast to the Commission or EP, believing that an incremental first step is often a better way of achieving a final goal than a single 'big bang' decision that might not be accepted by the member states.

The Secretariat has assisted in the drafting process, often having the power of the pen, and has brokered several key deals. But leadership by the Secretariat mostly affects the efficiency dimension of intergovernmental negotiations, ensuring that joint gains are reached, whereas the distributive effects of Secretariat leadership are smaller, though sometimes significant as the case of flexibility in the 1996–7 IGC shows. When the Secretariat has departed from this quiet behind-the-scenes leadership and more openly pursued its own interests, it was quickly cut out of the loop by Presidencies. Good examples of this was are the 2000 IGC, where the Portuguese Presidency excluded the Secretariat from many of its traditional roles, and the decision to create a more inclusive Convention Secretariat for the

European Convention after it became apparent how influential the Council Secretariat was in the Charter Convention in 2000 (see Chapter 7).

Concluding, the most effective strategies for EU institutional leadership were behind-the-scenes and low-profile leadership, attempting to push outcomes closer towards the 'upper edge' of realism.

Discussing the findings

This book shows that EU institutions are not the motors of integration that supranationalists have contended, nor are they the impotent actors of intergovernmentalist theorizing. In the following, I will briefly relate my findings to the two poles of the debate, and then conclude by comparing my model and findings with Pollack's rational choice institutionalism.

Liberal Intergovernmentalism

Liberal intergovernmentalism enjoys the status of being an anti-paradigm in integration theory – a theory that all other theories use as their negative point of reference. This status is due partly to the provocative nature of Moravcsik's strongly governmentalist argument, but owes a lot also to the strength and depth of his scholarly arguments themselves. That being said, this book takes issue with Moravcsik on four points.

First, Moravcsik argues that when bargaining costs are low *relative* to the gains of cooperation, governments will have incentives to mobilize all of the necessary resources to overcome these costs (Moravcsik, 1999a, p. 273). Therefore EU institutions have no comparative advantages in the provision of leadership, making them 'redundant, futile, and sometimes even counterproductive' (ibid., pp. 269–70). But based upon hard primary sources, I contend that in the vast majority of issues in intergovernmental negotiations in the EU, governments are reliant upon the provision of expertise by EU institutions. If we lower the level of aggregation from broad positions to more detailed knowledge of complex issues and the actual drafting of legal texts, there are indications that EU institutions have comparative informational advantages.

While all governments perhaps had a fully synoptic knowledge of the EU in the 1960s and 1970s, the EU is so complex today that only actors that specialize in EU affairs and devote many resources to it, and also have long institutional memories, fully understand all of the intricacies of the issues in intergovernmental negotiations. Smaller governments simply do not have the resources, while large governments have two problems. First, civil servants in national foreign ministries are often shifted to different desks, meaning, for example, that they do not have the same hands-on experience with multiple IGCs as the Secretariat. Secondly, even when certain national governments are able to rival the level of information possessed by EU institutions, this information is often perceived to be biased by other governments. Therefore, on substantive issues governments often rely upon the Commission for advice and assistance, whereas on legal issues the Council Secretariat Legal Service is utilized. And often the bargaining situation itself is so complex that only the Secretariat with its vast experience in brokering deals in the Council has a complete picture of possible compromises, trade-offs, and zones of agreement. These informational advantages are most evident vis-à-vis smaller governments, which then becomes crucial when they hold the Presidency. As these governments chairing the negotiations often draw extensively upon either the Commission or Council Secretariat, this gives the institutions channels for influencing the proceedings.

Secondly, Moravcsik developed his theory *before* the institutionalist turn in political science in the early 1990s, and Moravcsik has not since embraced the insight of institutionalism that institutional position itself can be a power resource in negotiations (on institutionalism, see Hall and Taylor, 1996; March and Olsen, 1989). The consequence of this downplaying of institutional position is that Moravcsik posits that bargaining strength is only determined by the relative dependence of a state upon agreement. My findings clearly show the impact of institutional position for EU institutions. For example, the delegation by the Luxembourg Presidency in 1985 of agenda-setting power to the Commission was crucial for the ability of the Commission to shape the substantive agenda of the IGC and the final outcome. My findings are also echoed by newer rational choice institutionalist research both on daily EU policy-making and on treaty reform negotiations (e.g. Pollack, 2003; Tallberg, 2003a, 2004).

Thirdly and related to the point on intergovernmental bargaining, Moravcsik appears to deny that the way actors play their cards in negotiations matter. For example, in his analysis of the 1996–7 IGC together with Nicolaïdis, he sidesteps the question of why France was relatively unsuccessful given its relative power (Moravcsik and Nicolaïdis, 1999, p. 75). But France, like the Commission in the European Convention, tabled many contradictory positions during the 1996–7 IGC and effectively played itself out of influence (see Deloche-Gaudez, 2002). As was repeatedly seen in the analyses for the Commission, poor negotiating tactics could ruin a favourable initial position. Further, the Council Secretariat for the most part played its cards exceedingly well, and successfully exploited its opportunities for providing leadership.

Finally, Moravcsik does concede that the Council Secretariat can be important, but defines the problem away by arguing that the Secretariat merely acts on governmental preferences. But as shown by this study, the Secretariat cannot always be termed a 'neutral' actor, and was an insider with institutional preferences that did not always reflect governmental preferences (see Chapters 3–7). This strengthens that contention that leadership by EU institutions does indeed matter in even the most intergovernmental forum of the EU.

Supranationalist approaches

Early neo-functionalism argued that leadership by the Commission was a vital element in EU negotiations that helped governments upgrade their common interests (Haas, 1958, 1961; Lindberg, 1963). An active Commission could advance proposals that capitalized upon demands for integration, pushing the EU in a more pro-integrative direction (Haas, 1961, pp. 367–9). Yet the focus of early neo-functionalism was upon explaining how and when national interests converged *prior to* intergovernmental conferences, and the process within intergovernmental negotiations whereby these converging interests were translated into outcomes was underspecified.

Neo-functionalism underwent a series of major revisions after the Empty Chairs crisis in 1965–6, and a large number of competing versions emerged. Of most relevance to the present study was Lindberg and Scheingold's modified neo-functionalist theory (Lindberg and Scheingold, 1970). Building upon the insights of early neo-functionalism, they created an Easton-inspired system model of integration, where demands for integration and leadership at both the supranational and national level were key inputs into the system (ibid., p. 113). The model then went on to describe supranational leadership, stating that the Commission provided task-oriented leadership by supplying organizing skills, making proposals, and in general facilitating and assisting the intergovernmental bargaining process by for example translating all of the interests of national actors into package deals (ibid., p. 129). Active supranational leadership was seen to be a necessary but not sufficient condition for the integration process to progress (p. 130), but they also argued that national leadership was more important in the major 'transformative' decisions (p. 244).

While the leadership model in this book echoes some of the propositions of Lindberg and Scheingold's model, my leadership model provides clearer hypotheses for *how* the provision of successful leadership by EU institutions *varies* depending upon the negotiating context and how actors play their cards. Secondly, my findings do not fully support their contention that national leadership is more important in the major 'transformative' decisions. In the 1985 IGC, Commission leadership was vital in ensuring the major transformation of the then European Community through the Internal Market. In the PU IGC, while the final TEU reflects a Franco-German compromise between a stronger Europe and an intergovernmental Europe, both governments were dependent upon the Council Secretariat providing the actual legal formula that enabled them to agree upon this compromise. Finally, the Commission played a key facilitating role in the fifth enlargement, which was a task that no other actor could have lifted. Without the Commission, it is difficult to envisage that ten new member states would have joined the EU on 1 May 2004.

Turning to newer supranationalist approaches, the transactionalist approach of Stone Sweet and Sandholtz, or the social constructivist approach of Christiansen and Jørgensen do not specify the dynamics by which demands for integration are translated into outcomes (Christiansen and Jørgensen, 1998, 1999; Stone Sweet and Sandholtz, 1998, 1999). Christiansen and Jørgensen for example stated that 'At most, they [governments] bargained over the way in which existing trends in the integration process . . . were formally incorporated into the treaty' (1999, p. 15). But as was seen in this book, there is nothing pre-determined about the actual form for how demands are incorporated into the treaties, and the translation of vague 'demands' for integration into treaty text is often a winding path with many twists and turns. This is best seen in the negotiation of issues such as EMU and flexibility. Crucially, leadership is necessary to translate vague demands into outcomes, and even more importantly, who provides leadership is vital for how demands are incorporated into the treaties. Outcomes are very different depending upon whether for example France, the Commission, or Denmark plays a leadership role.

Rational choice institutionalism

One of Pollack's greatest strengths is his argument that the question of supranational entrepreneurship or leadership is not an either/or, but is more of a 'yes under certain conditions' (Pollack, 1997, 2003). Based upon principal–agent theorizing more broadly, Pollack argues that the formal institutional position of an actor matters (Pollack, 2003, pp. 47–56). Further, EU institutions (agents) should matter when governments (principals) have unclear preferences, and when agents have comparative informational advantages (ibid.). These points are reflected in the arguments made in my theoretical model on the importance of comparative informational advantages, governmental preferences and institutional position. But my model goes further by specifying more clearly the impact of the negotiating context, and also discussing the impact of choice of strategy upon actor success in shaping outcomes.

And Pollack's actual empirical analysis of treaty reform negotiations echoes Moravcsik's findings by stating first that EU institutions *do not* have formal institutional powers and are therefore forced to rely on creating 'focal points' around which governmental preferences can converge, and secondly that EU institutions generally *do not* have comparative informational advantages (Pollack, 1999; 2003, pp. 53–6). But Pollack appears to discount the importance of the 'informal' delegation of powers, such as when Presidencies give the Council Secretariat the pen in drafting all treaty texts in a treaty reform negotiation, or when governments quietly ask the Commission to broker key compromises in enlargement negotiations. Finally, as argued above, bargaining costs in intergovernmental negotiations are often so high that most governments are forced to rely upon the expertise of the Council Secretariat and Commission for legal and substantive knowledge, and assistance in brokering key deals.

The implications for the democratic deficit of the Union

This book has shown that governments were not fully in control of the grand bargains of integration since the mid-1980s. While most of the leadership provided by EU institutions has had the effect of improving the efficiency of intergovernmental bargaining processes, EU institutions also helped push the process forward in a more pro-integrative direction than would otherwise have been agreed upon. If governments are fully in control, then there is naturally no 'democratic deficit' (Moravcsik, 2002). But if governments are not fully in control, what implications does this have for national democracies and the democratic deficit in the EU? Does leadership by non-democratic EU institutions increase the democratic deficit of the EU, or can it be argued based upon an efficiency paradigm of democracy that EU institutions are merely helping governments deliver outputs that citizens demand?

There are at least three discernible means whereby the EU can be democratically legitimated. First, *participatory* legitimacy involves being directly linked electorally with voters (see Jolly, 2003; Lord and Magnette, 2004; Newman, 2001 for discussions of democracy, legitimacy and the EU and Rosamond, 2001). Secondly, the EU could also be legitimated by *efficiency* concerns, meaning that the EU is able to deliver outputs demanded by citizens (Lord and Magnette, 2004). A third approach is based upon *procedural* legitimacy, meaning that the EU can be legitimate democratically when it observes certain procedures, such as transparency and legal certainty (ibid.).

Neither the Commission nor Council Secretariat are democratically legitimated. At the highest level they are only indirectly democratic, as key figures in the Secretariat and Commission are appointed by democratically elected governments. But at lower levels, both institutions are non-democratic bureaucracies, where appointments are based upon merit, with considerations of nationality to ensure a mixed representation of nationalities (see Stevens and Stevens, 2001). The European Parliament is a democratically elected representative of the citizens of the EU, but given the low level of participation in EP elections, and the relative importance of non-European issues in EP elections, questions can be raised about the true democratic representativity of the EP. And with the exception of the European Convention, the EP has not had a significant impact upon the grand bargains of integration in the past two decades.

The creation of the EU was based upon ideas of technical efficiency and planning, and the EU was not intended to be a democratic community (Drake, 2000a; Rittberger, 2001, p. 701). But have citizens supported the pro-integrative push by non-democratic EU institutions in the past two decades? In the following I will try to get closer to an answer to this question by looking at trends in public support for integration.

There are unfortunately many problems associated with using opinion polls in general, and Eurobarometer in particular. One problem is anticipation, where an EU institution adopts positions based upon what it believes will be popular. Secondly, there are many indications that the general level of knowledge of citizens about European affairs is often disappointingly low, and therefore answers to polls might reflect myths or national factors more than real responses based upon the issues. For instance, at the start of the 1996–7 IGC, 60 per cent of EU citizens were unaware that an IGC

FIGURE 9.2   *Net support for EU membership, 1979 to 2003*

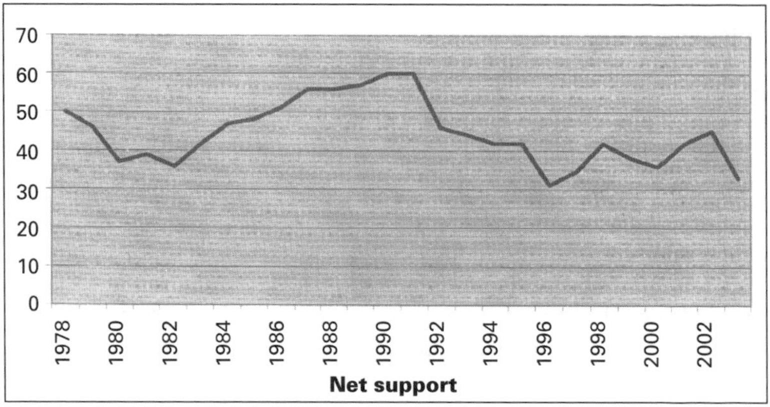

Source: Eurobarometer, Autumn polls 1978–2003.

was being held (polled April–May 1996, Eurobarometer, no. 45, p. 54). Therefore, the figures utilized in the following are *only* used heuristically to indicate broad trends.

One indicator of support could be the net support of EU citizens of the EU over time. Figure 9.2 illustrates, based upon Eurobarometer polls, the net support of citizens of EU membership by subtracting the number of respondents answering that EU membership is a 'bad thing' from the number saying that EU membership is a 'good thing'.

Figure 9.2 illustrates that there was a broad and strengthening 'permissive consensus' among citizens in the mid- to late 1980s, whereas there was a sharp drop in support in 1991, and that levels of support in the 1990s until the present were at the same level as in the early 1980s. While it could be argued that the integrative steps taken in the 1985 and 1990–1 IGCs were reflected in relatively high levels of support, a 'not-so-permissive-consensus' developed in the early 1990s (Laursen, 1994), and therefore further integrative steps in the 1990s and early 2000s were not supported as strongly by citizens. But in contrast, when citizens were asked about the *desired* speed of integration of Europe on a scale from 1 to 7, there is no real difference in levels from 1990 until 2000 (see Eurobarometer, no. 53, p. 29). In 1990 the aggregate desired speed was 5.0, whereas it was 4.8 in 2000, with only slight variations from 4.4 to 5.1 during the period (ibid.). Compared with citizens perceptions of the actual level of integration, citizens polled ensured that they wanted more integration than was being delivered throughout the period (ibid.).

When we look at areas where EU institutions have mattered in specific treaty-reform negotiations compared with opinion polls for IGCs in the 1980s and 1990s, in the 1985 IGC many of the Commission's attempts to push the outcome in a pro-integrative direction were supported by citizens. A broad majority of citizens supported majority voting in 1985, with 61 per cent of those replying supporting majority voting for important decisions and only 39 per cent wanting to keep unanimity (Eurobarometer, no. 24, p. 84). A majority was also positive about the creation of a European political union, with 16 per cent very much for and 27 per cent to some extent for, whereas 43 per cent were indifferent (Eurobarometer, no. 23, p. 51). But Commission attempts to create a European currency were not as strongly supported, with 38 per cent against and 32 per cent were for, with 21 per cent answering 'don't mind' (Eurobarometer, no. 23, p. 18).

In the autumn of 1990, strong majorities supported: the creation of a common security and defence policy (66 per cent for, 15 per cent against), the introduction of EP co-decision (64 per cent for, 14 per cent against), and a social charter (67 per cent answered a 'good thing', 4 per cent a 'bad thing'), whereas weaker majorities existed for a single currency (55 per cent for, 23 per cent against) or a common foreign policy (51 per cent for, 26 per cent against) (Eurobarometer, no. 34, p. 24, 32). Based upon these figures, Commission leadership in creating EMU had the same level of support as Commission attempts to create an EC-level foreign policy!

In the spring of 1996 only 43 per cent of citizens polled supported allowing EU citizens to be candidates in local elections in other member states, which was included in the Treaty of Amsterdam, whereas 66 per cent supported a common foreign policy that was only marginally strengthened by the Treaty (Eurobarometer, no. 45, p. 57). A clear majority of citizens supported strengthening the role of the EP in 1995 (54 per cent for, 23 per cent against) (ibid., no. 43, p. 40). Further, majorities supported joint EU decision-making on many of the JHA issues that were communitarized in the Treaty – issues where Commission leadership was important (Eurobarometer, no. 45, p. 61).

The picture regarding whether citizens supported pro-integrative steps is therefore murky. In some issues such as a common foreign policy, a majority of citizens supported strengthening EU-level decision-making, whereas governments themselves only took hesitant steps, and EU institutions were unable to significantly affect outcomes. Other steps where EU institutions were important such as the EMU had relatively lower levels of citizen support. It is therefore difficult to conclude that citizens latently supported EU institutional leadership that pushed integration further than governments left to their own devices would have agreed.

This picture is further complicated by looking at levels of support for enlargement. In autumn 2000, a time where the Commission was acting as the 'champion of enlargement' and was playing a major leadership role, only 44 per cent of polled citizens supported enlargement, 35 per cent were against and 21 per cent answered 'do not know' (Eurobarometer, no. 58, p. 76). But levels of support for enlargement increased significantly in 2001, and by late 2002, 52 per cent supported, 30 per cent were against and 18 per cent answered 'do not know' (ibid.).

Concluding, there is little evidence that indicates that citizens have either strongly supported or strongly opposed the pro-integrative steps in which EU institutions have played a major role. Referendums in the early 1990s seemed to indicate that citizens opposed further developments towards political union, but EMU was at least as unpopular as these steps (for more, see Laursen and Vanhoonacker, 1994). In general, leadership by EU institutions has not pushed integration forward uniformly in the areas in which citizens desired further integrative steps. We cannot therefore argue that leadership by EU institutions is legitimate based solely upon efficiency concerns, that is, providing outputs that citizens demand. There are therefore substantial democratic problems raised by non-democratic EU institutions providing significant leadership in major EU intergovernmental negotiations.

One solution to the democratic problem is to use Conventions to prepare future intergovernmental negotiations on treaty reform. Chapter 7 clearly showed that the democratically legitimated EP had a strong leadership role in the European Convention, although the subsequent IGC among democratically legitimated governments was mostly about removing what governments viewed as the most onerous EP 'fingerprints' from the final Constitutional Treaty. But if we incorporate procedural legitimacy concerns, the open and inclusive Convention method is far superior in democratic terms than the closed-door and exclusive IGC method.

Yet there is a democratic paradox here, for while the process might have been more democratic and open than past rounds of treaty reform, the results are less likely to survive popular referendums than past rounds of treaty reform. In the past, treaty reforms have resulted in treaties that built upon the existing treaties, such as the Treaty of Nice. These treaties were so complex and arcanely written that only EU experts understood them. But the Constitutional Treaty is much clearer and simpler, which could have the disadvantage of providing strong ammunition to Eurosceptics and opponents in coming referendums. This is the democratic paradox of the treaty reform process, and could perhaps prove to be the Achilles heel of the Convention method.

The future of the Union

The Brussels Summit debacle in December 2003 showed with alarming clarity that strong leadership will be increasingly necessary in the history-making negotiations of European integration. In the case of the Italian Presidency, the lesson was that a Presidency ignores the Council Secretariat at its own peril. As predicted by the leadership model in this book, an EU-25 without strong and legitimate leadership will drift listlessly from one sub-optimal outcome to another.

There are multiple possible sources of leadership in the future EU-25. Leadership might be supplied by a new 'President' or 'Chairperson' of the European Council, or by a revamped Presidency. Another source might be the increasing signs that a 'big three' directorate will attempt to take over the role traditionally played by the Franco-German motor. But a 'big-three' directorate is unlikely to be acceptable to a majority of member states, and therefore will be unable to provide legitimate leadership.

What are the implications for the future for the Commission, Council Secretariat and EP? My findings show that the Commission should go back to the basics, and attempt to provide the type of leadership that was so successful in the 1985 IGC and the fifth enlargement negotiations. Another point is that it should be active in institutional politics prior to intergovernmental negotiations, attempting to carve out privileged institutional positions such as the chair of influential agenda-setting committees, or taking part in the drafting process. The Secretariat should at all costs not attempt to play the higher-profile role seen in the 2000 IGC, but should attempt to regain its role of being the 'right hand person' of the Presidency or whichever actor will be chairing future intergovernmental negotiations.

Finally, the EP should fight to preserve the Convention method, as it naturally grants it a much better platform for its leadership attempts than in the traditional IGC method (see Figure 9.1). But while the EP was quite successful in providing leadership in the European Convention, the EP should in a future Convention be more aware of 'red lines' for key national governments. If EP leadership had not for example ensured the introduction of a double majority voting system, a matter which at the end of the day had no real impact upon the EP, the 2003–4 IGC would not have had so many problems in reaching an acceptable conclusion.

References

Ackrill, Robert W. (2000) 'CAP Reform 1999: A Crisis in the Making?', *Journal of Common Market Studies,* vol. 38, no. 2, pp. 343–53.

Agence Europe (AE), Europe Daily Bulletins, diverse issues.

Allison, Graham and Philip Zelikow (1999) *Essence of Decision: Explaining the Cuban Missile Crisis*, 2nd edn. New York: Longman.

Alter, Karen J. (2001) *Establishing the Supremacy of European Law: The Making of an International Rule of Law in Europe.* Oxford: Oxford University Press.

Armstrong, Kenneth and Simon Bulmer (1998) *The Governance of the Single European Market.* Manchester: Manchester University Press.

Avery, Graham (1995) 'The Commission's Perspective on the Enlargement Negotiations', SEI Working Paper No. 12.

Avery, Graham (2004) 'The Enlargement Negotiations', in Fraser Cameron (ed.), *The Future of Europe: Enlargement and Integration.* London: Routledge, Chapter 3.

Bachrach, Peter and Morton S. Baratz (1962) 'The Two Faces of Power', *American Political Science Review,* vol. 56, no. 4, pp. 942–52.

Bachrach, Peter and Morton S. Baratz (1963) 'Decisions and Nondecisions: An Analytical Framework', *American Political Science Review,* vol. 57, no. 3, September 1963, pp. 632–42.

Bailer, Stefanie (2004) 'Bargaining Success in the European Union', *European Union Politics,* vol. 5, issue 1, pp. 99–123.

Bailer, Stefanie and Gerald Schneider (2000) 'The Power of Legislative Hot Air: Informal Rules and the Enlargement Debate in the European Parliament', *Journal of Legislative Studies,* vol. 6, no. 2, Summer 2000, pp. 19–44.

Bainbridge, Timothy (2000) *The Penguin Companion to European Union*, 2nd edn. London: Penguin Books.

Barrera, Mario and Ernst B. Haas (1969) 'The Operationalization of Some Variables Related to Regional Integration: A Research Note', *International Organization*, vol. 23, issue 1, winter 1969, pp. 150–60.

Baun, Michael J. (1995/96) 'The Maastricht Treaty as High Politics: Germany, France, and European Integration', *Political Science Quarterly*, vol. 110, no. 4, pp. 605–24.

Baun, Michael J. (2000) *A Wider Europe: The Process and Politics of European Union enlargement.* Lanham: Rowman and Littlefield Publishers, Inc.

Beach, Derek (1998) 'The Negotiation of the Europe Agreements with Poland, Hungary, and Czechoslovakia: A Three-Level Game', *TKI*

Working Papers on European Integration and Regime Formation, no. 31/98. Esbjerg: Sydjysk Universitetsforlag.

Beach, Derek (2001) *Between Law and Politics: The Relationship Between the European Court of Justice and EU Member States*. Copenhagen: DJØF Publishing.

Beach, Derek (2002) 'The Negotiation of the Amsterdam Treaty – When Theory Meets Reality', in Finn Laursen (ed.), *The Amsterdam Treaty: National Preference Formation, Interstate Bargaining, Outcome and Ratification*. Odense: Odense University Press, pp. 593–637.

Beach, Derek (2004) 'The Unseen Hand in Treaty Reform Negotiations: the role and impact of the Council Secretariat', *Journal of European Public Policy*. vol. 11, no. 3, June 2004, pp. 408–39.

Benelux (1992) 'The Community's Enlargement: The Benelux memorandum submitted to the European Council in Lisbon', Europe Documents, Agence Internationale d'Information pour la Press, no. 1789, 27 June 1992.

Bercovitch, Jacob (1984) 'Problems and Approaches in the Study of Bargaining and Negotiation', *Political Science*, vol. 36, no. 2, December 1984, pp. 125–44.

Bercovitch, Jacob (1996a) 'The Structure and Diversity of Mediation in International Relations', in Jacob Bercovitch and Jeffrey Z. Rubin (eds), *Mediation in International Relations*. New York: St. Martin's Press, pp. 1–29.

Bercovitch, Jacob (1996b) 'Introduction: Thinking About Mediation', in Jacob Bercovitch (ed.), *Resolving International Conflicts – The Theory and Practice of Mediation*. London: Lynne Rienner Publishers, pp. 1–9.

Bercovitch, Jacob and Allison Houston (1996) 'The Study of International Mediation: Theoretical Issues and Empirical Evidence', in Jacob Bercovitch (ed.), *Resolving International Conflicts – The Theory and Practice of Mediation*. London: Lynne Rienner Publishers, pp. 11–35.

Beuter, Rita (2002) 'Germany: Safeguarding the EMU and the Interests of the Länder', in Finn Laursen (ed.) *The Amsterdam Treaty: National Preference Formation, Interstate Bargaining, Outcome and Ratification*. Odense: Odense University Press, pp. 93–120.

Blair, Tony (2000) Prime Minister's Speech to the Polish Stock Exchange, 6 October 2000.

Bornschier, Volker (2000) 'Western Europe's Move Toward Political Union', in Volker Bornschier (ed.), *State-Building in Europe: The Revitalization of Western European Integration*. Cambridge: Cambridge University Press, pp. 3–37.

Branch, Ann P. and Jakob C. Øhrgaard (1999) 'Trapped in the Supranational-Intergovernmental Dichotomy: A response to Stone Sweet and Sandholtz', *Journal of European Public Policy*, vol. 6, no. 1, March 1999, pp. 123–43.

Bräuninger, Thomas, Tanja Cornelius, Thomas König and Thomas Schuster (2001) 'The Dynamics of European Integration: A Constitutional Analysis of the Amsterdam Treaty', in Gerald Schneider and Mark Aspinwall (eds), *The Rules of Integration: Institutionalist Approaches to the Study of Europe.* Manchester: Manchester University Press, pp. 46–68.

Brown, L. Neville and Tom Kennedy (2000) *The Court of Justice of the European Communities.* 5th edn., London: Sweet and Maxwell.

Brown, Tony (2003) 'National Parliaments in the Convention on the Future of Europe', *Federal Trust Constitutional Online Papers*, no. 31/03, November 2003, published online at: http://www.fedtrust.co.uk/.

Budden, Philip (2002) 'Observations on the Single European Act and "Relaunch of Europe": A Less "Intergovernmental" Reading of the 1985 Intergovernmental Conference', *Journal of European Public Policy*, vol. 9, no. 1, February 2002, pp. 76–97.

Bulletin of the European Communities, various issues.

Bulmer, Simon J. (1994) 'The Governance of the European Union: A New Institutionalist Approach', *Journal of Public Politics*, vol. 13, no. 4, pp. 351–80.

Burley, Anne-Marie and Walter Mattli (1993) 'Europe Before the Court: A Political Theory of Legal Integration', *International Organization*, vol. 47, no. 1, winter 1993, pp. 41–76.

Cameron, David R. (1992) 'The 1992 Initiative: Causes and Consequences', in Sbragia, Alberta M. (ed.) *Europolitics: Institutions and Policymaking in the "New" European Community.* Washington, DC: Brookings Institution, s. 23–74.

Cameron, Fraser (2000) 'The Commission's Perspective', in Jackie Gower and John Redmond (eds), *Enlarging the European Union: The Way Forward.* Aldershot: Ashgate, s. 13–25.

Carnevale, Peter J. and Sharon Arad (1996) 'Bias and Impartiality in International Mediation', in Jacob Bercovitch (ed.), *Resolving International Conflicts – The Theory and Practice of Mediation.* London: Lynne Rienner Publishers, pp. 39–53.

CDU/CSU (1994) 'Reflections on European Policy', in *Agence Europe, Europe Documents*, no. 1895/96, 7 September 1994.

Charlemagne (1994) 'L'equilibre entre les etats membres', in *L'equilibre européen. Etudes rassemblées et publiées en hommage B. Niels Ersbøll.* Brussels: Edition provisoire, pp. 69–78.

Christiansen, Thomas (2002) 'The Role of Supranational Actors in EU Treaty Reform', *Journal of European Public Policy*, vol. 9, no. 1, February 2002, pp. 33–53.

Christiansen, Thomas (2003) 'Out of the Shadows: The General Secretariat of the Council of Ministers', in R.M. van Schendelen and R. Scully (eds), *The Unseen Hand: Unelected Legislators in the EU.* London: Frank Cass.

Christiansen, Thomas and Knud Erik Jørgensen (1998) 'Negotiating Treaty Reform in the European Union: The Role of the European Commission', *International Negotiation*, vol. 3, no. 3, pp. 435–52.

Christiansen, Thomas and Knud Erik Jørgensen (1999) 'The Amsterdam Process: A Structurationist Perspective on EU Treaty Reform', *European Integration online Papers (EIoP)*, vol. 3, no. 1. Published on Internet site http://eiop.or.at/eiop/texte/1999-001a.htm.

Christiansen, Thomas, Gerda Falkner and Knud Erik Jørgensen (2002) 'Theorizing EU Treaty Reform: Beyond Diplomacy and Bargaining', *Journal of European Public Policy*, vol. 9, no. 1, February 2002, pp. 12–32.

Christoffersen, Poul Skytte (1992) *Traktaten om Den Europæiske Union – Baggrund, Forhandling, Resultat*. København: Jurist- og Økonomforbundets Forlag.

Church, Clive H. and David Phinnemore (2002) *The Penguin Guide to the European Treaties: From Rome to Maastricht, Amsterdam, Nice and Beyond*. London: Penguin.

Cloos, J., G. Reinesch, D. Vignes, and J. Weyland (1993) *Le Traité de Maastricht. Genèse, Analyse, Commentaire*. Brussels: Bruylant.

Closa, Carlos (2004a) 'The Value of Institutions: Mandate and Self-Mandate in the Convention Process', *Politique Européenne*, vol. 13, primtemps 2004.

Closa, Carlos (2004b) 'The Convention Method and the Transformation of EU Constitutional Politics', in Erik Oddvar Eriksen, John Erik Fossum and Agustín Menédez (eds), *Developing a Constitution for Europe*. London: Routledge, pp. 183–206.

Cockfield, Lord A. (1994) *The European Union: Creating the Single Market*. Chichester: Chancery Law Publishing.

Committee for the Study of EMU (1989) *Report on Economic and Monetary Union in the European Community*. Luxembourg: Office for Official Publications of the European Communities.

Coombes, David (1970) *Politics and Bureaucracy in the European Community: A Portrait of the Commission of the EEC*. London: George Allen and Unwin Ltd.

Corbett, Richard (1987) 'The 1985 Intergovernmental Conference and the Single European Act', in Roy Pryce (ed.), *The Dynamics of European Union*. London: Croom Helm, pp. 238–72.

Corbett, Richard (1992) 'The Intergovernmental Conference on Political Union', *Journal of Common Market Studies*, vol. XXX, no. 3, September 1992, pp. 271–98.

Corbett, Richard (1993) *The Treaty of Maastricht*. Harlow: Longman Group UK Limited.

Corbett, Richard (1998) *The European Parliament's Role in Closer EU Integration*. Basingstoke, Macmillan.

Corbett, Richard, Francis Jacobs and Michael Shackleton (1995) *The European Parliament*. 3rd edn. London: Cartermill Publishing.

Corbett, Richard, Francis Jacobs and Michael Shackleton (2003) *The European Parliament*. 5th edn. London: John Harper Publishing.

Council of the European Communities (1990) *The Council of the European Communities*. Luxembourg: Office for Official Publications of the European Communities.

Council Secretariat (2002) Personal correspondence of the author with the General Secretariat of the Council's Direction générale A 1 / Personnel – Administration, Brussels, 2 October 2002.

Cox, Robert W. and Harold K. Jacobsen (1973) 'The Framework for Inquiry', in Robert W. Cox, Harold K. Jacobsen *et al.*, *The Anatomy of Influence – Decision Making in International Organizations*. London: Yale University Press, pp. 1–36.

Crombez, Cristophe, Bernard Steunenberg, and Richard Corbett (2000) 'Forum Section: Understanding the EU Legislative Process', *European Union Politics*, vol. 1, no. 3, pp. 365–85.

Dahl, Robert (1957) 'The Concept of Power', *Behavioural Science*, vol. 2, pp. 201–15.

Daugbjerg, Carsten and Alan Swinbank (2004) 'The CAP and EU Enlargement: Prospects for an Alternative Strategy to Avoid the Lock-In of CAP Support', *Journal of Common Market Studies*, vol. 42, issue 1, pp. 99–119.

de Búrca, Gráinne (2001) 'The Drafting of the European Union Charter of Fundamental Rights', *European Law Review*, vol. 26, no. 2, April 2001, pp. 126–38.

Dehaene, Jean-Luc (1999) *The Institutional Implications of Enlargement: Report to the European Commission*. Brussels, 18 October 1999.

Dehousse, Franklin (1999) *Amsterdam: The Making of a Treaty*. London: London European Research Centre.

Deloche-Gaudez, Florence (2001) *The Convention on a Charter of Fundamental Rights: A Method for the Future*. Notre Europe, Research and Policy Paper no. 15, November 2001.

Deloche-Gaudez, Florence (2002) 'France: A Member State Losing Influence?', in Finn Laursen (ed.), *The Amsterdam Treaty: National Preference Formation, Interstate Bargaining, Outcome and Ratification*. Odense: Odense University Press, pp. 139–60.

Delors, Jacques (1989) 'Europe: Embarking on a New Course', in *1992 and After. Contemporary European Affairs*, vol. 1, no ½, 1989, pp. 15–28.

den Boer, Monica (2002) 'A New Area of Freedom, Security and Justice' in Finn Laursen (ed.), *The Amsterdam Treaty: National Preference Formation, Interstate Bargaining, Outcome and Ratification*. Odense: Odense University Press, pp. 509–35.

de Ruyt, Jean (1987) *L'Acte Unique Europeen: Commentaire.* Brussels: Editions de l'Université Libre de Bruxelles.

Dessai, Suraje (2001) 'Why Did The Hague Climate Conference Fail?', *Environmental Politics,* vol. 10, no. 3, autumn 2001, pp. 139–44.

Devuyst, Youri (1998) 'Treaty Reform in the European Union: The Amsterdam Process', *Journal of European Public Policy*, vol. 5, no. 4, December 1998, pp. 615–31.

Digeser, Peter (1992) 'The Fourth Face of Power', *Journal of Politics*, vol. 54, no. 4, November 1992, pp. 977–1007.

Dinan, Desmond (1997) 'The Commission and the Reform Process', in Geoffrey Edwards and Alfred Pijpers (eds), *The Politics of European Treaty Reform: The 1996 Intergovernmental Conference and Beyond.* London: Pinter.

Dinan, Desmond (1999) *Ever Closer Union: An Introduction to European Integration.* Basingstoke: Macmillan.

Dinan, Desmond (2000) 'The Commission and the Intergovernmental Conferences', in Neill Nugent (ed.), *At the Heart of the Union: Studies of the European Commission.* 2nd edn. London: Macmillan, pp. 250–69.

Dinan, Desmond and Sophie Vanhoonacker (2000–2001) 'IGC 2000 Watch' Parts 1–4, in *ECSA Review*, vol. 13, nos 2–4, 2000 and vol. 14, no. 1, 2001.

Drake, Helen (2000) *Jacques Delors: Perspectives on a European Leader.* London: Routledge.

Due, Ole (2000) 'Regeringskonferencen og det judicielle system i EU', *EU-ret og Menneskeret'*, vol. 7, no. 2, June 2000, pp. 45–51.

Dupont, Christophe and Guy-Olivier Faure (1991) 'The Negotiation Process', in Victor A. Kremenyuk (ed.) *International Negotiation: Analysis, Approaches, Issues.* San Francisco, CA: Jossey-Bass Publishers, pp. 40–57.

Dyson, Kenneth (1994) *Elusive Union: The Process of Economic and Monetary Union in Europe.* London: Longman.

Dyson, Kenneth and Kevin Featherstone (1999) *The Road to Maastricht: Negotiating Economic and Monetary Union.* Oxford: Oxford University Press.

Economist, The (2000a) various issues.

Economist, The (2000b) 'At Two in the Morning', vol. 357, issue 8201, 12/16/2000, p. 26.

Economist, The (2000c) 'Raining on Chirac's Parade', vol. 357, issue 8201, 12/16/2000, p. 28.

Economist, The (2003) 'Who Killed the Constitution?', vol. 369, issue 8355, 12/20/2003, pp. 71–3.

Edwards, Geoffrey and David Spence (1997) 'The Commission in Perspective', in Geoffrey Edwards and David Spence (eds), *The European Commission.* 2nd edn. London: Cartermill Publishing, pp. 1–32.

Elgström, Ole (2001) ' "The Honest Broker"? – The EU Council Presidency as a Mediator', Paper presented at the 4th Pan-European International Relations Conference, Canterbury, 8–10 September 2001.

Elgström, Ole (2003) ' "The Honest Broker"? The Council Presidency as a Mediator', in Ole Elgström (ed.) *European Union Council Presidencies: A Comparative Analysis*. London: Routledge, pp. 38–54.

EPP – ED Group in the European Parliament (2003) *The Road to an Enlarged Union: 1993–2003*. Brussels: EPP – ED Group in the European Parliament.

Epstein, Lee and Jeffrey A. Segal (2000) 'Measuring Issue Salience', *American Journal of Political Science*, vol. 44, no. 1, January 2000, pp. 66–83.

Ersbøll, Niels (1994) The European Union: The Immediate Priorities', *International Affairs*, vol. 70, no. 3, pp. 413–19.

Europaudvalget (2000a) 'EU-Kommissionen fremlægger konkrete tekstforslag til institutionel reform af EU-traktaterne', Info-note I 72, 03 februar 2000.

Europaudvalget (2000b) 'Portugisisk EU-formandskab ønsker at udvide dagsorden for regeringskonferencen', Info-note, bilag 57, 1999–00.

Europaudvalget (2000c) 'Europa-Kommissionen præsenterer ekspertrapport om todeling af EU-traktaterne', Info-note, bilag 152, 1999–00.

European Commission (1985) *Completing the Internal Market*. Brussels, COM (85) 310 final, 1985.

European Commission (1986) *Nineteenth General Report on the Activities of the European Communities 1985*. Luxembourg: Office of Official Publications. 1986.

European Commission (1990a) *Proposal for a Draft Treaty Amending the Treaty Establishing the European Economic Community with a View to Achieving Economic and Monetary Union*. 21 August 1990.

European Commission (1990b) *Draft Treaty Amending the Treaty Establishing the European Community with a View to Achieving Economic and Monetary Union*. Brussels, 10 December 1990 (SEC(90) 2500).

European Commission (1990c) *XXIII General Report of the activities of the European Community in 1989*. Brussels/Luxembourg: The European Community. 1990.

European Commission (1991a) 'Intergovernmental Conferences: Contributions by the Commission', *Bulletin of the European Communities*, supplement 2/91. Luxembourg: Office for the Official Publications of the European Communities.

European Commission (1991c) *General Report of the activities of the European Community in 1990*. Brusells/Luxembourg: The European Community. 1991.

European Commission (1991b) *One Market, One Money: An Evaluation of the Potential Benefits and Costs of Forming an Economic and Monetary*

Union in the European Community. Luxembourg: Office of Official Publications.

European Commission (1992) 'Europe and the Challenge of Enlargement', Europe Documents, Agence Internationale d'Information pour la Press, no. 1790, 3 July 1992.

European Commission (1994a) *The Europe Agreements and Beyond.* COM (94) 320 Final, Brussels, 13 July 1994.

European Commission (1994b) *Follow Up to Commission Communication on 'The Europe Agreements and Beyond: A Strategy to Prepare the Countries of Central and Eastern Europe for Accession'*. COM (94) 361 final, Brussels, 27 July 1994.

European Commission (1995a) *White Paper on the Preparation of the Associated Countries of Central and Eastern Europe for Integration into the Internal Market of the Union.* COM (95) 163 final, Brussels, 3 May 1995.

European Commission (1995b) *Report of 10 May 1995 on the Operation of the Treaty on European Union.*

European Commission (1996) *Reinforcing Political Union and Preparing for Enlargement.* Commission Opinion of 28 February 1996, COM (96) 90 final, 28 February 1996.

European Commission (1996) *General Report of the activities of the European Union.* Brussels/Luxembourg: 1996.

European Commission (1997) *Agenda 2000: For a Stronger and Wider Europe.* COM (97) 2000 final.

European Commission (1998) *Proposals for Council Regulations Concerning the Reform of the Common Agricultural Policy.* COM (1998).

European Commission (1999a) *Composite Paper: Reports on Progress Towards Accession by Each of the Candidate Countries.* COM (99), 4 November 1999.

European Commission (1999b) *Adapting the Institutions to Make a Success of Enlargement.* Contribution by the European Commission to Preparations for the Intergovernmental Conference on Institutional Issues. COM (99) 592, 10 November 1999.

European Commission (2000a) *Adapting the Institutions to Make a Success of Enlargement – Commission Opinion.* Commission Opinion in Accordance with Article 48 of the Treaty on European Union on the Calling of a Conference of Representatives of the Governments of the Member States to Amend the Treaties. COM (2000) 34, 26 January 2000.

European Commission (2000b) *Additional Commission Contribution to the Intergovernmental Conference on Institutional Reform: Reform of the Community Courts.* Official Journal, COM (2000) 109 final, 01 March 2000, Luxembourg: Office for Official Publications of the European Communities.

European Commission (2000c) *Commission Communication – A Basic Treaty for the European Union.* Brussels, COM (2000) 434 final, 12 July 2000.

European Commission (2000d) *Enlargement Strategy Paper.* European Commission, 8 November 2000.

European Commission (2001) *Information Note – The Free Movement of Workers in the Context of Enlargement.* 6 March 2001, European Commission. Available at internet site: http://europa.eu.int/comm/enlargement/docs/pdf/migration enl.pdf

European Commission (2003) *General Report of the activities of the Euopean Union.* Brussels/Luxembourg: 2003.

European Commission (2002a) *Communication from the Commission – A Project for the European Union.* Brussels, 22 May 2002, COM (2002) 247 Final.

European Commission (2002b) *Contribution to a Preliminary Draft Constitution – Feasibility Study (Penelope).* Brussels, 4 December 2002.

European Commission (2002c) *Communicatino from the Commission on the Institutional Architecture – For the European Union – Peace, Freedom and Solidarity.* Brussels, 5 December 2002, COM (2002) 728 final.

European Commission (2002d) *Towards the Enlarged Union: Strategy Paper and Report of the European Commission on the Progress Towards Accession by Each of the Candidate Countries.* Brussels, 9 October 2002, COM (2002) 700 final.

European Commission (2003a) *A Constitution for the Union – Opinion of the Commission, Pursuant to Article 48 of the Treaty on European Union, on the Conference of Representatives of the Member States' Governments Convened to Revise the Treaties.* Brussels, 19 September 2003, COM (2003) 548 final.

European Commission (2003) *General Report of the activities of the European Union.* Brussels/Luxembourg: 2003.

European Communities (2000) *The Community Budget: The Facts in Figures.* Luxembourg: Office for Official Publications of the European Communities.

European Communities (2003) *Draft Treaty Establishing a Constitution for Europe.* Luxembourg: Office for Official Publications of the European Communities, 2003.

European Council (1990) *The Council of the European Community.* Luxembourg: Office for Official Publications of the European Communities.

European Council (1993) *European Council at Copenhagen 21–22 June 1993: Presidency Conclusions.* Europe Documents. Agence Internationale d'Information pour la Presse. No. 1844/45, 24 June 1993.

European Council (1994) *European Council at Corfu 24–25 June, 1994: Presidency Conclusions.* SN 150/94, 24–25 June 1994.

European Council (1995) *Madrid European Council 15 and 16 December 1995: Presidency Conclusions.* SN 400/95, 16 December 1995.

European Counil (1996) *Florence European Council.* SN 300/96. 21 June 1996.

European Council (1997a) *Amsterdam European Council.* SN 150/97, 16 June 1997.

European Council (1997b) *Luxembourg European Council.* SN 400/97, 12 December 97.

European Council (1999a) *Presidency Conclusion: Berlin European Council 24 and 25 March 1999.* SN 100/1/99 rev, 25 March 1999.

European Council (1999b) *Presidency Conclusions: Cologne European Council.* SN 150/99, 3–4 June 1999.

European Council (1999c) *Presidency Conclusions: Helsinki European Council.* SN 300/99, 10–11 December 1999.

European Council (2000a) *Presidency Conclusions: Feira European Council.* 19–20 June 2000.

European Council (2000b) *Presidency Conclusion: Nice European Council Meeting 7, 8 and 9 December 2000.* SN 400/1/00, 8 December 2000.

European Council (2001) *Presidency Conclusions: European Council Meeting in Laeken. 14 and 15 December 2001.* SN 300/1/01 Rev 1, Brussels, 14 December 2001.

European Council (2002) *Brussels European Council, 24 and 25 October 2002: Presidency Conclusions.* Brussels, 26 November 2002, 14702/02.

European Council (2003) *Thessaloniki European Council: Presidency Conclusions.* Brussels, 1 October 2003, 11683/03, POLGEN 55.

European Liberal Democrats (2001) *Preparing for Enlargement.* Published on internet site: http://eldi.europarl.eu.int/1/BDNJHLMDJDIFCBAMI-JECLHPFPDBD94187E9DWWA35ETE4Q/docs/DLS/2000-ADMIN-0183-EN.pdf

European Parliament (1984) *Draft Treaty establishing the European Union.* Luxembourg, March.

European Parliament (1990) *Resolution on the Intergovernmental Conference in the Context of the Parliament's Strategy for European Union.* Official Journal, no. C 96, 17 April 1990.

European Parliament (1992) *Resolution on the Results of the Intergovernmental Conferences.* A3-0123/92, Europe Documents, Agence Internationale d'Information pour la Presse. No. 1769, 10 April 1992.

European Parliament (1993) *Report on the Structure of the European Union with Regard to its Enlargement and the Creation of a Europe-Wide Order.* 20 January 1993, A3-0189/92, PE152.242/def.

European Parliament (1996a) *Resolution on i) Parliament's Opinion on the convening of the IGC; and ii) Evaluation of the Work of the Reflection*

Group and Definition of the Political Priorities of the European Parliament with a View to the Intergovernmental Conference.

European Parliament (1996b) *Resolution on the White Paper 'Preparing the Associated Countries of Central and Eastern Europe for Integration into the Internal Market of the Union'*, OJ No. 141, 13/05/1996m p. 135, 17 April 1996, A4-0101/96, PE215.521/def.

European Parliament (1996c) *Resolution on the Financing of the Enlargement of the European Union*, OJ No. C 020, 20/01/1997, p. 134, 12 December 1996, A4-0353/96, PE218.268/def.

European Parliament (1996d) *Summary of the Positions of the Member States and the European Parliament on the 1996 Intergovernmental Conference*. Luxembourg, 30 September 1996.

European Parliament (1996e) *Summary of the Positions of the Member States and the European Parliament on the 1996 Intergovernmental Conference*. Luxembourg, 4 December 1996.

European Parliament (1997a) *Resolution on the Treaty of Amsterdam.* 19 November 1997, A4-0347/97.

European Parliament (1997b) *Resolution on the Communication from the Commission 'Agenda 2000 – for a Stronger and Wider Union' (COM(97)2000 – C4-0371/97)*, 4 December 1997, A4-0368/97, PE224.336/def.

European Parliament (1997c) *Resolution on the Communication from the Commission 'Agenda 2000 – the 2000–2006 Financial Framework for the Union and the Future Financing System)*, 4 December 1997, A4-0331/97, PE223.701/def.

European Parliament (1999a) *The Role of the European Parliament in the Enlargement Process.* Briefing no. 38, Secretariat Working Party, Task-Force 'Enlargement', Luxembourg, 27 January 1999, PE 168.065.

European Parliament (1999b) *Resolution on the Preparation of the Reform of the Treaties and the next Intergovernmental Conference*. Agence Internationale d'Information pour la Presse. No. 2163, 26 November 1999, p. 1–6.

European Parliament (2000a) *Resolution of the European Parliament on the Convening of the Intergovernmental Conference*. 14094/1999 – C5-0341/1999 – 1999/0825(CNS) – PE 284.656.

European Parliament (2000b) *Summary of the Proceedings of the Intergovernmental Conference Between 14 February and 6 June 2000 on the Eve of the Feira European Council to be Held on 19 and 20 June*. Brussels, 7 June 2000, PE 286.924.

European Parliament (2000c) 'Notice to Members: Stage reached in the Work of the Intergovernmental Conference on the Eve of the Meeting of the European Council to be Held from 7 to 9 December 2000 in Nice.' Brussels, 29 November 2000, PE 294.718.

European Parliament (2000d) *European Parliament Resolution on the Outcome of the European Council on 7–11 December 2000 in Nice.* Brussels, 14 December 2000, B5-0938, 0939 and 0942/2000.

European Parliament (2000e) *European Parliament Resolution on the Enlargement of the European Union (COM(1999) 500 – C5-0341/2000 – 2000/2171 (COS))*, 4 October 2000, A5-0250/2000.

European Parliament (2001a) *The European Parliament in the Enlargement Process – An Overview.* Secretariat Working Party, Task-Force 'Enlargement', May 2001, Published on http://www.europarl.eu.int/enlargement/positionep/ep_overview_en/htm

European Parliament (2001b) *European Parliament Resolution on the Constitutional Process and the Future of the Union.* Brussels, 29 November 2001, A5-0368/2001.

European Parliament (2003a) *The European Parliament in the Enlargement Process – An Overview.* Secretariat Working Party, Task-Force "Enlargement", March 2003, DV\492865.EN. Published on http://www.europarl.eu.int/enlargement_new/positionep/pdf/ep_role_en.pdf

European Parliament (2003b) *European Parliament Resolution on the Draft Treaty Establishing a Constitution for Europe and the European Parliament's Opinion on the Convening of the Intergovernmental Conference (IGC).* Brussels, 24 September 2003, A5-0299/2003.

European Parliament (2003c) *European Parliament Resolution on the Financial Provisions in the Draft Treaty Establishing a Constitution for Europe.* Brussels, 20 November 2003, P5_TA(2003)0517.

European Parliament IGC Monitoring Group (2003) 'Comparative Tables Concerning the Positions of the Member States in the IGC', IGC Monitoring Group, The Secretariat, PE 337.089, 6 November 2003.

European Policy Centre (Belmont European Policy Centre/European Policy Centre) (1996–1997) *Challenge 96./Challenge Europe.* Brussels: IGC Intelligence Service, European Policy Centre.

Eurostat (2003) *Towards an Enlarged European Union: Key Indicators on Member States and Candidate Countries.* Luxembourg: Eurostat.

Falkner, Gerda (2002) 'How Intergovernmental are Intergovernmental Conferences? An Example from the Maastricht Treaty Reform', *Journal of European Public Policy,* vol. 9, no. 1, February 2002, pp. 98–119.

Fearon, James D. (1991) 'Counterfactuals and Hypothesis Testing in Political Science', *World Politics,* vol. 43, issue 2, January 1991, pp. 169–95.

Federal Trust (2003a) *EU Constitution Project Newsletter*, vol. 1, issue 7, November 2003.

Federal Trust (2003b) *EU Constitution Project Newsletter*, vol. 1, issue 8, December 2003.

Fielder, Nicola (2000) 'The origins of the Single Market', in Volker Bornschier (ed.), *State-building in Europe: The Revitalization of Western European Integration*. Cambridge: Cambridge University Press, pp. 75–92.

Finnemore, Martha and Kathryn Sikkink (1998) 'International Norm Dynamics and Political Change', *International Organization*, vol. 52, no. 4, autumn 1998, pp. 887–917.

Fischer, Joschka (2000) 'From Confederacy to Federation – Thoughts on the Finality of European Integration', Speech by Joschka Fischer at the Humboldt University in Berlin, 12 May 2000. Available on http://www.auswaertiges-amt.de/www/en/index_html.

Forster, Anthony (1999) *Britain and the Maastricht Negotiations*. Basingstoke: MacMillan Press Ltd.

Franco, Marc (1999) 'The enlargement: The European Commission's Viewpoint', in Victoria Curzon Price, Alice Landau and Richard G. Whitman (eds), *The Enlargement of the European Union: Issues and Strategies*. London: Routledge, pp. 67–75.

Friis, Lykke (1996) *When Europe Negotiates: From Europe Agreements to Eastern Enlargement*. Copenhagen: Institute of Political Science, University of Cophenhagen.

Friss, Lykke (1997) *When Europe negotiates: From Europe Agreements to Eastern Enlargement*. Copenhagen: Institute of Political Science, University of Copenhagen Ph.D. thesis.

Friis, Lykke (1998) ' "The End of the Beginning" of Eastern Enlargement – Luxembourg Summit and Agenda-Setting.' *European Integration online Papers (EIoP)*, vol. 2, no. 7, http://eiop.or.at/eiop/texte/1998–007a.htm

Friis, Lykke and Anna Jarosz-Friis (2001) 'When the going gets tough: the EU's enlargement negotiations with Poland', *Journal of European Integration*, vol. 23, no. 1, pp. 29–61.

Friis, Lykke and Anna Jarosz-Friis (2002) *Countdown to Copenhagen: Big Bang or Fizzle in the EU's Enlargement Process?* Copenhagen: Danish Institute of International Affairs.

Galloway, David (1999) 'Keynote Article: *Agenda 2000* – Packaging the Deal', *Journal of Common Market Studies*, vol. 37, Annual Review, September 1999, pp. 9–35.

Galloway, David (2001) *The Treaty of Nice and Beyond – Realities and Illusions of Power in the EU*. Sheffield: Sheffield University Press.

Garrett, Geoffrey and George Tsebelis (1996) 'An Institutional Critique of Intergovernmentalism', *International Organization*, vol. 50, no. 2, spring 1996, pp. 269–99.

Garrett, Geoffrey and George Tsebelis (2001) 'The Institutional Foundations of Intergovernmentalism and Supranationalism in the European Union', *International Organization*, vol. 55, no. 2, spring 2001, pp. 357–90.

Garrett, Geoffrey and Barry Weingast (1993) 'Ideas, Interests, and Institutions: Constructing the European Community's Internal Market', in Judith Goldstein and Robert O. Keohane (eds), *Ideas and Foreign Policy : Beliefs, Institutions, and Political Change*. London: Cornell University Press, pp. 173–206.

Gazzo, Marina (1985a) *Towards European Union: From the "Crocodile" to the European Council in Milan (28–29 June 1985), Volume 1. Documents selected and introduced by Marina Gazzo*. Brussels: Agence Europe.

Gazzo, Marina (1985b) *Towards European Union: From the 'Crocodile' to the European Council in Milan (28–29 June 1985), Supplement: Updated to 10.7.1985*. Brussels: Agence Europe.

Gazzo, Marina (1986) *Towards European Union: From the European Council in Milan to the Signing of the European Single Act, Volume 2. Documents Selected and Introduced by Marina Gazzo*. Brussels: Agence Europe.

General Secretariat of the Council (2002) Personal correspondance with the General Secretariat of the Council's DG A1 Personnel – Administration. Dated 2 October 2002.

George, Stephen (1996) 'The Approach of the British Government to the 1996 Intergovernmental Conference of the European Union', *Journal of European Public Policy*, vol. 3, no. 1, pp. 45–62.

Gil Ibañez, Alberto (1992) 'Spain and European Political Union', in Finn Laursen and Sophie Vanhoonacker (eds), *The Intergovernmental Conference on Political Union. Institutional Reforms, New Policies and International Identity of the European Community*. Maastricht: European Institute of Public Administration, pp. 99–114.

Gillingham, John (2003) *European Integration 1950–2003: Superstate or New Market Economy?* Cambridge: Cambridge University Press.

Grant, Charles (1994) *Delors: Inside the House that Jacques Built*. London: Nicholas Brealey Publishing.

Gray, Mark (2000) 'Negotiating EU Treaties: The Case for a New Approach', in Edward Best, Mark Gray and Alexander Stubb (eds), *Rethinking the European Union: IGC 2000 and Beyond*. Maastricht: European Institute of Public Administration, pp. 263–80.

Gray, Mark (2001) 'The European Commission and Treaty Reform', Speech given to Nuffield College, University of Oxford, May 2001.

Gray, Mark (2002) 'Negotiating the Treaty of Amsterdam: The role and influence of the European Commission', in Finn Laursen (ed.), *The Amsterdam Treaty: National Preference Formation, Interstate Bargaining, Outcome and Ratification*. Odense: Odense University Press, pp. 381–404.

Gray, Mark and Alexander Stubb (2001) 'The Treaty of Nice: Negotiating a Poisoned Chalice?', *Journal of Common Market Studies*, vol. 39, Annual Review EU 2001, September 2001, pp. 5–23.

Greve, Morten F. and Knud E. Jørgensen (2002) 'Treaty Reform as Constitutional Politics – A longitudinal view', *Journal of European Public Policy,* vol. 9, no. 1, February 2002, pp. 54–75.

Grevi, Giovanni (2004) 'Light and shade of a Quasi-Constitution: An Assessment', EPC Issue Paper No. 14, 23 June 2004.

Grieco, Joseph (1995) 'The Maastricht Treaty, Economic and Monetary Union and the Neo-Realist Research Programme', *Review of International Studies,* vol. 21, s.21–40.

Griller, S., D.P. Droutsas, G. Falkner, K. Forgó and M. Nentwich (2000) *The Treaty of Amsterdam: Facts, Analysis, Prospects.* Wien: Springer.

Grilli, Enzo (1993) *The European Community and the Developing Countries.* Cambridge: Cambridge University Press.

Haas, Ernst B. (1958) *The Uniting of Europe. Political, Social and Economic Forces, 1950–1957.* Stanford, CA: Stanford University Press.

Haas, Ernst B. (1961) 'International Integration: The European and the Universal Process', *International Organization,* vol. 15, issue 3, summer 1961, pp. 366–92.

Haas, Ernst B. (1970) 'The Study of Regional Integration: Reflections on the Joy and Anguish of Pretheorizing', *International Organization,* vol. 24, issue 4, pp. 607–46.

Haas, Ernst B. (1990) *When Knowledge is Power: Three Models of Change in International Organizations.* Berkeley, CA: University of California Press.

Haas, Peter (1992) 'Introduction: Epistemic Communities and International Policy Co-ordination', *International Organization,* vol. 46, no. 1, pp. 1–35.

Habeeb, William Mark (1988) *Power and Tactics in International Negotiation.* Baltimore, MD: Johns Hopkins University Press.

Hall, Peter and Rosemary C.R. Taylor (1996) 'Political Science and the three New Institutionalisms', *Political Studies,* vol. 44, pp. 936–57.

Halligan, Aoife (2003) 'The End of a Long and Bumpy Road?', *Convention Intelligence,* 16 June 2003. Brussels: European Policy Centre.

Hampson, Fen Osler with Michael Hart (1995) *Multilateral Negotiations: Lessons from Arms Control, Trade, and the Environment.* Baltimore, MD: The Johns Hopkins University Press.

Harris, Geoffrey (2000) 'A European Parliament Perspective', in Jackie Gower and John Redmond (eds), *Enlarging the European Union: The Way Forward.* Aldershot: Ashgate, s. 26–35.

Hartley, Trevor (2003) *T.* 5th edn. Oxford University Press.

Hayes-Renshaw, Fiona and Helen Wallace (1997) *The Council of Ministers.* Basingstoke: Macmillan.

Heisenberg, Dorothee (1999) *The Mark of the Bundesbank: Germany's Role in European Monetary Cooperation.* London: Lynne Rienner Publishers.

Hix, Simon (1994) 'The Study of the European Community: The Challenge to Comparative Politics', *West European Politics*, vol. 17, no. 1, pp. 1–30.

Hix, Simon (1999) *The Political System of the European Union*. Basingstoke: Macmillan.

Hix, Simon (2002) 'Constitutional Agenda-Setting Through Discretion in Rule Interpretation: Why the European Parliament Won at Amsterdam', *British Journal of Political Science*, vol. 32, Issue 2, pp. 259–80.

Hoffmann, Stanley (1966) 'Obstinate or Obsolete: The Fate of the Nation State and the Case of Western Europe', *Daedalus*, vol. 93, no. 3, pp. 862–915.

Holbrooke, Richard (1998) *To End a War*. New York: Random House.

Hooghe, Liesbet (2001) *The European Commission and the Integration of Europe: Images of Governance*. Cambridge: Cambridge University Press.

Hopmann, P. Terrence (1996) *The Negotiation Process and the Resolution of International Conflicts*. Columbia: University of South Carolina Press.

House of Lords (2000) *Select Committee on European Union – European Union – Eleventh Report*. 18 July 2000.

Huang, David W.F. (2002) 'On Institution Building of the European Union and Asia–Pacific Economic Cooperation', Paper presented at international conference on 'Exploring Federalism and Integration: The EU, Taiwan and Korea', 26–27 October, 2002 Berlin, Germany.

Hughes, James, Gwendolyn Sasse and Claire Gordon (2003) 'EU Enlargement and Power Assymmetries: Conditionality and the Commission's Role in Regionalisation in Central and Eastern Europe', Working Paper 49/03, Sussex European Institute.

Irish Presidency (2004) *European – Working Together: Programme of the Irish Presidency of the European Union, January–June 2004*. PRN1487.

Isaksen, Susanne, and Toft, Ole, and Bødtcher-Hansen, Jens (1998) *En traktat bliver til : Amsterdam-traktaten : forberedelse, forhandling og resultat*. Albertslund: Schultz.

Jabko, Nicolas (1999) 'In the Name of the Market: How the European Commission Paved the Way for Monetary Union', *Journal of European Public Policy*, vol. 6, no. 3, September 1999, pp. 475–95.

Jacobs, Francis, Richard Corbett and Michael Shackleton (1995) *The European Parliament*. 3rd edn. London: Cartermill International Ltd.

Jolly, Mette (2003) 'Debating Democracy in the European Union: Four Paradigms.' Paper presented to Federal Trust workshop, 2nd workshop of the UACES Study Group, From the Convention to the IGC, London 10–11 July 2003.

Jones, Bryan (2001) *Politics and the Architecture of Choice: bounded rationality and governance*. Chicago: University of Chicago Press.

Jonsson, Håkan and Hans Hegeland (2003) 'Konventet bakom kulisserna – om arbetsmetoden och förhandlingsspelat i Europeiska konventet', SIEPS Working Paper, 2003:2u.

Krasner, Stephen D. (1991) 'Global Communications and National Power: Life on the Pareto Frontier', *World Politics*, vol. 43, no. 3, April 1991, pp. 336–66.

Kressel, K., Dean G. Priutt *et al.* (1989) *Mediation Research: Process and Effectiveness of Third-Party Intervention.* San Francisco, CA: Jossey-Bass.

Kugler, Jacek and John H.P. Williams (1994) 'The Politics Surrounding the Creation of the EC Bank: The Last Stumbling Block to Integration', in Bruce Bueno de Mesquita and Frans N. Stokman (eds), *European Community Decision Making: Models, Applications, and Comparisons.* New Haven: Yale University Press, pp. 185–212.

Landau, Alice (2004) 'Negotiating the Enlargement', in Paul Meerts and Franz Cede (eds), *Negotiating European Union.* Basingstoke: Palgrave Macmillan.

Laursen, Finn (1992) 'Explaining the Intergovernmental Conference', in Finn Laursen and Sophie Vanhoonacker (eds) *The Intergovernmental Conference on Political Union. Institutional Reforms, New Policies and International Identity of the European Community.* Maastricht: European Institute of Public Administration, pp. 229–48.

Laursen, Finn (1994) 'The Not-So-Permissive Consensus: Thoughts on the Maastricht Treaty and the Future of European Integration', in Finn Laursen and Sophie Vanhoonacker (eds), *The Ratification of the Maastricht Treaty: Issues, Debates and Future Implications.* Maastricht: European Institute of Public Administration, pp. 295–318.

Laursen, Finn (2001) *Nice-traktaten: Baggrund, Kommentar, Perspektiver.* København: Den Danske Europabevægelse.

Laursen, Finn (ed.) (2002) *The Amsterdam Treaty: National Preference Formation, Interstate Bargaining, Outcome and Ratification.* Odense: Odense University Press.

Laursen, Finn and Sophie Vanhoonacker (1992) (eds) *The Intergovernmental Conference on Political Union. Institutional Reforms, New Policies and International Identity of the European Community.* Maastricht: European Institute of Public Administration.

Laursen, Finn and Sophie Vanhoonacker (1994) (eds) *The Ratification of the Maastricht Treaty: Issues, Debates and Future Implications.* Maastricht: European Institute of Public Administration.

Lax, David A. and James K. Sebenius (1986) *The Manager as Negotiator.* New York: Free Press.

Lequesne, Christian (2001) 'The French Presidency: The Half Success of Nice', *Journal of Common Market Studies*, vol. 39, Annual Review, September 2001, pp. 47–50.

Lindberg, Leon N. (1963) *The Political Dynamics of European Economic Integration.* Stanford, CA: Stanford University Press.

Lindberg, Leon N. (1966) 'Integration as a Source of Stress on the European Community System', *International Organization*, vol. xx, no. 2, Spring 1966, pp. 233–65.

Lindberg, Leon N. and Stuart A. Scheingold (1970) *Europe's Would-Be Polity: Patterns of Change in the European Community*. Englewood Cliffs, NJ: Prentice-Hall, Inc.

Lipsius, Justus (1995) 'The 1996 Intergovernmental Conference', *European Law Review*, vol. 20, no. 3, pp. 235–67.

Lloréns, Felipe Basabe (2002) 'Spain: A "Difficult" Negotiation Partner?', in Finn Laursen (ed.), *The Amsterdam Treaty: National Preference Formation, Interstate Bargaining, Outcome and Ratification*. Odense: Odense University Press, pp. 311–39.

Lodge, Juliet (1998) 'Negotiations in the European Union: The 1996 Intergovernmental Conference', *International Negotiation*, vol. 3, pp. 481–505.

Lord, Christopher and Paul Magnette (2004) 'E Pluribus Unum? Creative Disagreements about Legitimacy in the EU', *Journal of Common Market Studies*, vol. 42, no. 1, pp. 183–202.

Ludlow, Peter (2002) *The Laeken Council*. Brussels: Eurocomment.

Ludlow, Peter (2004a) *The Making of the New Europe: The European Councils in Brussels and Copenhagen 2002*. Brussels: Eurocomment.

Ludlow, Peter (2004b) 'Brussels Breakdown', *Prospect*, issue 95, February 2004. Downloaded from http://www.prospect-magazine.co.uk.

Lukes, Steven (1974) *Power: A Radical View*. Basingstoke: Macmillan.

Lyck, Lise (1992) 'Environmental Policy', in Lise Lyck (ed.), *Denmark and EC Membership Evaluated*. London: Pinter Publishers, pp. 139–44.

Majone, Giandomenico (1996) 'The European Commission as Regulator', in Giandomenico Majone (ed.), *Regulating Europe*. London: Routledge, pp. 61–82.

Malnes, Raino (1995) ' "Leader" and "Entrepreneur" in International Negotiations: A Conceptual Analysis', *European Journal of International Relations*, vol. 1, no. 1, pp. 87–112.

March, James G. and Johan P. Olsen (1984) 'The New Institutionalism: Organizational Factors in Political Life', *American Political Science Review*, vol. 78, no. 3, pp. 734–49.

March, James G. and Johan P. Olsen (1989) *Rediscovering Institutions: The Organizational Basis of Politics*. New York: Free Press.

Maurer, Andreas (2002) 'The European Parliament', in Finn Laursen (ed.) *The Amsterdam Treaty: National Preference Formation, Interstate Bargaining and Outcome*. Odense: Odense University Press.

Mayhew, Alan (1998) *Recreating Europe – The European Union's Policy towards Central and Eastern Europe*. Cambridge: Cambridge University Press.

Mazzucelli, Colette (1997) *France and Germany at Maastricht: Politics and Negotiations to Create the European Union*. New York: Garland Publishing, Inc.

McAllister, Richard (1997) *From EC to EU: An Historical and Political Survey*. London: Routledge.

McDonagh, Bobby (1998) *Original Sin in a Brave New World: An Account of the Negotiation of the Treaty of Amsterdam*. Dublin: Institute of European Affairs.

Meier, Kenneth J. (1989) 'Bureaucratic Leadership in Public Organizations', in Bryan D. Jones (ed.), *Leadership and Politics: New Perspectives in Political Science*. Lawrence: University Press of Kansas, pp. 267–88.

Menon, Anand (1998) 'France and the IGC of 1996', *Journal of European Public Policy*, vol. 3, no. 2, pp.231–52.

Menon, Anand (2003) 'Britain and the Convention on the Future of Europe', *International Affairs*, vol. 79, no. 5, pp. 963–78.

Metcalfe, David (1998) 'Leadership in European Union Negotiations: The Presidency of the Council', *International Negotiation,* vol. 3, pp. 413–34.

Meunier, Sophie and Kalypso Nicolaïdis (1999) 'Who Speaks for Europe? The Delegation of Trade Authority in the European Union', *Journal of Common Market Studies,* vol. 37, no. 3, September 1999, pp. 477–501.

Middlemas, Keith (1995) *Orchestrating Europe: The Informal Politics of European Union 1973–1995*. London: Fontana Press.

Midgaard, Knut and Arild Underdal (1977) 'Multiparty Conferences', in Daniel Druckman (ed.), *Negotiations: Social-psychological perspectives*. London: Sage Publications, pp. 329–46.

Milward, Alan S. (1993) 'Conclusions: The Value of History', in Alan S. Milward (ed.), *The Frontier of National Sovereignty: History and Theory, 1945–1992*. London: Routledge, pp. 182–201.

Milward, Alan S. and Vibeke Sørensen (1993) 'Interdependence or Integration? A National Choice', in Alan S. Milward (ed.), *The Frontier of National Sovereignty: History and Theory, 1945–1992*. London: Routledge, pp. 1–32.

Moravcsik, Andrew (1993) 'Preferences and Power in the European Community: A Liberal Intergovernmentalist Approach', *Journal of Common Market Studies*, vol. 31, no. 4, December 1993, pp. 473–524.

Moravcsik, Andrew (1995) 'Liberal Intergovernmentalism and Integration: A Rejoinder', *Journal of Common Market Studies*, vol. 33, no. 4, December 1995, pp. 611–28.

Moravcsik, Andrew (1998) *The Choice for Europe: Social Purpose and State Power from Messina to Maastricht*. Ithaca, NY: Cornell University Press.

Moravcsik, Andrew (1999a) 'A New Statecraft? Supranational Entrepreneurs and International Cooperation', *International Organization,* vol. 53, no. 2, spring 1999, pp. 267–306.

Moravcsik, Andrew (1999b) 'Theory and Method in the Study of International Negotiation: A Rejoinder to Oran Young', *International Organization,* vol. 53, no. 4, autumn 1999, pp. 811–14.

Moravcsik, Andrew (2002) 'In Defence of the "Democratic Deficit":
Reassessing Legitimacy in the European Union', *Journal of Common Market Studies*, vol. 40, no. 4, pp. 603–24.

Moravcsik, Andrew and Kalypso Nicolaïdis (1999) 'Explaining the Treaty of Amsterdam: Interests, Influence, Institutions', *Journal of Common Market Studies,* vol. 37, no. 1, March 1999, pp. 59–85.

Neuhold, Christine (2001) ' "You Can't Always Get What You Want". An Analysis of the Role of the European Parliament and the European Commission at the Nice Intergovernmental Conference', Paper prepared for delivery at the 4th Pan-European IR Conference, Canterbury, 8–10 September 2001.

Newman, Marc (2001) 'Democracy and accountability in the EU', in Jeremy Richardson (ed.) *European Union: Power and Policy-Making*, London: Routledge.

Niemann, Arne (1998) 'The PHARE Programme and the Concept of Spillover: Neofunctionalism in the Making', *Journal of European Public Policy*, vol. 5, no. 3, September 1998, pp. 428–46.

Norman, Peter (2003) *The Accidental Constitution: The Story of the European Convention*. Brussels: Eurocomment.

Nugent, Neill (1999) *The Government and Politics of the European Union*. 4th edn. London: Macmillan.

Nugent, Neill (ed.) (2000a) *At the Heart of the Union – Studies of the European Commission*. 2nd edn. London: Macmillan.

Nugent, Neill (2000b) *The European Commission*. Basingstoke: Palgrave Macmillan.

Nugent, Neill (ed.) (2004) *European Union Enlargement*. Basingstoke: Palgrave Macmillan.

Nuttall, Simon (1997) 'The Commission and foreign policy-making', in Geoffrey Edwards and David Spence (eds), *The European Commission*. 2nd edn., London: Cartermill International Ltd, pp. 303–20.

Padoa-Schioppa, Tommaso (2000) *The Road to Monetary Union in Europe: The Emperor, The Kings, and the Genies*. Oxford: Oxford University Press.

Padoa-Schioppa, Tommaso *et al.* (1987) *Efficiency, Stability and Equity: A Strategy for the Evolution of the Economic System of the European Community*. Oxford: Oxford University Press.

Parliamentary Group of the Party of European Socialists (2002) *Our Goal: The Reunification of Europe*. February 2002. Brussels: Parliamentary Group of the Party of European Socialists.

Pedersen, Thomas (1998) *Germany, France, and the integration of Europe : A Realist Interpretation*. London: Pinter.

Pedersen, Thomas (2002) 'Cooperative Hegemony: Power, Ideas and Institutions in Regional Integration', *Review of International Studies*, vol. 28, issue 4, pp. 677–96.

Peterson, John (1995) 'Decision-making in the European Union: Towards a Framework for Analysis', *Journal of European Public Policy*, vol. 2, no. 1, March 1995, pp. 69–93.

Peterson, John (1999) 'The Santer Era: The European Commission in Normative, Historical and Theoretical Perspective', *Journal of European Public Policy*, vol. 6, no. 1, March 1999, pp. 46–65.

Peterson, John and Elizabeth Bomberg (1999) *Decision-Making in the European Union*. Basingstoke: Macmillan.

Petite, Michel (1998) 'The Treaty of Amsterdam', Harvard Law School – Jean Monnet Chair Working Paper, no. 2, 1998.

Petite, Michel (2000) ' The IGC and the European Commission', in Edward Best, Mark Gray and Alexander Stubb (eds), *Rethinking the European Union: IGC 2000 and Beyond*. Maastricht: European Institute of Public Administration, pp. 61–6.

Pfetsch, Frank R. (1999) 'Institutions Matter: Negotiating the European Union', in Peter Berton, Hiroshi Kimura and William I. Zartmann (eds), *International Negotiation: Actors, Structure/Process, Values*. New York: St. Martin's Press, pp. 191–222.

Pierson, Paul (1996) 'The Path to European Integration', *Comparative Political Studies*, vol. 21, issue 1, pp. 123–64.

Piris, Jean-Claude (1999) 'Does the European Union have a Constitution? Does it Need One?', *European Law Review*, vol. 24, no. 6, December 1999, pp. 557–85.

Pollack, Mark A. (1997) 'Delegation, Agency, and Agenda Setting in the European Community', *International Organization*, vol. 51, no. 1, winter 1997, pp. 99–134.

Pollack, Mark A. (1999) 'Delegation, Agency and Agenda Setting in the Treaty of Amsterdam', *European Integration Online Papers (EIoP)*, vol. 3 (1999), no. 6, published at Internet site: http://eiop.or.at/eiop/texte/1999-006a.htm.

Pollack, Mark A. (2003) *The Engines of Integration. Delegation, Agency and Agenda Setting in the European Union*. Oxford: Oxford University Press.

Raiffa, Howard (1982) *The Art and Science of Negotiation*. Cambridge, MA: Harvard University Press.

Reflection Group (1995) *Reflection Group's Report of 5 December 1995*. SN 520/95 REFLEX 21. Brussels.

Rittberger, Berthold (2001) 'Which Institutions for Post-War Europe? Explaining the Institutional Design of Europe's First Community', *Journal of European Public Policy*, vol. 8, no. 5, October 2001, pp. 673–708.

Rittberger, Berthold (2003) 'The Creation and Empowerment of the European Parliament', *Journal of Common Market Studies*, vol. 41, no. 2, pp. 203–25.

Rosamond, Ben (2000) *Theories of European Integration*. Basingstoke: Macmillan.

Ross, George (1995) *Jacques Delors and European Integration*. Cambridge: Polity Press.

Sandholtz, Wayne (1992) *High-Tech Europe: The Politics of International Cooperation*. Berkeley, CA: University of California Press.

Sandholtz, Wayne (1993) 'Choosing Union: Monetary Politics and Maastricht', *International Organization*, vol. 47, no. 1, winter 1993, pp. 1–39.

Sandholtz, Wayne and Alec Stone Sweet (1999) 'European Integration and Supranational Governance Revisited: Rejoinder to Branch and Øhrgaard', *Journal of European Public Policy*, vol. 6, no. 1, March 1999, pp. 144–54.

Sandholtz, Wayne and John Zysman (1989) '1992: Recasting the European Bargain', *World Politics*, vol. 41, no. 1, pp. 95–128.

Sandholtz, Wayne and Alec Stone Sweet (eds) (1998) *European Integration and Supranational Governance*. Oxford: Oxford University Press.

Scharpf, Fritz (1997) *Games Real Actors Play: Actor-Centered Institutionalism in Policy Research*. Oxford: Westview Press.

Schimmelfennig, Frank (2001) 'The Community Trap: Liberal Norms, Rhetorical Action, and the Eastern Enlargement of the European Union', *International Organization*, vol. 55, no. 1, winter 2001, pp. 47–80.

Schmitter, Philippe C. (1969) 'Three Neo-Functional Hypotheses about International Integration', *International Organization*, vol. 23, issue 1, winter 1969, pp. 161–6.

Schmitter, Philippe C. (1970) 'A Revised Theory of Regional Integration', in Leon N. Lindberg and Stuart A. Scheingold (eds), *Regional Integration: Theory and Research*. Cambridge, MA: Harvard University Press, pp. 232–64.

Schneider, Gerald and Lars-Erik Cederman (1994) 'The Change of Tide in Political Cooperation: A Limited Information Model of European Integration', *International Organization*, vol. 48, issue 4, pp. 633–62.

Schout, Adriaan and Sophie Vanhoonacker (2001) 'The Presidency as Broker? Lessons from Nice', Paper prepared for delivery at the 4th Pan-European IR Conference, Canterbury, 8–10 September, 2001.

Scully, Roger M. (1997) 'The European Parliament and the Co-Decision Procedure: A Reassessment', *The Journal of Legislative Studies*, vol. 3, no. 3, pp. 58–73.

Sebenius, James K. (1983) 'Negotiation Arithmetic: Adding and Subtracting Issues and Parties', *International Organization*, vol. 37, no. 2, spring 1983, pp. 281–316.

Sebenius, James K. (1984) *Negotiating the Law of the Sea*. Cambridge, MA: Harvard University Press.

Sebenius, James K. (1991) 'Negotiation Analysis', in Victor A. Kremenyuk (ed.), *International Negotiation: Analysis, Approaches, Issues*. Oxford: Jossey-Bass Publishers, pp. 203–15.

Sebenius, James K. (1992) 'Challenging Conventional Explanations of International Cooperation: Negotiation Analysis and the Case of Epistemic Communities', *International Organization*, vol. 46, no. 1, winter 1992, pp. 323–65.

Serger, Sylvia Schwaag (2001) *Negotiating CAP Reform in the European Union – Agenda 2000*. Lund: Swedish Institute for Food and Agricultural Economics, Report 2001:4.

Sherrington, Phillipa (2000) *The Council of Ministers: Political Authority in the European Union*. London: Pinter.

Simon, Herbert A. (1997) *Adminstrative Behavior: A Study of Decision-Making Processes in Administrative Organizations*. 4th edn. New York: The Free Press.

Sjöstedt, Gunnar (1994) 'Negotiating the Uruguay Round of the General Agreement of Tariffs and Trade' in I. William Zartman (ed.) *International Multilaterla Negotiations*. San Fransisco: Jossey-Bass Publishers.

Sjöstedt, Gunnar (1999) 'Leadership in multilateral negotiations: crisis or transition?', in Peter Berton, Hiroshi Kimura and I. William Zartman (eds) *International Negotiation*. New York: St. Martin's Press, pp. 223–56.

Sjöstedt, Gunnar (1999) 'Leadership in Multilateral Negotiations: Crisis or Transition?', in Peter Berton, Hiroshi Kimura and William I. Zartmann (eds), *International Negotiation: Actors, Structure/Process, Values*. New York: St. Martin's Press, pp. 223–53.

Smith, Karen E. (2003) 'The Evolution and Application of EU Membership Conditionality', in Marise Cremona (ed.), *The Enlargement of the European Union*. Oxford: Oxford University Press, pp. 105–39.

Stacey, Jeffrey (2003) 'Displacement of the Council Via Informal Dynamics? Comparing the Commission and Parliament', *Journal of European Public Policy*, vol. 10, no. 6, December 2003, pp. 936–55.

Stein, Arthur A. (1982) 'Coordination and Collaboration: Regimes in an Anarchic World', *International Organization*, vol. 36, no. 2, Spring 1982, pp. 299–324.

Stenelo, Lars-G. (1972) *Mediation in International Relations*. Lund: Studentlitteratur.

Stevens, Anne and Handley Stevens (2001) *Brussels Bureaucrats? The Administration of the European Union*. Basingstoke: Palgrave Macmillan.

Stone Sweet, Alec and Wayne Sandholtz (1998) 'Integration, Supranational Governance, and the Institutionalization of the European Polity', in Wayne Sandholtz and Alec Stone Sweet (eds), *European Integration and Supranational Governance*. Oxford: Oxford University Press, pp. 1–26.

Stone Sweet, Alec, Wayne Sandholtz and Neil Fligstein (eds) (2001) *The Institutionalization of Europe*. Oxford: Oxford University Press.

Stuart, Gisela (2003) *The Making of Europe's Constitution*. Fabian Ideas, no. 609. London: Fabian Society.

Stubb, Alexander (1998) *Flexible Integration and the Amsterdam Treaty: Negotiating Differentiation in the 1996–97 IGC*. Dissertation submitted for the degree of Doctor of Philosophy at the London School of Economics and Political Science, Michaelmas Term, December 1998.

Stubb, Alexander (2002) *Negotiating Flexibility in the European Union*. Basingstoke: Palgrave Macmillan.

Svensson, Anna-Carin (2000) *In the Service of the European Union: The Role of the Presidency in Negotiating the Amsterdam Treaty – 1995–97*. Uppsala: Acta Universitatis Upsaliensis – Skrifter utgivna av statsveten-skapliga föreningen i Uppsala.

Sverdrup, Ulf (2000) 'Precedents and Present Events in the European Union: An Institutional Perspective on Treaty Reform', in Karlheinz Neunreither and Antje Wiener (eds), *European Integration After Amsterdam: Institutional Dynamics and Prospects for Democracy*. Oxford: Oxford University Press, pp. 241–65.

Sverdrup, Ulf (2002) 'An institutionalist perspective on treaty reform: contextualizing the Amsterdam and Nice Treaties', *Journal of European Public Policy*, vol. 9, no. 1, pp. 120–40.

Tallberg, Jonas (2002a) 'The Power of the Chair in International Bargaining', Paper presented at the 2002 ISA Annual Convention, New Orleans, 24–27 March 2002.

Tallberg, Jonas (2002b) 'First Pillar: The Domestic Politics of Treaty Reform in Environment and Employment', in Finn Laursen (ed.), *The Amsterdam Treaty: National Preference Formation, Interstate Bargaining, Outcome and Ratification*. Odense: Odense University Press, pp. 453–72.

Tallberg, Jonas (2003a) 'The Agenda-Shaping Powers of the EU Council Presidency', *Journal of European Public Policy*, vol. 10, no. 1, pp. 1–20.

Tallberg, Jonas (2003b) *European governance and supranational institutions: making states comply*. London: Routledge.

Tallberg, Jonas (2004) *The Power of the Chair: Leadership and Negotiation in the European Union*. Unpublished manuscript.

Torreblanca, José I. (2001) *The Reuniting of Europe: Promises, Negotiations and Compromises*. Aldershot: Ashgate.

Touval, Saadia (2002) *Mediation in the Yugoslav Wars*. New York: Palgrave.

Tranholm-Mikkelsen, Jeppe (1991) 'Neo-Functionalism: Obstinate or Obsolete? A Reappraisal in the Light of the New Dynamism of the EC', *Millennium: Journal of International Studies,* vol. 20, no. 1, pp. 1–22.

Tsebelis, George (1990) *Nested Games: Rational Choice in Comparative Politics*. Berkeley, CA: University of California Press.

Tsebelis, George and Geoffrey Garrett (1997) 'Agenda Setting, Vetoes and the European Union's Co-Decision Procedure', *Journal of Legislative Studies*, vol. 3, no. 3, pp. 74–92.

Tsebelis, George and Geoffrey Garrett (2001) 'The Institutional Foundations of Intergovernmentalism and Supranationalism in the European Union', *International Organization*, vol. 55, no. 2, spring 2001, pp. 357–90.

Tsoukalis, Loukas (2000) 'Economic and Monetary Union: Political Conviction and Economic Uncertainty', in Helen Wallace and William Wallace (eds), *Policy-Making in the European Union.* 4th edn. Oxford: Oxford University Press, pp. 149–78.

Ulveman, Michael and Thomas Lauritzen (2003) *I spidsen for Europa: Det danske EU-formandskab – en historie om triumf og magtopgør.* København: People's Press.

Underdal, Arild (1983) 'Causes of Negotiation Failure', *European Journal of Political Research*, vol. 11, pp. 183–95.

Underdal, Arild (1991) The Outcomes of Negotiation', in Victor A. Kremenyuk (ed.) *International Negotiation: Analysis, Approaches, Issues.* San Francisco, CA: Jossey-Bass Publishers, pp. 100–16.

Underdal, Arild (1994) 'Leadership Theory: Rediscovering the Arts of Management', in I. William Zartman (ed.) *International Multilateral Negotiation: Approaches to the Management of Complexity.* San Francisco, CA: Jossey-Bass Publishers, pp. 178–97.

Underdal, Arild (2002) 'The outcomes of Negotiation', in Victor A. Kremenyuk (ed.), *International Negotiation: Analysis, Approaches, Issues*, 2nd Edition. San Francisco, CA: Jossey-Bass Publishers, pp. 100–17.

Vanhoonacker, Sophie (1992) 'The European Parliament', in Finn Laursen and Sophie Vanhoonacker (eds), *The Intergovernmental Conference on Political Union: Institutional Reforms, New Policies, and International Identity of the European Community.* Maastricht: European Institute of Public Administration, pp. 215–28.

Verdun, Amy (1999) 'The Role of the Delors Committee in the Creation of EMU: An Epistemic Community', *Journal of European Public Policy*, vol. 6, no. 2, June 1999, pp. 308–28.

Wall, James A. and Ann Lynn (1993) 'Mediation: A Current Review', *Journal of Conflict Resolution,* vol. 37, no. 1, March 1993, pp. 160–94.

Wall, James A., John B. Stark and Rhetta L. Standifer (2001) 'Mediation: A Current Review and Theory Development', *Journal of Conflict Resolution*, vol. 45, no. 3, June 2001, pp. 370–91.

Wallace, Helen (1990) 'Making Multilateral Negotiations Work', in William Wallace (ed.), *The Dynamics of European Integration.* London: The Royal Institute of International Affairs, pp. 213–28.

Watkins, Michael (1999) 'Negotiating in a Complex World', *Negotiation Journal*, vol. 15, no. 3, July 1999, pp. 245–70.

Wehr, Paul and John Paul Lederach (1996) 'Mediating Conflict in Central America', in Jacob Bercovitch (Ed.) *Resolving International Conflicts – The Theory and Practice of Mediation*. London: Lynne Rienner Publishers, pp. 55–74.

Weiler, Joseph H.H. (1993) 'Journal to an Unknown Destination: A Retrospective and Prospective of the European Court of Justice in the Arena of Political Integration', *Journal of Common Market Studies*, vol. 31, no. 4, December 1993, pp. 417–46.

Wester, Robert (1992) 'The European Commission', in Finn Laursen and Sophie Vanhoonacker (eds), *The Intergovernmental Conference on Political Union: Institutional Reforms, New Policies, and International Identity of the European Community*. Maastricht: European Institute of Public Administration, pp. 205–14.

Westlake, Martin (1999) *The Council of the European Union*, rev edn. London: John Harper Publishing.

Wood, Pia Christina (1995) 'The Franco-German Relationship in the Post-Maastricht Era', in Carolyn Rhodes and Sonia Mazey (eds), *The States of the European Union Volume 3 – Building a European Polity?* Boulder, CO: Lynne Rienner Publishers Inc., pp. 221–44.

Working Party (2000) 'Report by the Working Party on the Future of the European Communities' Legal System', January 2000.

Young, Oran R. (1991) 'Political Leadership and Regime Formation: On the Development of Institutions in International Society', *International Organization*, vol. 45, no. 3, summer 1991, pp. 281–308.

Young, Oran R. (1999) 'Comment on Andrew Moravcsik, "A new state-craft? Supranational Entrepreneurs and International Cooperation" ', *International Organization*, vol. 53, no. 4, autumn 1999, pp. 805–9.

Zartman, William I. (2002) 'The Structure of Negotiation', in Victor A. Kremenyuk (ed.), *International Negotiation: Analysis, Approaches, Issues*. 2nd edn. San Francisco, CA: Jossey-Bass Publishers, pp. 71–84.

Zartman, I. William and Maureen R. Berman (1982) *The Practical Negotiator*. New Haven: Yale Univeristy Press.

Ziltener, Patrick (2000) 'Tying up the Luxembourg Package of 1985', in Volker Bornschier (ed.), *State-Building in Europe: The Revitalization of Western European Integration*. Cambridge, MA: Cambridge University Press, pp. 38–72.

Index